Oracle Exadata
Survival Guide

David Fitzjarrell

Mary Mikell Spence

Apress®

Oracle Exadata Survival Guide

ISBN-13 (pbk): 978-1-4302-6010-3

ISBN-13 (electronic): 978-1-4302-6011-0

Trademarked names, logos, and images may appear in this book. Rather than use a trademark symbol with every occurrence of a trademarked name, logo, or image, we use the names, logos, and images only in an editorial fashion and to the benefit of the trademark owner, with no intention of infringement of the trademark.

The use in this publication of trade names, trademarks, service marks, and similar terms, even if they are not identified as such, is not to be taken as an expression of opinion as to whether or not they are subject to proprietary rights.

While the advice and information in this book are believed to be true and accurate at the date of publication, neither the authors nor the editors nor the publisher can accept any legal responsibility for any errors or omissions that may be made. The publisher makes no warranty, express or implied, with respect to the material contained herein.

President and Publisher: Paul Manning
Lead Editor: Jonathan Gennick
Development Editor: Tom Welsh
Technical Reviewer: Arup Nanda
Editorial Board: Steve Anglin, Mark Beckner, Ewan Buckingham, Gary Cornell, Louise Corrigan, James DeWolf,
    Jonathan Gennick, Jonathan Hassell, Robert Hutchinson, Michelle Lowman, James Markham,
    Matthew Moodie, Jeff Olson, Jeffrey Pepper, Douglas Pundick, Ben Renow-Clarke, Dominic Shakeshaft,
    Gwenan Spearing, Matt Wade, Steve Weiss, Tom Welsh
Coordinating Editor: Anamika Panchoo
Copy Editor: Michael G. Laraque
Compositor: SPi Global
Indexer: SPi Global
Artist: SPi Global
Cover Designer: Anna Ishchenko

Distributed to the book trade worldwide by Springer Science+Business Media New York, 233 Spring Street, 6th Floor, New York, NY 10013. Phone 1-800-SPRINGER, fax (201) 348-4505, e-mail orders-ny@springer-sbm.com, or visit www.springeronline.com. Apress Media, LLC is a California LLC and the sole member (owner) is Springer Science + Business Media Finance Inc (SSBM Finance Inc). SSBM Finance Inc is a Delaware corporation.

For information on translations, please e-mail rights@apress.com, or visit www.apress.com.

Apress and friends of ED books may be purchased in bulk for academic, corporate, or promotional use. eBook versions and licenses are also available for most titles. For more information, reference our Special Bulk Sales–eBook Licensing web page at www.apress.com/bulk-sales.

Any source code or other supplementary materials referenced by the author in this text is available to readers at www.apress.com. For detailed information about how to locate your book's source code, go to www.apress.com/source-code/.

Dedicated to Shari, Gabi, Zachary, Nammy, and Paw Paw, without whom this book would not have been written

—David Fitzjarrell

Contents at a Glance

Contents

About the Authors

David Fitzjarrell is a Senior Oracle Database Administrator living in the Denver/Boulder area of Colorado. He has over 24 years of experience in various industries and is currently working with Exadata in a large-scale OLTP and ERP retail environment. He started with Oracle Version 6.0 and has worked with almost every release since, concentrating on the areas of physical administration and performance tuning. He has been the Social Media Director for the Rocky Mountain Oracle Users Group, contributes monthly articles for databasejournal.com, participates in various Oracle forums and newsgroups, and writes an Oracle-centric blog at http://dfitzjarrell.wordpress.com.

Mary Mikell Spence, a Senior Oracle Database Administrator living in Metropolitan Atlanta, Georgia, has worked in the IT field since graduating from Georgia Tech in 1983. Beginning her career as an application developer, she has worked with Oracle since 1991. Her Oracle experience has involved everything from database design and architecture through backup and recovery. She began working with Oracle E-Business Suite 11i as an ERP DBA in 2000 while on a large migration and upgrade project; the past couple of years have found her working on a similar project—this time, on Exadata with a multi-terabyte ERP database. Mary may be found on LinkedIn at http://www.linkedin.com/in/mmspence.

About the Technical Reviewer

Arup Nanda has been an Oracle DBA for more than 18 years (and counting), working on all aspects of Oracle database, from modeling, performance tuning, backup, and disaster recovery to security and, more recently, Exadata. Currently, he is the global database lead at a major multinational corporation near New York, managing, among other things, several Exadata installations. Arup has coauthored five books, published more than 500 articles on *Oracle Magazine, Oracle Technology Network*, and in other publications; presented about 300 sessions at various Oracle technology conferences all over the world; and delivered 30 Oracle Celebrity Seminar series courses. He is an editor for *SELECT Journal*—the IOUG publication, a member of the Board of Directors of the Exadata SIG, an Oracle ACE Director, and a member of the Oak Table Network. Acknowledging his professional expertise and involvement in the user community, Oracle awarded him the "DBA of the Year" title in 2003 and "Architect of the Year" in 2012.

Acknowledgments

Successes are never the result of a single person's actions; many seen, and unseen, individuals contribute in many ways to ensure completion of a project. With that thought in mind, I express my heartfelt gratitude to those who helped me start and finish this book. First and foremost, I thank my loving wife, Shari, for giving me confidence, feedback, and several severe kicks in the pants to keep me on schedule. I wasn't the most pleasant person to deal with when deadlines loomed and the words sometimes wouldn't flow; she stuck with me and kept me going like no one else possibly could. Next are our two wonderful children, Gabi and Zachary, who understood that Daddy had more work to do long after the normal workday was over. I know it was hard on them to muster the patience they so bravely displayed, especially since they were 11 and 8, respectively, when this whole project started. They are truly awesome. My coconspirator, Mary, was also a trouper, providing not only insight but a much-needed second opinion, which helped tremendously when something that made perfect sense to me didn't quite turn the light on with her. This made me step back and seek a different perspective on my work. I think it has made for a more focused text, clearing up any ambiguities my tunnel vision might have created. Then there's Kellyn Pot'Vin, who hauled me on to the Board of Directors of the Rocky Mountain Oracle Users Group (RMOUG) and sentenced me to be the Social Media Director for a year, an honor which caused my wife to laugh. ("You?!? You're not very social." "Remember, these are Oracle nerds." "Oh, then you actually stand a chance.") Kellyn's insistence and persistence paid off handsomely; I have met wonderful members of the Oracle community who have been so supportive of this effort, including Amy Caldwell, Sarah Cleaver, Rebecca Mitchell, Jeff Smith, and Leighton Nelson. To these people, I am deeply and profoundly indebted.

—David Fitzjarrell

Introduction

This book was borne from our personal experiences with managing, configuring, and migrating databases and applications to the Exadata platform. Along the way, we took notes, tried this, tried that, and eventually came to an understanding of what Exadata could do and how it does it. We didn't go into great detail on the inner workings of the system (Kerry Osborne, Randy Johnson, and Tanel Pöder have already provided an excellent text at that level), opting instead to provide a guide for the working DBA who may not have time to read through and digest a "nuts and bolts" book. Thus, this book is designed to lead the DBA through what we feel are the most important aspects and concepts of Exadata, without getting bogged down in details. We recommend having access to an Exadata machine, so you can try the scripts, queries, and commands provided and see the results firsthand. Having an interactive experience with Exadata will, we think, make some of the concepts easier to understand.

Our goal in writing this book was to provide experienced Oracle DBAs with the tools and knowledge to take on Exadata, hopefully without fear. No attempt is made to explain how Oracle works—this is not a "learn Oracle by doing" text. Our intent is to leverage the existing knowledge of field-proven and time-tested Oracle professionals, so that they can successfully adapt what they already know to the Exadata platform.

CHAPTER 1

■ ■ ■

Exadata Basics

Since its introduction in September 2008, Exadata has fast become both a familiar term and a familiar presence in the IT/database realm. The system has undergone several changes in its short history, from storage solution to complete database appliance. Although it is not yet a household name, the number of Exadata installations has increased to the point where it will soon become commonplace in data centers across the country. So, what *is* Exadata? It might be better to begin by stating what Exadata isn't. Exadata is not

- the greatest thing since sliced bread;
- the only database machine that can single-handedly eliminate every occurrence of contention in your application;
- the long-awaited silver bullet to solve all of your other database performance problems;
- a black box, constructed by the wizards of Middle Earth, understandable only to the anointed few.

What *Is* Exadata?

Now that you know what Exadata isn't, let's discuss what it is. Exadata is a system, composed of matched and tuned components providing enhancements available with no other configuration, that can improve the performance of the database tier. This system includes database servers, storage servers, an internal InfiniBand network with switches, and storage devices (disks), all configured by Oracle Advanced Customer Support personnel to meet the customer's requirements. (Changes to that configuration, including changing the default storage allocations between the data and recovery disk groups, can be made with assistance from Oracle Advanced Customer Support.) Figure 1-1 illustrates the general layout of an Exadata system.

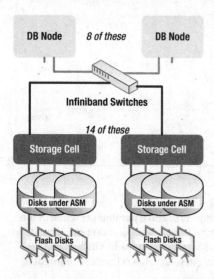

Figure 1-1. *General layout of an Exadata system*

Can Exadata improve every situation? No, but it wasn't designed to. Originally designed as a data warehouse/business intelligence appliance, the releases from V2 on have added Online Transaction Processing (OLTP) applications. Yet not every feature of Exadata is applicable to every query, application, or situation that may arise. Chances are good that if your application is not suffering from contention issues, Exadata may provide reduced response time and better throughput than systems using off-the-shelf components.

Exadata did not start out being what it is today; originally, it was conceived as an open-source storage solution for RAC (Real Application Clusters) installations, intended to address the problem of transferring large volumes of data across the grid infrastructure, known internally within Oracle as SAGE (Storage Appliance for Grid Environments). In September 2008, Oracle unveiled the HP Oracle Database Machine, spotlighting the Exadata Storage Servers. At that time, Exadata referred only to the storage server components, although the HP Oracle Database Machine included all of the components found in later releases of the Exadata product.

The system was marketed as a data warehouse solution. Then, a year later, Exadata V2 was released, this time marketed as a complete and integrated database appliance, including database servers, storage servers, an internal InfiniBand network, and software designed so the components worked in concert as a unified whole. Oracle marketed this appliance as the first database machine for OLTP, so now Exadata was the machine of choice for both data warehousing and OLTP systems. The following year (2010) saw the release of Exadata X2, which continued the improvements by adding a second configuration (X2-8) to the mix. This provided customers with two options for a full-rack implementation. And in September 2012, Exadata X3 hit the market, improving performance yet again and offering a fifth configuration option, the Eighth Rack.

Available Configurations

The X3 series of Exadata machines, which replaced the X2 series, is available in the following five configurations:

> *X3-2 Eighth Rack*: Two database servers, each with two eight-core Xeon processors with eight cores enabled and 256GB of RAM, three storage servers, and thirty-six disk drives
>
> *X3-2 Quarter Rack*: Two database servers, each with two eight-core Xeon processors and 256GB of RAM, three storage servers, and thirty-six disk drives

X3-2 Half Rack: Four database servers, each with two eight-core Xeon processors and 256GB of RAM, seven storage servers, eighty-four disk drives, and a spine switch for expansion

X3-2 Full Rack: Eight database servers, each with two eight-core Xeon processors and 256GB of RAM, fourteen storage servers, one hundred sixty-eight disk drives, and a spine switch for expansion

X3-8 Full Rack: Two database servers, each with eight ten-core Xeon processors and 2TB of RAM, fourteen storage servers, one hundred sixty-eight disk drives, a spine switch for expansion, and no keyboard/video/mouse module

In general, the X3 series of Exadata machines is twice as powerful as the discontinued X2 series on a "like for like" comparison. As mentioned earlier, in the X3-2 series, there is a new Eighth Rack configuration that provides slightly less computing power (a total of sixteen processor cores, eight of which are enabled) than the X2-2 Quarter Rack (which offered a total of twelve processor cores, all of which were enabled). This reduces the licensing costs as compared to the X3-2 Quarter Rack, making the Eighth Rack a very suitable and cost-effective X3-2 entry point into the Exadata arena.

Storage

How much raw storage you have depends on whether you choose High Capacity or High Performance drives—High Capacity Serial Attached SCSI (SAS) drives have 3TB each of raw storage running at 7,200RPM and the High Performance drives have 600GB each running at 15,000RPM. For a Quarter Rack configuration with High Capacity disks, 108TB of total raw storage is provided, with roughly 40TB available for data after normal Automatic Storage Management (ASM) redundancy is configured. Using High Performance disks, the total raw storage for a Quarter Rack machine is 21.1TB, with approximately 8.4TB of usable data storage with normal ASM redundancy. High redundancy reduces the storage by roughly another third on both configurations; the tradeoff is the additional ASM mirror in case of disk failure, as high redundancy provides two copies of the data. Normal redundancy provides one copy.

The disks are accessed through the storage servers (or cells), running their own version of Linux with a subset of the Oracle kernel built in. It is interesting to note that there is no direct access to the storage from the database servers; the only way they can "see" the disks is through ASM. In the X3-2 Quarter Rack and Eighth Rack configurations, there are three storage cells, with each storage cell controlling twelve disks. Each storage server provides two six-core Xeon processors and 24GB of RAM. Between the various configurations of Exadata, the differences become the number of database servers (often referred to as *compute nodes*) and the number of storage servers or cells—the greater the number of storage cells, the more storage the Exadata machine can control internally. As previously noted, the storage servers also run an integrated Oracle kernel. This allows the database servers to "pass off" (or offload) parts of qualifying queries, so that the database servers only have to handle the reduced data volume of the result sets, rather than scanning every data or index block for the objects of interest. This is known as a Smart Scan. How Smart Scans work and what triggers them are covered in Chapter 2.

Smart Flash Cache

Another part of the Exadata performance package is the Smart Flash Cache, 384GB of solid-state flash storage for each storage cell, configured across four Sun Flash Accelerator F20 PCIe cards. With a Quarter Rack configuration (three storage servers/cells), 1.1TB of flash storage is available; a Full Rack provides 5.3TB of flash storage. The flash cache is usable as a smart cache to service large volumes of random reads, or it can be configured as flash disk devices and mounted as an ASM disk group. That topic will be covered in greater depth in Chapter 4.

Even More Storage

Expansion racks consist of both storage servers and disk drives. There are three different configurations available: Quarter Rack, Half Rack, and Full Rack, any of which can connect to any Oracle Exadata machine. For the Quarter Rack configuration, an additional spine switch will be necessary; the IP address for the spine switch is left unassigned during configuration, so that if one is installed, the address will be available, with no need to reconfigure the machine.

Besides adding storage, these racks also add computing power for Smart Scan operations, with the smallest expansion rack containing four storage servers and forty-eight disk drives, adding eight six-core CPUs to the mix. The largest expansion rack provides 18 storage servers with 216 disk drives. Actual storage will depend on whether the system is using High Capacity or High Performance disk drives; the drive types cannot be mixed in a single Exadata machine/expansion rack configuration, so if the Exadata system is using High Capacity drives, the expansion rack must also contain High Capacity disks, if those disks are being added to existing disk groups.

One reason for this requirement is that ASM stripes the data across the total number of drives in a disk group, thus the size and geometry of the disk units must be uniform across the storage tier. It is not necessary for the disks of the expansion rack to be added to an existing disk group; a completely separate disk group can be created from that storage. You cannot mix storage types within the expansion rack, but the disk type does not need to match that of the host system, if a separate disk group is to be created from that storage. The beauty of these expansion racks is that they integrate seamlessly with the existing storage on the host Exadata system. If these disks are added to existing disk groups, ASM automatically triggers a rebalance to evenly distribute the extents across the total number of available disks.

Things to Know

An Exadata system, available in four configurations, is a complex arrangement of database servers, storage servers, disk drives, and an internal InfiniBand network with modifications designed to address many performance issues in a unique way. It's the first system with a "divide-and-conquer" approach to query processing that can dramatically improve performance and reduce query response time. It also includes Smart Flash Cache, a write-back cache that can handle large volumes of reads and is designed for Online Transaction Processing (OLTP) systems. This cache can also be configured as flash disk devices. Additional storage is available in the form of Exadata Expansion Racks, which can be added to any Exadata configuration to extend the storage and add storage-cell computing power. The storage in the expansion rack can be the same type (High Capacity, High Performance) as in the Exadata Machine; however, in some cases, Oracle recommends High Capacity drives for expansion racks, regardless of the storage found in the host Exadata system.

Moving on, we'll discuss the various performance enhancements Exadata provides and how, at least in a limited way, these enhancements are implemented. This is not meant to be an exhaustive text but a "getting started" guide to help lead you through the maze. There are other, more technical, texts you can read to gain a deeper knowledge of the machine, but with this book's background in hand, it will be easier to understand what Exadata does that other systems can't.

CHAPTER 2

▪▪▪

Smart Scans and Offloading

One of the enhancements provided by Exadata is the Smart Scan, a mechanism by which parts of a query can be offloaded, or handed off, to the storage servers for processing. This "divide-and-conquer" approach is one reason Exadata is able to provide such stellar performance. It's accomplished by the configuration of Exadata, where database servers and storage cells offer computing power and the ability to process queries, owing to the unique storage server software running on the storage cells.

Smart Scans

Not every query qualifies for a Smart Scan, as certain conditions must be met. Those conditions are as follows:

- A full table scan or full index scan must be used, in addition to direct-path reads.

- One or more of the following simple comparison operators must be in use:

    - =

    - <

    - >

    - >=

    - =<

    - BETWEEN

    - IN

    - IS NULL

    - IS NOT NULL

Smart Scans will also be available when queries are run in parallel, because direct-path reads are executed by default, by parallel query slaves. Of course, the other conditions must also be met: parallel only ensures that direct-path reads are used. What does a Smart Scan do to improve performance? It reduces the amount of data the database servers must process to return results. The offloading process divides the workload among the compute nodes and the storage cells, involves more CPU resources, and returns smaller sets of data to the receiving process.

Instead of reading 10,000 blocks of data to return 1,000 rows, offloading allows the storage cells to perform some of the work with access and filter predicates and to send back only the rows that meet the provided criteria. Similar in operation to parallel query slaves, the offloading process divides the work among the available storage cells, and each cell returns any qualifying rows stored in that particular subset of disks. And, like parallel query, the result "pieces" are merged into the final result set. Offloading also reduces inter-instance transfer between nodes, which, in turn, reduces latching and global locking. Latching, in particular, consumes CPU cycles. Less latching equates to a further reduction in CPU cycles, enhancing performance. The net "savings" in CPU work and execution time can be substantial; queries that take minutes to execute on non-Exadata systems can sometimes be completed in seconds as a result of using Smart Scans.

Plans and Metrics

Execution plans can report Smart Scan activity, if they are the actual plans generated by the optimizer at runtime. Qualifying plans will be found in the V$SQL_PLAN and DBA_HIST_SQL_PLAN views and will be generated by autotrace, when the ON option is used, or can be found by enabling a 10046 trace and processing the resulting trace file through tkprof. Using autotrace in EXPLAIN mode may not provide the same plan as generated at runtime, because it can still use rule-based optimizer decisions to generate plans. The same holds true for EXPLAIN PLAN. (We have seen cases where EXPLAIN PLAN and a 10046 trace differed in the reported execution plan.) The tkprof utility also offers an explain mode, and it, too, can provide misleading plans. By default, tkprof provides the actual plan from the execution, so using the command-line explain option is unnecessary.

Smart Scans are noted in the execution plan in one of three ways:

- TABLE ACCESS STORAGE FULL

- INDEX STORAGE FULL SCAN

- INDEX STORAGE FAST FULL SCAN

The presence of one or more of these operations does not mean that a Smart Scan actually occurred; other metrics should be used to verify Smart Scan execution. The V$SQL view (and, for RAC databases, GV$SQL) has two columns that provide further information on cell offload execution, io_cell_offload_eligible_bytes and io_cell_offload_returned_bytes. These are populated with relevant information regarding cell offload activity for a given sql_id, provided a Smart Scan was actually executed.

The io_cell_offload_eligible_bytes column reports the bytes of data that qualify for offload. This is the volume of data that can be offloaded to the storage cells during query execution. The io_cell_offload_returned_bytes column reports the number of bytes returned by the regular I/O path. These are the bytes that were not offloaded to the cells. The difference between these two values provides the bytes actually offloaded during query execution. If no Smart Scan were used, the values for both columns would be 0. There will be cases where the column io_cell_offload_eligible_bytes will be equal to 0, but the column io_cell_offload_returned_bytes will not. Such cases will usually, but not always, be referencing either fixed views (such as GV$SESSION_WAIT) or other data dictionary views (V$TEMPSEG_USAGE, for example). Such queries are not considered eligible for offload. (The view isn't offloadable, because it may expose memory structures resident on the database compute nodes, but that doesn't indicate they don't qualify for a Smart Scan [one or more of the base tables to that view might qualify].) The presence of projection data in VSQL_PLAN/GVSQL_PLAN is proof enough that a Smart Scan was executed.

Looking at a query where a Smart Scan is executed, using the smart_scan_ex.sql script, we see

```
SQL> select *
  2  from emp
  3  where empid = 7934;

    EMPID EMPNAME                                         DEPTNO
--------- ----------------------------------------- ----------
     7934 Smorthorper7934                                    15

Elapsed: 00:00:00.21
```

Execution Plan

Plan hash value: 3956160932

```
----------------------------------------------------------------------------------
| Id | Operation                  | Name | Rows | Bytes | Cost (%CPU)| Time     |
----------------------------------------------------------------------------------
|  0 | SELECT STATEMENT           |      |    1 |    28 | 6361   (1)| 00:00:01 |
|* 1 | TABLE ACCESS STORAGE FULL  | EMP  |    1 |    28 | 6361   (1)| 00:00:01 |
----------------------------------------------------------------------------------
```

Predicate Information (identified by operation id):

```
   1 - storage("EMPID"=7934)
       filter("EMPID"=7934)
```

Statistics

```
       1  recursive calls
       1  db block gets
   40185  consistent gets
   22594  physical reads
     168  redo size
     680  bytes sent via SQL*Net to client
     524  bytes received via SQL*Net from client
       2  SQL*Net roundtrips to/from client
       0  sorts (memory)
       0  sorts (disk)
       1  rows processed
```

SQL>

Notice that the execution plan reports, via the TABLE ACCESS STORAGE FULL operation, that a Smart Scan is in use. Verifying that with a quick query to V$SQL we see

```
    SQL>select  sql_id,
  2  io_cell_offload_eligible_bytes qualifying,
  3  io_cell_offload_eligible_bytes - io_cell_offload_returned_bytes actual,
  4  round((((io_cell_offload_eligible_bytes - io_cell_offload_returned_bytes)/io_cell_offload_
     eligible_bytes)*100, 2) io_saved_pct,
  5  sql_text
  6  from v$sql
  7  where io_cell_offload_returned_bytes> 0
  8  and instr(sql_text, 'emp') > 0
  9  and parsing_schema_name = 'BING';
```

```
SQL_ID          QUALIFYING    ACTUAL  IO_SAVED_PCT SQL_TEXT
-------------   ----------    ------  ------------ -------------------------------------
gfjb8dpxvpuv6   185081856   42510928        22.97 select * from emp where empid = 7934
```

SQL>

The savings in I/O, as a percentage of the total eligible bytes, was 22.97 percent, meaning Oracle processed almost 23 percent *less* data than it would have had a Smart Scan not been executed. Setting cell_offload_processing=false in the session, the query is executed again, using the no_smart_scan_ex.sql script, as follows:

```
SQL> alter session set cell_offload_processing=false;

Session altered.

Elapsed: 00:00:00.00
SQL>
SQL> select *
  2  from emp
  3  where empid = 7934;

    EMPID EMPNAME                                            DEPTNO
---------- -------------------------------------------- ----------
      7934 Smorthorper7934                                     15

Elapsed: 00:00:03.73

Execution Plan
----------------------------------------------------------
Plan hash value: 3956160932

-----------------------------------------------------------------------------------
| Id  | Operation                | Name  | Rows  | Bytes | Cost (%CPU)| Time     |
-----------------------------------------------------------------------------------
|   0 | SELECT STATEMENT         |       |     1 |    28 |  6361   (1)| 00:00:01 |
|*  1 |  TABLE ACCESS STORAGE FULL| EMP   |     1 |    28 |  6361   (1)| 00:00:01 |
-----------------------------------------------------------------------------------

Predicate Information (identified by operation id):
---------------------------------------------------

   1 - filter("EMPID"=7934)

Statistics
----------------------------------------------------------
          1  recursive calls
          1  db block gets
      45227  consistent gets
      22593  physical reads
          0  redo size
        680  bytes sent via SQL*Net to client
        524  bytes received via SQL*Net from client
          2  SQL*Net roundtrips to/from client
          0  sorts (memory)
          0  sorts (disk)
          1  rows processed
```

```
SQL>
SQL> set autotrace off timing off
SQL>
SQL> select sql_id,
  2  io_cell_offload_eligible_bytes qualifying,
  3  io_cell_offload_eligible_bytes - io_cell_offload_returned_bytes actual,
  4  round(((io_cell_offload_eligible_bytes - io_cell_offload_returned_bytes)/io_cell_offload_
     eligible_bytes)*100, 2) io_saved_pct,
  5  sql_text
  6  from v$sql
  7  where io_cell_offload_returned_bytes > 0
  8  and instr(sql_text, 'emp') > 0
  9  and parsing_schema_name = 'BING';

no rows selected

SQL>
```

In the absence of a Smart Scan, the query executed in 3.73 seconds and processed the entire 185081856 bytes of data. Because offload processing was disabled, the storage cells provided no assistance with the query processing. It is interesting to note that the execution plan reports TABLE ACCESS STORAGE FULL, a step usually associated with a Smart Scan. The absence of predicate information and the "no rows selected" result for the offload bytes query prove that a Smart Scan was not executed. Disabling cell offload processing created a noticeable difference in execution time, proving the power of a Smart Scan.

Smart Scan performance can also outshine the performance provided by an index for larger volumes of data by allowing Oracle to reduce the I/O by gigabytes, or even terabytes, of data when returning rows satisfying the query criteria. There are also cases where a Smart Scan is not the best performer; an index is added to the table and the same set of queries is executed a third time, again using the smart_scan_ex.sql script:

```
SQL> create index empid_idx on emp(empid);

Index created.

SQL>
SQL> set autotrace on timing on
SQL>
SQL> select *
  2  from emp
  3  where empid = 7934;

    EMPID EMPNAME                                         DEPTNO
---------- ----------------------------------------- ----------
     7934 Smorthorper7934                                 15


Elapsed: 00:00:00.01

Execution Plan
----------------------------------------------------------------
Plan hash value: 1109982043
```

```
----------------------------------------------------------------------------------
| Id | Operation                   | Name      | Rows | Bytes | Cost(%CPU)| Time     |
----------------------------------------------------------------------------------
|  0 | SELECT STATEMENT            |           |    1 |    28 |    4  (0)| 00:00:01|
|  1 |  TABLE ACCESS BY INDEX ROWID| EMP       |    1 |    28 |    4  (0)| 00:00:01|
|* 2 |   INDEX RANGE SCAN          | EMPID_IDX |    1 |       |    3  (0)| 00:00:01|
----------------------------------------------------------------------------------

Predicate Information (identified by operation id):
---------------------------------------------------

   2 - access("EMPID"=7934)

Statistics
---------------------------------------------------------------
     1  recursive calls
     0  db block gets
     5  consistent gets
     2  physical reads
   148  redo size
   684  bytes sent via SQL*Net to client
   524  bytes received via SQL*Net from client
     2  SQL*Net roundtrips to/from client
     0  sorts (memory)
     0  sorts (disk)
     1  rows processed
SQL>
SQL> set autotrace off timing off
SQL>
SQL>select sql_id,
  2  io_cell_offload_eligible_bytes qualifying,
  3  io_cell_offload_returned_bytes actual,
  4  round(((io_cell_offload_eligible_bytes - io_cell_offload_returned_bytes)/io_cell_offload_
     eligible_bytes)*100, 2) io_saved_pct,
  5  sql_text
  6  from v$sql
  7  where io_cell_offload_returned_bytes> 0
  8  and instr(sql_text, 'emp') > 0
  9  and parsing_schema_name = 'BING';

no rows selected

SQL>
```

Notice that an index range scan was chosen by the optimizer, rather than offloading the predicates to the storage cells. The elapsed time for the index-range scan was considerably less than the elapsed time for the Smart Scan, so, in some cases, a Smart Scan may not be the most efficient path to the data. This also illustrates an issue with existing indexes, as the optimizer may select an index that makes the execution path worse, which explains why some Exadata sources recommend dropping indexes to improve performance. Although it may eventually be decided that dropping an index is best for the overall performance of a query or group of queries, no such recommendation is offered here, as each situation is different and needs to be evaluated on a case-by-case basis; what's good for one Exadata system and application may not be good for another. The only way to know, with any level of certainty, whether or not to drop a particular index is to test and evaluate the results in an environment as close to production as possible.

Smart Scan Optimizations

A Smart Scan uses various optimizations to accomplish its task. There are three major optimizations a Smart Scan implements: Column Projection, Predicate Filtering, and storage indexes. Because storage indexes will be covered in detail in the next chapter, this discussion will concentrate on the first two optimizations. Suffice it to say, for now, that storage indexes are not like conventional indexes, in that they inform Exadata where *not* to look for data. That may be confusing at this point, but it will be covered in depth later. The primary focus of the next sections will be Column Projection and Predicate Filtering.

Column Projection

What is Column Projection? It's Exadata's ability to return only the columns requested by the query. In conventional systems using commodity hardware, Oracle will fetch the data blocks of interest in their entirety from the storage cells, loading them into the buffer cache. Oracle then extracts the columns from these blocks, filtering them at the end to return only the columns in the select list. Thus, the entire rows of data are returned to be further processed before displaying the final results. Column Projection does the filtering *before* it gets to the database server, returning only columns in the select list and, if applicable, those columns necessary for join operations. Rather than return the entire data block or row, Exadata returns only what it needs to complete the query operation. This can considerably reduce the data processed by the database servers.

Take, as an example, a table with 45 columns and a select list that contains 7 of those columns. Column Projection will return only those 7 columns, rather than the entire 45, reducing the database server workload appreciably. Let's add a two-column join condition to the query and another two columns from another table with 71 columns; Column Projection will return the nine columns from the select list and the four columns in the join condition (presuming the join columns are not in the select list). Thirteen columns are much less data than 116 columns (the 45 from the first table and the 71 from the second), which is one reason Smart Scans can be so fast. Column Projection information is available from either the PROJECTION column from V$SQL_PLAN or from the DBMS_XPLAN package, so you can choose which of the two is easier for you to use; the projection information is returned only if the "+projection" parameter is passed to the DISPLAY_CURSOR function, as was done in this example (again from smart_scan_ex.sql), which makes use of both methods of retrieving the Column Projection data:

```
SQL> select *
  2  from emp
  3  where empid = 7934;

    EMPID EMPNAME                                          DEPTNO
---------- ---------------------------------------- ----------
      7934 Smorthorper7934                                  15

Elapsed: 00:00:00.16

SQL> select sql_id,
  2          projection
  3  from v$sql_plan
  4  where sql_id = 'gfjb8dpxvpuv6';
```

```
SQL_ID         PROJECTION
------------- --------------------------------------------------------------------
gfjb8dpxvpuv6 "EMPID"[NUMBER,22], "EMP"."EMPNAME"[VARCHAR2,40], "EMP"."DEPTNO"[NUMBER,22]

SQL>
SQL> select *
  2  from table(dbms_xplan.display_cursor('&sql_id','&child_no', '+projection'));
Enter value for sql_id: gfjb8dpxvpuv6
Enter value for child_no:

PLAN_TABLE_OUTPUT
--------------------------------------------------------------------------------SQL_ID
gfjb8dpxvpuv6, child number 0
-------------------------------------
select * from emp where empid = 7934

Plan hash value: 3956160932


-------------------------------------------------------------------------------
| Id  | Operation                | Name | Rows | Bytes | Cost (%CPU)| Time     |
-------------------------------------------------------------------------------
|   0 | SELECT STATEMENT         |      |      |       | 6361 (100)|           |
|*  1 |   TABLE ACCESS STORAGE FULL| EMP |    1 |    28 | 6361   (1)| 00:00:01 |
-------------------------------------------------------------------------------

Predicate Information (identified by operation id):
---------------------------------------------------

   1 - storage("EMPID"=7934)
       filter("EMPID"=7934)

Column Projection Information (identified by operation id):
----------------------------------------------------------

1 - "EMPID"[NUMBER,22], "EMP"."EMPNAME"[VARCHAR2,40],
    "EMP"."DEPTNO"[NUMBER,22]


29 rows selected.

SQL>
```

As only three columns were requested, only those three columns were returned by the storage servers (proven by the Column Projection Information section of the autotrace report), making the query execution much more efficient. The database servers had no need to filter the result set rows to return only the desired columns.

Predicate Filtering

Where Column Projection returns only the columns of interest from a select list or join condition, Predicate Filtering is the mechanism used by Exadata to return only the rows of interest. Such filtering occurs at the storage cells, which reduces the volume of data the database servers must process. The predicate information is passed on to the storage servers during the course of Smart Scan execution, so performing the filtering operation at the storage server level is a logical choice. Because the data volume to the database servers is reduced, so is the load on the database server CPUs. The preceding example used both Column Projection and Predicate Filtering to rapidly return the result set; using both is a powerful combination not available from systems configured from individual, unmatched components.

Basic Joins

Depending on the query, join processing can also be offloaded to the storage servers, and these are processed using an interesting construct known as a *bloom filter*. These are not new, nor are they exclusive to Exadata, as Oracle has used them in query processing since Oracle Database Version 10g Release 2, primarily to reduce traffic between parallel query slaves. What is a bloom filter? Named after Burton Howard Bloom, who came up with the concept in the 1970s, it's an efficient data structure used to quickly determine if an element has a high probability of being a member of a given set. It's based on a bit array that allows for rapid searches and returns one of two results: either the element is probably in the set (which can produce false positives) or the element is definitely not in the set. The filter cannot produce false negatives, and the incidence of false positives is relatively rare. Another advantage to bloom filters is their small size relative to other data structures used for similar purposes (self-balancing binary search trees, hash tables, or linked lists). The possibility of false positives necessitates the addition of another filter to eliminate them from the results, yet such a filter doesn't add appreciably to the process time and, therefore, goes relatively unnoticed.

When bloom filters are used for a query on an Exadata system, the filter predicate *and* the storage predicate will list the SYS_OP_BLOOM_FILTER function as being called. This function includes the additional filter to eliminate any false positives that could be returned. It's the storage predicate that provides the real power of the bloom filter on Exadata. Using a bloom filter to pre-join the tables at the storage server level reduces the volume of data the database servers need to process and can significantly reduce the execution time of the given query.

An example of bloom filters in action follows; the bloom_fltr_ex.sql script was executed to generate this output.

```
SQL> --
SQL> -- Create sample tables
SQL> --
SQL> -- Create them parallel, necessary
SQL> -- to get a Smart Scan on these tables
SQL> --
SQL> create table emp(
  2      empid   number,
  3      empnmvarchar2(40),
  4      empsal  number,
  5      empssn  varchar2(12),
  6      constraint emp_pk primary key (empid)
  7  ) parallel 4;

Table created.

SQL>
```

```
SQL> create table emp_dept(
  2        empid    number,
  3        empdept  number,
  4        emploc   varchar2(60),
  5     constraint emp_dept_pk primary key(empid)
  6  ) parallel 4;

Table created.

SQL>
SQL> create table dept_info(
  2        deptnum number,
  3        deptnm  varchar2(25),
  4     constraint dept_info_pk primary key(deptnum)
  5  ) parallel 4;

Table created.
SQL>
SQL> --
SQL> -- Load sample tables with data
SQL> --
SQL> begin
  2          for i in 1..2000000 loop
  3                  insert into emp
  4                     values(i, 'Fnarm'||i, (mod(i, 7)+1)*1000, mod(i,10)||mod(i,10)||mod(i,10)||'-
'||mod(i,10)||mod(i,10)||'-'||mod(i,10)||mod(i,10)||mod(i,10)||mod(i,10));
  5                  insert into emp_dept
  6                    values(i, (mod(i,8)+1)*10, 'Zanzwalla'||(mod(i,8)+1)*10);
  7                      commit;
  8          end loop;
  9          insert into dept_info
 10          select distinct empdept, case when empdept = 10 then 'SALES'
 11                                         when empdept = 20 then 'PROCUREMENT'
 12                                         when empdept = 30 then 'HR'
 13                                         when empdept = 40 then 'RESEARCH'
 14                                         when empdept = 50 then 'DEVELOPMENT'
 15                                         when empdept = 60 then 'EMPLOYEE RELATIONS'
 16                                         when empdept = 70 then 'FACILITIES'
 17                                         when empdept = 80 then 'FINANCE' end
 18          from emp_dept;
 19
 20 end;
 21 /

PL/SQL procedure successfully completed.

SQL>
SQL> --
SQL> -- Run join query using bloom filter
SQL> --
SQL> -- Generate execution plan to prove bloom
SQL> -- filter usage
```

14

```
SQL> --
SQL> -- Also report query execution time
SQL> --
SQL> set autotrace on
SQL> set timing on
SQL>
SQL> select /*+ bloom join 2 parallel 2 use_hash(empemp_dept) */ e.empid, e.empnm, d.deptnm,
e.empsal
  2  from emp e join emp_depted on (ed.empid = e.empid) join dept_info d on (ed.empdept = d.deptnum)
  3  where ed.empdept = 20;
```

EMPID EMPNM	DEPTNM	EMPSAL
904505 Fnarm904505	PROCUREMENT	1000
907769 Fnarm907769	PROCUREMENT	3000
909241 Fnarm909241	PROCUREMENT	5000
909505 Fnarm909505	PROCUREMENT	3000
909641 Fnarm909641	PROCUREMENT	6000
910145 Fnarm910145	PROCUREMENT	6000
...		
155833 Fnarm155833	PROCUREMENT	7000
155905 Fnarm155905	PROCUREMENT	2000
151081 Fnarm151081	PROCUREMENT	1000
151145 Fnarm151145	PROCUREMENT	2000

250000 rows selected.

Elapsed: 00:00:14.27

Execution Plan

Plan hash value: 2643012915

```
---------------------------------------------------------------------------------------------------
| Id  | Operation                    | Name        | Rows | Bytes | Cost (%CPU)| Time     | TQ    |IN-OUT| PQ Distrib |
---------------------------------------------------------------------------------------------------
|   0 | SELECT STATEMENT             |             | 218K |   21M | 1376   (1)| 00:00:01 |       |      |            |
|   1 |  PX COORDINATOR              |             |      |       |           |          |       |      |            |
|   2 |   PX SEND QC (RANDOM)        | :TQ10002    | 218K |   21M | 1376   (1)| 00:00:01 | Q1,02 | P->S | QC (RAND)  |
|*  3 |    HASH JOIN                 |             | 218K |   21M | 1376   (1)| 00:00:01 | Q1,02 | PCWP |            |
|   4 |     PX RECEIVE               |             | 218K |   11M |  535   (1)| 00:00:01 | Q1,02 | PCWP |            |
|   5 |      PX SEND BROADCAST       | :TQ10001    | 218K |   11M |  535   (1)| 00:00:01 | Q1,01 | P->P | BROADCAST  |
|   6 |       NESTED LOOPS           |             | 218K |   11M |  535   (1)| 00:00:01 | Q1,01 | PCWP |            |
|   7 |        BUFFER SORT           |             |      |       |           |          | Q1,01 | PCWC |            |
|   8 |         PX RECEIVE           |             |      |       |           |          | Q1,01 | PCWP |            |
|   9 |          PX SEND BROADCAST   | :TQ10000    |      |       |           |          |       | S->P | BROADCAST  |
|  10 |           TABLE ACCESS BY INDEX ROWID| DEPT_INFO   |   1 |   27 |   1   (0)| 00:00:01 |       |      |            |
|* 11 |            INDEX UNIQUE SCAN  |DEPT_INFO_PK |   1 |       |   1   (0)| 00:00:01 |       |      |            |
|  12 |        PX BLOCK ITERATOR     |             | 218K | 5556K |  534   (1)| 00:00:01 | Q1,01 | PCWC |            |
|* 13 |TABLE ACCESS STORAGE FULL     | EMP_DEPT    | 218K | 5556K |  534   (1)| 00:00:01 | Q1,01 | PCWP |            |
|  14 |     PX BLOCK ITERATOR        |             |1690K |   77M |  839   (1)| 00:00:01 | Q1,02 | PCWC |            |
|* 15 |TABLE ACCESS STORAGE FULL     | EMP         |1690K |   77M |  839   (1)| 00:00:01 | Q1,02 | PCWP |            |
---------------------------------------------------------------------------------------------------
```

```
Predicate Information (identified by operation id):
---------------------------------------------------

   3 - access("ED"."EMPID"="E"."EMPID")
  11 - access("D"."DEPTNUM"=20)
  13 - storage("ED"."EMPDEPT"=20)
       filter("ED"."EMPDEPT"=20)
  15 - storage(SYS_OP_BLOOM_FILTER(:BF0000,"E"."EMPID"))
       filter(SYS_OP_BLOOM_FILTER(:BF0000,"E"."EMPID"))
Note
-----
   - dynamic sampling used for this statement (level=2)


Statistics
----------------------------------------------------------
     60  recursive calls
    174  db block gets
  40753  consistent gets
  17710  physical reads
   2128  redo size
9437983  bytes sent via SQL*Net to client
 183850  bytes received via SQL*Net from client
  16668  SQL*Net roundtrips to/from client
      6  sorts (memory)
      0  sorts (disk)
 250000  rows processed

SQL>
```

In less than 15 seconds, 250,000 rows were returned from a three-table join of over 4 million rows. The bloom filter made a dramatic difference in how this query was processed and provided exceptional performance given the volume of data queried. If offload processing is turned off, the bloom filter still is used at the database level:

```
SQL> select /*+ bloom join 2 parallel 2 use_hash(empemp_dept) */ e.empid, e.empnm, d.deptnm,
e.empsal
  2  from emp e join emp_depted on (ed.empid = e.empid) join dept_info d on (ed.empdept = d.deptnum)
  3  where ed.empdept = 20;
```

EMPID	EMPNM	DEPTNM	EMPSAL
380945	Fnarm380945	PROCUREMENT	6000
373361	Fnarm373361	PROCUREMENT	3000
373417	Fnarm373417	PROCUREMENT	3000
373441	Fnarm373441	PROCUREMENT	6000
...			
203529	Fnarm203529	PROCUREMENT	5000
202417	Fnarm202417	PROCUREMENT	6000
202425	Fnarm202425	PROCUREMENT	7000
200161	Fnarm200161	PROCUREMENT	4000

```
250000 rows selected.
```

Elapsed: 00:00:16.60

Execution Plan

Plan hash value: 2643012915

| Id | Operation | Name | Rows | Bytes | Cost (%CPU)| Time | TQ |IN-OUT| PQ Distrib |

0	SELECT STATEMENT		218K	21M	1376 (1)	00:00:01			
1	PX COORDINATOR								
2	PX SEND QC (RANDOM)	:TQ10002	218K	21M	1376 (1)	00:00:01	Q1,02	P->S	QC (RAND)
* 3	HASH JOIN		218K	21M	1376 (1)	00:00:01	Q1,02	PCWP	
4	PX RECEIVE		218K	11M	535 (1)	00:00:01	Q1,02	PCWP	
5	PX SEND BROADCAST	:TQ10001	218K	11M	535 (1)	00:00:01	Q1,01	P->P	BROADCAST
6	NESTED LOOPS		218K	11M	535 (1)	00:00:01	Q1,01	PCWP	
7	BUFFER SORT						Q1,01	PCWC	
8	PX RECEIVE						Q1,01	PCWP	
9	PX SEND BROADCAST	:TQ10000						S->P	BROADCAST
10	TABLE ACCESS BY INDEX ROWID	DEPT_INFO	1	27	1 (0)	00:00:01			
* 11	INDEX UNIQUE SCAN	DEPT_INFO_PK	1		1 (0)	00:00:01			
12	PX BLOCK ITERATOR		218K	5556K	534 (1)	00:00:01	Q1,01	PCWC	
* 13	TABLE ACCESS STORAGE FULL	EMP_DEPT	218K	5556K	534 (1)	00:00:01	Q1,01	PCWP	
14	PX BLOCK ITERATOR		1690K	77M	839 (1)	00:00:01	Q1,02	PCWC	
* 15	TABLE ACCESS STORAGE FULL	EMP	1690K	77M	839 (1)	00:00:01	Q1,02	PCWP	

Predicate Information (identified by operation id):
----

   3 - access("ED"."EMPID"="E"."EMPID")
  11 - access("D"."DEPTNUM"=20)
  13 - filter("ED"."EMPDEPT"=20)
  15 - filter(SYS_OP_BLOOM_FILTER(:BF0000,"E"."EMPID"))

Statistics
----
        33 recursive calls
       171 db block gets
     40049 consistent gets
     17657 physical reads
         0 redo size
   9437503 bytes sent via SQL*Net to client
    183850 bytes received via SQL*Net from client
     16668 SQL*Net roundtrips to/from client
         5 sorts (memory)
         0 sorts (disk)
    250000 rows processed

SQL>

Without the storage level execution of the bloom filter, the query execution time increased by 2.33 seconds, a 16.3 percent increase. For longer execution times, this difference can be significant. It isn't the bloom filter that gives Exadata such power with joins, it's the fact that Exadata can execute it not only at the database level but also at the storage level, something commodity hardware configurations can't do.

Offloading Functions

Functions are an interesting topic with Exadata, as far as Smart Scans are concerned. Oracle implements two basic types of functions: single-row functions, such as TO_CHAR(), TO_NUMBER(), CHR(), LPAD(), which operate on a single value and return a single result, and multi-row functions, such as AVG(), LAG(), LEAD(), MIN(), MAX(), and others, which operate on multiple rows and return either a single value or a set of values. Analytic functions are included in this second function type. The single-row functions are eligible to be offloaded and, thus, can qualify a query for a Smart Scan, because single-row functions can be divided among the storage servers to process data. Multi-row functions such as AVG(), MIN(), and MAX()must be able to access the entire set of table data, an action not possible by a Smart Scan with the storage architecture of an Exadata machine. The minimum number of storage servers in the smallest of Exadata configurations is three, and the storage is fairly evenly divided among these. This makes it impossible for one storage server to access the entire set of disks. Thus, the majority of multi-row functions cannot be offloaded to the storage tier; however, queries that utilize these functions may still execute a Smart Scan, even though the function cannot be offloaded, as displayed by executing the agg_smart_scan_ex.sql script; only the relevant output from that script is reproduced here.

```
SQL> select avg(sal)
  2  from emp;

  AVG(SAL)
----------
 2500000.5

Elapsed: 00:00:00.49

Execution Plan
----------------------------------------------------------
Plan hash value: 2083865914
```

Id	Operation	Name	Rows	Bytes	Cost (%CPU)	Time
0	SELECT STATEMENT		1	6	7468 (1)	00:00:01
1	SORT AGGREGATE		1	6		
2	TABLE ACCESS STORAGE FULL	EMP	5000K	28M	7468 (1)	00:00:01

```
Statistics
----------------------------------------------------------
          1  recursive calls
          1  db block gets
      45123  consistent gets
      26673  physical reads
          0  redo size
```

```
  530  bytes sent via SQL*Net to client
  524  bytes received via SQL*Net from client
    2  SQL*Net roundtrips to/from client
    0  sorts (memory)
    0  sorts (disk)
    1  rows processed

SQL>
SQL> set autotrace off timing off
SQL>
SQL> select sql_id,
  2  io_cell_offload_eligible_bytes qualifying,
  3  io_cell_offload_eligible_bytes - io_cell_offload_returned_bytes actual,
  4  round((((io_cell_offload_eligible_bytes - io_cell_offload_returned_bytes)/io_cell_offload_
     eligible_bytes)*100, 2) io_saved_pct,
  5  sql_text
  6  from v$sql
  7  where io_cell_offload_returned_bytes > 0
  8  and instr(sql_text, 'emp') > 0
  9  and parsing_schema_name = 'BING';

SQL_ID         QUALIFYING    ACTUAL  IO_SAVED_PCT SQL_TEXT
-------------  ----------  ----------  ------------  -----------------------------------------------------
2cqn6rjvp8qm7  218505216   54685152         22.82  select avg(sal) from emp
>
SQL>
```

A Smart Scan returned almost 23 percent less data to the database servers, making their work a bit easier. Because the AVG() function isn't offloadable and there is no WHERE clause in the query, the savings came from Column Projection, so Oracle returned only the data it needed (values from the SAL column) to compute the average. COUNT() is also not an offloadable function, but queries using COUNT() can also execute Smart Scans, as evidenced by the following example, also from agg_smart_scan_ex.sql. ()

```
SQL> select count(*)
  2  from emp;

  COUNT(*)
----------
   5000000

Elapsed: 00:00:00.34

Execution Plan
----------------------------------------------------------
Plan hash value: 2083865914
```

```
--------------------------------------------------------------------
| Id  | Operation               | Name | Rows  | Cost (%CPU)| Time     |
--------------------------------------------------------------------
|   0 | SELECT STATEMENT        |      |     1 | 7460   (1)| 00:00:01 |
|   1 |  SORT AGGREGATE         |      |     1 |           |          |
|   2 |   TABLE ACCESS STORAGE FULL| EMP | 5000K| 7460   (1)| 00:00:01 |
--------------------------------------------------------------------
```

Statistics

```
-------------------------------------------------------------
          1  recursive calls
          1  db block gets
      26881  consistent gets
      26673  physical reads
          0  redo size
        526  bytes sent via SQL*Net to client
        524  bytes received via SQL*Net from client
          2  SQL*Net roundtrips to/from client
          0  sorts (memory)
          0  sorts (disk)
          1  rows processed
```

```
SQL>
SQL> set autotrace off timing off
SQL>
SQL> select sql_id,
  2  io_cell_offload_eligible_bytes qualifying,
  3  io_cell_offload_eligible_bytes - io_cell_offload_returned_bytes actual,
  4  round(((io_cell_offload_eligible_bytes - io_cell_offload_returned_bytes)/io_cell_offload_
     eligible_bytes)*100, 2) io_saved_pct,
  5  sql_text
  6  from v$sql
  7  where io_cell_offload_returned_bytes > 0
  8  and instr(sql_text, 'emp') > 0
  9  and parsing_schema_name = 'BING';

SQL_ID        QUALIFYING   ACTUAL IO_SAVED_PCT SQL_TEXT
------------- ---------- ---------- ------------ ----------------------------------------------
6tds0512tv661 218505216  160899016        73.64 select count(*) from emp

SQL>
SQL> select sql_id,
  2          projection
  3  from v$sql_plan
  4  where sql_id = '&sql_id';
Enter value for sql_id: 6tds0512tv661
old   4: where sql_id = '&sql_id'
new   4: where sql_id = '6tds0512tv661'
```

```
SQL_ID        PROJECTION
------------- -----------------------------------------------------------
6tds0512tv661 (#keys=0) COUNT(*)[22]

SQL>
SQL> select *
  2 from table(dbms_xplan.display_cursor('&sql_id','&child_no', '+projection'));
Enter value for sql_id: 6tds0512tv661
Enter value for child_no: 0
old   2: from table(dbms_xplan.display_cursor('&sql_id','&child_no', '+projection'))
new   2: from table(dbms_xplan.display_cursor('6tds0512tv661','0', '+projection'))

PLAN_TABLE_OUTPUT
--------------------------------------------------------------------------------------------------
SQL_ID  6tds0512tv661, child number 0
-------------------------------------
select count(*) from emp

Plan hash value: 2083865914

-----------------------------------------------------------------------
| Id  | Operation              | Name | Rows  | Cost (%CPU)| Time     |
-----------------------------------------------------------------------
|   0 | SELECT STATEMENT       |      |       |  7460 (100)|          |
|   1 |  SORT AGGREGATE        |      |     1 |            |          |
|   2 |   TABLE ACCESS STORAGE FULL| EMP  | 5000K|  7460   (1)| 00:00:01 |
-----------------------------------------------------------------------

Column Projection Information (identified by operation id):
----------------------------------------------------------

   1 - (#keys=0) COUNT(*)[22]

23 rows selected.

SQL>
```

   The savings from the Smart Scan for the COUNT() query are impressive. Oracle only had to process approximately one-fourth of the data that would have been returned by a conventionally configured system.

   Because there are so many functions available in an Oracle database, which of the many can be offloaded? Oracle provides a data dictionary view, V$SQLFN_METADATA, which answers that very question. Inside this view is a column named, appropriately enough, OFFLOADABLE, which indicates, for every Oracle-supplied function in the database, if it can be offloaded. As you could probably guess, it's best to consult this view for each new release or patch level of Oracle running on Exadata. For 11.2.0.3, there are 393 functions that are offloadable, quite a long list by any standard. The following is a tabular output of the full list produced by the offloadable_fn_tbl.sql script.

>	<	>=	<=
=	!=	OPTTAD	OPTTSU
OPTTMU	OPTTDI	OPTTNG	TO_NUMBER
TO_CHAR	NVL	CHARTOROWID	ROWIDTOCHAR
OPTTLK	OPTTNK	CONCAT	SUBSTR
LENGTH	INSTR	LOWER	UPPER
ASCII	CHR	SOUNDEX	ROUND
TRUNC	MOD	ABS	SIGN
VSIZE	OPTTNU	OPTTNN	OPTDAN
OPTDSN	OPTDSU	ADD_MONTHS	MONTHS_BETWEEN
TO_DATE	LAST_DAY	NEW_TIME	NEXT_DAY
OPTDDS	OPTDSI	OPTDIS	OPTDID
OPTDDI	OPTDJN	OPTDNJ	OPTDDJ
OPTDIJ	OPTDJS	OPTDIF	OPTDOF
OPTNTI	OPTCTZ	OPTCDY	OPTNDY
OPTDPC	DUMP	OPTDRO	TRUNC
FLOOR	CEIL	DECODE	LPAD
RPAD	OPTITN	POWER	SYS_OP_TPR
TO_BINARY_FLOAT	TO_NUMBER	TO_BINARY_DOUBLE	TO_NUMBER
INITCAP	TRANSLATE	LTRIM	RTRIM
GREATEST	LEAST	SQRT	RAWTOHEX
HEXTORAW	NVL2	LNNVL	OPTTSTCF
OPTTLKC	BITAND	REVERSE	CONVERT
REPLACE	NLSSORT	OPTRTB	OPTBTR
OPTR2C	OPTTLK2	OPTTNK2	COS
SIN	TAN	COSH	SINH
TANH	EXP	LN	LOG
>	<	>=	<=
=	!=	OPTTVLCF	TO_SINGLE_BYTE
TO_MULTI_BYTE	NLS_LOWER	NLS_UPPER	NLS_INITCAP
INSTRB	LENGTHB	SUBSTRB	OPTRTUR
OPTURTB	OPTBTUR	OPTCTUR	OPTURTC
OPTURGT	OPTURLT	OPTURGE	OPTURLE
OPTUREQ	OPTURNE	ASIN	ACOS
ATAN	ATAN2	CSCONVERT	NLS_CHARSET_NAME
NLS_CHARSET_ID	OPTIDN	TRIM	TRIM
TRIM	SYS_OP_RPB	OPTTM2C	OPTTMZ2C
OPTST2C	OPTSTZ2C	OPTIYM2C	OPTIDS2C
OPTDIPR	OPTXTRCT	OPTITME	OPTTMEI
OPTITTZ	OPTTTZI	OPTISTM	OPTSTMI
OPTISTZ	OPTSTZI	OPTIIYM	OPTIYMI
OPTIIDS	OPTIDSI	OPTITMES	OPTITTZS
OPTISTMS	OPTISTZS	OPTIIYMS	OPTIIDSS
OPTLDIIF	OPTLDIOF	TO_TIME	TO_TIME_TZ
TO_TIMESTAMP	TO_TIMESTAMP_TZ	TO_YMINTERVAL	TO_DSINTERVAL
NUMTOYMINTERVAL	NUMTODSINTERVAL	OPTDIADD	OPTDISUB
OPTDDSUB	OPTIIADD	OPTIISUB	OPTINMUL
OPTINDIV	OPTCHGTZ	OPTOVLPS	OPTOVLPC
OPTDCAST	OPTINTN	OPTNTIN	CAST
SYS_EXTRACT_UTC	GROUPING	SYS_OP_MAP_NONNULL	OPTT2TTZ1
OPTT2TTZ2	OPTTTZ2T1	OPTTTZ2T2	OPTTS2TSTZ1
OPTTS2TSTZ2	OPTTSTZ2TS1	OPTTSTZ2TS2	OPTDAT2TS1

OPTDAT2TS2	OPTTS2DAT1	OPTTS2DAT2	SESSIONTIMEZONE
OPTNTUB8	OPTUB8TN	OPTITZS2A	OPTITZA2S
OPTITZ2TSTZ	OPTTSTZ2ITZ	OPTITZ2TS	OPTTS2ITZ
OPTITZ2C2	OPTITZ2C1	OPTSRCSE	OPTAND
OPTOR	FROM_TZ	OPTNTUB4	OPTUB4TN
OPTCIDN	OPTSMCSE	COALESCE	SYS_OP_VECXOR
SYS_OP_VECAND	BIN_TO_NUM	SYS_OP_NUMTORAW	SYS_OP_RAWTONUM
SYS_OP_GROUPING	TZ_OFFSET	ADJ_DATE	ROWIDTONCHAR
TO_NCHAR	RAWTONHEX	NCHR	SYS_OP_C2C
COMPOSE	DECOMPOSE	ASCIISTR	UNISTR
LENGTH2	LENGTH4	LENGTHC	INSTR2
INSTR4	INSTRC	SUBSTR2	SUBSTR4
SUBSTRC	OPTLIK2	OPTLIK2N	OPTLIK2E
OPTLIK2NE	OPTLIK4	OPTLIK4N	OPTLIK4E
OPTLIK4NE	OPTLIKC	OPTLIKCN	OPTLIKCE
OPTLIKCNE	SYS_OP_VECBIT	SYS_OP_CONVERT	ORA_HASH
OPTTINLA	OPTTINLO	SYS_OP_COMP	SYS_OP_DECOMP
OPTRXLIKE	OPTRXNLIKE	REGEXP_SUBSTR	REGEXP_INSTR
REGEXP_REPLACE	OPTRXCOMPILE	OPTCOLLCONS	TO_BINARY_DOUBLE
TO_BINARY_FLOAT	TO_CHAR	TO_CHAR	OPTFCFSTCF
OPTFCDSTCF	TO_BINARY_FLOAT	TO_BINARY_DOUBLE	TO_NCHAR
TO_NCHAR	OPTFCSTFCF	OPTFCSTDCF	OPTFFINF
OPTFDINF	OPTFFNAN	OPTFDNAN	OPTFFNINF
OPTFDNINF	OPTFFNNAN	OPTFDNNAN	NANVL
NANVL	REMAINDER	REMAINDER	ABS
ABS	ACOS	ASIN	ATAN
ATAN2	CEIL	CEIL	COS
COSH	EXP	FLOOR	FLOOR
LN	LOG	MOD	MOD
POWER	ROUND	ROUND	SIGN
SIGN	SIN	SINH	SQRT
SQRT	TAN	TANH	TRUNC
TRUNC	OPTFFADD	OPTFDADD	OPTFFSUB
OPTFDSUB	OPTFFMUL	OPTFDMUL	OPTFFDIV
OPTFDDIV	OPTFFNEG	OPTFDNEG	OPTFCFEI
OPTFCDEI	OPTFCFIE	OPTFCDIE	OPTFCFI
OPTFCDI	OPTFCIF	OPTFCID	OPTIAND
OPTIOR	OPTMKNULL	OPTRTRI	OPTNINF
OPTNNAN	OPTNNINF	OPTNNNAN	NANVL
REMAINDER	OPTFCFINT	OPTFCDINT	OPTFCINTF
OPTFCINTD	OPTDMO	PREDICTION	PREDICTION_PROBABILITY
PREDICTION_COST	CLUSTER_ID	CLUSTER_PROBABILITY	FEATURE_ID
FEATURE_VALUE	SYS_OP_ROWIDTOOBJ	OPTENCRYPT	OPTDECRYPT
SYS_OP_OPNSIZE	SYS_OP_COMBINED_HASH	REGEXP_COUNT	OPTDMGETO
SYS_DM_RXFORM_N	SYS_DM_RXFORM_CHR	SYS_OP_BLOOM_FILTER	OPTXTRCT_XQUERY
OPTORNA	OPTORNO	SYS_OP_BLOOM_FILTER_LIST	OPTDM
OPTDMGE			

You will note there appear to be duplications of the function names; each function has a unique func_id, although the names may not be unique. This is the result of overloading, providing multiple versions of the same function that take differing numbers and/or types of arguments.

Virtual Columns

Virtual columns are a welcome addition to Oracle. They allow tables to contain values calculated from other columns in the same table. An example would be a TOTAL_COMP column made up of the sum of salary and commission. These column values are not stored physically in the table, so an update to a base column of the sum, for example, would change the resulting value the virtual column returns. As with any other column in a table, a virtual column can be used as a partition key, used in constraints, or used in an index, and statistics can also be gathered on them. Even though the values contained in a virtual column aren't stored with the rest of the table data, they (or, rather, the calculations used to generate them) can be offloaded, so Smart Scans are possible. This is illustrated by running smart_scan_virt_ex.sql. The following is the somewhat abbreviated output.

```
SQL> create table emp (empid number not null,
  2                     empname varchar2(40),
  3                     deptno        number,
  4                     sal           number,
  5                     comm          number,
  6                     ttl_comp      number generated always as (sal + nvl(comm, 0)) virtual );

Table created.

SQL>
SQL> begin
  2          for i in 1..5000000 loop
  3                  insert into emp(empid, empname, deptno, sal, comm)
  4                  values (i, 'Smorthorper'||i, mod(i, 40)+1, 900*(mod(i,4)+1), 200*mod(i,9));
  5          end loop;
  6
  7          commit;
  8 end;
  9 /

PL/SQL procedure successfully completed.

SQL>
SQL> set echo on
SQL>
SQL> exec dbms_stats.gather_schema_stats('BING')

PL/SQL procedure successfully completed.

SQL>
SQL> set autotrace on timing on
SQL>
SQL> select *
  2  from emp
  3  where ttl_comp > 5000;
```

EMPID	EMPNAME	DEPTNO	SAL	COMM	TTL_COMP
12131	Smorthorper12131	12	3600	1600	5200
12167	Smorthorper12167	8	3600	1600	5200
12203	Smorthorper12203	4	3600	1600	5200
12239	Smorthorper12239	40	3600	1600	5200
12275	Smorthorper12275	36	3600	1600	5200
...					
4063355	Smorthorper4063355	36	3600	1600	5200
4063391	Smorthorper4063391	32	3600	1600	5200
4063427	Smorthorper4063427	28	3600	1600	5200

138888 rows selected.

Elapsed: 00:00:20.09

Execution Plan

Plan hash value: 3956160932

```
--------------------------------------------------------------------------------
| Id  | Operation               | Name | Rows  | Bytes | Cost (%CPU)| Time     |
--------------------------------------------------------------------------------
|   0 | SELECT STATEMENT        |      | 232K  | 8402K |  7520   (2)| 00:00:01 |
|*  1 |  TABLE ACCESS STORAGE FULL| EMP  | 232K  | 8402K |  7520   (2)| 00:00:01 |
--------------------------------------------------------------------------------
```

Predicate Information (identified by operation id):

```
   1 - storage("TTL_COMP">5000)
       filter("TTL_COMP">5000)
```

```
SQL> select  sql_id,
  2          io_cell_offload_eligible_bytes qualifying,
  3          io_cell_offload_eligible_bytes - io_cell_offload_returned_bytes actual,
  4          round(((io_cell_offload_eligible_bytes - io_cell_offload_returned_bytes)/io_cell_
offload_eligible_bytes)*100, 2) io_saved_pct,
  5          sql_text
  6  from v$sql
  7  where io_cell_offload_returned_bytes > 0
  8  and instr(sql_text, 'emp') > 0
  9  and parsing_schema_name = 'BING';
```

SQL_ID	QUALIFYING	ACTUAL	IO_SAVED_PCT	SQL_TEXT
6vzxd7wn8858v	218505216	626720	.29	select * from emp where ttl_comp > 5000

```
SQL>
SQL> select sql_id,
  2          projection
  3  from v$sql_plan
  4  where sql_id = '6vzxd7wn8858v';

SQL_ID        PROJECTION
------------- --------------------------------------------------------------
6vzxd7wn8858v
6vzxd7wn8858v "EMP"."EMPID"[NUMBER,22], "EMP"."EMPNAME"[VARCHAR2,40], "EMP
              "."DEPTNO"[NUMBER,22], "SAL"[NUMBER,22], "COMM"[NUMBER,22]


SQL>
```

Updating the COMM column, which in turn updates the TTL_COMP virtual column, and modifying the query to look for a higher value for TTL_COMP skips more of the table data.

```
SQL> update emp
  2  set comm=2000
  3  where sal=3600
  4  and mod(empid, 3) = 0;

416667 rows updated.

SQL>
SQL> commit;

Commit complete.

SQL> set autotrace on timing on
SQL>
SQL> select *
  2  from emp
  3  where ttl_comp > 5200;

    EMPID EMPNAME                                     DEPTNO        SAL       COMM   TTL_COMP
---------- ---------------------------------------- ---------- ---------- ---------- ----------
    12131 Smorthorper12131                              12       3600       2000       5600
    12159 Smorthorper12159                              40       3600       2000       5600
    12187 Smorthorper12187                              28       3600       2000       5600
    12215 Smorthorper12215                              16       3600       2000       5600
    12243 Smorthorper12243                               4       3600       2000       5600
    12271 Smorthorper12271                              32       3600       2000       5600
...
  4063339 Smorthorper4063339                            20       3600       2000       5600
  4063367 Smorthorper4063367                             8       3600       2000       5600
  4063395 Smorthorper4063395                            36       3600       2000       5600
  4063423 Smorthorper4063423                            24       3600       2000       5600

416667 rows selected.
```

```
Elapsed: 00:00:43.85

Execution Plan
------------------------------------------------------------
Plan hash value: 3956160932

------------------------------------------------------------------------
| Id  | Operation                | Name | Rows  | Bytes | Cost (%CPU)| Time     |
------------------------------------------------------------------------
|   0 | SELECT STATEMENT         |      | 138K| 5018K| 7520   (2)| 00:00:01 |
|*  1 |   TABLE ACCESS STORAGE FULL| EMP  | 138K| 5018K| 7520   (2)| 00:00:01 |
------------------------------------------------------------------------

Predicate Information (identified by operation id):
---------------------------------------------------

   1 - storage("TTL_COMP">5200)
       filter("TTL_COMP">5200)

SQL> set autotrace off timing off
SQL>
SQL> select  sql_id,
  2           io_cell_offload_eligible_bytes qualifying,
  3           io_cell_offload_eligible_bytes - io_cell_offload_returned_bytes actual,
  4           round(((io_cell_offload_eligible_bytes - io_cell_offload_returned_bytes)/io_cell_
offload_eligible_bytes)*100, 2) io_saved_pct,
  5           sql_text
  6  from v$sql
  7  where io_cell_offload_returned_bytes > 0
  8  and instr(sql_text, 'emp') > 0
  9  and parsing_schema_name = 'BING';

SQL_ID          QUALIFYING      ACTUAL IO_SAVED_PCT SQL_TEXT
-------------   -----------   ---------   -----------  --------------------------------------
6vzxd7wn8858v   218505216      626720         .29 select * from emp where ttl_comp > 5000
62pvf6c8bng9k   218505216    69916712          32 update emp set comm=2000 where sal=3600 and m
                                                   od(empid, 3) = 0

bmyygpg0uq9p0   218505216   152896792       69.97 select * from emp where ttl_comp > 5200

SQL>
SQL> select sql_id,
  2          projection
  3  from v$sql_plan
  4  where sql_id = '&sql_id';
Enter value for sql_id: bmyygpg0uq9p0
old   4: where sql_id = '&sql_id'
new   4: where sql_id = 'bmyygpg0uq9p0'
```

```
SQL_ID        PROJECTION
------------- ------------------------------------------------------------
bmyygpg0uq9p0
bmyygpg0uq9p0 "EMP"."EMPID"[NUMBER,22], "EMP"."EMPNAME"[VARCHAR2,40], "EMP
              "."DEPTNO"[NUMBER,22], "SAL"[NUMBER,22], "COMM"[NUMBER,22]


SQL>
```

Things to Know

Smart Scans are the lifeblood of Exadata. They provide processing speed unmatched by commodity hardware. Queries are eligible for Smart Scan processing if they execute full table or full index scans, include offloadable comparison operators, and utilize direct reads.

Smart Scan activity is indicated by three operations in a query plan: TABLE ACCESS STORAGE FULL, INDEX STORAGE FULL SCAN, and INDEX STORAGE FAST FULL SCAN. Additionally, two metrics from VSQL/GVSQL (io_cell_offload_eligible_bytes, io_cell_offload_returned_bytes) indicate that a Smart Scan has been executed. The plan steps alone cannot provide proof of Smart Scan activity; the VSQL/GVSQL metrics must also be non-zero to know that a Smart Scan was active.

Exadata provides the exceptional processing power of Smart Scans through the use of Predicate Filtering, Column Projection, and storage indexes (a topic discussed solely in Chapter 3). Predicate Filtering is the ability of Exadata to return only the rows of interest to the database servers. Column Projection returns only the columns of interest, those in the select list, and those in a join predicate. Both of these optimizations reduce the data the database servers must process to return the final results. Also of interest is offloading, the process whereby Exadata offloads, or passes off, parts of the query to the storage servers, allowing them to do a large part of the work in query processing. Because the storage cells have their own CPUs, this also reduces the CPU usage on the database servers, the one point of contact between Exadata and the users.

Joins "join" in on the Exadata performance enhancements, as Exadata utilizes bloom filters to pre-process qualifying joins to return the results from large table joins in far less time than either a hash join or nested loop join could provide.

Some functions are also offloadable to the storage cells, but owing to the nature of the storage cell configuration, generally, only single-row functions are eligible. A function not being offloadable does not disqualify a query from executing a Smart Scan, and you will find that queries using some functions, such as AVG() and COUNT(), will report Smart Scan activity. In Oracle Release 11.2.0.3, there are 393 functions that qualify as offloadable. The V$SQLFN_METADATA view indicates offloadable functions through the OFFLOADABLE column, populated with YES for qualifying functions.

Virtual columns—columns where the values are computed from other columns in the same table—are also offloadable, even though the values in those columns are dynamically generated at query time, so tables that have them are still eligible for Smart Scans.

CHAPTER 3

■ ■ ■

Storage Indexes

Storage indexes may be the most misunderstood and confusing part of Exadata. The name conjures images of conventional index structures, such as the B-tree index, bitmap index, LOB index, and others, but this is a far different construct, with a very different purpose, from any index you may have seen outside of Exadata. Designed and implemented in a unique fashion, with a purpose that is very different from any conventional index, a storage index catalogs data in uniform pieces and records the barest minimum of information an index could contain. Although the data is minimal, the storage index could be one of the most powerful pieces of Exadata.

An Index That Isn't

Storage indexes are dynamically created in 1MB segments for a given table, stored in memory, and built based on offloaded predicates. A maximum of eight columns per segment can be indexed, and each segment records the column name, the minimum value for that segment, the maximum value for that segment, and whether any NULL values exist in that 1MB "chunk."

Columns are indexed on a first-come, first-served basis; Exadata doesn't take, for example, the first eight columns in the table and index those but indexes columns as they appear in the query predicates. It's also possible that every 1MB segment for a given table could have differing columns indexed. It's more likely, although not guaranteed, that many of the indexed segments will contain the same column list.

The indexes can also be built from multiple sets of query predicates. If a query has four columns in its WHERE clause and no storage index yet exists for the queried table, those four columns create it. If another query offloads five additional columns from that same table to the storage cells, the first four listed columns round out the storage index for the table segments accessed. The second query may also access more table segments than the previous query; if no index exists in those additional segments, all five columns are indexed. On and on this can go until all the 1MB table segments have a storage index associated with them, each consisting of the eight-column maximum. Those indexes will remain resident in memory until CELLSRV is restarted or the storage cell itself is rebooted. A reboot or restart erases them, and the whole process starts over again, dynamically building storage indexes as the storage cells receive offloaded predicate information.

This is one reason why, in systems running a good number of ad hoc queries, the storage indexes created after a reboot or restart of CELLSRV may not be exactly the same as the ones that were in use before the storage cell was shut down. Slight changes in performance can result from such storage index rebuilds, which should be the expected behavior. Exadata systems running prepackaged applications, such as an ERP system, have a better chance of re-creating the same storage indexes that existed before the storage tier was restarted, since the majority of the queries offloaded to the storage cells offload the same predicates, in the same order, regardless of when they are executed (the beauty of "canned" queries). This doesn't mean that prepackaged applications will create the same storage indexes after a restart of the storage cells, just that the possibility is far more likely to occur.

A storage index doesn't look like any index you've encountered before, but it doesn't behave like one either. A simplified visualization might look like Figure 3-1 (the image is courtesy of Richard Foote, who has a wealth of knowledge about Oracle indexes).

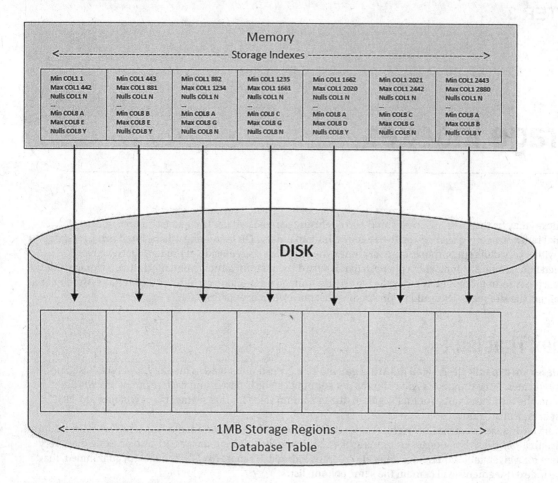

Figure 3-1. Storage index structure

Each storage segment for a table is associated with a memory region in each storage cell; each memory region contains the index data for the table storage segment it is mapped to. As Oracle processes a Smart Scan it also scans these index regions, looking for possible matches (segments that could contain the desired value or values) while skipping the segments it can ignore (those having no possibility of containing the desired value). It's the ability to skip reading "unnecessary" data segments, segments where the desired data cannot be found, that gives storage indexes their power.

Given that glorious, although long, description, it isn't difficult to understand why storage indexes can be confusing. But they don't need to be.

Don't Look Here

Unlike a B-tree index, designed and implemented to tell Oracle where data *is,* a storage index is designed to allow Oracle to skip, or bypass, storage segments, basically telling Oracle where data *isn't*. To explain further, a B-tree index contains the exact value or values indexed, plus the rowid for each row in the table. The presence of the rowid pinpoints where the particular index key is found, allowing Oracle to zero in on the precise location for the desired key or keys. Thus, a B-tree index reports the exact location for each index key. Storage indexes have no exact locations stored.

For each offloaded query, a Smart Scan will use a storage index, provided one is available. Remember: These are dynamically created when predicates are offloaded to the storage cells, so some tables may not have a storage index created yet. When one exists, Oracle, through the storage cells, will scan a storage index and see if the column or columns of interest are present and whether the desired value falls within the minimum/maximum range recorded for the column or columns in a given segment. If the column is indexed and the desired value falls outside of the recorded range, that 1MB segment is skipped, creating instant I/O savings.

A storage index will also be used by IS NULL and IS NOT NULL predicates, because there is a bit set to indicate the presence of NULL values in an index segment. Depending on the data, a query either looking for or avoiding NULL values could bypass most of the table data, making the result set return much more quickly than on a conventionally configured system. A query must qualify for a Smart Scan before it will use a storage index; thus, it must meet all of the criteria for Smart Scan execution. Those conditions are listed in the previous chapter, so they won't be repeated here.

An interesting aspect of a storage index is its effectiveness, which is based on the location of key data in the table. For a conventional B-tree index, this is called the Clustering Factor, a function of how far Oracle must "trave" in the table to arrive at the location of the next key in the index. As one would expect, a fairly low value for the Clustering Factor is a good thing; unfortunately, that can only be guaranteed if the table data is ordered by the index key. Ordering the data to improve the Clustering Factor for one index most often makes the Clustering Factors for any remaining indexes worse. Likewise, a storage index has a pseudo–"Clustering Factor" in that the location of indexed key values can affect how well a storage index is used and whether or not it provides real I/O savings. Unlike with a B-tree index, clustering the keys close to each other in the table enhances the performance, and since there is only one storage index per table, adverse effects are few. Of course, after the initial data loading of a heap table, there is no guarantee that the ordering will be preserved, as inserts and deletes can shift the data keys outside of the desired groupings. Still, it would take a tremendous volume of inserts and deletes to entirely undo the key clustering that was originally established.

Remember that cell maintenance will cause storage index segments to be lost, forcing storage index creation from offloaded predicates once the cell or cells are back online. If those predicates create storage index segments different from those that were lost, the originally established key clustering may no longer be beneficial. Situations wherein the search key is scattered across the entire table can result in a 0 byte savings for the query, as there may be no segment that does not contain the desired value within the specified range. Table data relatively clustered with respect to the search key provides varying degrees of I/O reduction, depending on how closely the search keys are grouped. Low cardinality columns, those containing values such as True, False, Yes, No, or limited-range numeric values fare better when clustered than columns having a wide range of values or columns enforcing Unique and Primary Key constraints. Examples in the next two sections use a low cardinality column (SUITABLE_FOR_FRYING) containing one of two values, "Yes" and "No," to illustrate both conditions.

I Used It

To know if a storage index has provided any benefit to a query, a statistic, "cell physical IO bytes saved by storage index," will record the bytes the storage index allowed Oracle to bypass. This is a cumulative metric, meaning that the prior value is incremented each time the storage index allowed Oracle to skip reading data segments in the currently connected session (as reported by V$MYSTAT) or for a given session (in GV$SESSTAT). (Creating a new session or reestablishing a connection [using "connect <user>/<pass>" at the SQL> prompt] will reset the session-level counter.)

To illustrate this, two queries will be executed, after some initial setup not shown in the examples, that illustrate that a storage index allowed Oracle to skip reading data and that the byte savings value reported by Oracle is, indeed, cumulative. The storage_index_ex.sql script was used to generate this output, and running this on your own system will display the setup as well as the output shown here, plus the parts that were edited owing to their size. The log file this script generates is extremely large; it does include both sets of examples, however, and requires only a single execution to provide the entire set of results. The second example, run immediately after the first and starting with reconnecting as the schema owner, executes the same two queries. The connections will be reestablished between the two statements, which will show the actual savings for each query.

Two tables are created and populated, then the queries are run; the following shows the results of that first run:

```
SQL> select /*+ parallel(4) */
  2  count(*)
  3  from chicken_hr_tab
  4  where suitable_for_frying = 'Yes';

  COUNT(*)
----------
   2621440

SQL> select *
  2  from v$mystat
  3  where statistic# = (select statistic# from v$statname where name = 'cell physical
     IO bytes saved by storage index');

       SID STATISTIC#      VALUE
---------- ---------- ----------
      1107        247 1201201152

SQL> select /*+ parallel(4) */
  2  chicken_id, chicken_name, suitable_for_frying
  3  from chicken_hr_tab
  4  where suitable_for_frying = 'Yes';

CHICKEN_ID CHICKEN_NAME         SUI
---------- -------------------- ---
  38719703 Frieda               Yes
  38719704 Edie                 Yes
  38719705 Eunice               Yes
...
  37973451 Eunice               Yes
  37973452 Fran                 Yes

2621440 rows selected.

SQL> select *
  2  from v$mystat
  3  where statistic# = (select statistic# from v$statname where name = 'cell physical
     IO bytes saved by storage index');

       SID STATISTIC#      VALUE
---------- ---------- ----------
      1107        247 2281971712

SQL>
```

For the first query, approximately 1GB of data was bypassed to provide the record count; the second query skipped an additional 1GB of table data. That isn't obvious from the output shown, as the value displayed is, as noted before, the cumulative result. You may not need to know the bytes skipped by each query, so the cumulative count could be exactly what you want. The cumulative count, though, will also display unchanged for queries that do not execute a Smart Scan, so careful attention must be paid to the output of the V$MYSTAT query. If you do want individual savings figures, then you can produce those results as well; in this case, queries that do not meet Smart Scan criteria will return a 0 byte total. As noted previously, the script reconnects between queries; this produces results that better illustrate the I/O savings the storage index provides on a per-query basis:

```
SQL> connect bing/#######
Connected.
SQL> select /*+ parallel(4) */
  2  count(*)
  3  from chicken_hr_tab
  4  where suitable_for_frying = 'Yes';

  COUNT(*)
----------
  2621440


SQL> select *
  2  from v$mystat
  3  where statistic# = (select statistic# from v$statname where name = 'cell physical
     IO bytes saved by storage index');

       SID STATISTIC#      VALUE
---------- ---------- ----------
      1233        247 1080770560


SQL> connect bing/#######
Connected.
SQL> select /*+ parallel(4) */
  2  chicken_id, chicken_name, suitable_for_frying
  3  from chicken_hr_tab
  4  where suitable_for_frying = 'Yes';

CHICKEN_ID CHICKEN_NAME         SUI
---------- -------------------- ---
  38719703 Frieda               Yes
  38719704 Edie                 Yes
...
  37973451 Eunice               Yes
  37973452 Fran                 Yes

2621440 rows selected.

SQL>
SQL> select *
  2  from v$mystat
  3  where statistic# = (select statistic# from v$statname where name = 'cell physical
     IO bytes saved by storage index');

       SID STATISTIC#      VALUE
---------- ---------- ----------
      1233        247 1080770560

SQL>
```

33

Now it's obvious how much data was skipped for each query. For the initial run, there were also 120,430,592 bytes skipped when loading the data. (After the initial insert statements were executed, a series of "insert into … select … from …" statements were used to further populate the table.) The second run shows the actual savings the storage index provided for each query.

Oracle can skip table segments based on information the storage index provides, but because the index data is very basic, some "false positives" can occur. Oracle may find that a given segment satisfies the search criteria, because the searched-for value falls between the minimum and maximum values recorded for that segment, but, in reality, the minimum and maximum values hide the fact that the actual desired value does not exist in that particular segment.

In such cases, Oracle reads through the segment and comes up empty-handed, as no rows meeting the exact query criteria were found, even though the storage index indicated otherwise. Depending on how well grouped the keys are in the table, more segments than one would expect could be read, segments that produce no results, because the indexed values "falsely" indicate that a row or rows may exist. In this next example, a count of records having a TALENT_CD of 4 is desired. The data is loaded so that TALENT_CD values 3 and 5 are placed in the same table segments, and the rest of the TALENT_CD values are loaded into the remaining segments. This will provide the conditions to create a "false positive" result from the storage index:

```
SQL> insert /*+ append */
  2  into chicken_hr_tab (chicken_name, talent_cd, retired, retire_dt, suitable_for_frying, fry_dt)
  3  select
  4  chicken_name, talent_cd, retired, retire_dt, suitable_for_frying, fry_dt from chicken_hr_tab2
  5  where talent_cd in (3,5);

1048576 rows created.

Elapsed: 00:01:05.10
SQL> commit;

Commit complete.

Elapsed: 00:00:00.01
SQL> insert /*+ append */
  2  into chicken_hr_tab (chicken_name, talent_cd, retired, retire_dt, suitable_for_frying, fry_dt)
  3  select
  4  chicken_name, talent_cd, retired, retire_dt, suitable_for_frying, fry_dt from chicken_hr_tab2
  5  where talent_cd not in (3,5);

37748736 rows created.

Elapsed: 00:38:09.12
SQL> commit;

Commit complete.

Elapsed: 00:00:00.00
SQL>
SQL> exec dbms_stats.gather_table_stats(user, 'CHICKEN_TALENT_TAB', cascade=>true,
estimate_percent=>null);

PL/SQL procedure successfully completed.
```

```
Elapsed: 00:00:00.46
SQL> exec dbms_stats.gather_table_stats(user, 'CHICKEN_HR_TAB', cascade=>true,
estimate_percent=>null);

PL/SQL procedure successfully completed.

Elapsed: 00:00:31.66
SQL>
SQL> set timing on
SQL>
SQL> connect bing/bongo$tar
Connected.
SQL> alter session set parallel_force_local=true;

Session altered.

Elapsed: 00:00:00.00
SQL> alter session set parallel_min_time_threshold=2;

Session altered.

Elapsed: 00:00:00.00
SQL> alter session set parallel_degree_policy=manual;

Session altered.

Elapsed: 00:00:00.00
SQL>
SQL>
SQL> set timing on
SQL>
SQL> select /*+ parallel(4) */
  2  chicken_id
  3  from chicken_hr_tab
  4  where talent_cd = 4;

    CHICKEN_ID
---------------
      60277401
      60277404
...
      72320593
      72320597
      72320606
      72320626

4718592 rows selected.

Elapsed: 00:03:17.92
SQL>
```

```
SQL> select *
  2  from v$mystat
  3  where statistic# = (select statistic# from v$statname where name = 'cell physical
     IO bytes saved by storage index');

           SID      STATISTIC#           VALUE
--------------- --------------- ---------------
           915             247               0

Elapsed: 00:00:00.01
SQL>
```

▨ **Note**   The manner in which the data was loaded set the minimum and maximum values for TALENT_CD such that the storage index could not ignore any of the blocks, even though there are segments that do not contain the desired value.

The minimum and maximum values stored for an indexed segment don't guarantee that the desired value will be found, just that there is a high probability that the value exists in the associated table segment.

Even though this example was intentionally created to provide such a condition, it is also likely that this could occur in a production system, as normally occurring data changes (through inserts, updates, and deletes) could create this same sort of situation.

Or Maybe I Didn't

Data clustering plays a big part in whether a storage index provides any benefit. In the preceding example, great care was taken to load the data in a manner that would make a storage index beneficial to the query. Values of interest (those in the WHERE clause) were loaded, so that one or more of the 1MB table segments storage indexes operate upon contained values that could be skipped. In the next example, data was loaded in a fairly fast and convenient manner; the initial table population resulted in rows containing the value of interest (SUITABLE_FOR_FRYING is 'Yes') being scattered across the table and thus being found in every 1MB storage index segment. Subsequent loading of the data, using a simple "insert into ... select from ..." syntax, preserved that scattering and rendered the storage index basically useless for the given query. (It is a common practice to consider that a storage index was "not used" when the "cell physical IO bytes saved by storage index" statistic is 0, which isn't true. The storage index was used; there is no question about that, but it provided no benefit in the form of reduced I/O, as Oracle could not skip any of the 1MB data segments in its search for the desired rows.) Looking at the run where the storage index "key" data was scattered across the entire table, the following results were seen:

```
SQL> select /*+ parallel(4) */
  2  count(*)
  3  from chicken_hr_tab
  4  where suitable_for_frying = 'Yes';

  COUNT(*)
----------
   2621440
```

```
SQL>
SQL> select *
  2  from v$mystat
  3  where statistic# = (select statistic# from v$statname where name = 'cell physical
     IO bytes saved by storage index');

       SID STATISTIC#      VALUE
---------- ---------- ----------
      1304        247          0

SQL> select /*+ parallel(4) */
  2  chicken_id, chicken_name, suitable_for_frying
  3  from chicken_hr_tab
  4  where suitable_for_frying = 'Yes';

CHICKEN_ID CHICKEN_NAME          SUI
---------- --------------------- ---
  38699068 Pickles               Yes
  38699070 Frieda                Yes
  ...
  10116134 Pickles               Yes
  10116136 Frieda                Yes

2621440 rows selected.

SQL>
SQL> select *
  2  from v$mystat
  3  where statistic# = (select statistic# from v$statname where name = 'cell physical
     IO bytes saved by storage index');

       SID STATISTIC#      VALUE
---------- ---------- ----------
      1304        247          0

SQL> select /*+ parallel(4) */
  2  h.chicken_name, t.talent, h.suitable_for_frying
  3  from chicken_hr_tab h join chicken_talent_tab t on (t.talent_cd = h.talent_cd)
  4  where h.talent_cd = 5;

CHICKEN_NAME    TALENT                                          SUI
--------------- ----------------------------------------------- ---
Cat             Accountant                                      No
Cat             Accountant                                      No
Cat             Accountant                                      No
Cat             Accountant                                      No
...
Cat             Accountant                                      No
Cat             Accountant                                      No

524288 rows selected.
```

```
SQL>
SQL> select *
  2   from v$mystat
  3   where statistic# = (select statistic# from v$statname where name = 'cell physical
     IO bytes saved by storage index');

       SID STATISTIC#      VALUE
---------- ---------- ----------
      1304        247          0

SQL>
```

Since there is no 1MB segment that does not contain the searched-for value, the storage index cannot tell Oracle to skip any of them, which is reflected in the VALUE column from V$MYSTAT for the "cell physical IO bytes saved by storage index" statistic. (In 11.2.0.3, the statistic number for this event is 247, but it's best to actually query on the statistic name, as Oracle can, and has, reassigned statistic numbers for existing statistics, as new ones are added in newer versions.) Again, this does not mean that this storage index was not used; it does mean that no I/O savings were realized by using it.

Execution Plan Doesn't Know

Execution plans won't report storage index usage, because, frankly, the optimizer doesn't know whether a Smart Scan will or will not be used for a given query. The only certain monitoring method, outside of enabling tracing at the CELLSRV level, is through the "cell physical IO bytes saved by storage index" statistic. Chapter 9 will cover how to enable CELLSRV tracing; starting CELLSRV tracing requires a restart of the cell, which causes the storage index segments to be dropped.

Looking at the previous queries, showing (and not showing) storage index savings adding the execution plans to the generated output verifies that the optimizer won't report any information on the storage indexes in use:

```
SQL> set autotrace on
SQL>
SQL> select /*+ parallel(4) */
  2   h.chicken_name, t.talent, h.suitable_for_frying
  3   from chicken_hr_tab h join chicken_talent_tab t on (t.talent_cd = h.talent_cd)
  4   where h.talent_cd = 5;

CHICKEN_NAME         TALENT                                    SUI
-------------------- ----------------------------------------- ---
Cat                  Accountant                                No
Cat                  Accountant                                No
Cat                  Accountant                                No
Cat                  Accountant                                No
Cat                  Accountant                                No
...
Cat                  Accountant                                No
Cat                  Accountant                                No
Cat                  Accountant                                No
Cat                  Accountant                                No

524288 rows selected.
```

Execution Plan

Plan hash value: 793882093

```
-------------------------------------------------------------------------------------------------
| Id |Operation                |Name              |Rows |Bytes|Cost(%CPU)| Time | TQ |IN-OUT |PQ Distrib|
-------------------------------------------------------------------------------------------------
|  0 |SELECT STATEMENT         |                  |7759K| 207M|11742 (1)| 00:00:01|    |       |          |
|  1 | PX COORDINATOR          |                  |     |     |         |         |    |       |          |
|  2 |  PX SEND QC (RANDOM)    |:TQ10001          |7759K| 207M|11742 (1)| 00:00:01|Q1,01|P->S|QC (RAND)|
|  3 |   MERGE JOIN            |                  |7759K| 207M|11742 (1)| 00:00:01|Q1,01|PCWP|          |
|  4 |    SORT JOIN            |                  |7759K| 103M|11739 (1)| 00:00:01|Q1,01|PCWP|          |
|  5 |     PX BLOCK ITERATOR   |                  |7759K| 103M|11739 (1)| 00:00:01|Q1,01|PCWC|          |
| *6 |TABLE ACCESS STORAGE FULL|CHICKEN_HR_TAB    |7759K| 103M|11739 (1)| 00:00:01|Q1,01|PCWP|          |
| *7 |    SORT JOIN            |                  |    1|  14 |   3(34)| 00:00:01|Q1,01|PCWP|          |
|  8 |     PX RECEIVE          |                  |    1|  14 |   2 (0)| 00:00:01|Q1,01|PCWP|          |
|  9 |      PX SEND BROADCAST  |:TQ10000          |    1|  14 |   2 (0)| 00:00:01|Q1,00|P->P|BROADCAST|
| 10 |       PX BLOCK ITERATOR |                  |    1|  14 |   2 (0)| 00:00:01|Q1,00|PCWC|          |
|*11 |TABLE ACCESS STORAGE FULL|CHICKEN_TALENT_TAB|    1|  14 |   2 (0)| 00:00:01|Q1,00|PCWP|          |
-------------------------------------------------------------------------------------------------
```

Predicate Information (identified by operation id):

```
   6 - storage("H"."TALENT_CD"=5)
       filter("H"."TALENT_CD"=5)
   7 - access("T"."TALENT_CD"="H"."TALENT_CD")
       filter("T"."TALENT_CD"="H"."TALENT_CD")
  11 - storage("T"."TALENT_CD"=5)
       filter("T"."TALENT_CD"=5)
```

Note

   - Degree of Parallelism is 4 because of hint

Statistics

```
        25  recursive calls
         0  db block gets
    152401  consistent gets
    151444  physical reads
         0  redo size
   9018409  bytes sent via SQL*Net to client
    384995  bytes received via SQL*Net from client
     34954  SQL*Net roundtrips to/from client
         8  sorts (memory)
         0  sorts (disk)
    524288  rows processed
```

```
SQL>
SQL> set autotrace off
SQL>
SQL> select *
  2  from v$mystat
  3  where statistic# = (select statistic# from v$statname where name = 'cell physical
     IO bytes saved by storage index');

       SID STATISTIC#      VALUE
---------- ---------- ----------
         3        247   92028928

SQL>
```

The only evidence of storage index usage is the output from the final query in this example. No mention of storage indexes appears in the execution plan output.

The More, the Merrier

Data distribution plays a large part in storage index performance, but that's not the only data-related area that can impact Smart Scan execution and, as a result, storage index usage. Table size can also determine whether a storage index can be utilized. Serial direct path reads are generally utilized for large objects; small tables rarely trigger Smart Scans. How big does a table have to be to trigger a Smart Scan, and thus use a storage index? For the scripts shown here, the smallest table size that would guarantee a Smart Scan generated 40 extents, consuming 335,544,320 bytes. Smaller table sizes were tried, with no Smart Scans executed; however, with the loading method used, a smaller table size that would trigger a Smart Scan may not have been generated. Since exhaustive testing was not completed, there may be smaller tables that will trigger Smart Scan executions.

Size isn't the only factor in whether a Smart Scan will be triggered. Partitioned tables can create an interesting situation where the overall table size is sufficient to trigger a Smart Scan, but the sizes of the individual partitions aren't. Such a situation is created by the storage_index_part_ex.sql script. Again, the initial setup isn't shown, in order to concentrate on the end results. There are five partitions created and populated for this version of the table, with a deliberate attempt to evenly spread the data across all of the partitions. The names and row counts for each partition are shown as follows:

```
SQL> select count(*) from chicken_hr_tab partition(chick1);
      COUNT(*)
---------------
       1966080

SQL> select count(*) from chicken_hr_tab partition(chick2);

      COUNT(*)
---------------
       1966080

SQL> select count(*) from chicken_hr_tab partition(chick3);

      COUNT(*)
---------------
       1966080
```

```
SQL> select count(*) from chicken_hr_tab partition(chick4);

     COUNT(*)
---------------
      1966080

SQL> select count(*) from chicken_hr_tab partition(chick5);

     COUNT(*)
---------------
      1835008

SQL>
```

Overall, the table is large enough to ensure that a Smart Scan will be executed, and if the query involves a large percentage of the table data, a Smart Scan will, indeed, be run. It's the relatively small sizes of the individual partitions that can cause them to not qualify for a Smart Scan. Now that the stage is properly set, the same queries from the previous example are executed, and the Smart Scan results are reported. The changes between the examples are the partitioned table and the partition key distribution, which make a marked difference in Smart Scan execution and the benefit a storage index provides. The results, as Exadata reports them, are as follows:

```
SQL> select /*+ parallel(4) */
  2  count(*)
  3  from chicken_hr_tab
  4  where suitable_for_frying = 'Yes';

     COUNT(*)
---------------
      655360

SQL>
SQL> select *
  2  from v$mystat
  3  where statistic# = (select statistic# from v$statname where name = 'cell physical
     IO bytes saved by storage index');

           SID      STATISTIC#           VALUE
--------------- --------------- ---------------
          1434             247       187088896

SQL>
SQL> select /*+ parallel(4) */
  2  chicken_id, chicken_name, suitable_for_frying
  3  from chicken_hr_tab
  4  where suitable_for_frying = 'Yes';
```

```
    CHICKEN_ID CHICKEN_NAME            SUI
--------------- -------------------- ---
    2411502 Frieda                   Yes
...
    9507995 Fran                     Yes
    9507996 Eunice                   Yes

655360 rows selected.

SQL>
SQL> select  sql_id,
  2  io_cell_offload_eligible_bytes qualifying,
  3  io_cell_offload_eligible_bytes - io_cell_offload_returned_bytes actual,
  4  round(((io_cell_offload_eligible_bytes - io_cell_offload_returned_bytes)/io_cell_offload_
     eligible_bytes)*100, 2) io_saved_pct,
  5  sql_text
  6  from v$sql
  7  where io_cell_offload_returned_bytes > 0
  8  and instr(sql_text, 'suitable_for_frying') > 0
  9  and parsing_schema_name = 'BING';

SQL_ID          QUALIFYING       ACTUAL       IO_SAVED_PCT
-------------- --------------- --------------- ---------------
SQL_TEXT
--------------------------------------------------------------------------------------------------
8hgwndn3tj7xg        315211776       223167616            70.8
select /*+ parallel(4) */ chicken_id, chicken_name, suitable_for_frying from chicken_hr_tab where
suitable_for_frying = 'Yes'


c1486fx9pv44n        315211776       230036536           72.98
select /*+ parallel(4) */ count(*) from chicken_hr_tab where suitable_for_frying = 'Yes'


9u65az96tvhj5         62111744        22646696           36.46
select /*+ parallel(4) */ h.chicken_name, t.talent, h.suitable_for_frying from chicken_hr_tab h join
chicken_talent_tab t on (t.talent_cd = h.talent_cd) where h.talent_cd = 5

SQL>
SQL> select *
  2  from v$mystat
  3  where statistic# = (select statistic# from v$statname where name = 'cell physical
     IO bytes saved by storage index');

            SID      STATISTIC#            VALUE
--------------- --------------- ---------------
           1434             247        282230784

SQL>

SQL> select /*+ parallel(4) */
  2  h.chicken_name, t.talent, h.suitable_for_frying
  3  from chicken_hr_tab h join chicken_talent_tab t on (t.talent_cd = h.talent_cd)
  4  where h.talent_cd = 5;
```

```
CHICKEN_NAME          TALENT                              SUI
------------------    ----------------------------------  ---
Hazel                 Accountant                          No
Red                   Accountant                          No
Amanda                Accountant                          No
Dolly                 Accountant                          No
...
Terry                 Accountant                          No
Beulah                Accountant                          No
Calcutta              Accountant                          No

1835008 rows selected.

SQL>
SQL> select  sql_id,
  2  io_cell_offload_eligible_bytes qualifying,
  3  io_cell_offload_eligible_bytes - io_cell_offload_returned_bytes actual,
  4  round(((io_cell_offload_eligible_bytes - io_cell_offload_returned_bytes)/io_cell_offload_
     eligible_bytes)*100, 2) io_saved_pct,
  5  sql_text
  6  from v$sql
  7  where io_cell_offload_returned_bytes > 0
  8  and instr(sql_text, 'suitable_for_frying') > 0
  9  and parsing_schema_name = 'BING';

SQL_ID            QUALIFYING         ACTUAL        IO_SAVED_PCT
-------------   ----------------  ----------------  ----------------
SQL_TEXT
------------------------------------------------------------------------------------------------
8hgwndn3tj7xg     315211776         223167616          70.8
select /*+ parallel(4) */ chicken_id, chicken_name, suitable_for_frying from chicken_hr_tab where
suitable_for_frying = 'Yes'

c1486fx9pv44n     315211776         230036536          72.98
select /*+ parallel(4) */ count(*) from chicken_hr_tab where suitable_for_frying = 'Yes'

9u65az96tvhj5     62242816          26925984           43.26
select /*+ parallel(4) */ h.chicken_name, t.talent, h.suitable_for_frying from chicken_hr_tab h join
chicken_talent_tab t on (t.talent_cd = h.talent_cd) where h.talent_cd = 5

SQL>
```

So far, so good, as Smart Scans are being executed as expected. Reconnecting as the schema owner and adding another query, a different picture emerges. Between each query of the partitioned table, the session statistics are reset by again reconnecting as the schema owner, as follows:

```
SQL> connect bing/#########
Connected.
SQL>
```

```
SQL> select /*+ parallel(4) */
  2   count(*)
  3   from chicken_hr_tab
  4   where suitable_for_frying = 'Yes';

       COUNT(*)
---------------
         655360

SQL>
SQL> select  sql_id,
  2   io_cell_offload_eligible_bytes qualifying,
  3   io_cell_offload_eligible_bytes - io_cell_offload_returned_bytes actual,
  4   round(((io_cell_offload_eligible_bytes - io_cell_offload_returned_bytes)/io_cell_
     offload_eligible_bytes)*100, 2) io_saved_pct,
  5   sql_text
  6   from v$sql
  7   where io_cell_offload_returned_bytes > 0
  8   and instr(sql_text, 'suitable_for_frying') > 0
  9   and parsing_schema_name = 'BING';

SQL_ID              QUALIFYING         ACTUAL       IO_SAVED_PCT
-------------  ----------------  ---------------  ----------------
SQL_TEXT
--------------------------------------------------------------------------------------------
8hgwndn3tj7xg        315211776       223167616          70.8
select /*+ parallel(4) */ chicken_id, chicken_name, suitable_for_frying from chicken_hr_tab where
suitable_for_frying = 'Yes'

c1486fx9pv44n        315211776       230036536          72.98
select /*+ parallel(4) */ count(*) from chicken_hr_tab where suitable_for_frying = 'Yes'

9u65az96tvhj5         62242816        26925984          43.26
select /*+ parallel(4) */ h.chicken_name, t.talent, h.suitable_for_frying from chicken_hr_tab h join
chicken_talent_tab t on (t.talent_cd = h.talent_cd) where h.talent_cd = 5

SQL>

SQL> select *
  2   from v$mystat
  3   where statistic# = (select statistic# from v$statname where name = 'cell physical
     IO bytes saved by storage index');

            SID    STATISTIC#           VALUE
---------------  ---------------  ---------------
           1434            247        50757632

SQL>
SQL> connect bing/#########
Connected.
```

```
SQL>
SQL> select /*+ parallel(4) */
  2  sum(chicken_id)
  3  from chicken_hr_tab
  4  where suitable_for_frying = 'Yes';

SUM(CHICKEN_ID)
---------------
  4166118604642

SQL>
SQL> select  sql_id,
  2  io_cell_offload_eligible_bytes qualifying,
  3  io_cell_offload_eligible_bytes - io_cell_offload_returned_bytes actual,
  4  round((((io_cell_offload_eligible_bytes - io_cell_offload_returned_bytes)/io_cell_
     offload_eligible_bytes)*100, 2) io_saved_pct,
  5  sql_text
  6  from v$sql
  7  where io_cell_offload_returned_bytes > 0
  8  and instr(sql_text, 'suitable_for_frying') > 0
  9  and parsing_schema_name = 'BING';

SQL_ID          QUALIFYING        ACTUAL        IO_SAVED_PCT
-------------   ---------------   ---------------   ---------------
SQL_TEXT
------------------------------------------------------------------------------------------
8hgwndn3tj7xg      315211776        223167616             70.8
select /*+ parallel(4) */ chicken_id, chicken_name, suitable_for_frying from chicken_hr_tab where
suitable_for_frying = 'Yes'

c1486fx9pv44n      315211776        230036536            72.98
select /*+ parallel(4) */ count(*) from chicken_hr_tab where suitable_for_frying = 'Yes'

9u65az96tvhj5       62242816         26925984            43.26
select /*+ parallel(4) */ h.chicken_name, t.talent, h.suitable_for_frying from chicken_hr_tab h join
chicken_talent_tab t on (t.talent_cd = h.talent_cd) where h.talent_cd = 5

SQL>
SQL> select *
  2  from v$mystat
  3  where statistic# = (select statistic# from v$statname where name = 'cell physical
     IO bytes saved by storage index');

          SID     STATISTIC#           VALUE
---------------   ---------------   ---------------
         1434            247               0

SQL>
SQL> connect bing/#########
Connected.
SQL>
```

```
SQL> select /*+ parallel(4) */
  2  chicken_id, chicken_name, suitable_for_frying
  3  from chicken_hr_tab
  4  where suitable_for_frying = 'Yes';

    CHICKEN_ID CHICKEN_NAME          SUI
--------------- -------------------- ---
       9539150 Frieda               Yes
       9539151 Frieda               Yes
...
       9489101 Eunice               Yes
       9489102 Eunice               Yes

655360 rows selected.

SQL>
SQL> select  sql_id,
  2  io_cell_offload_eligible_bytes qualifying,
  3  io_cell_offload_eligible_bytes - io_cell_offload_returned_bytes actual,
  4  round(((io_cell_offload_eligible_bytes - io_cell_offload_returned_bytes)/io_cell_
     offload_eligible_bytes)*100, 2) io_saved_pct,
  5  sql_text
  6  from v$sql
  7  where io_cell_offload_returned_bytes > 0
  8  and instr(sql_text, 'suitable_for_frying') > 0
  9  and parsing_schema_name = 'BING';

SQL_ID             QUALIFYING         ACTUAL        IO_SAVED_PCT
------------- --------------- --------------- ---------------
SQL_TEXT
--------------------------------------------------------------------------------------
8hgwndn3tj7xg       315211776       223167616             70.8
select /*+ parallel(4) */ chicken_id, chicken_name, suitable_for_frying from chicken_hr_tab where
suitable_for_frying = 'Yes'

c1486fx9pv44n       315211776       230036536            72.98
select /*+ parallel(4) */ count(*) from chicken_hr_tab where suitable_for_frying = 'Yes'

9u65az96tvhj5        62242816        26925984            43.26
select /*+ parallel(4) */ h.chicken_name, t.talent, h.suitable_for_frying from chicken_hr_tab h join
chicken_talent_tab t on (t.talent_cd = h.talent_cd) where h.talent_cd = 5

SQL>
SQL> select *
  2  from v$mystat
  3  where statistic# = (select statistic# from v$statname where name = 'cell physical
     IO bytes saved by storage index');
```

```
            SID        STATISTIC#         VALUE
------------    ----------------    ----------------
         1434           247                0

SQL>
SQL> connect bing/#########
Connected.
SQL>
SQL> select /*+ parallel(4) */
  2   h.chicken_name, t.talent, h.suitable_for_frying
  3   from chicken_hr_tab h join chicken_talent_tab t on (t.talent_cd = h.talent_cd)
  4   where h.talent_cd = 5;

CHICKEN_NAME        TALENT                                              SUI
------------------  --------------------------------------------------  ---
Jennifer            Accountant                                          No
Constance           Accountant                                          No
Rachel              Accountant                                          No
Katy                Accountant                                          No
...
Calcutta            Accountant                                          No
Jennifer            Accountant                                          No

1835008 rows selected.

SQL>
SQL> select  sql_id,
  2   io_cell_offload_eligible_bytes qualifying,
  3   io_cell_offload_eligible_bytes - io_cell_offload_returned_bytes actual,
  4   round(((io_cell_offload_eligible_bytes - io_cell_offload_returned_bytes)/io_cell_
       offload_eligible_bytes)*100, 2) io_saved_pct,
  5   sql_text
  6   from v$sql
  7   where io_cell_offload_returned_bytes > 0
  8   and instr(sql_text, 'suitable_for_frying') > 0
  9   and parsing_schema_name = 'BING';

SQL_ID          QUALIFYING          ACTUAL          IO_SAVED_PCT
-------------   ----------------    ----------------  ----------------
SQL_TEXT
--------------------------------------------------------------------------------
8hgwndn3tj7xg      315211776           223167616              70.8
select /*+ parallel(4) */ chicken_id, chicken_name, suitable_for_frying from chicken_hr_tab where
suitable_for_frying = 'Yes'

c1486fx9pv44n      315211776           230036536              72.98
select /*+ parallel(4) */ count(*) from chicken_hr_tab where suitable_for_frying = 'Yes'

9u65az96tvhj5       62242816            26925984              43.26
select /*+ parallel(4) */ h.chicken_name, t.talent, h.suitable_for_frying from chicken_hr_tab h join
chicken_talent_tab t on (t.talent_cd = h.talent_cd) where h.talent_cd = 5
```

```
SQL> select *
  2  from v$mystat
  3  where statistic# = (select statistic# from v$statname where name = 'cell physical
     IO bytes saved by storage index');

            SID       STATISTIC#          VALUE
--------------- ---------------- ---------------
           1434              247              0

SQL>
```

No benefit was realized from a storage index for the last query, because it didn't execute a Smart Scan; the partitions are too small, individually, to trigger Smart Scan execution. Also, the first query computing the sum was not offloaded. This is proven by the fact that the query text is not listed among the SQL statements that were offloaded at one time or another, using another incarnation of the table and data.

NULLs

NULL searches are treated in a slightly different yet more efficient manner in Exadata. Unlike non-NULL table data, which is indexed by the minimum and maximum values for the listed column, the presence of NULLs is flagged by a bit for each column present in the storage index. Storage regions containing NULLs for the indexed columns have this bit set, which makes searching for NULLs a very fast operation, as Oracle only need search for segments where this NULL indicator bit shows that NULLs are present. Avoiding NULLs is also just as efficient, as Oracle only needs to read table segments where the NULL indicator bit is not set.

Proving this is another example, utilizing the previous data-loading strategy, clustering the desired values together to get the most "bang for the buck" out of the storage index. NULL values were added to the mix, so that three values now exist for the SUITABLE_FOR_FRYING column. Timing has been enabled to show the elapsed time for each query execution, so the total time for each query can be noted, and the session-level statistics were reset by reconnecting between queries, so it's easier to see how many bytes the storage index skipped for each search condition:

```
SQL>
SQL> connect bing/#########
Connected.
SQL>
SQL> set timing on
SQL>
SQL> select /*+ parallel(4) */
  2  count(*)
  3  from chicken_hr_tab
  4  where suitable_for_frying = 'Yes';

      COUNT(*)
---------------
       1572864

Elapsed: 00:00:00.80
SQL>
```

```
SQL> select *
  2  from v$mystat
  3  where statistic# = (select statistic# from v$statname where name = 'cell physical
     IO bytes saved by storage index');

           SID      STATISTIC#           VALUE
--------------   ---------------   ---------------
          1111             247       566501376

Elapsed: 00:00:00.00
SQL>
SQL> connect bing/#########
Connected.
SQL>
SQL> set timing on
SQL>
SQL> select /*+ parallel(4) */
  2  count(*)
  3  from chicken_hr_tab
  4  where suitable_for_frying is null;

       COUNT(*)
---------------
        1048576

Elapsed: 00:00:00.23
SQL>
SQL> select *
  2  from v$mystat
  3  where statistic# = (select statistic# from v$statname where name = 'cell physical
     IO bytes saved by storage index');

           SID      STATISTIC#           VALUE
--------------   ---------------   ---------------
          1111             247      1141440512

Elapsed: 00:00:00.00
SQL>
```

The IS NULL query executed in less than one-third of the time required for the query searching for "employees" ready to be sent to the fryer and skipped almost twice the number of bytes, because very few of the table segments contain NULL values. Again, this speed is partly due to not having to check minimum and maximum values for the specified column. Using this strategy, "false positives" won't occur, as Oracle doesn't flag segments that *may* have NULLs, only those segments where NULLs are actually present.

Needing to "Rebuild"

Storage indexes are memory-resident structures. As long as there is power to the storage cells, those indexes remain valid. Of course, using memory instead of more permanent physical media makes these indexes transient and subject to maintenance windows, power outages, and memory-card failures. There is no method to back up a storage index, and there really is no need to do so, given that storage indexes take very little time to build. The build process is not, as mentioned previously, the resource-intensive operation that building a "permanent" index would be. Using the term *rebuild* to replace dropped storage indexes is, to our minds, a misnomer, as there is no script to build them, and it's just as likely that the storage indexes built after a restart of the storage cells will not match the storage indexes in place prior to the outage.

Because storage indexes are built on data stored in 1MB segments, it doesn't take long to scan that segment of the table to find the minimum and maximum values an indexed column contains and note whether NULL values can or do exist. Building storage indexes after an outage is not the same resource-intensive operation that creating more permanent indexes can be. Building or rebuilding a B-tree index, for example, can take hours and can noticeably consume CPU and disk resources, whereas building a storage index is hardly noticeable during the course of day-to-day operations, doesn't hamper other sessions while it is being built, and completes in a mere fraction of the time. True, the information in a storage index is nothing like that of a B-tree index, but it doesn't need to be to serve its intended purpose.

Each storage server, or cell, has its own storage indexes, so losing one cell won't drop the indexes in the remaining cells, which means that only the storage indexes found in the problem cell will have to be created again. One of the good aspects of a storage index is that the index for each 1MB segment does not need to match the indexes representing the other table segments. Because tables are striped across the disks in a disk group, the table data is spread across all of the storage cells and, as a result, each table will have storage index segments in each of the storage cells. Issues with one cell won't create a situation where no storage indexes exist, so queries can still benefit from the index segments in the unaffected cells. In addition, the redundancy in ASM places the redundant data on a different storage cell from the primary source. This allows Exadata to lose a storage cell or apply patches in a rolling manner and not lose access to data.

Patching and software upgrades are probably the most likely reasons for storage indexes to be built, as CELLSRV needs to be stopped before some patching operations or software upgrades can begin. The size and scope of patching or upgrades will determine the fate of the storage indexes: database server patching/upgrades won't touch the storage cells, so storage indexes will remain intact, and patching/upgrades involving the storage tier or the entire Exadata machine will drop storage indexes. Firmware issues affecting physical disks will also cause storage index "rebuilds" as the storage cells themselves, including the operating system, will have to be restarted. True, storage firmware issues and Exadata upgrades are not common occurrences, but they can happen, so it's good to remember that storage indexes will have to be built once the storage firmware has been patched or the storage servers have been upgraded, either as storage maintenance or as part of an entire Exadata patch/upgrade, and the storage cells have been rebooted.

Another reason for storage indexes to be re-created involves maintenance on the flash cache hardware, the Sun flash PCIe cards. Four of these cards are installed into each storage server, providing 384GB of flash storage. Occasionally, these units need maintenance or replacement, which results in the affected storage cell being powered down. Although not directly related to the storage, they are part of the storage-cell architecture, and it should be noted that flash cache problems can require downtime to correct.

Remember that a Smart Scan can occur without a storage index being present. Losing storage indexes to maintenance windows or power outages isn't going to appreciably affect performance while they are being created. The time that they are missing will also be brief, as the first offloadable query after the storage cells are again up and running will start the build process all over again, and each subsequent offloaded query will contribute to those indexes until they are complete. It may not even be noticeable to the end users running queries, as time differences will likely be small in comparison to the previous runtimes when the storage indexes were available.

Things to Know

Storage indexes are memory-resident structures, not permanent database objects. They are built or modified dynamically when predicates are offloaded to the storage cells. Each index segment can index up to eight columns, plus the presence of NULLs, and index data segments that are 1MB in size. The index segments are built on a first-come, first-served basis; offloaded predicates are added to the index until the eight-column limit per segment is attained. More than one query can add columns to a storage index for a table. The index segments contain the column name, the minimum value for that segment, the maximum value for that segment, and whether or not that segment contains NULL values for the included column, indicated by a bit in the segment structure. When storage indexes exist, they are always used by Smart Scans; not every query can benefit from a storage index, though, as values may be scattered across the table segments, causing Oracle to read each segment. A storage index is like a probability matrix, indicating only the possibility that a value exists in the indexed table segment and, as such, "false positives" can occur. Such "false positives," created when the minimum and maximum values for a column in an index segment bracket the desired value but the desired value is not actually present in that segment, can also cause Oracle to read every table segment and provide no byte savings.

A storage index isn't like a conventional B-tree index: it isn't used to find where data is; it's used to know where data isn't. Scanning the minimum and maximum values for a column in a given storage segment can allow Oracle to eliminate locations to search. Since each storage index segment indexes a 1MB storage "chunk" of a table, creating a storage index is a fairly fast operation, done "on the fly" during query processing. Also, eliminating 1MB pieces of a table can quickly provide speed to a query: the less data Oracle needs to sift through, the faster the result set will be returned. In some ways, a storage index is really an anti-index, since it's used to eliminate locations to search, rather than pinpoint exactly where the desired data resides.

NULL values are treated differently, and more efficiently, than non-NULL search criteria, as Oracle only needs to read the NULL bit in the index. This can speed up queries by eliminating storage segments much faster than assessing minimum and maximum value pairs. Queries using the IS NULL and IS NOT NULL comparison operators can often return in a fraction of the time of queries where actual data values are used.

How data is loaded into a table also affects how efficient and fast a storage index can be. Tables where like values are clustered together can eliminate more storage segments than if the data values of interest are scattered across the entire table. The fewer storage segments that contain the value or values of interest allow Oracle to eliminate more storage segments from being read, returning the results much faster than would be possible with random data loading. Of course it's not possible to optimize storage indexes for every column they may contain, just as it isn't possible to generate the optimal Clustering Factor for every B-tree index created against a table.

Size can play a big part in the creation of storage indexes, and partitioned tables, in particular, can suffer from realizing no benefit from a storage index, if the partition or partitions being queried are small with respect to the overall table size. Querying the entire table without using partition pruning would realize savings from the use of the storage index.

Monitoring storage index benefits from the database server is an easy task. A single statistic named "cell physical IO bytes saved by storage index" in the V$SESSTAT and V$MYSTAT views records the bytes saved in a cumulative fashion, for each session in V$SESSTAT and for the current session in V$MYSTAT. Logging out and logging in again, or using connect to establish a new session, will reset this statistic to 0. This can be a useful technique to report exactly how many bytes were saved for a particular query by executing a single query after each connect is made. It's also useful to determine if any benefit was realized by using the storage index. Some queries won't benefit, because they aren't offloadable or the data was spread across every storage segment for the table or tables of interest.

Replacing storage indexes can be necessary for several reasons. Patching, software and/or hardware maintenance, and power outages are the major causes for this to occur. A less common cause for this is PCIe flash storage card maintenance or replacement, as that maintenance requires that the affected storage cell be powered down. Because they are basic indexes, containing a bare minimum of information, they are easy and fast to create and place very little load on the system. Only the affected storage cells will lose storage indexes, so if only one cell goes down, only those indexes will have to be built again.

■ ■ ■

## CHAPTER 4

Smart Flash Cache

The Smart Flash Cache can wear many hats: it's a cache; it's a flash component of the log writer process; and it can be configured as flash disk. Because this component is so versatile, it's worthwhile to see how it works, what it does, what it's made of, and how it can be configured as one or more ASM disk groups.

Flash Me

The Smart Flash Cache provides Exadata with the ability to deliver a high I/O-per-second (IOPS) rate, by caching frequently accessed data and allowing it to be read directly from flash memory, rather than from disk or RAM. It does this by caching frequently used table and index blocks for later use, thus absorbing the work repeated reads can create. Control file reads and writes, along with file header reads and writes, are also cached. Unlike conventional systems, though, the flash cache is smart and won't cache duplicate blocks written for ASM redundancy, nor will it cache I/O related to backup processes and data-pump exports.

The Smart Flash Cache behaves like a disk, but it isn't one. Comprising 4 Sun Flash PCIe cards per storage cell, each with 96GB of flash storage, the Smart Flash Cache totals 384GB of available space. For the X3 Eighth Rack configuration, the total flash storage is 4.8TB, and for the Quarter Rack configuration, the total flash storage available is 2.4TB. An X3 Half Rack has 11.2TB of flash storage, and the Full Rack provides 22.4TB. By comparison, the X2 Exadata Quarter Rack configuration has 1.1TB of available flash storage, and the Half Rack has 2.6TB, with the Full Rack providing 5.3TB. A basic block diagram of one of the cards is shown in Figure 4-1.

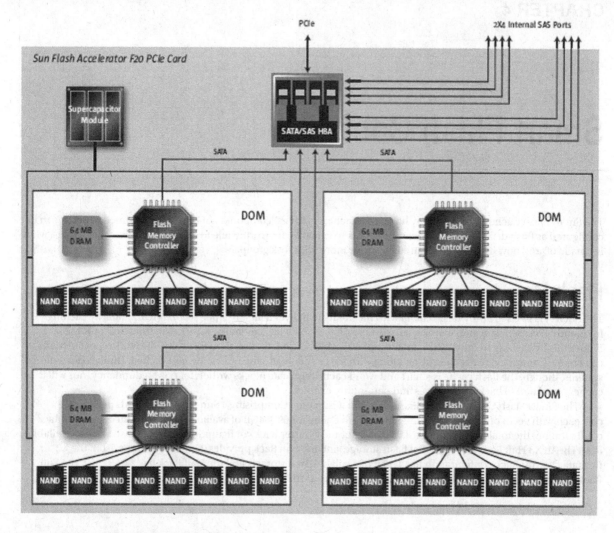

Figure 4-1. *Sun Flash Accelerator F20 PCIe Card block diagram*

At installation, the Exadata system is configured with almost all of the PCIe flash storage used as flash cache, with a small portion of this storage configured for flash logs. The DBA can, fairly easily, reconfigure the flash cache by resizing it, rebuilding it, or creating flash "disks" accessible to ASM. Smart Flash Cache is built on flash disks, which are not the same as the virtual flash disks a DBA can create to provide flash storage usable by ASM. Connecting to a storage cell and viewing the flash-cache detail using CellCLI shows the composition of the configured flash cache:

```
CellCLI> list flashcache detail
        name:                    myexa1cel01_FLASHCACHE
        cellDisk:
FD_07_myexa1cel01,FD_12_myexa1cel01,FD_15_myexa1cel01,FD_13_myexa1cel01,FD_04_myexa1cel01,FD_14_
myexa1cel01,FD_00_myexa1cel01,FD_10_myexa1cel01,FD_03_myexa1cel01,FD_09_myexa1cel01,FD_08_myexa1
cel01,FD_02_myexa1cel01,FD_01_myexa1cel01,FD_11_myexa1cel01,FD_05_myexa1cel01,FD_06_myexa1cel01
        creationTime:            2013-03-16T12:16:39-05:00
        degradedCelldisks:
```

```
     effectiveCacheSize:     364.75G
     id:                     3dfc24a5-2591-43d3-aa34-72379abdf3b3
     size:                   364.75G
     status:                 normal

CellCLI>
```

Sixteen disks are used per storage cell, to build the Smart Flash Cache. Each Sun PCIe card has 4 such disks, each one 32GB in size, with 24GB of that as addressable, nonvolatile memory. Even though there is a total of 384GB of flash storage, notice that 19.25GB are reserved for flash log and other uses, which makes 22.875GB of flash storage available for flash-cache creation. Each card also contains 64MB of DRAM, used to buffer writes to the nonvolatile memory, and an Energy Storage Module (ESM). This module is actually a capacitor, which can provide enough power to flush data from the buffer to the nonvolatile memory, in the event of a power outage. Should the ESM fail, the volatile buffer area will be bypassed, allowing direct writes to the nonvolatile memory. As long as the flash disks are configured as Smart Flash Cache, losing the ESM poses no write penalties; the storage software treats Smart Flash Cache as a write-through cache, bypassing it and writing directly to disk. In the event that the flash disks are configured into a flash disk, group loss of the ESM will incur write penalties, as the dynamic cache is no longer available.

The expected lifetime of these PCIe cards is two years, since the ESM will lose its ability to hold a charge. Sun documentation states that these cards can be replaced without shutting down the system; Oracle Exadata documentation recommends the affected storage servers be powered down before such maintenance begins. Remember that the ASM fail groups are configured so that loss of one storage cell doesn't affect the running databases.

Rebuilding the flash cache for a storage cell using the `create flashcache all` command creates the same storage distribution found after Exadata installation; the DBA can create a smaller Smart Flash Cache on a storage cell, by specifying the `size` parameter, but not a larger one.

How It Works

The Smart Flash Cache is a per-cell caching mechanism, optimized for frequently accessed data. Whether an object will be considered for Smart Flash Cache use is determined in part by the CELL_FLASH_CACHE storage parameter set at object creation. Look at the CREATE TABLE statement for the EMP demonstration table:

```
CREATE TABLE "BING"."EMP"
(    "EMPNO" NUMBER(4,0) NOT NULL ENABLE,
     "ENAME" VARCHAR2(10),
     "JOB" VARCHAR2(9),
     "MGR" NUMBER(4,0),
     "HIREDATE" DATE,
     "SAL" NUMBER(7,2),
     "COMM" NUMBER(7,2),
     "DEPTNO" NUMBER(2,0)
) SEGMENT CREATION IMMEDIATE
 PCTFREE 10 PCTUSED 40 INITRANS 1 MAXTRANS 255
NOCOMPRESS LOGGING
 STORAGE(INITIAL 65536 NEXT 1048576 MINEXTENTS 1 MAXEXTENTS 2147483645
 PCTINCREASE 0 FREELISTS 1 FREELIST GROUPS 1
 BUFFER_POOL DEFAULT FLASH_CACHE DEFAULT CELL_FLASH_CACHE DEFAULT)
 TABLESPACE "USERS" ROWDEPENDENCIES
```

There are three possible values for this storage parameter, with DEFAULT conveniently being the default. This setting tells Oracle to utilize the Smart Flash Cache in the normal mode, caching data using the provided caching criteria and aging out cached data in accordance with the appropriate retention policy. In the case of the DEFAULT setting, this would be using a prioritized Least-Recently-Used algorithm (the oldest data is aged out first, a common LRU configuration). There are two other settings to which this storage parameter may be set: KEEP and NONE. The KEEP setting changes the LRU algorithm by maintaining the data in the cache for as long as possible, but, to prevent KEEP data from hogging the cache, no more than 80 percent of the configured cache is available for data tagged as KEEP. Unused KEEP blocks that exceed the additional aging policy are purged. Setting CELL_FLASH_CACHE to NONE disables the use of the Smart Flash Cache for that object.

Each read or write operation is associated with the following additional information:

- The CELL_FLASH_CACHE setting for the associated object

- A cache hint based on the purpose of the request.The available hints are:

    - CACHE, which causes the blocks to be cached. I/O for index lookups would be one type of request that would be cached.

    - NOCACHE, which would apply to mirrored blocks from ASM, log writes, or a request that is simply too large to put into the cache. This hint is set, regardless of whether CELL_FLASH_CACHE is set to DEFAULT or KEEP.

    - EVICT, to remove data from the cache. Activities that would use this hint would be ASM rebalance operations (which cause blocks to be moved from one disk to another, thus invalidating the cached entries, as they would reference the original physical location) and finding cached data that has exceeded the threshold for the LRU algorithm.

The Smart Flash Cache, in addition to the CELL_FLASH_CACHE setting and the provided hint, also takes into consideration I/O size, type, and the current cache load, when making decisions on how and what to process. Extremely large I/O requests will not be cached, nor will any I/O requests that could negatively impact throughput, because the cache is extremely busy.

Write operations that are cached are not affected by this caching, as write performance is neither improved nor diminished. CELLSRV performs the disk writes, sending acknowledgment to the database tier, so transactions can continue without interruption. The Smart Flash Cache then determines if the data is to be cached or not, making the disk writes independent of the data-caching process.

Reads are the transactions that reap the rewards of the Smart Flash Cache. For a read, CELLSRV determines if the data is already in the Smart Flash Cache; an in-memory hash table of the cached data is maintained, so Oracle can quickly determine if the desired blocks can be found there. The hash table lists the blocks not marked for eviction, so when a match is found, a cache lookup can be executed. Cached blocks may be evicted when the source blocks have changed since the cached data was written, space is needed for I/O from a current transaction and the blocks are at the top of the LRU list, the blocks are tagged as KEEP but have remained unused beyond the additional KEEP threshold, or when their lifetime has exceeded the standard LRU thresholds.

It is also possible to place a table or index into the Smart Flash Cache manually, using the ALTER TABLE <TABLE_NAME> STORAGE(FLASH_CACHE [NONE|DEFAULT|KEEP]) and ALTER INDEX <INDEX NAME> STORAGE(FLASH_CACHE [NONE|DEFAULT|KEEP]) commands. Specifying NONE prevents the table or index from using the Smart Flash Cache. DEFAULT sets the normal Smart Flash Cache behavior and is set by default when creating a table or an index; KEEP will place the table or index into the Smart Flash Cache, provided there is sufficient space, and won't age it out. Using the KEEP option indiscriminately can fill the Smart Flash Cache and leave no room for objects where the FLASH_CACHE setting is DEFAULT. The KEEP setting should be used for small tables (for example, smaller look-up tables) or indexes, to allow larger tables/indexes where the FLASH_CACHE storage parameter is set to DEFAULT to use the Smart Flash Cache.

Logging We Will Go

The configured flash storage on each cell isn't used solely for Smart Flash Cache, as Exadata also provides Smart Flash Log as an additional mechanism for redo log writes. Each configured flash disk has 32MB of its storage configured as Smart Flash Log; this totals 512MB of Smart Flash Log storage per storage cell. Using Smart Flash Log can speed up transaction processing, as the first write that reports completion triggers the continuation of transaction processing at the database tier.

Redo log writes are sent to both disk and the Smart Flash Log. Once the log writer process (LGWR) receives an acknowledgment that a write is completed, transaction processing continues. It doesn't matter which write, to the Smart Flash Log or to disk, completes first; it's the acknowledgment that triggers the database server to allow processing to proceed. Rest assured that all writes to Smart Flash Log are also written to disk. Just because Smart Flash Log finished first, it doesn't stop LGWR from completing its disk writes. In concept, the Smart Flash Log is very similar to using multiplexed redo logs, in that all configured logs are written, regardless of which log finished writing first.

It's a Disk

Smart flash disks are not just for the Smart Flash Cache and Smart Flash Log to use. It's possible to configure these devices as flash disks recognized by ASM to create a flash disk group.

A flash disk group can be created using the flash disks on one or more storage cells, but it does require resizing the existing Smart Flash Cache. Before starting this process, it should be decided how large these flash disks will be, because creating such disks is not for the faint of heart, as it requires, as the first step, dropping the existing flash cache:

```
CellCLI> drop flashcache
Flash cache myexa1cel01_flashcache successfully dropped
```

Once the flash cache is dropped, it can be created with the new size. To create a 100GB flash cache:

```
CellCLI> create flashcache all size=100G
Flash cache myexa1cel01_flashcache successfully created
```

The flash disks available for ASM will be created with the balance of the available flash storage, 264.75GB, so no size parameter need be used:

```
CellCLI> create gridddisk all flashdisk prefix=flash
GridDisk flash_FD_00_myexa1cel01 successfully created
GridDisk flash_FD_01_myexa1cel01 successfully created
...
GridDisk flash_FD_15_myexa1cel01 successfully created

CellCLI> list griddisk
...
        flash_FD_00_myexa1cel01                 active
        flash_FD_01_myexa1cel01                 active
        ...
        Flash_FD_15_myexa1cel01                 active
CellCLI>
```

The choice can be made to create one or more sets of flash disks, by reconfiguring the Smart Flash Cache on only one storage cell, two storage cells, or even all of the available storage servers. Using the same prefix across storage servers allows all of the flash disks to be assigned to a single disk group in a single statement, regardless of which storage cell is involved. It's also possible to create separate flash disk sets, by making the prefix cell-specific, so that multiple flash-based disk groups could be created simply by specifying the prefix name in the CREATE DISKGROUP command.

Creating the flash disk group is not difficult; careful attention to detail is necessary, however, if multiple flash disk prefixes are in use, so that the proper set of flash disks will be assigned to the proper disk group. The command syntax is straightforward, but, first, the environment on the database server has to be set, in order to access the ASM instance. The following script, sid, is a good way to set the environment:

```
################################################################
# Oracle sid selection script
#
# 13-May-2012 - Mary Mikell Spence
#                 Infocrossing
################################################################

ORASID=$ORACLE_SID

if [ -f /etc/oratab ]
then
    export ORATAB=/etc/oratab
else
    export ORATAB=/var/opt/oracle/oratab
fi

unset ORACLE_BASE

echo;
I=1
for SHOW_DB in `cat $ORATAB | grep -v "#" |  grep -v '*' | cut -f 1 -d :`
do
    OHOME=`grep -v '#' $ORATAB | grep -v '*' | grep "^$SHOW_DB:" | cut -d: -f 2`
    echo "$I - $SHOW_DB - $OHOME"
    I=`expr $I + 1`
done
echo;

GOOD_NAME=false
while [ "${GOOD_NAME}" = "false" ]
do
  echo "Enter selection by # or name [$ORASID]: "
  read CHOICE
  if [ "$CHOICE" = "" ]
  then
    GOOD_NAME=true
    CHOICE=$ORASID
  else
    I=1
    for DB_NAME in `cat $ORATAB | grep -v "#" |  grep -v '*' | cut -f 1 -d :`
    do
```

```
      if [ "$DB_NAME" = "$CHOICE" -o "$I" = "$CHOICE" ]
      then
        GOOD_NAME=true
        CHOICE=$DB_NAME
      fi
      I=`expr $I + 1`
    done
  fi
done

ORAENV_ASK=NO
ORACLE_SID=$CHOICE

. oraenv > /dev/null

echo; echo;
echo "************************************************"
echo "ORACLE_BASE...$ORACLE_BASE"
echo "ORACLE_HOME...$ORACLE_HOME"
echo "ORACLE_SID....$ORACLE_SID"
echo "************************************************"
echo;

unset ORATAB
unset GOOD_NAME
unset I
unset SHOW_DB
unset CHOICE
unset DB_NAME
unset OHOME
unset ORASID
```

Now that you have a way to set the environment, the stage is set to create a flash-based disk group:

```
[oracle@myexa1db01 dbm1 ~]$ . sid

1 - +ASM1 - /u01/app/11.2.0.3/grid
2 - dbm1 - /u01/app/oracle/product/11.2.0.3/dbhome_1
3 - client - /u01/app/oracle/product/11.2.0/client_1

Enter selection by # or name [dbm1]:
1

************************************************
ORACLE_BASE.../u01/app/oracle
ORACLE_HOME.../u01/app/11.2.0.3/grid
ORACLE_SID....+ASM1
************************************************

[oracle@myexa1db01 +ASM1 ~]$ sqlplus / as sysasm

SQL*Plus: Release 11.2.0.3.0 Production on Tue Apr 30 10:11:09 2013

Copyright (c) 1982, 2011, Oracle.  All rights reserved.
```

```
Connected to:
Oracle Database 11g Enterprise Edition Release 11.2.0.3.0 - 64bit Production
With the Real Application Clusters and Automatic Storage Management options

SYS@+ASM1> col path format a45
SYS@+ASM1> select path, header_status
  2  from v$asm_disk
  3  where path like 'o/%/flash%'
  4  /

PATH                                          HEADER_STATU
--------------------------------------------- ------------
o/192.168.10.5/flash_FD_00_myexa1cel01        CANDIDATE
o/192.168.10.5/flash_FD_01_myexa1cel01        CANDIDATE
o/192.168.10.5/flash_FD_02_myexa1cel01        CANDIDATE
o/192.168.10.5/flash_FD_03_myexa1cel01        CANDIDATE
o/192.168.10.5/flash_FD_04_myexa1cel01        CANDIDATE
o/192.168.10.5/flash_FD_05_myexa1cel01        CANDIDATE
o/192.168.10.5/flash_FD_06_myexa1cel01        CANDIDATE
o/192.168.10.5/flash_FD_07_myexa1cel01        CANDIDATE
o/192.168.10.5/flash_FD_08_myexa1cel01        CANDIDATE
o/192.168.10.5/flash_FD_08_myexa1cel01        CANDIDATE
o/192.168.10.5/flash_FD_10_myexa1cel01        CANDIDATE
o/192.168.10.5/flash_FD_11_myexa1cel01        CANDIDATE
o/192.168.10.5/flash_FD_12_myexa1cel01        CANDIDATE
o/192.168.10.5/flash_FD_13_myexa1cel01        CANDIDATE
o/192.168.10.5/flash_FD_14_myexa1cel01        CANDIDATE
o/192.168.10.5/flash_FD_15_myexa1cel01        CANDIDATE

16 rows selected.

SYS@+ASM1> create diskgroup flash_dg redundancy normal
  2  disk 'o/%/flash%'
  3  attribute 'compatible.rdbms' = '11.2.0.0.0',
  4  'compatible.asm' = '11.2.0.0.0',
  5  'cell.smart.scan.capable' = 'TRUE',
  6  'au_size' = '4M'
  7  /

Diskgroup created.

SYS@+ASM1>
```

A flash-based disk group is now available for use. Depending on the redundancy level in use (NORMAL, providing one copy of the data, or HIGH, providing two copies of the data), the useable storage for data will be one-half to one-third of the total space available. This makes flash-based disk groups considerably smaller than their disk-based counterparts. For this example, remember that the total available flash space was 264.75GB. NORMAL redundancy was specified, so this flash disk group has about 132GB available. Using HIGH redundancy, the total available space would be about 88GB.

Monitoring

Monitoring Smart Flash Cache on the database servers is very similar, and just as limited, as monitoring Smart Scans from them, as only one metric is available from V$SYSSTAT that records flash cache activity: "cell flash cache read hits." On the other hand, monitoring the Smart Flash Cache from the storage servers provides more detail and diagnostic data, although there is no way to monitor the full storage tier from a single location; thus, the statistics are for the portion of the total flash cache on the given storage server.

Storage Server Tools

Through the CellCLI utility, a number of statistics are available to monitor flash cache usage. You can view the metrics and their descriptions using the LIST METRICDEFINITION command. To return the flash cache metrics and their descriptions, the following command can be used:

```
CellCLI> list metricdefinition attributes name, description where objectType = 'FLASHCACHE'
```

The metrics and descriptions are listed in Table 4-1.

Table 4-1. *Storage Cell Flash Cache Metrics and Their Descriptions*

FC_BYKEEP_OVERWR	""Number of megabytes pushed out of the FlashCache because of space limit for 'keep' objects"
FC_BYKEEP_OVERWR_SEC	"Number of megabytes per second pushed out of the FlashCache because of space limit for 'keep' objects"
FC_BYKEEP_USED	"Number of megabytes used for 'keep' objects on FlashCache"
FC_BY_USED	"Number of megabytes used on FlashCache"
FC_IO_BYKEEP_R	"Number of megabytes read from FlashCache for 'keep' objects"
FC_IO_BYKEEP_R_SEC	"Number of megabytes read per second from FlashCache for 'keep' objects"
FC_IO_BYKEEP_W	"Number of megabytes written to FlashCache for 'keep' objects"
FC_IO_BYKEEP_W_SEC	"Number of megabytes per second written to FlashCache for 'keep' objects"
FC_IO_BY_R	"Number of megabytes read from FlashCache"
FC_IO_BY_R_MISS	"Number of megabytes read from disks because not all requested data was in FlashCache"
FC_IO_BY_R_MISS_SEC	"Number of megabytes read from disks per second because not all requested data was in FlashCache"
FC_IO_BY_R_SEC	"Number of megabytes read per second from FlashCache"
FC_IO_BY_R_SKIP	"Number of megabytes read from disks for I/O requests that bypass FlashCache"
FC_IO_BY_R_SKIP_SEC	"Number of megabytes read from disks per second for I/O requests that bypass FlashCache"
FC_IO_BY_W	"Number of megabytes written to FlashCache"
FC_IO_BY_W_SEC	"Number of megabytes per second written to FlashCache"

(continued)

Table 4-1. (*continued*)

FC_IO_ERRS	"Number of I/O errors on FlashCache"
FC_IO_RQKEEP_R	"Number of read IO requests for 'keep' objects satisfied from FlashCache"
FC_IO_RQKEEP_R_MISS	"Number of read I/O requests for 'keep' objects that did not find all data in FlashCache"
FC_IO_RQKEEP_R_MISS_SEC	"Number of read I/O requests per second for 'keep' objects that did not find all data in FlashCache"
FC_IO_RQKEEP_R_SEC	"Number of read I/O requests for 'keep' objects per second satisfied from FlashCache"
FC_IO_RQKEEP_R_SKIP	"Number of read I/O requests for 'keep' objects that bypass FlashCache"
FC_IO_RQKEEP_R_SKIP_SEC	"Number of read I/O requests per second for 'keep' objects that bypass FlashCache"
FC_IO_RQKEEP_W	"Number of I/O requests for 'keep' objects that resulted in FlashCache being populated with data"
FC_IO_RQKEEP_W_SEC	"Number of I/O requests per second for 'keep' objects that resulted in FlashCache being populated with data"
FC_IO_RQ_R	"Number of read I/O requests satisfied from FlashCache"
FC_IO_RQ_R_MISS	"Number of read I/O requests that did not find all data in FlashCache"
FC_IO_RQ_R_MISS_SEC	"Number of read I/O requests per second that did not find all data in FlashCache"
FC_IO_RQ_R_SEC	"Number of read I/O requests satisfied per second from FlashCache"
FC_IO_RQ_R_SKIP	"Number of read I/O requests that bypass FlashCache"
FC_IO_RQ_R_SKIP_SEC	"Number of read I/O requests per second that bypass FlashCache"
FC_IO_RQ_W	"Number of I/O requests that resulted in FlashCache being populated with data"
FC_IO_RQ_W_SEC	"Number of I/O requests per second that resulted in FlashCache being populated with data"

These metrics are cumulative, from the time CELLSRV was started. To list the current value for one or more of the metrics, the LIST METRICCURRENT statement is used. The output reports the cumulative statistics for a single storage cell; the same command will have to be run on all remaining storage cells, to monitor the activity for the entire Smart Flash Cache.

Use the LIST METRICCURRENT statement to return Smart Flash Cache metrics for the given storage cell:

```
CellCLI> list metriccurrent where objectType = 'FLASHCACHE'

    FC_BYKEEP_OVERWR          FLASHCACHE        0.000 MB
    FC_BYKEEP_OVERWR_SEC      FLASHCACHE        0.000 MB/sec
    FC_BYKEEP_USED            FLASHCACHE        0.000 MB
    FC_BY_USED                FLASHCACHE        365,322 MB
    FC_IO_BYKEEP_R            FLASHCACHE        0.000 MB
    FC_IO_BYKEEP_R_SEC        FLASHCACHE        0.000 MB/sec
    FC_IO_BYKEEP_W            FLASHCACHE        0.047 MB
```

```
     FC_IO_BYKEEP_W_SEC             FLASHCACHE        0.000 MB/sec
     FC_IO_BY_R                     FLASHCACHE        60,257,512 MB
     FC_IO_BY_R_MISS                FLASHCACHE        12,592,252 MB
     FC_IO_BY_R_MISS_SEC            FLASHCACHE        0.891 MB/sec
     FC_IO_BY_R_SEC                 FLASHCACHE        21.193 MB/sec
     FC_IO_BY_R_SKIP                FLASHCACHE        567,179,945 MB
     FC_IO_BY_R_SKIP_SEC            FLASHCACHE        3.681 MB/sec
     FC_IO_BY_W                     FLASHCACHE        22,170,046 MB
     FC_IO_BY_W_SEC                 FLASHCACHE        4.028 MB/sec
     FC_IO_ERRS                     FLASHCACHE        0
     FC_IO_RQKEEP_R                 FLASHCACHE        0 IO requests
     FC_IO_RQKEEP_R_MISS            FLASHCACHE        0 IO requests
     FC_IO_RQKEEP_R_MISS_SEC        FLASHCACHE        0.0 IO/sec
     FC_IO_RQKEEP_R_SEC             FLASHCACHE        0.0 IO/sec
     FC_IO_RQKEEP_R_SKIP            FLASHCACHE        0 IO requests
     FC_IO_RQKEEP_R_SKIP_SEC        FLASHCACHE        0.0 IO/sec
     FC_IO_RQKEEP_W                 FLASHCACHE        3 IO requests
     FC_IO_RQKEEP_W_SEC             FLASHCACHE        0.0 IO/sec
     FC_IO_RQ_R                     FLASHCACHE        6,638,504,145 IO
requests
     FC_IO_RQ_R_MISS                FLASHCACHE        373,704,323 IO
requests
     FC_IO_RQ_R_MISS_SEC            FLASHCACHE        28.5 IO/sec
     FC_IO_RQ_R_SEC                 FLASHCACHE        2,688 IO/sec
     FC_IO_RQ_R_SKIP                FLASHCACHE        1,010,237,424 IO
requests
     FC_IO_RQ_R_SKIP_SEC            FLASHCACHE        16.7 IO/sec
     FC_IO_RQ_W                     FLASHCACHE        1,096,872,236 IO
requests
     FC_IO_RQ_W_SEC                 FLASHCACHE        326 IO/sec
```

Metrics for objects where the storage clause sets CELL_FLASH_CACHE to KEEP can be isolated and reported, for example:

```
CellCLI> list metriccurrent where objectType = 'FLASHCACHE' and name like '.*KEEP.*'
     FC_BYKEEP_OVERWR               FLASHCACHE        0.000 MB
     FC_BYKEEP_OVERWR_SEC           FLASHCACHE        0.000 MB/sec
     FC_BYKEEP_USED                 FLASHCACHE        0.000 MB
     FC_IO_BYKEEP_R                 FLASHCACHE        0.000 MB
     FC_IO_BYKEEP_R_SEC             FLASHCACHE        0.000 MB/sec
     FC_IO_BYKEEP_W                 FLASHCACHE        0.047 MB
     FC_IO_BYKEEP_W_SEC             FLASHCACHE        0.000 MB/sec
     FC_IO_RQKEEP_R                 FLASHCACHE        0 IO requests
     FC_IO_RQKEEP_R_MISS            FLASHCACHE        0 IO requests
     FC_IO_RQKEEP_R_MISS_SEC        FLASHCACHE        0.0 IO/sec
     FC_IO_RQKEEP_R_SEC             FLASHCACHE        0.0 IO/sec
     FC_IO_RQKEEP_R_SKIP            FLASHCACHE        0 IO requests
     FC_IO_RQKEEP_R_SKIP_SEC        FLASHCACHE        0.0 IO/sec
     FC_IO_RQKEEP_W                 FLASHCACHE        3 IO requests
     FC_IO_RQKEEP_W_SEC             FLASHCACHE        0.0 IO/sec

CellCLI>
```

It is also possible to exclude those same metrics by changing the statement slightly:

```
CellCLI> list metriccurrent where objectType = 'FLASHCACHE' and name not like '.*KEEP.*'
         FC_BY_USED              FLASHCACHE      365,290 MB
         FC_IO_BY_R              FLASHCACHE      60,267,646 MB
         FC_IO_BY_R_MISS         FLASHCACHE      12,592,880 MB
         FC_IO_BY_R_MISS_SEC     FLASHCACHE      1.568 MB/sec
         FC_IO_BY_R_SEC          FLASHCACHE      23.065 MB/sec
         FC_IO_BY_R_SKIP         FLASHCACHE      567,186,500 MB
         FC_IO_BY_R_SKIP_SEC     FLASHCACHE      5.888 MB/sec
         FC_IO_BY_W              FLASHCACHE      22,171,791 MB
         FC_IO_BY_W_SEC          FLASHCACHE      2.865 MB/sec
         FC_IO_ERRS              FLASHCACHE      0
         FC_IO_RQ_R              FLASHCACHE      6,639,787,345 IO requests
         FC_IO_RQ_R_MISS         FLASHCACHE      373,724,226 IO requests
         FC_IO_RQ_R_MISS_SEC     FLASHCACHE      50.2 IO/sec
         FC_IO_RQ_R_SEC          FLASHCACHE      2,927 IO/sec
         FC_IO_RQ_R_SKIP         FLASHCACHE      1,010,251,273 IO requests
         FC_IO_RQ_R_SKIP_SEC     FLASHCACHE      19.4 IO/sec
         FC_IO_RQ_W              FLASHCACHE      1,096,966,059 IO requests
         FC_IO_RQ_W_SEC          FLASHCACHE      170 IO/sec

CellCLI>
```

Performance metrics aren't the only values collected for the Smart Flash Cache. You can see what is in the cache, using the LIST FLASHCACHECONTENT command. To see which attributes are available to view or that can be used to filter the output, the FLASHCACHECONTENT object can be described:

```
CellCLI> describe flashcachecontent
         cachedKeepSize
         cachedSize
         dbID
         dbUniqueName
         hitCount
         hoursToExpiration
         missCount
         objectNumber
         tableSpaceNumber
```

A specific database can be targeted using either dbUniqueName or dbID. The objectNumber and tableSpaceNumber attributes are specific to a given dbUniqueName/dbID, so they should be used in conjunction with either dbUniqueName or dbID. To view the unique database name, the object number, the KEEP size, the cache size, the hit count, and miss count for objects from the DBM database, the command would be as follows:

```
CellCLI> list flashcachecontent where dbUniqueName = 'DBM' and hitcount > 99 attributes
dbUniqueName, objectNumber, cachedKeepSize, cachedSize, hitcount, misscount
         DBM     2       0       172032          1889    350
         DBM     8       0       81920           168     7
         DBM     104     0       622592          170     48
         DBM     225     0       2654208         382     247
         DBM     227     0       1081344         173     77
         DBM     268     0       1859584         770     25
```

DBM	271	0	65536	298	5
DBM	272	0	65536	383	4
DBM	421	0	2064384	8120	772
DBM	424	0	589824	2391	63
DBM	425	0	122880	372	17
DBM	466	0	196608	612	37
DBM	469	0	131072	462	4
...					
DBM	48306	0	32768	242	120
DBM	48406	0	196608	102	12
DBM	48464	0	237568	116	110
DBM	48466	0	1220608	247	104
DBM	48663	0	802816	142	52
DBM	48705	0	917504	101	20
DBM	48840	0	2334720	170	31
DBM	48972	0	2138112	176	104
DBM	4294967294	0	376832	25674712	181405

CellCLI>

By default, the LIST FLASHCACHECONTENT command reports the dbID, tableSpaceNumber and objectNumber. To return other attributes, they need to be listed in the command, using the attributes clause, as was done in this example.

Notice that among all of the attributes available at the storage-cell level, the object name is not one of them. This can easily be reported from the database servers by querying DBA_OBJECTS, using the objectNumber reported by CellCLI, which maps to the DATA_OBJECT_ID column:

```
SQL> select owner, object_type, object_name
  2  from dba_objects
  3  where data_object_id = 5888;

OWNER                OBJECT_TYPE         OBJECT_NAME
-------------------- ------------------- ---------------------------------
SYS                  INDEX               WRI$_ADV_MSG_GRPS_IDX_01

SQL>
```

A script can be written to generate the output from the LIST FLASHCACHECONTENT command and place it into a text file on the database server, for example:

```
/usr/bin/ssh celladmin@myexa1cel01-priv.7-11.com "cellcli -e list flashcachecontent where
dbUniqueName = '$1' attributes dbUniquename,objectNumber,hitcount,misscount,cachedSize"
/usr/bin/ssh celladmin@myexa1cel02-priv.7-11.com "cellcli -e list flashcachecontent where
dbUniqueName = '$1' attributes dbUniquename,objectNumber,hitcount,misscount,cachedSize"
/usr/bin/ssh celladmin@myexa1cel03-priv.7-11.com "cellcli -e list flashcachecontent where
dbUniqueName = '$1' attributes dbUniquename,objectNumber,hitcount,misscount,cachedSize"
```

A second script would be used to execute the first script and send the output to a file:

```
/home/oracle/bin/cellcli_flashcache_mon_nohdrs.sh $1 > /home/oracle/ext_tbls/flash_mon.txt
```

The database name of interest is passed to the second script on the command line. The generated file can then be used to create an external table, which can be joined to the DBA_OBJECTS view to report Smart Flash Cache activity by object name. As an example:

```
SQL> create or replace directory admin_dat_dir as '/home/oracle/ext_tbls';

Directory created.

SQL> create or replace directory admin_log_dir as '/home/oracle/logs';

Directory created.

SQL> create or replace directory admin_bad_dir as '/home/oracle/bad';

Directory created.

SQL>
SQL> CREATE TABLE flashmon_ext
  2                     (db_name    varchar2(12),
  3                      object_id  number,
  4                      hitct      number,
  5                      missct     number,
  6                      cachesz    number
  7                     )
  8       ORGANIZATION EXTERNAL
  9       (
 10         TYPE ORACLE_LOADER
 11         DEFAULT DIRECTORY admin_dat_dir
 12         ACCESS PARAMETERS
 13         (
 14           records delimited by newline
 15           badfile admin_bad_dir:'flashmon_ext%a_%p.bad'
 16           logfile admin_log_dir:'flashmon_ext%a_%p.log'
 17           fields terminated by whitespace
 18           missing field values are null
 19           ( db_name, object_id, hitct, missct, cachesz
 20           )
 21       )
 22         LOCATION ('flash_mon.txt')
 23       )
 24       PARALLEL
 25       REJECT LIMIT UNLIMITED;

Table created.

SQL>
```

The first directory contains the text file generated from CellCLI and the LIST FLASHCACHECONTENT command. The next two directories are for the logfile and badfile, which could be generated by SQL*Loader. Finally, we create the external table. Because the text file shouldn't change names or locations, generating a new file won't cause the external table to become invalid. Thus, the data can be refreshed at any time, and the external table will still be usable.

After the external table is created, it's a simple task of writing the query to map object_name to object_id:

```
SQL> select f.db_name, o.object_name, f.hitct, f.missct, f.cachesz
  2  from flashmon_ext f left outer join dba_objects o on (o.data_object_id = f.object_id);
```

DB_NAME	OBJECT_NAME	HITCT	MISSCT	CACHESZ
DBM	ICOL$	407479	9163	40828928
DBM	ICOL$	425912	11731	59179008
DBM	ICOL$	575450	44509	31588352
DBM	I_USER1	33	4	32768
DBM	CON$	159	60	32768
DBM	CON$	447	67	98304
DBM	UNDO$	49	2	32768
DBM	C_COBJ#	4782	572	2129920
DBM	C_COBJ#	9077	984	3178496
DBM	C_COBJ#	8120	968	4358144
DBM	I_OBJ#	2320	65	557056
DBM	I_OBJ#	1323	17	327680
DBM	I_OBJ#	1742	30	327680
DBM	I_IND1	280	19	458752
DBM	I_IND1	1160	44	196608
DBM	I_IND1	1405	35	131072
DBM	I_CDEF2	6150	516	425984
DBM	I_CDEF2	1332	78	720896
DBM	I_CDEF2	3483	210	2031616
DBM	I_OBJ5	49088	2555	9732096
DBM	I_OBJ5	16742	1144	8192000

...

In this example, the flashmon_ext table contains 16,202 rows, because data was collected across all three available storage cells. This explains the apparent duplication of object names in the output; each storage cell can cache the same object at the same time. Even though the object names may be duplicated, the cache size, hit count, and miss count are usually different.

It is not unusual to find object_id values in the four billion range, and these object_ids won't match to any object in DBA_OBJECTS. One source of object_ids in that range would be the V$FIXED_TABLE and GV$FIXED_TABLE views; however, none of the listed object_id values in the flashmon_ext table in that range matches any of those objects. In the absence of global temporary tables, the objects in question are undo segments.

Database Server Tools

There isn't much to see at the database layer, unfortunately. A single statistic, "cell flash cache read hits," is all that is available. As with the other metrics, this is cumulative, because the instance started as reported in V$SYSSTAT and for the duration of the current session in V$MYSTAT. The easiest way to measure the Smart Flash Cache activity for a SQL statement is to query V$MYSTAT before and after the statement is executed. Doing this in SQL*Plus offers the ability to save the query results in variables for use after the statement has completed, as follows:

```
SQL> select statistic#, value
  2  from v$mystat
  3  where statistic# in (select statistic# from v$statname where name = 'cell flash cache read hits');
```

```
STATISTIC#       VALUE
---------- ----------
       605          1

SQL>
SQL> select count(*)
  2  from emp;

  COUNT(*)
----------
   7340032

SQL>
SQL> column    val new_value endval
SQL>
SQL> select statistic#, value val
  2  from v$mystat
  3  where statistic# in (select statistic# from v$statname where name = 'cell flash cache read hits');

STATISTIC#       VAL
---------- ----------
       605        857

SQL>
SQL>
SQL> select &endval - &beginval flash_hits
  2  from dual;

FLASH_HITS
----------
       856

SQL>
```

What a Performer

As part of the balanced I/O subsystem, the Smart Flash Cache provides measurable performance improvements over non-Exadata systems. Cell single-block read times can regularly fall into the 1 millisecond or less range, which compares favorably with non-Exadata systems using Solid State Disk (SSD). The major difference is Exadata's ability to process larger I/O loads and maintain this level of performance. Because Exadata is a balanced system, with matched and tuned components, performance won't suffer until the physical limits of CPU and/or memory are reached.

Things to Know

Smart Flash Cache provides the ability to deliver high I/O-per-second rates by caching frequently accessed table and index blocks, allowing them to be read directly from flash memory.

The Smart Flash Cache is composed of 4 Sun Flash PCIe cards per storage cell, each with 96GB of flash storage. For an Exadata system with 3 storage cells, the total flash storage available is 1.125TB. The expected lifetime of these PCIe cards is two years, because the storage capacitor will lose its ability to hold a charge over time. According to Sun, the cards can be replaced individually, without shutting down the storage cell. Oracle, however, recommends a storage cell to be powered down before any maintenance.

The Smart Flash Cache is a per-cell caching mechanism, optimized for frequently accessed data. Whether an object will be considered for Smart Flash Cache use is determined in part by the CELL_FLASH_CACHE storage parameter set when that object is created.

Write operations are not affected by this caching. CELLSRV performs the disk writes, sending acknowledgment to the database tier, so transactions can continue without interruption. The Smart Flash Cache then determines if the data is to be cached or not, making the disk writes independent of the data-caching process.

An in-memory hash table is maintained of the cached data, so Oracle can quickly determine if the desired blocks can be found there. The hash table lists the blocks not marked for eviction, so when a match is found, a cache lookup can be executed.

Cached blocks may be evicted when the source blocks have changed since the cached data was written, space is needed for I/O from a current transaction, the blocks are tagged as KEEP but have remained unused beyond the additional KEEP threshold, or when their lifetime has exceeded the standard LRU thresholds.

Each configured flash disk has 32MB of its storage configured as Smart Flash Log; this totals 512MB of Smart Flash Log storage per storage cell. Redo log writes are sent to both disk and the Smart Flash Log. Once the log writer process (LGWR) receives an acknowledgment that a write is completed, either to the redo log or the Smart Flash Log area, transaction processing continues.

A flash disk group can be created using the flash disks on one or more storage cells; doing so requires resizing the existing Smart Flash Cache. One or more sets of flash disks can be created by reconfiguring the Smart Flash Cache on only one storage cell, two storage cells, or all of the available storage servers. The redundancy level chosen will determine the useable storage available; the maximum will be one-half the total space available, with the minimum being one-third of the total available space.

Monitoring the Smart Flash Cache from the storage cells provides a greater range of metrics than monitoring it from the database servers. One metric, "cell flash cache read hits," is the only indicator of flash cache activity on the database tier. The storage cells provide more than 30 metrics recording Smart Flash Cache activity, but, unfortunately, each cell has to be monitored individually. It's possible to script the storage-cell monitoring and populate an external table in the database, so that object names, in place of object ids, can identify the cached segments.

Some cached segments cannot be mapped to an object name. UNDO segments may be found in the Smart Flash Cache, with object id values greater than four billion.

CHAPTER 5

■■■

Parallel Query

Unlike other areas of Exadata, parallel query execution uses the same Oracle Release 11.2 functionality as non-Exadata systems. Because Exadata is, at its heart, a data-warehousing system, and efficient handling and processing of data-warehouse workloads was a primary design goal, parallel query processing is an important feature. Remember that Smart Scans and offloading rely on direct-path reads, the same read functionality that is used by parallel query slaves. In Release 11.2, Oracle has provided three improvements to the earlier attempts at controlling parallel execution. These improvements, along with the processing power of Exadata, make this feature more manageable, more scalable, and less likely to saturate server resources, such as memory and CPU, than earlier releases of the database. The first of those improvements that we will discuss is parallel statement queuing.

Getting into the Queue

Parallel query has been available in Oracle releases since version 7, and, when used with care, can significantly improve statement performance. On the other hand, when overused, it can bring the database server to its knees. Multiple users, all choosing parallel execution, can saturate CPU resources to the point that the benefits of parallel query become the curse of parallel query. Until Release 11.2, there was no way to control parallel execution by multiple users on the same system. That changed with parallel statement queuing. This was implemented because Exadata is a system designed to handle mixed workloads, allowing both data-warehouse and Online Transaction Processing applications to run and ensuring that neither suffers at the hands of the other. With parallel statement queuing, Exadata has a way to both separate the different types of workloads and also "rein in" parallel statements that otherwise would be too resource-intensive for a multiuser system.

Old School

To give some perspective on how parallel statement queuing has improved parallel query performance, it is necessary to examine the tool Oracle provided to manage this feature in earlier releases. The parallel_adaptive_multi_user parameter is quite a powerful tool, but it can create varying performance by deciding, at runtime, whether to parallelize a statement or not. It also determines how many slaves should be employed for a parallelized query. With this mechanism, the parallelism can go down dramatically, depending on the system resources in use at the moment the decision is made, which is the time the execution starts.

Statements can go from having 16 or more parallel slaves for one execution to having absolutely none the next time the same statement is executed. Remember that once the degree of parallelism (DOP) is set, it cannot be altered; the statement must run to completion at the assigned DOP, which may be one. The statement also cannot benefit from resources freed during its execution; if ten parallel query slaves become available during the serial execution of that statement, they cannot be repurposed to provide a higher DOP and, as a result, a shorter execution time.

As an example, you have a statement that was assigned 24 parallel query slaves the last time it was run, with a resulting execution time of 1 minute. A short spike in activity occurs at the time this statement starts its next execution, downgrading it to a serial operation. Several seconds later, this spike is over; the statement is stuck, executing serially for possibly 24 minutes or longer. With no apparent rhyme or reason for this seemingly erratic behavior (from the user's perspective), such inconsistent performance can make for unhappy users and very confused, unhappy developers.

The New Method

Parallel adaptive multi user was a good start at controlling parallel execution, based on available resources, but version 11.2 introduces parallel statement queuing to the mix, allowing parallel execution to be placed on hold, until sufficient resources become available.

■ **Note** It is best to set `parallel_adaptive_multi_user` to `FALSE` to prevent these two features from conflicting with each other. When both are enabled, we have seen parallel queries take much longer to execute.

How it works is simple, really. Enable the feature by setting `parallel_degree_policy` to `AUTO`. Next, set `parallel_servers_target` to the number of parallel slaves you want. The easy part is that you run your queries; Oracle takes care of the rest for you. In basic terms, a statement will be queued if it will require more parallel slaves than there are currently available. Once the required number of slaves are freed, the statement executes.

The V$SQL_MONITOR and GV$SQL_MONITOR views report on the execute status of submitted statements; basically, these views report that a statement is DONE (in some form), EXECUTING, or, if parallel statement queuing is enabled, QUEUED. Given that information, it isn't difficult to see which statements are waiting in the parallel statement queue. The standard EMP table from the demobld.sql script was used, although it was loaded with a very large number of records:

```
SQL> select count(*)
  2  from emp;

  COUNT(*)
-------------
 15032385536

SQL>
```

We chose to select the average salary from our large version of the EMP table from 12 different sessions. We then queried V$SQL_MONITOR to see how many of those sessions ended up in the queue. The query produced the following output:

```
SQL> select sid, sql_id, sql_exec_id, sql_text
  2  from v$sql_monitot monitor
  3  where status = 'QUEUED'
  4  order by 3;

       SID SQL_ID        SQL_EXEC_ID SQL_TEXT
---------- ------------- ----------- -------------------------------------
      1532 5du23va3p3ad0    16777216 select avg(sal) from emp
      1059 5du23va3p3ad0    16777217 select avg(sal) from emp
      1628 5du23va3p3ad0    16777218 select avg(sal) from emp
       865 5du23va3p3ad0    16777219 select avg(sal) from emp
```

```
 205 5du23va3p3ad0    16777220 select avg(sal) from emp
2199 5du23va3p3ad0    16777221 select avg(sal) from emp
1542 5du23va3p3ad0    16777222 select avg(sal) from emp
 159 5du23va3p3ad0    16777223 select avg(sal) from emp
1888 5du23va3p3ad0    16777224 select avg(sal) from emp
1234 5du23va3p3ad0    16777225 select avg(sal) from emp
 705 5du23va3p3ad0    16777226 select avg(sal) from emp

11 rows selected.

SQL>
```

The sql_exec_id is, basically, a run number indicating the statement's position in the queue. It is also possible for the sql_exec_id to be the same for all queued statements (indicating simultaneous execution), if the sum of the parallel resources required for execution doesn't exceed the maximum available for the database.

Control Issues

There may be times when you want to have some control over parallel statement queuing behavior. If you simply turn it on and let it run, it's a first-in, first-out (FIFO) queue. It's possible to bypass the queue using a hint. It's also possible to use parallel statement queuing, even if the feature isn't enabled at the database level.

Two parameters are available that can affect parallel statement queuing, and the foremost of those is parallel_servers_target. The value for this parameter sets the number of parallel server processes Oracle can run before placing statements in the queue. There is a formula for computing the default value, as follows:

```
((4*cpu_count)*parallel_threads_per_cpu)*active number of instances
```

Given an Exadata X3-2 with the following settings:

```
cpu_count                       24
parallel_threads_per_cpu         4
```

and two active instances, the default setting would be computed as follows:

$$((4*24)*4)*2 = 768$$

This is a value that is much higher than you'd ever want to set; the calculation, as written, will compute a value intended to utilize all of the available resources for parallel query processes. Also, a setting that high would seriously impact OLTP transactions, as they could possibly starve, should a long-running, resource-intensive parallel query commandeer the available CPU and memory.

Like pga_aggregate_target, this parameter sets a target value, not a limit. There can be more parallel server processes running than the parameter initially configures. This can occur because the number of parallel slaves assigned to a statement may be up to twice the DOP setting. As an example, a system has parallel_servers_target set to 4 and Auto DOP set a degree of parallelism of 4. The statement could have up to 8 parallel query processes attached to it, which is greater than the target setting. Parallel query processes are assigned, in part, based on available resources, so occasionally, exceeding the parallel_servers_target setting isn't a problem. The statement may end up in the parallel statement queue, but it won't fail to run, because it's using more parallel query slaves than parallel_servers_target would lead you to believe are allowed.

The second parameter to affect parallel statement queuing is a hidden parameter, _parallel_statement_queuing. The values for this parameter are TRUE and FALSE, with TRUE being the default setting when parallel_degree_policy is set to AUTO. It can be set independently of parallel_degree_policy, to enable and disable this feature.

Even when parallel statement queuing is active it's possible to bypass the queue entirely, with a hint. The NO_STATEMENT_QUEUING hint allows you to immediately execute parallel queries that otherwise would have been placed into the queue. Checking the queue for them is fruitless, as they do not appear with a status of "QUEUED." Querying VSQL/GVSQL joined to V$SESSION/GV$SESSION will reveal that they are, indeed, running. Not only do they jump the queue, they also can spawn parallel query slaves in excess of the setting for parallel_servers_target.

If you don't have parallel statement queuing enabled, you can still use it with another hint: STATEMENT_QUEING. This will queue statements, should parallel resoures be scarce at the time the statement starts execution.

Necessary Settings

In addition to parallel statement queuing (which we just covered), Oracle has provided automatic degree of parallelism (Auto DOP) and in-memory parallel execution. All three are enabled when parallel_degree_policy is set to AUTO. Auto DOP allows the database to calculate the degree of parallelism on a query-by-query basis; we will discuss this in more detail in a separate section. This is the one improvement that requires a bit of effort to get working, as Oracle won't activate this feature, if the I/O system has not been calibrated.

We will discuss I/O calibration in more detail later on in this chapter. For now, you should know that it's not a task to be executed during business hours.

I/O calibration is just one part of parallel query processing configuration; several database initialization parameters control some aspect of parallel query execution. These parameters, their settings, and which features or aspects of parallel query execution they affect are listed in Table 5-1.

Table 5-1. *Parameters Affecting Parallel Query Execution*

Name	Default	Description
parallel_adaptive_multi_user	TRUE	Enable adaptive setting of degree for multiple-user streams.
parallel_automatic_tuning	FALSE	Enable intelligent defaults for parallel execution parameters.
parallel_degree_limit	CPU	Limit placed on degree of parallelism. Values range from CPU, I/O, and an integer value of 2 or greater.
parallel_degree_policy	MANUAL	Policy used to compute the degree of parallelism (MANUAL/LIMITED/AUTO).
parallel_execution_message_size	16384	Message buffer size for parallel execution.
parallel_force_local	FALSE	Force single-instance execution.
parallel_instance_group		Instance group to use for all parallel operations. Can restrict parallel operations to a subset of the RAC instances available.
parallel_io_cap_enabled	FALSE	Enable capping of DOP by I/O bandwidth.
parallel_max_servers	240	Maximum parallel query servers per instance.
parallel_min_percent	0	Minimum percent of threads required for parallel query.
parallel_min_servers		Minimum parallel query servers per instance.
parallel_min_time_threshold	AUTO	Threshold above which a plan is a candidate for parallelization (in seconds). Can also be set to a numeric value, including 0.
parallel_servers_target	240	Instance target in terms of number of parallel servers.
parallel_threads_per_cpu	2	Number of parallel execution threads per CPU. Used in various parallel query computations.

Parallel statement queuing and in-memory_parallel execution rely on the `parallel_servers_target` and the `parallel_min_time_threshold` parameter settings. We have discussed parallel statement queuing at the beginning of this chapter; in-memory parallel execution will be discussed in its own section.

My Friend Auto

Auto DOP is a change in parallel operations introduced in Oracle Release 11.2. In prior releases of the database, parallel operations relied on hints at the query level or on the `DEGREE` and `INSTANCES` settings for the object in use. It is an unfortunate reality that a single DOP setting is rarely appropriate for all queries, at all times, for a given object. Arriving at usable values for the DOP that makes the query execution more efficient than serial execution and doesn't adversely impact other queries and statements is a time-consuming trial-and-error process. It requires the development team to understand the platform in use and the workload that the system will be experiencing when the statement is executed. Another issue with the DOP: it cannot change during statement execution. Auto DOP was designed to overcome such problems, and it's done its job admirably.

Calibrate Me

Auto DOP, when enabled and activated, causes Oracle to evaluate each statement, to determine if it should run in parallel. The DOP is set once this decision has been made.

■ **Note**   It is important to note that simply enabling Auto DOP doesn't get it working; it needs to be activated by running an I/O calibration in each database where you want Auto DOP available.

The optimizer evaluates serial execution time and, in general, if that estimated time exceeds the setting for `parallel_min_time_threshold`, the statement will be executed in parallel. By default, this parameter is set to `AUTO`, providing a threshold value of 10 seconds. This parameter can be altered at the system level or at the session level, to implement a lower or higher parallel triggering threshold.

A supplied package, DBMS_RESOURCE_MANAGER, provides the CALIBRATE_IO procedure that is used to generate a random read-only workload across all RAC instances on the cluster. The procedure takes five parameters, two input values (number of disks and maximum estimated disk latency), and three output variables to receive the computed values for maximum I/Os per second, the maximum megabytes per second, and the calculated latency. An anonymous PL/SQL block can be used to call the procedure and return the computed metrics, as follows:

```
Set serveroutput on size 1000000
Declare
        Calc_lat        number;
        Calc_iops       number;
        Calc_mbps       number;
Begin

        Dbms_resource_manager.calibrate_io(&dsks,&maxlat, Calc_iops, Calc_mbps, Calc_lat);

        Dbms_output.put_line('Max IOPS          : '||Calc_iops);
        Dbms_output.put_line('Max mbytes-per-sec: '||Calc_mbps);
        Dbms_output.put_line('Calc. latency     : '||Calc_lat);
End;
/
```

As stated earlier in the chapter, before Auto DOP is activated, the I/O system has to be calibrated. This must be done for each different database running on the Exadata system.

■ **Note**   It cannot be stressed enough that I/O calibration is a resource-intensive operation and should not be run on a system experiencing heavy workloads. This is an "after-hours" operation that will take about 15 minutes or more to run. Your patience will be rewarded when Auto DOP is functional.

A view, V$IO_CALIBRATION_STATUS, reports whether or not this calibration has been run. A database in need of calibration will show these results when V$IO_CALIBRATION_STATUS is queried:

```
SQL> select *
  2  from v$io_calibration_status;

STATUS        CALIBRATION_TIME
------------- -------------------------------------------------------------
NOT AVAILABLE

SQL>
```

Queries that would be executed in parallel on calibrated systems run serially on databases that have not had I/O calibration run. The execution plan returns an informative message about the Auto DOP calculations, immediately visible after query execution when autotrace is enabled:

```
SQL> select count(*)
  2  from dba_objects
  3  /

  COUNT(*)
----------
    369952

Execution Plan
----------------------------------------------------------
Plan hash value: 3660875064
```

Id	Operation	Name	Rows	Bytes	Cost (%CPU)	Time
0	SELECT STATEMENT		1		1099 (2)	00:00:14
1	SORT AGGREGATE		1			
2	VIEW	DBA_OBJECTS	320K		1099 (2)	00:00:14
3	UNION-ALL					
* 4	FILTER					
* 5	HASH JOIN		320K	21M	1092 (2)	00:00:14
6	INDEX FULL SCAN	I_USER2	845	3380	5 (0)	00:00:01
* 7	HASH JOIN		320K	20M	1085 (2)	00:00:14
8	INDEX FULL SCAN	I_USER2	845	18590	5 (0)	00:00:01
* 9	TABLE ACCESS STORAGE FULL	OBJ$	320K	13M	1078 (2)	00:00:13
10	NESTED LOOPS		1	30	4 (0)	00:00:01
* 11	INDEX RANGE SCAN	I_OBJ4	1	10	3 (0)	00:00:01

```
|* 12 |       INDEX RANGE SCAN        | I_USER2 |    1 |   20 |    1   (0)| 00:00:01 |
|* 13 |        HASH JOIN              |         |   29 |  232 |    7  (15)| 00:00:01 |
|  14 |         INDEX FULL SCAN       | I_LINK1 |   29 |  116 |    1   (0)| 00:00:01 |
|  15 |         INDEX FULL SCAN       | I_USER2 |  845 | 3380 |    5   (0)| 00:00:01 |
       ------------------------------------------------------------------------------
---

          Predicate Information (identified by operation id):
          ---------------------------------------------------

4 - filter("O"."TYPE#"<>4 AND "O"."TYPE#"<>5 AND "O"."TYPE#"<>7 AND "O"."TYPE#"<>8
          AND "O"."TYPE#"<>9 AND "O"."TYPE#"<>11 AND "O"."TYPE#"<>12 AND "O"."TYPE#"<>13 AND
          "O"."TYPE#"<>14 AND "O"."TYPE#"<>22 AND "O"."TYPE#"<>87 AND "O"."TYPE#"<>88 OR
          BITAND("U"."SPARE1",16)=0 OR ("O"."TYPE#"=4 OR "O"."TYPE#"=5 OR "O"."TYPE#"=7 OR
          "O"."TYPE#"=8 OR "O"."TYPE#"=9 OR "O"."TYPE#"=10 OR "O"."TYPE#"=11 OR "O"."TYPE#"=12
          OR "O"."TYPE#"=13 OR "O"."TYPE#"=14 OR "O"."TYPE#"=22 OR "O"."TYPE#"=87) AND
          ("U"."TYPE#"<>2 AND SYS_CONTEXT('userenv','current_edition_name')='ORA$BASE' OR
          "U"."TYPE#"=2 AND "U"."SPARE2"=TO_NUMBER(SYS_CONTEXT('userenv','current_edition_id'))
          OR  EXISTS (SELECT 0 FROM SYS."USER$" "U2",SYS."OBJ$" "O2" WHERE "O2"."TYPE#"=88 AND
          "O2"."DATAOBJ#"=:B1 AND "U2"."TYPE#"=2 AND "O2"."OWNER#"="U2"."USER#" AND
          "U2"."SPARE2"=TO_NUMBER(SYS_CONTEXT('userenv','current_edition_id')))))
5 - access("O"."SPARE3"="U"."USER#")
7 - access("O"."OWNER#"="U"."USER#")
9 - storage("O"."LINKNAME" IS NULL AND "O"."TYPE#"<>10 AND
          BITAND("O"."FLAGS",128)=0 AND "O"."NAME"<>'_NEXT_OBJECT' AND
          "O"."NAME"<>'_default_auditing_options_')
    filter("O"."LINKNAME" IS NULL AND "O"."TYPE#"<>10 AND BITAND("O"."FLAGS",128)=0
          AND "O"."NAME"<>'_NEXT_OBJECT' AND "O"."NAME"<>'_default_auditing_options_')
11 - access("O2"."DATAOBJ#"=:B1 AND "O2"."TYPE#"=88)
12 - access("O2"."OWNER#"="U2"."USER#" AND "U2"."TYPE#"=2 AND
          "U2"."SPARE2"=TO_NUMBER(SYS_CONTEXT('userenv','current_edition_id')))
     filter("U2"."SPARE2"=TO_NUMBER(SYS_CONTEXT('userenv','current_edition_id')))
13 - access("L"."OWNER#"="U"."USER#")
```

Note

   - **automatic DOP: skipped because of IO calibrate statistics are missing**

```
Statistics
----------------------------------------------------------
         17  recursive calls
          2  db block gets
       4788  consistent gets
       4772  physical reads
          0  redo size
        528  bytes sent via SQL*Net to client
        524  bytes received via SQL*Net from client
          2  SQL*Net roundtrips to/from client
          0  sorts (memory)
          0  sorts (disk)
          1  rows processed

SQL>
```

Running the calibration process is simple and straightforward, and we pass to our script the number of disks and an expected latency of 10. The procedure returns the actual latency, along with the maximum IOPs and the maximum megabytes per second the storage system can support:

```
SQL> @calibrate_io
Enter value for dsks: 36
Enter value for maxlat: 10
old   7:     dbms_resource_manager.calibrate_io (&dsks, &maxlat, Calc_iops, Calc_mbps, Calc_lat);
new   7:     dbms_resource_manager.calibrate_io (36, 10, Calc_iops, Calc_mbps, Calc_lat);
Max IOPS          : 1022
Max mbytes-per-sec: 2885
Calc. latency     : 11

PL/SQL procedure successfully completed.

Elapsed: 00:07:10.57
SQL>
```

Once this calibration has completed, a query of V$IO_CALIBRATE_STATUS reports a different result than it did previously:

```
SQL> select *
  2  from v$io_calibration_status;

STATUS         CALIBRATION_TIME
-------------  ------------------------------------------------------------
READY          08-APR-13 11.24.49.977 AM

SQL>
```

If you query V$IO_CALIBRATION_STATUS during an I/O calibration run, the view will report results similar to the following output:

```
SQL> select *
  2  from v$io_calibration_status;

STATUS         CALIBRATION_TIME
-------------  ------------------------------------------------------------
IN PROGRESS    01-APR-12 09.34.13.083 AM

SQL>
```

The CALIBRATION_TIME value reported will be from the previous run; it's the IN PROGRESS status that lets you know that I/O calibration is running.

Querying DBA_RSRC_IO_CALIBRATE reveals all the current calibration statistics recorded after a completed run:

```
SQL> select num_physical_disks, max_iops, max_mbps, max_pmbps, latency
  2  from dba_rsrc_io_calibrate;

NUM_PHYSICAL_DISKS   MAX_IOPS   MAX_MBPS   MAX_PMBPS   LATENCY
------------------   --------   --------   ---------   --------
                36       1022       2885         289        11

SQL>
```

After I/O calibration has been successfully completed, if the query or statement in question meets or exceeds the serial execution time represented by the parallel_min_time_threshold parameter, then Auto DOP will set the degree of parallelism, regardless of whether any of the objects are explicitly set for parallel execution. You may find that once I/O calibration is completed, some tasks may take longer to complete because they are queued. This may occur because the parallel resources allocated may not be sufficient for all the queries and statements that qualify for parallel execution. There is a Metalink Note, document id 1393405.1, that explains how to delete the I/O calibration statistics. In summary, there is a single table, RESOURCE_IO_CALIBRATE$, that the two views are based on. Deleting the data from this table clears the I/O calibration statistics, so that Auto DOP will no longer function. Statements in the queue at the time the statistics are deleted will remain in the queue until executed; no additional statements will be queued after the I/O calibration statistics are deleted. This is not as drastic a measure as it may appear at first, because DBMS_RESOURCE_MANAGER.CALIBRATE_IO deletes any existing I/O calibration values before it generates the current statistics, using this same statement, as a portion of the tkprof output shows:

```
SQL ID: bzhku92rujah0 Plan Hash: 256968859

delete from resource_io_calibrate$
```

call	count	cpu	elapsed	disk	query	current	rows
Parse	1	0.01	0.00	0	0	0	0
Execute	1	0.00	0.00	0	1	0	0
Fetch	0	0.00	0.00	0	0	0	0
total	2	0.01	0.00	0	1	0	0

```
Misses in library cache during parse: 1
Optimizer mode: ALL_ROWS
Parsing user id: SYS   (recursive depth: 1)
Number of plan statistics captured: 1
```

Rows (1st)	Rows (avg)	Rows (max)	Row Source Operation
0	0	0	DELETE RESOURCE_IO_CALIBRATE$ (cr=1 pr=0 pw=0 time=26 us)
0	0	0	TABLE ACCESS FULL RESOURCE_IO_CALIBRATE$ (cr=1 pr=0 pw=0 time=21 us cost=2 size=0 card=1)

****

Make It So

I/O calibration isn't the only factor in enabling Auto DOP, as the parameter parallel_degree_policy must be set to AUTO or LIMITED. By default, it is set to MANUAL, which disables the three parallel features of Oracle Release 11.2: Auto DOP, parallel statement queuing, and in-memory parallel execution. The three available settings, and their effects on these features, are listed in Table 5-2.

Table 5-2. How parallel_degree_policy Settings Affect Parallel Execution

Setting	Effect
MANUAL	Disables all three new parallel query features. Causes parallel processing reverts to the behavior of prior releases, parallelizing statements only if they are hinted or the object being queried is created with or altered to have a DEGREE greater than the default of 1.
LIMITED	Only Auto DOP is enabled with this setting; the remaining two new parallel features are disabled. With this setting, only queries against objects associated with a DEGREE of DEFAULT will be considered.
AUTO	All three new parallel features are enabled. Queries and statements will be evaluated for parallel execution, regardless of the DEGREE setting on the object or objects accessed.

Another parameter, this one "hidden," that affects one of the new features is _parallel_statement_queueing. When set to TRUE (the default), queuing is enabled, which allows Oracle to decide if a parallel statement can be executed at runtime or if it needs to wait in the queue until sufficient resources are available. And yet another "hidden" parameter, _parallel_cluster_cache_policy, controls whether in-memory parallel execution is available or not. A setting of cached enables this feature. On Exadata, this feature can be less useful; when it is enabled, the Smart Scan optimizations will not be available when the buffer cache is scanned. It's a choice of whether to use the full power of Smart Scans against the buffer cache or use in-memory parallel execution. This primarily applies to data warehouse workloads, as OLTP processes rarely require parallel processing. You should be aware, though, that Smart Scans accessing the buffer cache can be affected when in-memory parallel execution is configured.

With parallel_degree_policy set to AUTO, it doesn't matter if objects are created with a DEGREE greater than one, as the database decides which statements to run in parallel, how many parallel slaves to execute, and even how many RAC nodes to involve in the process. This is the beauty and power of Auto DOP.

Do It in Memory

The third parallel feature, in-memory parallel execution, can improve query performance when Smart Scans are not used. It is designed to use the buffer cache, is cluster aware, and can utilize all available RAC nodes. It is enabled when parallel_degree_policy is set to AUTO. Other parameters that can affect In-memory parallel execution are parallel_servers_target, pzrallel_min_time_threshold, parallel_degree_limit, and parallel_degree_policy. Low values for parallel_servers_target, parallel_degree_limit, and parallel_min_time_threshold make it more likely for in-memory parallel execution to run. Additionally, the parallel_force_local parameter can be set to TRUE to reduce the available parallel resources to only those on the local server that can also favor in-memory parallel execution. Non-parallel parameters that affect this improvement are sga_max_size and sga_target, which control the buffer cache size, among other areas of the SGA. Larger cache sizes can accommodate larger tables in memory, which can also make it more likely for this feature to run. Setting these parameters to low values can't guarantee that this feature will run, but you may have a better chance of using it, if you scale back these settings.

While it is true that memory is much faster than disk, a Smart Scan is designed to be fast and efficient when accessing data on disk. Column Projection and Predicate Filtering greatly reduce the volume of data processed by the database tier, speeding the query along. But if all of the data could be loaded and processed in memory, the execution time would be a fraction of the time it would take to process the same volume of data read from disk.

There are benefits to in-memory parallel execution.

- Physical I/O is essentially eliminated.

- Traffic between the database servers and the storage cells is eliminated.

- There is far lower latency for memory, as compared to either disk or flash storage.

These benefits cannot be taken alone, however, because the available resources of CPU and memory have to be considered. Functions that would be offloaded to the storage cells (data filtering and data decompression) during Smart Scan execution fall to the database servers to perform. This can increase the CPU cycles required to process data, and without the additional CPUs and memory of the storage servers, it can put a strain on database server performance. There is a chance that you will have these resources to spare, and an equally likely chance that you do not. Whether or not to use this feature is a decision only you can make, after carefully considering all the facts.

None of the Exadata systems we have worked on use in-memory parallel execution. This is likely a good thing, if the majority of queries use Smart Scans, because, as mentioned previously, none of the Smart Scan optimizations are available. Yes, it would eliminate disk I/O, but it also eliminates the extra CPUs the storage servers would provide for data filtering, decompression, and other operations. Even though it looks good in concept, on an Exadata system, using in-memory parallel execution could be less efficient than using a Smart Scan, because, in a Smart Scan, the storage servers share the workload and reduce the volume of data the database tier processes. In addition, queries that would see the greatest benefit would be those that normally wouldn't use a Storage Index, placing the entire table into memory. On Exadata systems where a good number of queries and statements don't use Smart Scans, and the tables are sized to fit entirely in the buffer cache, in-memory parallel execution could improve performance by eliminating disk I/O (in the form of physical reads), in favor of memory access (by using logical reads).

As noted earlier, when `parallel_degree_policy` is set to `AUTO`, all three of the parallel features are enabled. If you want to disable in-memory parallel execution, this can be done in one of two ways: either by setting `parallel_degree_policy` to `MANUAL` (a setting that disables all of the features) or by setting a hidden parameter, `_parallel_cluster_cache_policy`, to `ADAPTIVE`, which preserves availability of the Auto DOP and parallel statement queuing features. When Auto DOP is active, `_parallel_cluster_cache_policy` will be set to `CACHED`.

In-memory parallel execution is not the easiest feature to get to work on Exadata. We have yet to get it to function on our systems, even when setting unusually low thresholds for `parallel_min_time_threshold`, `parallel_servers_target`, and `parallel_degree_limit`. It also requires that an entire table fit into the buffer cache, which is not an easy accomplishment. Add to that the fact that the database servers are performing all the work, without the assistance of a Smart Scan to eliminate possibly large volumes of data, and it may be that a Smart Scan is really a better path to take. Again, the decision is one only you can make, after considering all aspects of both Smart Scan and in-memory parallel execution and the current workload on your system.

Things to Know

Parallel query processing is not exclusive to Exadata; it uses the same functionality available to any installation of Oracle 11.2. What makes it especially beneficial to Exadata is the fact that Exadata was designed, in the beginning, to support data warehousing, where parallel processing is utilized frequently.

There are three new features of parallel query processing that change how parallel queries perform. These are automatic degree of parallelism (Auto DOP), parallel statement queuing, and in-memory parallel processing. Of the three, the first two provide the greatest benefit to Exadata.

Auto DOP does just what its name suggests: it computes the degree of parallelism automatically based on available resources and system load. It is not enabled by default. An initialization parameter, `parallel_degree_policy`, must be set to `AUTO` or `LIMITED` to enable Auto DOP. By default, this parameter is set to `MANUAL`. When this parameter is set to `AUTO`, then all three new parallel query features are enabled.

I/O calibration is a must to get Auto DOP to function, and a provided procedure, `DBMS_RESOURCE_MANAGER.CALIBRATE_IO`, is used to generate and record the calibration data. Although it's fairly simple to execute, it is a time-consuming and resource-intensive operation and should not be attempted on a heavily used system.

I/O calibration results are visible in the V$IO_CALIBRATION_STATUS and DBA_RSRC_IO_CALIBRATE views. The results are stored in the `RESOURCE_IO_CALIBRATE$` table. When a query to V$IO_CALIBRATION_STATUS returns a status of `NOT AVAILABLE`, this indicates that I/O calibration has not been run. A status of COMPLETED, along with the completion date, proves the existence of valid calibration data.

There may be performance issues after enabling Auto DOP, such as queries taking a longer overall time to complete. It is possible to delete the I/O calibration statistics by deleting from the RESOURCE_IO_CALIBRATE$ table. This is not as drastic an action as it may first appear, as the DBMS_RESOURCE_MANAGER.CALIBRATE_IO procedure first executes this delete before generating new calibration data.

Parallel statement queuing is enabled through the following initialization parameters:

```
parallel_degree_policy
parallel_servers_target
```

Remember that setting parallel_degree_policy to AUTO enables all three new parallel query features, which is the only way to enable parallel statement queing. The parallel_servers_target should be set to the desired number of parallel slaves, which should be allowed. It is not, however, a hard limit, as this setting can be exceeded in some cases, because Auto DOP can set a number of parallel slaves, which is double the assigned DOP. It is not a common occurrence, so it's not an issue, should it happen.

The V$SQL_MONITOR and GV$SQL_MONITOR views record which statements are in the parallel statement queue. A status of QUEUED indicates which statements are waiting in the statement queue. In addition to reporting which statements are in the queue, these views also record the SQL_EXEC_ID, which indicates the order in which the queued statements will be executed. Normally, this is sequentially assigned, but if several of the queued statements can be executed in parallel simultaneously, the SQL_EXEC_ID can show the same value for several entries.

It is possible to control parallel statement queuing. Changing the value for parallel_servers_target affects when statements will be queued. A low value for parallel_servers_target can cause more statements to be queued, as the available parallel query resources have been reduced. Increasing this value can allow more statements to process before the queue is populated. Another way to control queuing is through hints. Parallel statement queuing can be bypassed for a statement, if the NO_STATEMENT_QUEUING hint is used. The hinted statement will bypass the statement queue, if the available resources are low enough to have caused it to be placed there and run immediately at the computed DOP. This is one case when the value for parallel_servers_target can be exceeded.

If parallel statement queuing is not enabled, by setting parallel_degree_policy to LIMITED or MANUAL or by setting the hidden parameter _parallel_statement_queuing to FALSE, selected statements can still be queued, using the STATEMENT_QUEUING hint. Using this hint causes Oracle to behave as though parallel statement queuing is enabled, but only affects statements that utilize this hint. This is useful when you want parallel statement queuing enabled only for statements you choose to queue if their parallel execution would impede the processing of other statements that are more important to the business.

In-memory parallel execution is the third new feature, and it's probably not one that most queries on Exadata would utilize. There is both good and bad to this feature. The good is the elimination of disk I/O, traffic between the database servers and the storage cells, and the fact that memory has a far lower latency than either disk or flash storage. The bad, on Exadata, is that because the disk I/O is eliminated, the Smart Scan optimizations are no longer available, the database servers must do all of the work of filtering and decompressing data, and the number of available CPUs diminishes as the storage servers are no longer involved in the query processing.

In-memory parallel execution can be disabled either by setting another hidden parameter, _parallel_cluster_cache_policy, to ADAPTIVE or by setting parallel_degree_policy to MANUAL, which turns off all of the new parallel query features.

In-memory parallel execution is rarely found on Exadata systems. It may be possible to have a query that would benefit more from in-memory parallel execution than by using a Smart Scan, but we haven't seen that happen on Exadata systems we support.

CHAPTER 6

■ ■ ■

Compression

Oracle Release 11.2 offers Advanced Compression, a way to reduce the overall size of your data by compressing commonly occurring values and strings with tokens, mnemonics that can represent much larger strings and values. Two types of compression are offered on systems not using Exadata-type storage: Basic and OLTP. Basic compression is available without the Advanced Compression licensing. A third compression option, Hybrid Columnar Compression (HCC), is available on Exadata systems and non-Exadata systems using Exadata-type storage. This is offered in two basic levels: QUERY and ARCHIVE.

These compression options provide space savings, reducing table sizes to almost half the uncompressed size. Of course, such features do not come without a price, and may not behave as you would expect them to. When used with caution and care, storage requirements can be reduced, sometimes significantly. It's knowing when to use compression and which compression level to implement that makes this a valuable, usable feature.

How Can I Compress Thee

There are three general levels of compression: Basic, OLTP, and Hybrid Columnar Compression (which we will refer to as HCC), available with Exadata. By far, the most aggressive of these is HCC, but it can throw in some surprises for the uninitiated. Also, be aware that only one Advanced Compression option can be in use for a nonpartitioned table; it can be OLTP or HCC but not both. Partitioned tables differ in that each partition can use different compression methods. For example, the current partition, partitioned by date, can use OLTP compression to make updates and inserts less time-consuming; partitions for the next six months can use QUERY LOW compression; and archive partitions (those older than six months) can use ARCHIVE HIGH compression to allow space savings for partitions that are no longer updated.

Basic

Basic compression is aptly named; it compresses table data simply and fairly quickly, resulting in considerable space savings:

```
SQL> select segment_name, bytes
  2  from user_segments;

SEGMENT_NAME                                 BYTES
-------------------------------------- -----------
DEPT                                         65536
SALGRADE                                     65536
DUMMY                                        65536
EMP                                      713031680
```

```
SQL> alter table emp move compress;

Table altered.

SQL> select segment_name, bytes
  2  from user_segments;

SEGMENT_NAME                              BYTES
-----------------------------------  ----------

DEPT                                      65536
SALGRADE                                  65536
DUMMY                                     65536
EMP                                   184549376
```

To affect the current data, as well as future inserts and updates, we have to move the table and compress it. A simple alter table emp compress; would have set the table for compression, but the current data would have remained unaffected, providing no immediate space savings. The move allowed Oracle to compress the existing data in the table.

OLTP

OLTP compression is the first of the Advanced Compression options, which require separate licensing to use. Unlike Basic compression, OLTP compression does provide for automatic compression after updates; however, it's performed in a batch-type operation on a block-by-block basis. It, too, can provide substantial savings on the storage tier:

```
SQL> select segment_name, bytes
  2  from user_segments;

SEGMENT_NAME                              BYTES
-----------------------------------  ----------

EMP                                   721420288
DEPT                                      65536
SALGRADE                                  65536
DUMMY                                     65536

SQL> alter table emp move compress for oltp;

Table altered.

SQL> select segment_name, bytes
  2  from user_segments;

SEGMENT_NAME                              BYTES
-----------------------------------  ----------

EMP                                   201326592
DEPT                                      65536
SALGRADE                                  65536
DUMMY                                     65536

SQL>
```

The compressed size using OLTP compression is a bit larger than that for Basic compression, but you get the added benefit of eventual recompression after updated blocks are filled. As updated blocks hit the compression threshold, they are compressed using the OLTP algorithm, so that it is not necessary to manually re-compress the table. This does, of course, leave the updated table in a mixed state of compressed and uncompressed blocks, but the uncompressed blocks will return to the compressed state, once the conditions for compression are reached.

Hybrid Columnar Compression (HCC)

Hybrid Columnar Compression is a compression option available only for tables residing on Exadata storage. (As well as Exadata, this includes Axiom, the SPARC SuperCluster, and the Sun ZFS Storage Appliance.) If you try this on any other system, you will receive the following informative message:

```
SQL> alter table emp move compress for query high;
alter table emp move compress for query high
         *
ERROR at line 1:
ORA-64307: hybrid columnar compression is not supported for tablespaces on this storage type

SQL>
```

The phrase *this storage type* means any storage other than those listed at the beginning of this section. With that in mind, we want to mention that HCC can be a showstopper for Data Guard, when the destination database is not on Exadata or using Exadata storage. Tables in the affected Data Guard instance will need to be uncompressed before transactions can be applied to them, so all of the space savings will be lost. This is also true for database backups when HCC is enabled. Restoring a backup where HCC compression is used to a non-Exadata system will necessitate uncompressing those tables. This can easily cause you to run out of storage before all the tables are uncompressed, if the storage requirements were determined from the Exadata side.

HCC works differently than the two options mentioned earlier in this chapter, as it reorganizes data into Compression Units (CU). How it works will be discussed in the next section. For the moment, we will concentrate on implementing HCC in its four forms and on how those forms differ. There are two basic types under the HCC banner, QUERY and ARCHIVE, each having the options of HIGH and LOW. The first pair of HCC options we will discuss falls under the QUERY type. We will then discuss the ARCHIVE type.

QUERY

This type is less aggressive than ARCHIVE, but it still initially compresses data more than OLTP compression. We first compress our EMP table forQUERY HIGH:

```
SQL>
SQL> --
SQL> -- Current storage for the EMP table
SQL> -- (this is simply a test table for this example)
SQL> --
SQL> select segment_name, sum(bytes) total_space
  2  from user_segments
  3  group by segment_name;
```

```
SEGMENT_NAME                          TOTAL_SPACE
------------------------------------  -----------
DEPT                                        65536
DUMMY                                       65536
EMP                                     713031680
EMP_IDX                                 478150656
SALGRADE                                    65536

Elapsed: 00:00:00.82
SQL>
SQL> --
SQL> -- Compress the table for query high (use HCC)
SQL> --
SQL> -- Note elapsed time to compress
SQL> --
SQL> alter table emp move compress for query high;

Table altered.

Elapsed: 00:00:35.65
SQL>
SQL> --
SQL> -- Index is now invalid
SQL> --
SQL> -- Must rebuild to make it usable
SQL> --
SQL> -- Note elapsed time
SQL> --
SQL> alter index emp_idx rebuild;

Index altered.

Elapsed: 00:01:13.70
SQL>
SQL> --
SQL> -- Current compression type, storage for table/index
SQL> -- initially after compression is enabled
SQL> --
SQL> select table_name, compression, compress_for
  2  from user_tables;

TABLE_NAME                    COMPRESS COMPRESS_FOR
----------------------------- -------- ------------
DEPT                          DISABLED
BONUS                         DISABLED
SALGRADE                      DISABLED
DUMMY                         DISABLED
EMP                           ENABLED  QUERY HIGH
```

```
Elapsed: 00:00:00.20
SQL>
SQL> select segment_name, sum(bytes) total_space
  2  from user_segments
  3  group by segment_name;

SEGMENT_NAME                        TOTAL_SPACE
----------------------------------- -----------
DEPT                                      65536
DUMMY                                     65536
EMP                                     8388608
EMP_IDX                               260046848
SALGRADE                                  65536

Elapsed: 00:00:00.03
SQL>
```

The resulting size is much smaller than either of the Basic or OLTP compression options. Even at the QUERY LOW compression rate, the size is still less than OLTP compression can provide:

```
SQL>
SQL> --
SQL> -- Initial storage
SQL> --
SQL> select segment_name, sum(bytes) total_space
  2  from user_segments
  3  group by segment_name;

SEGMENT_NAME                        TOTAL_SPACE
----------------------------------- -----------
DEPT                                      65536
DUMMY                                     65536
EMP                                   713031680
EMP_IDX                               478150656
SALGRADE                                  65536

Elapsed: 00:00:00.25
SQL>
SQL> --
SQL> -- Compress for QUERY LOW
SQL> --
SQL> -- Note elapsed time
SQL> --
SQL> alter table emp move compress for query low;

Table altered.

Elapsed: 00:00:16.16
SQL>
SQL> alter index emp_idx rebuild;
```

87

```
Index altered.

Elapsed: 00:00:43.08
SQL>
SQL> --
SQL> -- These figures are the same as those generated
SQL> -- AFTER the HCC compressed data was updated the first time
SQL> --
SQL> select table_name, compression, compress_for
  2  from user_tables;

TABLE_NAME                      COMPRESS COMPRESS_FOR
------------------------------- -------- ------------
DEPT                            DISABLED
BONUS                           DISABLED
SALGRADE                        DISABLED
DUMMY                           DISABLED
EMP                             ENABLED  QUERY LOW

Elapsed: 00:00:00.02
SQL>
SQL> select segment_name, sum(bytes) total_space
  2  from user_segments
  3  group by segment_name;

SEGMENT_NAME                         TOTAL_SPACE
------------------------------------ -----------
DEPT                                       65536
DUMMY                                      65536
EMP                                     14680064
EMP_IDX                                260046848
SALGRADE                                   65536

Elapsed: 00:00:00.02
SQL>
```

ARCHIVE

The HCC compression type ARCHIVE is definitely the most aggressive in terms of space savings, but it's also intended for data that is designated read-only and is or will be archived for occasional use. It certainly isn't intended for actively updated tables; the space savings would be lost due to uncompressing the data, to allow the updates and recompressing at the lower OLTP level. We'll compress our standard EMP table for ARCHIVE HIGH and see what space savings are generated:

```
SQL> --
SQL> -- Current storage for the EMP table
SQL> -- (this is simply a test table for this example)
SQL> --
SQL> select segment_name, sum(bytes) total_space
  2  from user_segments
  3  group by segment_name;
```

```
SEGMENT_NAME                          TOTAL_SPACE
------------------------------------- -----------
DEPT                                        65536
DUMMY                                       65536
EMP                                     713031680
EMP_IDX                                 478150656
SALGRADE                                    65536

Elapsed: 00:00:00.02
SQL>
SQL> --
SQL> -- Compress the table for archive high
SQL> --
SQL> -- Note elapsed time to compress
SQL> --
SQL> alter table emp move compress for archive high;

Table altered.

Elapsed: 00:00:38.55
SQL>
SQL> --
SQL> -- Index is now invalid
SQL> --
SQL> -- Must rebuild to make it usable
SQL> --
SQL> -- Note elapsed time
SQL> --
SQL> alter index emp_idx rebuild;

Index altered.

Elapsed: 00:00:39.45
SQL>
SQL> --
SQL> -- Current compression type, storage for table/index
SQL> -- initially after compression is enabled
SQL> --
SQL> select table_name, compression, compress_for
  2  from user_tables;

TABLE_NAME                    COMPRESS COMPRESS_FOR
----------------------------- -------- ------------
DEPT                          DISABLED
BONUS                         DISABLED
SALGRADE                      DISABLED
DUMMY                         DISABLED
EMP                           ENABLED  ARCHIVE HIGH
```

```
Elapsed: 00:00:00.02
SQL>
SQL> select segment_name, sum(bytes) total_space
  2   from user_segments
  3   group by segment_name;

SEGMENT_NAME                           TOTAL_SPACE
-------------------------------------- -----------
DEPT                                         65536
DUMMY                                        65536
EMP                                        4194304
EMP_IDX                                  260046848
SALGRADE                                     65536

Elapsed: 00:00:00.01
SQL>
```

The space savings are substantial, taking the table from its original size of 680 megabytes down to 4 megabytes, a savings of 99.41 percent. Using ARCHIVE LOW instead of ARCHIVE HIGH still produces impressive results:

```
SQL> --
SQL> -- Initial storage
SQL> --
SQL> select segment_name, sum(bytes) total_space
  2   from user_segments
  3   group by segment_name;

SEGMENT_NAME                           TOTAL_SPACE
-------------------------------------- -----------
DEPT                                         65536
DUMMY                                        65536
EMP                                      713031680
EMP_IDX                                  478150656
SALGRADE                                     65536

Elapsed: 00:00:01.31
SQL>
SQL> --
SQL> -- Compress for ARCHIVE LOW
SQL> --
SQL> -- Note elapsed time
SQL> --
SQL> alter table emp move compress for archive low;

Table altered.

Elapsed: 00:00:34.16
SQL>
SQL> alter index emp_idx rebuild;
```

```
Index altered.

Elapsed: 00:00:48.44
SQL>
SQL> --
SQL> -- These figures are the same as those generated
SQL> -- AFTER the HCC compressed data was updated the first time
SQL> --
SQL> select table_name, compression, compress_for
  2  from user_tables;

TABLE_NAME                       COMPRESS COMPRESS_FOR
-------------------------------- -------- ------------
DEPT                             DISABLED
BONUS                            DISABLED
SALGRADE                         DISABLED
DUMMY                            DISABLED
EMP                              ENABLED  ARCHIVE LOW

Elapsed: 00:00:00.03
SQL>
SQL> select segment_name, sum(bytes) total_space
  2  from user_segments
  3  group by segment_name;

SEGMENT_NAME                         TOTAL_SPACE
------------------------------------ -----------
DEPT                                       65536
DUMMY                                      65536
EMP                                      8388608
EMP_IDX                                260046848
SALGRADE                                   65536

Elapsed: 00:00:00.02
SQL>
```

Using ARCHIVE LOW, the table ends up twice as large as it did using ARCHIVE HIGH, but the table is 98.82 percent smaller than it was originally, before compression. This is the same level of compression afforded by QUERY HIGH.

Oracle provides a function in the DBMS_COMPRESSION package named GET_COMPRESSION_TYPE. This function returns a number representing the compression type and level in use for a given table. We have a query to report the owner, table_name, numeric compression id, and the type name for a given table. We pass in the owner and table name as inputs.

```
set verify off
select distinct
        '&&owner' owner,
        '&&tabname' table_name,
        dbms_compression.get_compression_type('&&owner','&&tabname', rowid) comp_typ,
        decode(dbms_compression.get_compression_type('&&owner','&&tabname', rowid),
               1, 'NONE',
```

```
             2, 'OLTP',
             4, 'QUERY HIGH',
             8, 'QUERY LOW',
            16, 'ARCHIVE HIGH',
            32, 'ARCHIVE LOW') type_name
from
        &&owner..&&tabname
/

Undefine owner
Undefine tabname
```

The output follows:

```
SQL> @get_compression_type.sql
Enter value for owner: BING
Enter value for tabname: EMP

OWNE TABL   COMP_TYP TYPE_NAME
---- ---- ---------- ------------
BING EMP          8 QUERY LOW

SQL>
```

The Nuts and Bolts of HCC

Using HCC causes some changes in how Oracle stores table data, altering the storage format from the usual heap-style block population to a column-centric format, still using data blocks, called Compression Units, or CUs. This is a logical change, as Compression Units consist of multiple Oracle blocks with a unique layout. First, Oracle collects a number of similar rows for a Compression Unit and organizes them in a columnar format, similar to Figure 6-1.

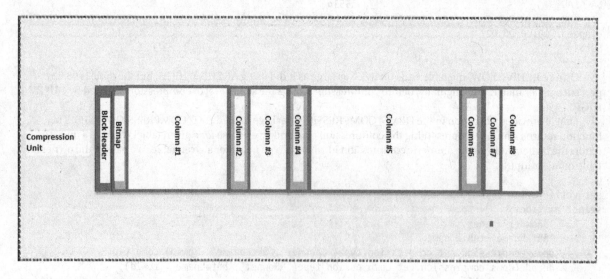

Figure 6-1. *Initial data organization for HCC Compression Unit*

Collecting rows of similar data makes it easier to compress the data using HCC, as common elements that can be replaced with tokens are colocated in the same Compression Unit. Oracle, by design, is a row-centric DBMS, so this interim structure is converted back to a row format, similar to Figure 6-2.

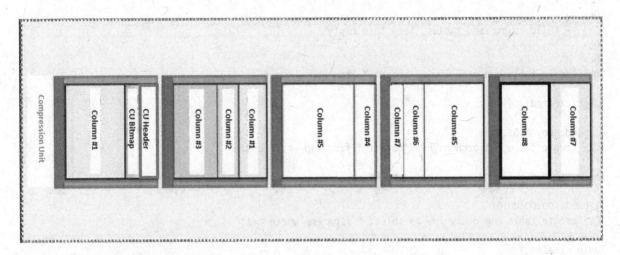

Figure 6-2. *HCC Compression Unit layout*

Five data blocks are used to store the data from this example, with each column being a row in the block. Some columns won't fit into a single block, so they are chained across multiple blocks, as illustrated. The block header is shown in red; the CU header is in the first block of the Compression Unit, as is the Compression Unit bitmap, showing where the rows are located. The data columns follow the CU Header and CU Bitmap rows in block 1, with Column 1 data starting at the third row of the block.

As mentioned previously, if a column won't fit entirely in a single block, it is chained across to the next block in the Compression Unit. This strategy continues until all the columns are stored. Because like data is stored together, HCC can provide exceptionally high compression ratios, as compared to either Basic or OLTP compression. Also, creating Compression Units in this fashion prevents rows from being split across CUs, so that an entire row can be read from a single CU.

Performance

Depending on whether you are inserting, updating, or querying data, the performance of compressed tables may not be what you would expect. Querying data is usually a fast operation. Inserting for all but OLTP compression requires parallel or direct load inserts, so that the newly inserted rows are compressed. Updates take longer, as the data has to be uncompressed before it can be updated. Carefully analyze how a table is used before deciding on compression; heavily updated tables are better served with OLTP compression than either of the HCC compression types. Remember that engineering is often described as the art of making tradeoffs. You can't have your cake and eat it too.

When You Load

Loading data into compressed tables, with the lone exception of OLTP compression, requires parallel or direct-path inserts. Of course, loading into compressed tables can take longer than the same process for noncompressed tables. We created empty tables using the various compression methods and loaded them from the EMP table we populated in earlier examples. The results of those loads, and the times required for those loads, are shown in the following example:

```
SQL>
SQL> --
SQL> -- Build compressed tables, keep them empty
SQL> --
SQL>
SQL> create table emp_arch_low as select * from emp where 0=1;

Table created.

Elapsed: 00:00:01.42
SQL> create table emp_arch_high as select * from emp where 0=1;

Table created.

Elapsed: 00:00:00.01
SQL> create table emp_query_low as select * from emp where 0=1;

Table created.

Elapsed: 00:00:00.01
SQL> create table emp_query_high as select * from emp where 0=1;

Table created.

Elapsed: 00:00:00.01
SQL> create table emp_oltp as select * from emp where 0=1;

Table created.

Elapsed: 00:00:00.01
SQL> create table emp_basic as select * from emp where 0=1;

Table created.

Elapsed: 00:00:00.01
SQL>
SQL> --
SQL> -- Create a copy of emp, uncompressed
SQL> --
SQL>
SQL> create table emp_nocomp as select * From emp where 0=1;

Table created.

Elapsed: 00:00:00.02
SQL>
SQL> --
SQL> --
SQL> -- We load the tables and see how long each
```

```
SQL> -- compression level takes
SQL> --
SQL> --
SQL>
SQL> insert /*+ append */ into emp_nocomp select * from emp;

14680064 rows created.

Elapsed: 00:00:06.51
SQL> insert /*+ append */ into emp_arch_low     select * from emp;

14680064 rows created.

Elapsed: 00:00:08.80
SQL> insert /*+ append */ into emp_arch_high select * from emp;

14680064 rows created.

Elapsed: 00:00:07.07
SQL> insert /*+ append */ into emp_query_low select * from emp;

14680064 rows created.

Elapsed: 00:00:07.30
SQL> insert /*+ append */ into emp_query_high select * from emp;

14680064 rows created.

Elapsed: 00:00:06.24
SQL> insert /*+ append */ into emp_oltp select * from emp;

14680064 rows created.

Elapsed: 00:00:08.10
SQL> insert /*+ append */ into emp_basic select * from emp;

14680064 rows created.

Elapsed: 00:00:07.66
SQL>
```

We have collected the data and presented it in Table 6-1, so that it's easier to understand.

Table 6-1. *Load Times and Data Volumes for Compressed Tables*

Table Name	Compression Type	Rows	Time to Load
emp_nocomp	None	14680064	6.51 seconds
emp_basic	Basic	14680064	7.66 seconds
emp_arch_low	Archive Low	14680064	8.80 seconds
emp_arch_high	Archive High	14680064	7.07 seconds
emp_query_low	Query Low	14680064	7.30 seconds
emp_query_high	Query High	14680064	6.24 seconds
emp_oltp	OLTP	14680064	8.10 seconds

For all but the QUERY HIGH compression, the load times exceed the time to load the uncompressed table. Your execution times may vary from those we generated, because they depend on the load the system is experiencing when you perform your test. If Smart Scans are used, some of the processing will be offloaded to the storage cells, allowing them to reduce the workload on the database servers. This can result in load times that are less than the time to load uncompressed data.

When You Query

Queries can also take longer to process when the data is compressed. Smart Scans also play a part here, as some of the work (such as uncompressing the data) falls to the storage cells, rather than the database servers. We have run the same query against each of the tables representing the various compression types; the results of those tests follow:

```
SQL>
SQL> --
SQL> -- Let's select from each table and see how long it takes
SQL> --
SQL>
SQL> select /*+ parallel 4 */ *
  2  from emp_nocomp
  3  where empno > 7930;

    EMPNO ENAME      JOB            MGR HIREDATE       SAL       COMM     DEPTNO
---------- ---------- --------- ---------- --------- ---------- ---------- ----------
      7934 MILLER     CLERK         7782 23-JAN-82      1300                    10
      7934 MILLER     CLERK         7782 23-JAN-82      1300                    10
      7934 MILLER     CLERK         7782 23-JAN-82      1300                    10
      7934 MILLER     CLERK         7782 23-JAN-82      1300                    10
...
      7934 MILLER     CLERK         7782 23-JAN-82      1300                    10
      7934 MILLER     CLERK         7782 23-JAN-82      1300                    10
      7934 MILLER     CLERK         7782 23-JAN-82      1300                    10

1048576 rows selected.
```

```
Elapsed: 00:01:25.90
SQL>
SQL> select /*+ parallel 4 */ *
  2  from emp_arch_low
  3  where empno > 7930;

    EMPNO ENAME      JOB             MGR HIREDATE        SAL       COMM     DEPTNO
---------- ---------- ---------- ---------- --------- ---------- ---------- ----------
      7934 MILLER     CLERK          7782 23-JAN-82       1300                     10
      7934 MILLER     CLERK          7782 23-JAN-82       1300                     10
      7934 MILLER     CLERK          7782 23-JAN-82       1300                     10
      7934 MILLER     CLERK          7782 23-JAN-82       1300                     10
...
      7934 MILLER     CLERK          7782 23-JAN-82       1300                     10
      7934 MILLER     CLERK          7782 23-JAN-82       1300                     10
      7934 MILLER     CLERK          7782 23-JAN-82       1300                     10

1048576 rows selected.

Elapsed: 00:01:42.92
SQL>
SQL> select /*+ parallel 4 */ *
  2  from emp_arch_high
  3  where empno > 7930;

    EMPNO ENAME      JOB             MGR HIREDATE        SAL       COMM     DEPTNO
---------- ---------- ---------- ---------- --------- ---------- ---------- ----------
      7934 MILLER     CLERK          7782 23-JAN-82       1300                     10
      7934 MILLER     CLERK          7782 23-JAN-82       1300                     10
      7934 MILLER     CLERK          7782 23-JAN-82       1300                     10
      7934 MILLER     CLERK          7782 23-JAN-82       1300                     10
...
      7934 MILLER     CLERK          7782 23-JAN-82       1300                     10
      7934 MILLER     CLERK          7782 23-JAN-82       1300                     10
      7934 MILLER     CLERK          7782 23-JAN-82       1300                     10

1048576 rows selected.

Elapsed: 00:01:33.90
SQL>
SQL> select /*+ parallel 4 */ *
  2  from emp_query_low
  3  where empno > 7930;

    EMPNO ENAME      JOB             MGR HIREDATE        SAL       COMM     DEPTNO
---------- ---------- ---------- ---------- --------- ---------- ---------- ----------
      7934 MILLER     CLERK          7782 23-JAN-82       1300                     10
      7934 MILLER     CLERK          7782 23-JAN-82       1300                     10
      7934 MILLER     CLERK          7782 23-JAN-82       1300                     10
      7934 MILLER     CLERK          7782 23-JAN-82       1300                     10
...
```

```
     7934 MILLER      CLERK           7782 23-JAN-82       1300                      10
     7934 MILLER      CLERK           7782 23-JAN-82       1300                      10
     7934 MILLER      CLERK           7782 23-JAN-82       1300                      10

1048576 rows selected.

Elapsed: 00:01:24.15
SQL>
SQL> select /*+ parallel 4 */ *
  2  from emp_query_high
  3  where empno > 7930;

    EMPNO ENAME      JOB              MGR HIREDATE          SAL       COMM     DEPTNO
---------- ---------- --------- ---------- --------- ---------- ---------- ----------
     7934 MILLER      CLERK           7782 23-JAN-82       1300                      10
     7934 MILLER      CLERK           7782 23-JAN-82       1300                      10
     7934 MILLER      CLERK           7782 23-JAN-82       1300                      10
     7934 MILLER      CLERK           7782 23-JAN-82       1300                      10
...
     7934 MILLER      CLERK           7782 23-JAN-82       1300                      10
     7934 MILLER      CLERK           7782 23-JAN-82       1300                      10
     7934 MILLER      CLERK           7782 23-JAN-82       1300                      10

1048576 rows selected.

Elapsed: 00:01:26.82
SQL>
SQL> select /*+ parallel 4 */ *
  2  from emp_oltp
  3  where empno > 7930;

    EMPNO ENAME      JOB              MGR HIREDATE          SAL       COMM     DEPTNO
---------- ---------- --------- ---------- --------- ---------- ---------- ----------
     7934 MILLER      CLERK           7782 23-JAN-82       1300                      10
     7934 MILLER      CLERK           7782 23-JAN-82       1300                      10
     7934 MILLER      CLERK           7782 23-JAN-82       1300                      10
     7934 MILLER      CLERK           7782 23-JAN-82       1300                      10
...
     7934 MILLER      CLERK           7782 23-JAN-82       1300                      10
     7934 MILLER      CLERK           7782 23-JAN-82       1300                      10
     7934 MILLER      CLERK           7782 23-JAN-82       1300                      10

1048576 rows selected.

Elapsed: 00:01:25.77
SQL>
SQL> select /*+ parallel 4 */ *
  2  from emp_basic
  3  where empno > 7930;
```

EMPNO	ENAME	JOB	MGR	HIREDATE	SAL	COMM	DEPTNO
7934	MILLER	CLERK	7782	23-JAN-82	1300		10
7934	MILLER	CLERK	7782	23-JAN-82	1300		10
7934	MILLER	CLERK	7782	23-JAN-82	1300		10
7934	MILLER	CLERK	7782	23-JAN-82	1300		10
...							
7934	MILLER	CLERK	7782	23-JAN-82	1300		10
7934	MILLER	CLERK	7782	23-JAN-82	1300		10
7934	MILLER	CLERK	7782	23-JAN-82	1300		10

```
1048576 rows selected.

Elapsed: 00:01:26.08
SQL>
```

The summarized data is shown in Table 6-2.

Table 6-2. *Query Execution Times for Compressed Tables*

Table Name	Rows Returned	Compression Level	Elapsed Time
emp_nocomp	1048576	None	00:01:25.90
emp_arch_low	1048576	Archive Low	00:01:42.92
emp_arch_high	1048576	Archive High	00:01:33.90
emp_query_low	1048576	Query Low	00:01:24.15
emp_query_high	1048576	Query High	00:01:26.82
emp_oltp	1048576	OLTP	00:01:25.77
emp_basic	1048576	Basic	00:01:26.08

Notice that all but the tables compressed for ARCHIVE HIGH and ARCHIVE LOW were very close in execution time to the uncompressed table. The execution plan is the same for all queries, as follows:

```
Execution Plan
-------------------------------------------------------------
Plan hash value: 398743904

--------------------------------------------------------------------------------
--------------------
| Id | Operation          | Name | Rows  | Bytes | Cost (%CPU)| Time     | TQ
|IN-OUT| PQ Distrib |
--------------------------------------------------------------------------------
--------------------
|  0 | SELECT STATEMENT   |      | 1088K |   90M | 13117   (1)| 00:00:01 |
|    |            |
|  1 |  PX COORDINATOR    |      |       |       |       |    |          |
|    |            |
```

```
|   2 |    PX SEND QC (RANDOM)        | :TQ10000  |  1088K|    90M| 13117   (1)| 00:00:01 | Q1,00 |
P->S | QC (RAND) |
|   3 |     PX BLOCK ITERATOR         |           |  1088K|    90M| 13117   (1)| 00:00:01 | Q1,00 |
PCWC |                |
|*  4 |      TABLE ACCESS STORAGE FULL| EMP_NOCOMP|  1088K|    90M| 13117   (1)| 00:00:01 | Q1,00 |
PCWP |                |
------------------------------------------------------------------------------------------------
--------------------------

Predicate Information (identified by operation id):
---------------------------------------------------

   4 - storage("EMPNO">7930)
       filter("EMPNO">7930)

Note
-----
   - dynamic sampling used for this statement (level=2)
   - automatic DOP: Computed Degree of Parallelism is 2
```

Auto DOP and a Smart Scan made the query times essentially no worse than for the uncompressed data, a testament to both features of Exadata. The Smart Scan also provided extra CPU cycles from the storage cells, as the data was uncompressed at the storage cells, rather than at the database servers.

When You Update

Updates pose a problem to Basic-level compression, as the data has to be uncompressed and remains so after the updates.

```
SQL> update emp set sal=sal*1.10 where empno = 7566;

1048576 rows updated.

SQL> select segment_name, bytes
  2  from user_segments;

SEGMENT_NAME                                BYTES
----------------------------------------- ----------
DEPT                                        65536
SALGRADE                                    65536
DUMMY                                       65536
EMP                                     243269632

SQL>
```

Notice that the overall bytes that EMP consumes increased after the updates were completed. Subsequent updates will cause the table to increase in size, as blocks are processed. The table will have to be compressed again to regain the initial savings, as follows:

```
SQL> alter table emp move compress;

Table altered.

SQL> select segment_name, bytes
  2  from user_segments;

SEGMENT_NAME                              BYTES
-----------------------------------  ----------
DEPT                                      65536
SALGRADE                                  65536
DUMMY                                     65536
EMP                                   184549376

SQL>
```

There is no provision for automatic compression after updates occur. Even though Basic compression is available without additional licensing, its use could be limited to tables that aren't updated or are updated infrequently.

Updates to compressed tables also take longer than they would for uncompressed tables, because the blocks affected by the update have to be uncompressed before the updates can occur. The elapsed time for a bulk update of a table compressed using Basic compression is as follows:

```
SQL> update emp set sal=sal*1.10 where empno = 7566;

1048576 rows updated.

Elapsed: 00:01:05.85
SQL>
```

This was executed on a system with no load and only one connected user. On more heavily loaded systems, the elapsed time can be greater and, interestingly, the table size can increase over the original size, if the bulk update affects a large portion of the table data.

```
SQL>
SQL> --
SQL> -- Current storage for the EMP table
SQL> -- (this is simply a test table for this example)
SQL> --
SQL> select segment_name, sum(bytes) total_space
  2  from user_segments
  3  group by segment_name;

SEGMENT_NAME                        TOTAL_SPACE
-----------------------------------  ----------
DEPT                                      65536
DUMMY                                     65536
```

```
EMP                               713031680
EMP_IDX                           469762048
SALGRADE                              65536


Elapsed: 00:00:01.46
SQL>
SQL> --
SQL> -- Compress the table basic
SQL> --
SQL> -- Note elapsed time to compress
SQL> --
SQL> alter table emp move compress;

Table altered.

Elapsed: 00:00:15.57
SQL>
SQL> --
SQL> -- Index is now invalid
SQL> --
SQL> -- Must rebuild to make it usable
SQL> --
SQL> -- Note elapsed time
SQL> --
SQL> alter index emp_idx rebuild;

Index altered.

Elapsed: 00:00:53.01
SQL>
SQL> --
SQL> -- Current compression type, storage for table/index
SQL> -- initially after compression is enabled
SQL> --
SQL> select table_name, compression, compress_for
  2  from user_tables;

TABLE_NAME                      COMPRESS COMPRESS_FOR
------------------------------- -------- ------------
DEPT                            DISABLED
BONUS                           DISABLED
SALGRADE                        DISABLED
DUMMY                           DISABLED
EMP                             ENABLED  BASIC

Elapsed: 00:00:00.03
SQL>
SQL> select segment_name, sum(bytes) total_space
  2  from user_segments
  3  group by segment_name;
```

```
SEGMENT_NAME                          TOTAL_SPACE
------------------------------------  -----------
DEPT                                        65536
DUMMY                                       65536
EMP                                     184549376
EMP_IDX                                 260046848
SALGRADE                                    65536

Elapsed: 00:00:00.02
SQL>
SQL> --
SQL> -- Perform an update on the compressed data
SQL> --
SQL> -- Note elapsed time to complete
SQL> --
SQL> update emp set sal=sal*1.08 where empno > 7350;

14680064 rows updated.

Elapsed: 00:14:25.18
SQL>
SQL> commit;

Commit complete.

Elapsed: 00:00:00.00
SQL>
SQL> --
SQL> -- Compression type has not changed in the
SQL> -- data dictionary but the consumed space
SQL> -- has increased beyond the original size
SQL> -- of the table
SQL> --
SQL> select table_name, compression, compress_for
  2  from user_tables;

TABLE_NAME                      COMPRESS COMPRESS_FOR
------------------------------- -------- ------------
DEPT                            DISABLED
BONUS                           DISABLED
SALGRADE                        DISABLED
DUMMY                           DISABLED
EMP                             ENABLED  BASIC

Elapsed: 00:00:00.03
SQL>
SQL> select segment_name, sum(bytes) total_space
  2  from user_segments
  3  group by segment_name;
```

```
SEGMENT_NAME                          TOTAL_SPACE
------------------------------------  -----------
DEPT                                        65536
DUMMY                                       65536
EMP                                     956301312
EMP_IDX                                 260046848
SALGRADE                                    65536

Elapsed: 00:00:00.01
SQL>
SQL> --
SQL> -- Perform a second update
SQL> --
SQL> -- Note elapsed time
SQL> --
SQL> update emp set sal=sal*1.08 where empno > 7350;

14680064 rows updated.

Elapsed: 00:03:48.95
SQL>
SQL> commit;

Commit complete.

Elapsed: 00:00:00.01
SQL>
SQL> --
SQL> -- Current storage consumed after second update
SQL> --
SQL> select table_name, compression, compress_for
  2  from user_tables;

TABLE_NAME                    COMPRESS COMPRESS_FOR
----------------------------  -------- ------------
DEPT                          DISABLED
BONUS                         DISABLED
SALGRADE                      DISABLED
DUMMY                         DISABLED
EMP                           ENABLED  BASIC

Elapsed: 00:00:00.03
SQL>
SQL> select segment_name, sum(bytes) total_space
  2  from user_segments
  3  group by segment_name;

SEGMENT_NAME                          TOTAL_SPACE
------------------------------------  -----------
DEPT                                        65536
DUMMY                                       65536
```

```
EMP                                      956301312
EMP_IDX                                  260046848
SALGRADE                                     65536


Elapsed: 00:00:00.01
SQL>
```

The table has gained size, due to the updates to compressed data using the Basic compression algorithm. Such behavior makes Basic compression an invalid option for actively updated tables.

OLTP compression makes it easier to keep a good portion of the space savings generated by the initial compression, although it may not be immediately realized, because not all of the updated blocks are filled. The following example illustrates this:

```
SQL>
SQL> --
SQL> -- Initial storage
SQL> --
SQL> select segment_name, sum(bytes) total_space
  2  from user_segments
  3  group by segment_name;


SEGMENT_NAME                         TOTAL_SPACE
------------------------------------ -----------
DEPT                                       65536
DUMMY                                      65536
EMP                                    713031680
EMP_IDX                                478150656
SALGRADE                                   65536


Elapsed: 00:00:00.03
SQL>
SQL> --
SQL> -- Compress for OLTP rather than QUERY HIGH
SQL> --
SQL> -- Note elapsed time
SQL> --
SQL> alter table emp move compress for oltp;


Table altered.


Elapsed: 00:00:19.36
SQL>
SQL> alter index emp_idx rebuild;


Index altered.


Elapsed: 00:00:52.12
SQL>
SQL> --
SQL> -- These figures are the same as those generated
SQL> -- AFTER the HCC compressed data was updated the first time
```

```
SQL> --
SQL> select table_name, compression, compress_for
  2  from user_tables;

TABLE_NAME                     COMPRESS COMPRESS_FOR
------------------------------ -------- ------------
DEPT                           DISABLED
BONUS                          DISABLED
SALGRADE                       DISABLED
DUMMY                          DISABLED
EMP                            ENABLED  OLTP

Elapsed: 00:00:00.04
SQL>
SQL> select segment_name, sum(bytes) total_space
  2  from user_segments
  3  group by segment_name;

SEGMENT_NAME                     TOTAL_SPACE
-------------------------------- -----------
DEPT                                   65536
DUMMY                                  65536
EMP                                201326592
EMP_IDX                            260046848
SALGRADE                               65536

Elapsed: 00:00:00.01
SQL>
SQL> --
SQL> -- Perform an update
SQL> --
SQL> -- Note elapsed time (less than the previous compressed update)
SQL> --
SQL> update emp set sal=sal*1.08 where empno > 7350;

14680064 rows updated.

Elapsed: 00:20:40.64
SQL>
SQL> commit;

Commit complete.

Elapsed: 00:00:00.01
SQL>
SQL> --
SQL> -- Current compression level and storage
SQL> --
SQL> -- Looks like the storage after the second
SQL> -- update to the HCC compressed data
```

```
SQL> --
SQL> select table_name, compression, compress_for
  2  from user_tables;

TABLE_NAME                      COMPRESS COMPRESS_FOR
------------------------------- -------- ------------
DEPT                            DISABLED
BONUS                           DISABLED
SALGRADE                        DISABLED
DUMMY                           DISABLED
EMP                             ENABLED  OLTP

Elapsed: 00:00:00.03
SQL>
SQL> select segment_name, sum(bytes) total_space
  2  from user_segments
  3  group by segment_name;

SEGMENT_NAME                         TOTAL_SPACE
------------------------------------ -----------
DEPT                                       65536
DUMMY                                      65536
EMP                                    511705088
EMP_IDX                                260046848
SALGRADE                                   65536

Elapsed: 00:00:00.01
SQL>
```

The overall table size is still less than it was originally. The partially filled data blocks are still in an uncompressed state, contributing to the size increase. As these blocks fill up, they will be automatically compressed in a batch-style operation, reducing the table size further.

Updates to data compressed using HCC reveal behavior you should expect, after reading the examples provided in this chapter. However, in this scenario, the compression algorithm changes, due to the updates. Originally compressed for QUERY HIGH after updates, the compression becomes OLTP and remains there until modified by you. The data dictionary still reports that HCC is in effect, and it is, but because of the updates, Oracle now treats this data as though it were compressed using the OLTP compression scheme. We will update data using the EMP table, compressed for QUERY HIGH, then compressed for QUERY LOW, to illustrate this behavior.

```
SQL> --
SQL> -- Perform an update on the compressed data
SQL> --
SQL> -- Note elapsed time to complete
SQL> --
SQL> update emp set sal=sal*1.08 where empno > 7350;

14680064 rows updated.

Elapsed: 00:42:34.40
SQL>
SQL> commit;
```

```
Commit complete.

Elapsed: 00:00:00.03
SQL>
SQL> --
SQL> -- Compression type has not changed in the
SQL> -- data dictionary but the consumed space
SQL> -- has increased to the level of a table
SQL> -- initially compressed for OLTP
SQL> --
SQL> select table_name, compression, compress_for
  2  from user_tables;

TABLE_NAME                       COMPRESS COMPRESS_FOR
-------------------------------- -------- ------------
DEPT                             DISABLED
BONUS                            DISABLED
SALGRADE                         DISABLED
DUMMY                            DISABLED
EMP                              ENABLED  QUERY HIGH

Elapsed: 00:00:00.03
SQL>
SQL> select segment_name, sum(bytes) total_space
  2  from user_segments
  3  group by segment_name;

SEGMENT_NAME                         TOTAL_SPACE
------------------------------------ -----------
DEPT                                       65536
DUMMY                                      65536
EMP                                    226492416
EMP_IDX                                721420288
SALGRADE                                   65536

Elapsed: 00:00:00.33
SQL>
SQL> --
SQL> -- Perform a second update
SQL> --
SQL> -- Note elapsed time
SQL> --
SQL> update emp set sal=sal*1.08 where empno > 7350;

14680064 rows updated.

Elapsed: 00:03:15.00
SQL>
SQL> commit;
```

```
Commit complete.

Elapsed: 00:00:00.02
SQL>
SQL> --
SQL> -- Current storage consumed after second update
SQL> --
SQL> select table_name, compression, compress_for
  2  from user_tables;

TABLE_NAME                     COMPRESS COMPRESS_FOR
------------------------------ -------- ------------
DEPT                           DISABLED
BONUS                          DISABLED
SALGRADE                       DISABLED
DUMMY                          DISABLED
EMP                            ENABLED  QUERY HIGH

Elapsed: 00:00:00.02
SQL>
SQL> select segment_name, sum(bytes) total_space
  2  from user_segments
  3  group by segment_name;

SEGMENT_NAME                       TOTAL_SPACE
---------------------------------- -----------
DEPT                                     65536
DUMMY                                    65536
EMP                                  452984832
EMP_IDX                              721420288
SALGRADE                                 65536

Elapsed: 00:00:00.21
SQL>
```

Note that the index associated with the table also increases in size after the first update and remains at that size during subsequent updates to the table. We will now perform the same updates to the EMP table compressed for QUERY LOW, as follows:

```
SQL> --
SQL> -- Perform an update
SQL> --
SQL> -- Note elapsed time (less than the previous compressed update)
SQL> --
SQL> update emp set sal=sal*1.08 where empno > 7350;

14680064 rows updated.

Elapsed: 00:47:52.75
SQL>
SQL> commit;
```

```
Commit complete.

Elapsed: 00:00:00.02
SQL>
SQL> --
SQL> -- Current compression level and storage
SQL> --
SQL> -- Looks like the storage after the second
SQL> -- update to the HCC compressed data
SQL> --
SQL> select table_name, compression, compress_for
  2  from user_tables;

TABLE_NAME                      COMPRESS COMPRESS_FOR
------------------------------- -------- ------------
DEPT                            DISABLED
BONUS                           DISABLED
SALGRADE                        DISABLED
DUMMY                           DISABLED
EMP                             ENABLED  QUERY LOW

Elapsed: 00:00:00.03
SQL>
SQL> select segment_name, sum(bytes) total_space
  2  from user_segments
  3  group by segment_name;

SEGMENT_NAME                         TOTAL_SPACE
------------------------------------ -----------
DEPT                                       65536
DUMMY                                      65536
EMP                                    243269632
EMP_IDX                                612368384
SALGRADE                                   65536

Elapsed: 00:00:00.49
SQL>
SQL> --
SQL> -- Perform a second update
SQL> --
SQL> -- Note elapsed time
SQL> --
SQL> update emp set sal=sal*1.08 where empno > 7350;

14680064 rows updated.

Elapsed: 00:02:20.24
SQL>
SQL> commit;

Commit complete.
```

```
Elapsed: 00:00:00.02
SQL>
SQL> --
SQL> -- Current storage consumed after second update
SQL> --
SQL> select table_name, compression, compress_for
  2  from user_tables;

TABLE_NAME                      COMPRESS COMPRESS_FOR
------------------------------- -------- ------------
DEPT                            DISABLED
BONUS                           DISABLED
SALGRADE                        DISABLED
DUMMY                           DISABLED
EMP                             ENABLED  QUERY LOW

Elapsed: 00:00:00.03
SQL>
SQL> select segment_name, sum(bytes) total_space
  2  from user_segments
  3  group by segment_name;

SEGMENT_NAME                         TOTAL_SPACE
------------------------------------ -----------
DEPT                                       65536
DUMMY                                       65536
EMP                                    511705088
EMP_IDX                                612368384
SALGRADE                                   65536

Elapsed: 00:00:02.80
SQL>
```

Note the slight size difference between the results from the updates to QUERY HIGH and QUERY LOW compression. The real differences are shown in the overall elapsed times to complete the desired updates. The first update to the table takes the longest time, as the fully compressed data is being uncompressed to complete the transaction. The second update takes longer than for an uncompressed table, but it still takes considerably less time than the initial update. This is one of the issues with using compression on an active table.

Using either of the ARCHIVE compression types, the situation is no different. Because the ARCHIVE levels provide the best initial compression ratios, it should be expected that updates to tables compressed in either of these two ways should take greater time to complete, especially the first update after compression has completed. We perform the same updates to these two compression levels, as we did to the other levels, and report the results. First, for ARCHIVE HIGH:

```
SQL> --
SQL> -- Perform an update on the compressed data
SQL> --
SQL> -- Note elapsed time to complete
SQL> --
SQL> update emp set sal=sal*1.08 where empno > 7350;
```

```
14680064 rows updated.

Elapsed: 00:50:36.26
SQL>
SQL> commit;

Commit complete.

Elapsed: 00:00:00.02
SQL>
SQL> --
SQL> -- Compression type has not changed in the
SQL> -- data dictionary but the consumed space
SQL> -- has increased to the level of a table
SQL> -- initially compressed for OLTP
SQL> --
SQL> select table_name, compression, compress_for
  2  from user_tables;

TABLE_NAME                      COMPRESS COMPRESS_FOR
------------------------------- -------- ------------
DEPT                            DISABLED
BONUS                           DISABLED
SALGRADE                        DISABLED
DUMMY                           DISABLED
EMP                             ENABLED  ARCHIVE HIGH

Elapsed: 00:00:00.03
SQL>
SQL> select segment_name, sum(bytes) total_space
  2  from user_segments
  3  group by segment_name;

SEGMENT_NAME                        TOTAL_SPACE
----------------------------------- -----------
DEPT                                      65536
DUMMY                                     65536
EMP                                   234881024
EMP_IDX                               679477248
SALGRADE                                  65536

Elapsed: 00:00:00.11
SQL>
SQL> --
SQL> -- Perform a second update
SQL> --
SQL> -- Note elapsed time
SQL> --
SQL> update emp set sal=sal*1.08 where empno > 7350;

14680064 rows updated.
```

```
Elapsed: 00:02:23.52
SQL>
SQL> commit;

Commit complete.

Elapsed: 00:00:00.02
SQL>
SQL> --
SQL> -- Current storage consumed after second update
SQL> --
SQL> select table_name, compression, compress_for
  2  from user_tables;

TABLE_NAME                        COMPRESS COMPRESS_FOR
--------------------------------- -------- ------------
DEPT                              DISABLED
BONUS                             DISABLED
SALGRADE                          DISABLED
DUMMY                             DISABLED
EMP                               ENABLED  ARCHIVE HIGH

Elapsed: 00:00:00.06
SQL>
SQL> select segment_name, sum(bytes) total_space
  2  from user_segments
  3  group by segment_name;

SEGMENT_NAME                        TOTAL_SPACE
--------------------------------- ------------
DEPT                                     65536
DUMMY                                    65536
EMP                                  452984832
EMP_IDX                              679477248
SALGRADE                                 65536

Elapsed: 00:00:03.00
SQL>
```

All the space savings from using ARCHIVE HIGH were lost, putting the table back into the range of OLTP compression after the same updates. Notice that the first update consumed about five more minutes of elapsed time, as compared to the QUERY-compressed tables. To finish out the space changes that can be expected from using HCC on active tables, we perform the same updates on our EMP table compressed for ARCHIVE LOW, as follows:

```
SQL>
SQL> --
SQL> -- Perform an update
SQL> --
SQL> -- Note elapsed time (less than the previous compressed update)
SQL> --
SQL> update emp set sal=sal*1.08 where empno > 7350;
```

```
14680064 rows updated.

Elapsed: 00:07:29.25
SQL>
SQL> commit;

Commit complete.

Elapsed: 00:00:00.02
SQL>
SQL> --
SQL> -- Current compression level and storage
SQL> --
SQL> -- Looks like the storage after the second
SQL> -- update to the HCC compressed data
SQL> --
SQL> select table_name, compression, compress_for
  2  from user_tables;

TABLE_NAME                       COMPRESS COMPRESS_FOR
-------------------------------- -------- ------------
DEPT                             DISABLED
BONUS                            DISABLED
SALGRADE                         DISABLED
DUMMY                            DISABLED
EMP                              ENABLED  ARCHIVE LOW

Elapsed: 00:00:00.03
SQL>
SQL> select segment_name, sum(bytes) total_space
  2  from user_segments
  3  group by segment_name;

SEGMENT_NAME                       TOTAL_SPACE
-------------------------------- -----------
DEPT                                   65536
DUMMY                                  65536
EMP                                218103808
EMP_IDX                            637534208
SALGRADE                               65536

Elapsed: 00:00:00.02
SQL>
SQL> --
SQL> -- Perform a second update
SQL> --
SQL> -- Note elapsed time
SQL> --
SQL> update emp set sal=sal*1.08 where empno > 7350;

14680064 rows updated.
```

```
Elapsed: 00:02:12.42
SQL>
SQL> commit;

Commit complete.

Elapsed: 00:00:00.03
SQL>
SQL> --
SQL> -- Current storage consumed after second update
SQL> --
SQL> select table_name, compression, compress_for
  2  from user_tables;

TABLE_NAME                       COMPRESS COMPRESS_FOR
-------------------------------- -------- ------------
DEPT                             DISABLED
BONUS                            DISABLED
SALGRADE                         DISABLED
DUMMY                            DISABLED
EMP                              ENABLED  ARCHIVE LOW

Elapsed: 00:00:00.06
SQL>
SQL> select segment_name, sum(bytes) total_space
  2  from user_segments
  3  group by segment_name;

SEGMENT_NAME                       TOTAL_SPACE
---------------------------------- -----------
DEPT                                     65536
DUMMY                                    65536
EMP                                  452984832
EMP_IDX                              637534208
SALGRADE                                 65536

Elapsed: 00:00:00.02
SQL>
```

Again, the total space consumed by the EMP table returns to the level of OLTP compression after two updates, so the space saved after the table was initially compressed has been lost.

Ratios—What to Expect

We have shown that when the data is initially compressed, HCC can provide a substantial reduction in table size. Reasonably accurate estimates can be obtained from Oracle.

What Oracle Thinks

To return a reasonably accurate compression ratio, the DBMS_COMPRESSION.GET_COMPRESSION_RATIO procedure can be used.

```
SQL>
SQL> --
SQL> -- Compute compression estimates
SQL> --
SQL>
SQL> set serveroutput on size 1000000
SQL>
SQL> declare
  2             blockct_comp      number;
  3             blockct_uncomp    number;
  4             rows_comp         number;
  5             rows_uncomp       number;
  6             comp_rat          number;
  7             comp_type         varchar2(40);
  8  begin
  9             dbms_compression.get_compression_ratio('&&tblspc','&&ownr','&&tblname',null,
            dbms_compression.comp_for_oltp, blockct_comp, blockct_uncomp,rows_comp, rows_uncomp,
            comp_rat, comp_type);
 10             dbms_output.put_line('Compression type: '||comp_type||'     Compression ratio (est):
            '||comp_rat);
 11             dbms_compression.get_compression_ratio('&&tblspc','&&ownr','&&tblname',null,
            dbms_compression.comp_for_query_low, blockct_comp, blockct_uncomp,rows_comp,
            rows_uncomp, comp_rat, comp_type);
 12             dbms_output.put_line('Compression type: '||comp_type||'     Compression ratio (est):
            '||comp_rat);
 13             dbms_compression.get_compression_ratio('&&tblspc','&&ownr','&&tblname',null,
            dbms_compression.comp_for_query_high, blockct_comp, blockct_uncomp,rows_comp,
            rows_uncomp, comp_rat, comp_type);
 14             dbms_output.put_line('Compression type: '||comp_type||'     Compression ratio (est):
            '||comp_rat);
 15             dbms_compression.get_compression_ratio('&&tblspc','&&ownr','&&tblname',null,
            dbms_compression.comp_for_archive_low, blockct_comp, blockct_uncomp,rows_comp,
            rows_uncomp, comp_rat, comp_type);
 16             dbms_output.put_line('Compression type: '||comp_type||'     Compression ratio (est):
            '||comp_rat);
 17             dbms_compression.get_compression_ratio('&&tblspc','&&ownr','&&tblname',null,
            dbms_compression.comp_for_archive_high, blockct_comp, blockct_uncomp,rows_comp,
            rows_uncomp, comp_rat, comp_type);
 18             dbms_output.put_line('Compression type: '||comp_type||'     Compression ratio (est):
            '||comp_rat);
 19  end;
 20  /
Enter value for tblspc: USERS
Enter value for ownr: BING
Enter value for tblname: EMP
old   9:           dbms_compression.get_compression_ratio('&&tblspc','&&ownr','&&tblname',null,
            dbms_compression.comp_for_oltp, blockct_comp, blockct_uncomp,rows_comp, rows_uncomp,
            comp_rat, comp_type);
new   9:           dbms_compression.get_compression_ratio('USERS','BING','EMP',null, dbms_compression.
            comp_for_oltp, blockct_comp, blockct_uncomp,rows_comp, rows_uncomp, comp_rat, comp_type);
```

```
old  11:        dbms_compression.get_compression_ratio('&&tblspc','&&ownr','&&tblname',null,
                dbms_compression.comp_for_query_low, blockct_comp, blockct_uncomp,rows_comp, rows_uncomp,
                comp_rat, comp_type);
new  11:        dbms_compression.get_compression_ratio('USERS','BING','EMP',null, dbms_compression.comp_
                for_query_low, blockct_comp, blockct_uncomp,rows_comp, rows_uncomp, comp_rat, comp_type);
old  13:        dbms_compression.get_compression_ratio('&&tblspc','&&ownr','&&tblname',null,
                dbms_compression.comp_for_query_high, blockct_comp, blockct_uncomp,rows_comp,
                rows_uncomp, comp_rat, comp_type);
new  13:        dbms_compression.get_compression_ratio('USERS','BING','EMP',null, dbms_compression.comp_
                for_query_high, blockct_comp, blockct_uncomp,rows_comp, rows_uncomp, comp_rat, comp_type);
old  15:        dbms_compression.get_compression_ratio('&&tblspc','&&ownr','&&tblname',null, dbms_
                compression.comp_for_archive_low, blockct_comp, blockct_uncomp,rows_comp, rows_
                uncomp, comp_rat, comp_type);
new  15:        dbms_compression.get_compression_ratio('USERS','BING','EMP',null, dbms_compression.comp_
                for_archive_low, blockct_comp, blockct_uncomp,rows_comp, rows_uncomp, comp_rat, comp_type);
old  17:        dbms_compression.get_compression_ratio('&&tblspc','&&ownr','&&tblname',null, dbms_
                compression.comp_for_archive_high, blockct_comp, blockct_uncomp,rows_comp, rows_
                uncomp, comp_rat, comp_type);
new  17:        dbms_compression.get_compression_ratio('USERS','BING','EMP',null, dbms_compression.comp_for_
                archive_high, blockct_comp, blockct_uncomp,rows_comp, rows_uncomp, comp_rat, comp_type);
Compression type: "Compress For OLTP"       Compression ratio (est): 3.5
Compression Advisor self-check validation successful. select count(*) on both Uncompressed and EHCC
Compressed format = 1000001 rows
Compression type: "Compress For Query Low"       Compression ratio (est): 51.1
Compression Advisor self-check validation successful. select count(*) on both Uncompressed and EHCC
Compressed format = 1000001 rows
Compression type: "Compress For Query High"       Compression ratio (est): 183.9
Compression Advisor self-check validation successful. select count(*) on both Uncompressed and EHCC
Compressed format = 1000001 rows
Compression type: "Compress For Archive Low"       Compression ratio (est): 183.9
Compression Advisor self-check validation successful. select count(*) on both Uncompressed and EHCC
Compressed format = 1000001 rows
Compression type: "Compress For Archive High"       Compression ratio (est): 189.8

PL/SQL procedure successfully completed.

Elapsed: 00:04:30.02
SQL>
```

Table 6-3 summarizes the estimated compression ratios for the various compression types.

Table 6-3. *Estimated Compression Ratios*

Compression Type	Estimated Ratio
OLTP	3.5
Query Low	51.1
Query High	183.9
Archive Low	183.9
Archive High	189.8

What You Get

The data in our EMP table was very compressible (simply, the same 14 rows loaded again and again, to reach our target size and row count), so the compression ratios should be impressive. Your data may not be as compressible (it likely isn't), so your estimates and actual ratios will probably differ. The actual ratios for our data agreed fairly well with the estimates; Table 6-4 summarizes those results.

Table 6-4. *Actual Observed Compression Ratios*

Compression Type	Actual Ratio
OLTP	3.5
Query Low	48.6
Query High	85.0
Archive Low	85.0
Archive High	170.0

Your results may differ, but for three out of the five listed compression types, Oracle did a very good job of estimating the compression ratios. Be aware that what Oracle reports may not be exactly what you get in actual use.

Things to Know

There are three general levels of compression, two of which require additional licensing: Basic, OLTP, and Hybrid Columnar Compression (HCC).

HCC has two types (QUERY and ARCHIVE), and each of those has two subtypes (HIGH and LOW), to provide four distinct levels of HCC. In general, QUERY-type compression is intended for somewhat active data, whereas ARCHIVE compression is intended for data that will be queried fairly infrequently and will not be updated.

HCC does its magic by collecting rows with similar data and compressing them into a Compression Unit (CU). Each unit is composed of multiple data blocks that contain entire rows of data across the CU. This makes it easier and more efficient for Oracle to return the data, because only one CU has to be accessed to return entire rows.

Compression levels vary with the compression type. Basic provides the least compression, and ARCHIVE HIGH provides the greatest space savings at the time of compression.

Loading data into compressed tables usually requires parallel processing and/or direct path loads (the latter supplied by SQL*Loader). The /*+ append */ hint parallelizes the inserts, allowing them to be compressed on insert. It can take longer to load compressed tables than it can uncompressed tables.

Queries are a mixed bag when it comes to execution times, as Smart Scans can make a query of compressed data run faster by offloading the uncompression activities to the storage cells. Queries of compressed data that don't use Smart Scans can run longer (and most likely will) than the same query run against uncompressed data.

Updates to compressed tables will cause the table to increase in size. Basic compression has no provision for automatic re-compression, so tables using this method will have to be periodically re-compressed if they are actively updated. OLTP compression will automatically re-compress data blocks that are full, making room for more uncompressed data. HCC compression silently reverts to OLTP after data is updated, so the original level of compression is lost, but the OLTP level of compression remains, including the automatic compression of full data blocks.

Compression ratios can be estimated by the DBMS_COMPRESSION.GET_COMPRESSION_RATIO procedure, and in many cases, will agree with the observed compression ratios on user data. Highly compressible data can show large discrepancies between the estimated and actual compression ratios, so do not be alarmed if you don't get exactly what Oracle predicts.

CHAPTER 7

▪▪▪

Exadata Cell Wait Events

The Oracle wait interface was first expanded in Oracle Release 8.1.x, to provide a window into Oracle performance. In subsequent releases, this interface has been improved and expanded, making Oracle a very well-instrumented database. Keeping tabs on where Oracle spends its time and how much time it consumes per event, the wait interface is an invaluable tool with which the database administrator (DBA) can diagnose performance issues. With Exadata, this wait interface has been expanded even further to include Exadata-specific wait events in support of the operations unique to this system. These events, and the actual operations they monitor, will be covered in this chapter. We will also cover existing, non-Exadata wait events that apply to Exadata operations.

What is a *wait event*? It is an event the database is waiting on, such as a disk read, that is timed and given a name. In release 11.2.0.3, there are 1150 named wait events listed in the V$EVENT_NAME view, 23 of which reference Exadata-specific operations. Of those, 17 are specific to the storage cells. These are the events we will cover in this chapter.

Available Nowhere Else

Because Exadata is using the same Oracle software available on non-Exadata systems, the list of wait events is the same, whether or not you're using Exadata. The difference is that some of these events are populated only on Exadata systems, which is the only reason they are available nowhere else.

Cell Events

Cell events are, obviously, events that will not be populated on non-Exadata systems or systems not using Exadata storage. There are 17 cell-related events in V$EVENT_NAME. These are listed in Table 7-1.

Table 7-1. *Cell Wait Events and Classes*

Cell worker idle	Idle
Cell manager cancel work request	Other
Cell smart flash unkeep	Other
Cell worker online completion	Other
Cell worker retry	Other
Cell manager closing cell	System I/O
Cell manager discovering disks	System I/O
Cell manager opening cell	System I/O
Cell smart incremental backup	System I/O
Cell smart restore from backup	System I/O
Cell list of blocks physical read	User I/O
Cell multiblock physical read	User I/O
Cell single block physical read	User I/O
Cell smart file creation	User I/O
Cell smart index scan	User I/O
Cell smart table scan	User I/O
Cell statistics gather	User I/O

These events will be covered in detail in a later section of this chapter.

Triggering Events

It is interesting to see which operations trigger the various cell wait events. This information is available in the DBA_HIST_ACTIVE_SESS_HISTORY view, as well as in V$SYSTEM_EVENT. It is likely that not every event listed in Table 7-1 will be reported in DBA_HIST_ACTIVE_SESS_HISTORY; however, one event may be triggered by a number of plan operations. The query we used to generate a list of events and associated operations follows:

```
SQL> select event , non_exa_event, operation ,count(*)
  2  from
  3  (select event,
  4          decode(event, 'cell smart table scan','',
  5  'cell smart index scan','',
  6  'cell statistics gather','',
  7  'cell smart incremental backup','',
  8  'cell smart file creation','',
  9  'cell smart restore from backup','',
 10  'cell single block physical read','db file sequential read',
 11  'cell multiblock physical read','db file scattered read',
 12  'cell list of blocks physical read','db file parallel read',
 13  'cell manager opening cell','',
```

```
14   'cell manager closing cell','',
15   'cell manager discovering disks','',
16   'cell worker idle','',
17   'cell smart flash unkeep','',
18   'cell worker online completion','',
19   'cell worker retry','',
20   'cell manager cancel work request','') non_Exa_event,
21          sql_plan_operation||' '||sql_plan_options operation
22   from dba_hist_active_sess_history
23   where event like 'cell%')
24   where operation <> ' '
25   group by event, non_exa_event, operation
26   order by 1
27   /
```

EVENT	NON_EXA_EVENT	OPERATION	COUNT(*)
cell list of blocks physical read	db file parallel read	DELETE	1
		INDEX RANGE SCAN	176
		INDEX STORAGE SAMPLE FAST FULL SCAN	1
		INDEX UNIQUE SCAN	65
		PX COORDINATOR	6
		TABLE ACCESS BY GLOBAL INDEX ROWID	2
		TABLE ACCESS BY INDEX ROWID	4412
		TABLE ACCESS BY LOCAL INDEX ROWID	4
		TABLE ACCESS STORAGE FULL	50
		TABLE ACCESS STORAGE SAMPLE BY ROWID RANGE	1
		UPDATE	1
cell multiblock physical read	db file scattered read	INDEX FULL SCAN	1
		INDEX RANGE SCAN	160
		INDEX SKIP SCAN	4
		INDEX STORAGE FAST FULL SCAN	14
		INDEX STORAGE SAMPLE FAST FULL SCAN	445
		INDEX UNIQUE SCAN	10
		LOAD TABLE CONVENTIONAL	2
		TABLE ACCESS BY INDEX ROWID	5819
		TABLE ACCESS BY LOCAL INDEX ROWID	4
		TABLE ACCESS STORAGE FULL	1627
		TABLE ACCESS STORAGE FULL FIRST ROWS	324
		TABLE ACCESS STORAGE SAMPLE BY ROWID RANGE	58
		UPDATE	1
cell single block physical read	db file sequential read	CREATE TABLE STATEMENT	1
		DDL STATEMENT	19
		DELETE	139
		FIXED TABLE FIXED INDEX	10
		FIXED TABLE FULL	338
		FOR UPDATE	12
		INDEX FULL SCAN	711
		INDEX RANGE SCAN	14281

```
                                             INDEX RANGE SCAN (MIN/MAX)                    26
                                             INDEX RANGE SCAN DESCENDING                   10
                                             INDEX SKIP SCAN                             2289
                                             INDEX STORAGE SAMPLE FAST FULL SCAN           64
                                             INDEX UNIQUE SCAN                           1100
                                             LOAD TABLE CONVENTIONAL                      372
                                             PX COORDINATOR                                3
                                             SELECT STATEMENT                             41
                                             SORT AGGREGATE                               30
                                             TABLE ACCESS BY GLOBAL INDEX ROWID            1
                                             TABLE ACCESS BY INDEX ROWID              103970
                                             TABLE ACCESS BY LOCAL INDEX ROWID           293
                                             TABLE ACCESS CLUSTER                         21
                                             TABLE ACCESS STORAGE FULL                    34
                                             TABLE ACCESS STORAGE FULL FIRST ROWS          1
                                             TABLE ACCESS STORAGE SAMPLE BY ROWID RANGE  449
                                             UPDATE                                      171

cell smart index scan                        INDEX STORAGE FAST FULL SCAN                  8

cell smart table scan                        TABLE ACCESS STORAGE FULL                  1180
                                             TABLE ACCESS STORAGE FULL FIRST ROWS          4

52 rows selected.

SQL>
```

The listing also contains the equivalent non-Exadata event, if one exists. In the following section, these events, their equivalent non-Exadata events, their description, and various parameters they supply will be discussed.

User I/O Events

Each of these events is associated with a wait class; there are four distinct wait classes for the cell events. The most populous wait class for cell events is the User I/O class, with seven of the seventeen events in this class. We will look at each event in that class in this section and see what it reports.

Cell Smart Table Scan

The cell smart table scan event records time against full-table scans that are offloaded to the storage cells. Because it can be used to determine if a statement utilized a Smart Scan, and thus benefited from offloading, it may be the most important wait event in the Exadata system. Remember that offloading only occurs during direct-path reads, so this event will, in general, replace the direct path read event. This is not to say that you won't see a direct path read event on an Exadata system, but it is much more likely to see time recorded against the cell smart table scan event. As this is a direct-path read, it returns the data directly to the program global area (PGA) of the user process requesting it, which includes parallel slave processes.

The use of an InfiniBand network changes the actual mechanism for direct-path reads, in comparison to non-Exadata systems. Each direct-path read request to the storage cells also contains a reference to the select list, join predicates—if they exist—and the query predicates. This allows the storage servers to filter the data and perform column projection before "handing over" the results to the database servers. Each data block processed by a Smart Scan has these optimizations applied to it; the database server processes that request. The data also have access to the

ASM extent map, so they can request the necessary allocation units, or AUs, from each storage cell. The storage cells then read these allocation units in the order of request and apply the Smart Scan optimizations to each AU, returning the projected columns from rows that satisfy the supplied filter criteria. As expected, this event will occur repeatedly when large scans are executed.

A 10046 trace is a good source for seeing this event recorded. We provide a small section of a large table scan, operating in parallel, as follows:

```
WAIT #46969064935512: nam='cell smart table scan' ela= 794053 cellhash#=88802347 p2=0 p3=0 obj#=133235
                                                                        tim=1371608209311673
WAIT #46969064935512: nam='cell smart table scan' ela= 151 cellhash#=88802347 p2=0 p3=0 obj#=133235
                                                                        tim=1371608209317400
WAIT #46969064935512: nam='PX Deq: Execution Msg' ela= 80 sleeptime/senderid=268566527 passes=1
                                          p3=7325501352 obj#=133235 tim=1371608209321134
WAIT #46969064935512: nam='cell smart table scan' ela= 116 cellhash#=88802347 p2=0 p3=0 obj#=133235
                                                                        tim=1371608209321618
WAIT #46969064935512: nam='cell smart table scan' ela= 39049 cellhash#=88802347 p2=0 p3=0 obj#=133235
                                                                        tim=1371608209360713
WAIT #46969064935512: nam='PX Deq: Execution Msg' ela= 138 sleeptime/senderid=268566527 passes=1
                                          p3=7325501352 obj#=133235 tim=1371608209361123
WAIT #46969064935512: nam='cell smart table scan' ela= 126 cellhash#=398250101 p2=0 p3=0 obj#=133235
                                                                        tim=1371608209361740
WAIT #46969064935512: nam='cell smart table scan' ela= 39318 cellhash#=398250101 p2=0 p3=0 obj#=133235
                                                                        tim=1371608209401129
WAIT #46969064935512: nam='PX Deq: Execution Msg' ela= 84 sleeptime/senderid=268566527 passes=1
                                          p3=7325501352 obj#=133235 tim=1371608209401312
WAIT #46969064935512: nam='cell smart table scan' ela= 100 cellhash#=398250101 p2=0 p3=0 obj#=133235
                                                                        tim=1371608209401875
WAIT #46969064935512: nam='cell smart table scan' ela= 44604 cellhash#=398250101 p2=0 p3=0 obj#=133235
                                                                        tim=1371608209446549
WAIT #46969064935512: nam='PX Deq: Execution Msg' ela= 76 sleeptime/senderid=268566527 passes=1
                                          p3=7325501352 obj#=133235 tim=1371608209446719
WAIT #46969064935512: nam='cell smart table scan' ela= 120 cellhash#=2520626383 p2=0 p3=0 obj#=133235
                                                                        tim=1371608209447214
WAIT #46969064935512: nam='cell smart table scan' ela= 223022 cellhash#=2520626383 p2=0 p3=0 obj#=133235
                                                                        tim=1371608209670288
WAIT #46969064935512: nam='PX Deq: Execution Msg' ela= 82 sleeptime/senderid=268566527 passes=1
                                          p3=7325501352 obj#=133235 tim=1371608209670463
WAIT #46969064935512: nam='cell smart table scan' ela= 103 cellhash#=2520626383 p2=0 p3=0 obj#=133235
                                                                        tim=1371608209670967
WAIT #46969064935512: nam='cell smart table scan' ela= 5520 cellhash#=2520626383 p2=0 p3=0 obj#=133235
                                                                        tim=1371608209676590
WAIT #46969064935512: nam='PX Deq: Execution Msg' ela= 90 sleeptime/senderid=268566527 passes=1
                                          p3=7325501352 obj#=133235 tim=1371608209676760
WAIT #46969064935512: nam='cell smart table scan' ela= 161 cellhash#=398250101 p2=0 p3=0 obj#=133235
                                                                        tim=1371608209677348
WAIT #46969064935512: nam='cell smart table scan' ela= 43339 cellhash#=398250101 p2=0 p3=0 obj#=133235
                                                                        tim=1371608209720745
WAIT #46969064935512: nam='PX Deq: Execution Msg' ela= 113 sleeptime/senderid=268566527 passes=1
                                          p3=7325501352 obj#=133235 tim=1371608209720974
WAIT #46969064935512: nam='cell smart table scan' ela= 132 cellhash#=2520626383 p2=0 p3=0 obj#=133235
                                                                        tim=1371608209721594
```

```
WAIT #46969064935512: nam='cell smart table scan' ela= 9462 cellhash#=2520626383 p2=0 p3=0 obj#=133235
                                                             tim=1371608209731125
WAIT #46969064935512: nam='PX Deq: Execution Msg' ela= 102 sleeptime/senderid=268566527 passes=1
                                                    p3=7325501352 obj#=133235 tim=1371608209731327
WAIT #46969064935512: nam='cell smart table scan' ela= 84 cellhash#=2520626383 p2=0 p3=0 obj#=133235
                                                             tim=1371608209732040
WAIT #46969064935512: nam='cell smart table scan' ela= 19 cellhash#=88802347 p2=0 p3=0 obj#=133235
                                                             tim=1371608209732081
```

Notice this section also includes a number of 'PX Deq: Execution Msg' events, proof of the parallel processing utilized during the query execution.

Parameters supplied by this event provide only the object id (obj#) and the cell hash number (cellhash#). Parameters P2 and P3 are unused. In contrast, the direct path-read event provides the object_id, the file number, the offset into the file (first dba), and the number of contiguous blocks read (block cnt), shown as follows:

```
WAIT #47901347109608: nam='direct path read' ela= 355651 file number=1 first dba=1474969 block cnt=3
                                                        obj#=243 tim=1371659720952304
WAIT #47901347109608: nam='direct path read' ela= 59 file number=1 first dba=1474980 block cnt=4
                                                        obj#=243 tim=1371659720952562
WAIT #47901347109608: nam='direct path read' ela= 16812 file number=1 first dba=1474984 block cnt=4
                                                        obj#=243 tim=1371659720969412
```

Note that on Exadata systems implementing direct-path reads (when the query or statement does not qualify for Smart Scan execution), there is no cell information provided, so it's not known which cell received and processed which request.

Cell Smart Index Scan

In the same manner as the cell smart table scan, the cell smart index scan records time against fast full-index scans that are offloaded to the storage cells, the only real difference being the object type being scanned.

On one of the most active systems, we have a total of 1184 cell smart table scans recorded in DBA_HIST_ACTIVE_SESS_HISTORY, while during that same time period only 8 cell smart index scans were reported. This may be due to the propensity of Oracle 11.2 to perform direct-path reads on serial table scans. There is a hidden parameter, _serial_direct_read, normally set to FALSE, that can be set to TRUE to favor this activity. Setting this event may create performance issues in heavily used production systems, so it's best to test this on a nonproduction system, using an environment as close to production as possible. Note that the parameter only specifies serial direct reads, not the object those reads operate upon, so indexes can also utilize this serial-read mechanism. Because indexes tend to be smaller than the tables they index, it's a good possibility their smaller size precludes use of the cell smart index scan event. Also, only fast full-index scans are eligible for cell smart index scans; index range scans and index full scans do not qualify.

In the same manner as the cell smart table scan event, the cell smart index scan event doesn't provide much information; only the cell hash number (cellhash#) and the object_id (obj#) are found in a 10046 trace file, with parameters P2 and P3 again unused.

```
WAIT #46969064936345: nam='cell smart index scan' ela= 178 cellhash#=2520626383 p2=0 p3=0 obj#=448299
                                                             tim=1371608209741332
WAIT #46969064936345: nam='cell smart index scan' ela= 462 cellhash#=2520626383 p2=0 p3=0 obj#=448299
                                                             tim=1371608209752118
```

Cell Single-Block Physical Read

This event is the Exadata equivalent of the db file sequential read event on non-Exadata systems. These are usually indicative of index access operations, including index block reads and table block reads by rowids provided from the index lookups, but other operations can also use this event when accessing single blocks.

Operations that generate the cell single block physical read event can be many, as shown by the following output from DBA_HIST_ACTIVE_SESS_HISTORY:

```
EVENT                          NON_EXA_EVENT             OPERATION                               COUNT(*)
-----                          -------------             ---------                               --------
cell single block physical read db file sequential read  CREATE TABLE STATEMENT                         1
                                                         DDL STATEMENT                                 19
                                                         DELETE                                       139
                                                         FIXED TABLE FIXED INDEX                       10
                                                         FIXED TABLE FULL                             338
                                                         FOR UPDATE                                    12
                                                         INDEX FULL SCAN                              711
                                                         INDEX RANGE SCAN                           14281
                                                         INDEX RANGE SCAN (MIN/MAX)                    26
                                                         INDEX RANGE SCAN DESCENDING                   10
                                                         INDEX SKIP SCAN                             2289
                                                         INDEX STORAGE SAMPLE FAST FULL SCAN           64
                                                         INDEX UNIQUE SCAN                           1100
                                                         LOAD TABLE CONVENTIONAL                      372
                                                         PX COORDINATOR                                 3
                                                         SELECT STATEMENT                              41
                                                         SORT AGGREGATE                                30
                                                         TABLE ACCESS BY GLOBAL INDEX ROWID             1
                                                         TABLE ACCESS BY INDEX ROWID               103970
                                                         TABLE ACCESS BY LOCAL INDEX ROWID            293
                                                         TABLE ACCESS CLUSTER                          21
                                                         TABLE ACCESS STORAGE FULL                     34
                                                         TABLE ACCESS STORAGE FULL FIRST ROWS           1
                                                         TABLE ACCESS STORAGE SAMPLE BY ROWID RANGE   449
                                                         UPDATE                                       171
```

The most common event in the preceding list is index access, accounting for 11 of the listed entries. Add to that the total occurrences of these events, and it's even more obvious that the most likely operation to mark time against this event is index access.

This event provides more information than the other events discussed thus far, reporting the cell hash number (cellhash#), the disk hash number (diskhash#), the total bytes passed during the operation (bytes), and the object_id (obj#). With this event, you know not only which object was accessed but from which disk, which cell, and how many bytes were read. The following is a small part of the output from grep on a 10046 trace file that shows these reported values:

```
WAIT #47185678513912: nam='cell single block physical read' ela= 13725 cellhash#=398250101
                      diskhash#=2110579711 bytes=8192 obj#=134196 tim=1364280947867845
WAIT #47185663242504: nam='cell single block physical read' ela= 562 cellhash#=398250101
                      diskhash#=736840779 bytes=8192 obj#=21 tim=1364280948818774
WAIT #47185660188840: nam='cell single block physical read' ela= 516 cellhash#=398250101
                      diskhash#=592573387 bytes=8192 obj#=69 tim=1364280948820595
WAIT #47185681467920: nam='cell single block physical read' ela= 518 cellhash#=398250101
                      diskhash#=323658058 bytes=8192 obj#=62 tim=1364280948828550
```

```
WAIT  #47185664116080:  nam='cell  single  block  physical  read'  ela=  593  cellhash#=2520626383
                            diskhash#=1392289187 bytes=8192 obj#=61 tim=1364280948829493
WAIT  #47185671820512:  nam='cell  single  block  physical  read'  ela=  520  cellhash#=2520626383
                            diskhash#=1878859599 bytes=8192 obj#=54 tim=1364280948832544
WAIT  #47185672026856:  nam='cell  single  block  physical  read'  ela=  536  cellhash#=88802347
                            diskhash#=1487722174 bytes=8192 obj#=37 tim=1364280948855726
WAIT  #47185676137528:  nam='cell  single  block  physical  read'  ela=  505  cellhash#=398250101
                            diskhash#=949169843 bytes=8192 obj#=75 tim=1364280948856712
WAIT  #47185663821624:  nam='cell  single  block  physical  read'  ela=  504  cellhash#=2520626383
                            diskhash#=372821781 bytes=8192 obj#=106 tim=1364280948857502
WAIT  #47185663821624:  nam='cell  single  block  physical  read'  ela=  510  cellhash#=88802347
                            diskhash#=2410699693 bytes=8192 obj#=104 tim=1364280948858089
WAIT  #47185671360600:  nam='cell  single  block  physical  read'  ela=  484  cellhash#=398250101
                            diskhash#=4004546112 bytes=8192 obj#=108 tim=1364280948859019
WAIT  #47185671360600:  nam='cell  single  block  physical  read'  ela=  508  cellhash#=2520626383
                            diskhash#=3373534499 bytes=8192 obj#=108 tim=1364280948859781
WAIT  #47185663242504:  nam='cell  single  block  physical  read'  ela=  499  cellhash#=398250101
                            diskhash#=736840779 bytes=8192 obj#=21 tim=1364280948860521
WAIT  #47185671976024:  nam='cell  single  block  physical  read'  ela=  519  cellhash#=88802347
                            diskhash#=2410699693 bytes=8192 obj#=4 tim=1364280948873162
WAIT  #47185678747440:  nam='cell  single  block  physical  read'  ela=  505  cellhash#=88802347
                            diskhash#=3487034449 bytes=8192 obj#=427 tim=1364280948876978
WAIT  #47185678747440:  nam='cell  single  block  physical  read'  ela=  504  cellhash#=88802347
                            diskhash#=351342063 bytes=8192 obj#=425 tim=1364280948877576
```

Cell Multiblock Physical Read

This event was renamed for Exadata systems, as the non-Exadata event is named db file scattered read, which is descriptive but not entirely accurate, as the blocks read may not be scattered but contiguous. Oracle 11.2 still reports multiblock reads using the db file scattered read event on non-Exadata systems, regardless of whether they are reading contiguous or scattered blocks. For Exadata systems, this event records time for contiguous multiblock reads.

A partial list of the operations that trigger this wait event follows:

EVENT	NON_EXA_EVENT	OPERATION	COUNT(*)
cell multiblock physical read	db file scattered read	INDEX FULL SCAN	1
		INDEX RANGE SCAN	160
		INDEX SKIP SCAN	4
		INDEX STORAGE FAST FULL SCAN	14
		INDEX STORAGE SAMPLE FAST FULL SCAN	445
		INDEX UNIQUE SCAN	10
		LOAD TABLE CONVENTIONAL	2
		TABLE ACCESS BY INDEX ROWID	5819
		TABLE ACCESS BY LOCAL INDEX ROWID	4
		TABLE ACCESS STORAGE FULL	1627
		TABLE ACCESS STORAGE FULL FIRST ROWS	324
		TABLE ACCESS STORAGE SAMPLE BY ROWID RANGE	58
		UPDATE	1

The output of processing another 10046 trace file with grep follows, showing how this event is reported:

```
WAIT  #47901352100880:  nam='cell  multiblock  physical  read' ela=  640  cellhash#=398250101
                        diskhash#=4004546112 bytes=65536 obj#=631 tim=1371659723908619
WAIT  #47901352100880:  nam='cell  multiblock  physical  read' ela=  844  cellhash#=398250101
                        diskhash#=4004546112 bytes=65536 obj#=631 tim=1371659723909603
WAIT  #47901352100880:  nam='cell  multiblock  physical  read' ela=  632  cellhash#=398250101
                        diskhash#=4004546112 bytes=65536 obj#=631 tim=1371659723910387
WAIT  #47901352100880:  nam='cell  multiblock  physical  read' ela=  620  cellhash#=398250101
                        diskhash#=4004546112 bytes=65536 obj#=631 tim=1371659723911140
WAIT  #47901352100880:  nam='cell  multiblock  physical  read' ela=  639  cellhash#=398250101
                        diskhash#=4004546112 bytes=65536 obj#=631 tim=1371659723911925
WAIT  #47901352100880:  nam='cell  multiblock  physical  read' ela=  653  cellhash#=398250101
                        diskhash#=2110579711 bytes=65536 obj#=631 tim=1371659723912743
WAIT  #47901352100880:  nam='cell  multiblock  physical  read' ela=  960  cellhash#=398250101
                        diskhash#=2110579711 bytes=65536 obj#=631 tim=1371659723913842
WAIT  #47901352100880:  nam='cell  multiblock  physical  read' ela=  841  cellhash#=398250101
                        diskhash#=2110579711 bytes=65536 obj#=631 tim=1371659723914879
WAIT  #47901352100880:  nam='cell  multiblock  physical  read' ela=  630  cellhash#=398250101
                        diskhash#=2110579711 bytes=65536 obj#=631 tim=1371659723915692
WAIT  #47901352100880:  nam='cell  multiblock  physical  read' ela=  726  cellhash#=398250101
                        diskhash#=2110579711 bytes=65536 obj#=631 tim=1371659723916608
WAIT  #47901352100880:  nam='cell  multiblock  physical  read' ela=  820  cellhash#=398250101
                        diskhash#=2110579711 bytes=65536 obj#=631 tim=1371659723917621
WAIT  #47901352100880:  nam='cell  multiblock  physical  read' ela=  687  cellhash#=398250101
                        diskhash#=2110579711 bytes=65536 obj#=631 tim=1371659723918461
WAIT  #47901352100880:  nam='cell  multiblock  physical  read' ela=  757  cellhash#=398250101
                        diskhash#=2110579711 bytes=65536 obj#=631 tim=1371659723919396
WAIT  #47901352100880:  nam='cell  multiblock  physical  read' ela= 13061  cellhash#=398250101
                        diskhash#=323658058 bytes=1048576 obj#=631 tim=1371659723933281
WAIT  #47901352100880:  nam='cell  multiblock  physical  read' ela= 11539  cellhash#=2520626383
                        diskhash#=1346328363 bytes=1048576 obj#=631 tim=1371659723946098
WAIT  #47901352100880:  nam='cell  multiblock  physical  read' ela= 14240  cellhash#=88802347
                        diskhash#=493540951 bytes=1048576 obj#=631 tim=1371659723964141
WAIT  #47901352100880:  nam='cell  multiblock  physical  read' ela=  7785  cellhash#=88802347
                        diskhash#=4062498200 bytes=163840 obj#=631 tim=1371659723973491
WAIT  #47901352100880:  nam='cell  multiblock  physical  read' ela=  597  cellhash#=398250101
                        diskhash#=949169843 bytes=32768 obj#=997 tim=1371659723976483
```

This event reports the same information as the cell single-block physical read event, that is, the cell hash (cellhash#), disk hash (diskhash#), total bytes passed (bytes), and the object_id (obj#).

Cell List of Blocks Physically Read

Originally called db file parallel read, on Exadata systems it was renamed to more accurately reflect the operations that trigger it. However, on non-Exadata systems, the originally named event is the one to which time is recorded. Interestingly, this event has nothing to do with parallel data manipulation language (DML) operations.

This event records time for multi-block reads when the blocks are *not* contiguous. This makes it easier to distinguish from contiguous multiblock reads. Again, a number of plan operations can trigger this event, as the following list shows:

EVENT	NON_EXA_EVENT	OPERATION	COUNT(*)
cell list of blocks physical read	db file parallel read	DELETE	1
		INDEX RANGE SCAN	176
		INDEX STORAGE SAMPLE FAST FULL SCAN	1
		INDEX UNIQUE SCAN	65
		PX COORDINATOR	6
		TABLE ACCESS BY GLOBAL INDEX ROWID	2
		TABLE ACCESS BY INDEX ROWID	4412
		TABLE ACCESS BY LOCAL INDEX ROWID	4
		TABLE ACCESS STORAGE FULL	50
		TABLE ACCESS STORAGE SAMPLE BY ROWID RANGE	1
		UPDATE	1

The four most "popular" plan operations on one of our databases are TABLE ACCESS BY INDEX ROWID, INDEX RANGE SCAN, INDEX UNIQUE SCAN, and TABLE ACCESS STORAGE FULL, in order of frequency.

Looking again at a 10046 trace file, it can be seen how this event is reported in the following output from grep:

```
WAIT #47901352100880: nam='cell list of blocks physical read' ela= 537 cellhash#=398250101
                diskhash#=2110579711 blocks=3 obj#=997 tim=1371659723985684
WAIT #47901352100880: nam='cell list of blocks physical read' ela= 574 cellhash#=398250101
                diskhash#=2110579711 blocks=4 obj#=997 tim=1371659723988550
WAIT #47901352100880: nam='cell list of blocks physical read' ela= 1723 cellhash#=398250101
                diskhash#=323658058 blocks=46 obj#=997 tim=1371659723998837
WAIT #47901352100880: nam='cell list of blocks physical read' ela= 1208 cellhash#=2520626383
                diskhash#=1346328363 blocks=36 obj#=997 tim=1371659724003584
WAIT #47901352100880: nam='cell list of blocks physical read' ela= 1567 cellhash#=2520626383
                diskhash#=4245410826 blocks=47 obj#=997 tim=1371659724010794
WAIT #47901352100880: nam='cell list of blocks physical read' ela= 632 cellhash#=398250101
                diskhash#=4080537574 blocks=4 obj#=997 tim=1371659724013129
WAIT #47901344458904: nam='cell list of blocks physical read' ela= 33814 cellhash#=398250101
                diskhash#=949169843 blocks=27 obj#=447547 tim=1371659793327488
WAIT #47901354882040: nam='cell list of blocks physical read' ela= 702 cellhash#=398250101
                diskhash#=949169843 blocks=7 obj#=4 tim=1371659807119269
WAIT #47901354882040: nam='cell list of blocks physical read' ela= 715 cellhash#=398250101
                diskhash#=323658058 blocks=8 obj#=4 tim=1371659807144991
WAIT #47901354882040: nam='cell list of blocks physical read' ela= 40454 cellhash#=398250101
                diskhash#=4080537574 blocks=61 obj#=4 tim=1371659807259159
WAIT #47901354882040: nam='cell list of blocks physical read' ela= 1135 cellhash#=398250101
                diskhash#=4080537574 blocks=17 obj#=4 tim=1371659807265443
WAIT #47901354882040: nam='cell list of blocks physical read' ela= 805 cellhash#=398250101
                diskhash#=4080537574 blocks=12 obj#=4 tim=1371659807266892
WAIT #47901354882040: nam='cell list of blocks physical read' ela= 198850 cellhash#=88802347
                diskhash#=2443481431 blocks=57 obj#=4 tim=1371659807516838
WAIT #47901354882040: nam='cell list of blocks physical read' ela= 1987 cellhash#=88802347
                diskhash#=987865679 blocks=31 obj#=4 tim=1371659807569906
WAIT #47901354882040: nam='cell list of blocks physical read' ela= 1733 cellhash#=88802347
                diskhash#=987865679 blocks=37 obj#=4 tim=1371659807574314
```

```
WAIT #47901354882040:  nam='cell list of blocks physical read' ela= 2216 cellhash#=88802347
                       diskhash#=4062498200 blocks=69 obj#=4 tim=1371659807579817
WAIT #47901354882040:  nam='cell list of blocks physical read' ela= 34220 cellhash#=88802347
                       diskhash#=4062498200 blocks=54 obj#=4 tim=1371659807615518
WAIT #47901354882040:  nam='cell list of blocks physical read' ela= 36753 cellhash#=398250101
                       diskhash#=949169843 blocks=126 obj#=4 tim=1371659807657273
WAIT #47901354882040:  nam='cell list of blocks physical read' ela= 2424 cellhash#=398250101
                       diskhash#=4004546112 blocks=89 obj#=4 tim=1371659807700181
WAIT #47901354882040:  nam='cell list of blocks physical read' ela= 2656 cellhash#=88802347
                       diskhash#=987865679 blocks=95 obj#=4 tim=1371659807707733
WAIT #47901354882040:  nam='cell list of blocks physical read' ela= 1534 cellhash#=2520626383
                       diskhash#=3381263565 blocks=15 obj#=4 tim=1371659807714012
WAIT #47901354882040:  nam='cell list of blocks physical read' ela= 1958 cellhash#=2520626383
                       diskhash#=3381263565 blocks=51 obj#=4 tim=1371659807719799
```

As with the other cell block-read events, this, too, reports the cell hash (cellhash#), disk hash (diskhash#), and the object_id of the scanned object (obj#). It differs by reporting the total number of noncontiguous blocks read (blocks).

Cell Smart File Creation

When data files are created or extended, data blocks must be formatted. On non-Exadata systems, this task falls to the database server, and the data file init write event collects time when this occurs. Exadata does things differently by having the storage cells perform this task, and as a result, the cell smart file creation wait event records time when data blocks are formatted. Note that a file does not have to be added to a tablespace for this wait to occur; the event actually records time against data block formatting.

It may seem strange to have this wait event in the User I/O category, but many times, data blocks are formatted due to DML operations, such as autoextending a data file or deleting data. Other operations that can trigger this event include updates, nonunique index creations, direct-path loads, and inserts using the /*+ append */ hint.

How can updates and deletes trigger the cell smart file creation wait event? As noted previously, the wait event actually records time for data block-formatting operations, and deletes can cause data blocks to be reformatted for reuse when those blocks no longer contain data. Updates can also trigger this event, as an update may trigger a data file extension or use of a new data block, if row chaining or migration occurs.

There is only one parameter returned when this event is triggered and that is the cell hash (cellhash#); all other parameters that could be passed are unused.

Cell Statistics Gather

This is a wait event that we feel is incorrectly categorized as User I/O, because it doesn't record time against disk I/O operations; rather, it records time reading from V$CELL_THREAD_HISTORY, V$CELL_REQUEST_TOTALS, and other X$ tables and V$ views referencing cell activities, as well as recursive queries against the AUD$ table.

Generating a 10046 trace file and using grep to find this event produces the following abbreviated output:

```
WAIT #47971177959976:  nam='cell statistics gather' ela= 235 cellhash#=0 p2=0 p3=0 obj#=384
                       tim=1372568877816026
WAIT #47971177959976:  nam='cell statistics gather' ela= 253 cellhash#=0 p2=0 p3=0 obj#=384
                       tim=1372568877836094
WAIT #47971177959976:  nam='cell statistics gather' ela= 256 cellhash#=0 p2=0 p3=0 obj#=384
                       tim=1372568877855930
WAIT #47971177959976:  nam='cell statistics gather' ela= 280 cellhash#=0 p2=0 p3=0 obj#=384
                       tim=1372568877882687
```

```
WAIT  #47971177959976: nam='cell statistics gather' ela= 276 cellhash#=0 p2=0 p3=0 obj#=384
                                                                         tim=1372568877902691
WAIT  #47971177959976: nam='cell statistics gather' ela= 256 cellhash#=0 p2=0 p3=0 obj#=384
                                                                         tim=1372568877921221
WAIT  #47971177959976: nam='cell statistics gather' ela= 318 cellhash#=0 p2=0 p3=0 obj#=384
                                                                         tim=1372568877940424
```

These waits are against the AUD$ table (object_id and data_object_id 384 in our database). The query executed in this trace file was not against AUD$ but against V$CELL and V$CELL_THREAD_HISTORY. The formatted output from tkprof from the trace file generated for the V$CELL_THREAD_HISTORY query follows:

```
SQL ID: fqv4mmcqsysbp Plan Hash: 3553215696

select *
From
 v$cell_thread_history
```

call	count	cpu	elapsed	disk	query	current	rows
Parse	1	0.00	0.00	0	4	0	0
Execute	1	0.00	0.00	0	0	0	0
Fetch	2775	0.13	0.15	0	0	0	41609
total	2777	0.13	0.15	0	4	0	41609

```
Misses in library cache during parse: 1
Optimizer mode: ALL_ROWS
Parsing user id: 401
Number of plan statistics captured: 1
```

Rows (1st)	Rows (avg)	Rows (max)	Row Source Operation
41609	41609	41609	FIXED TABLE FULL X$KCFISOSSN (cr=0 pr=0 pw=0 time=116083 us cost=0 size=676 card=1)

Elapsed times include waiting on following events:

Event waited on	Times Waited	Max. Wait	Total Waited
SQL*Net message to client	2775	0.00	0.00
cell statistics gather	66	0.00	0.02
SQL*Net message from client	2775	2.63	12.53
row cache lock	9	0.00	0.00
library cache lock	2	0.00	0.00
library cache pin	2	0.00	0.00

```
********************************************************************************
```

System I/O Events

There are five cell-specific events in this wait class, and three of these events rarely accumulate any appreciable time. The two backup events do accrue time during backup and recovery operations and are interesting not only for what operations have time recorded against them but also for the operations that you think would accrue time but do not. We list the non-backup events in Table 7-2.

Table 7-2. *Cell Startup and Shutdown Wait Events*

Event	Description
Cell manager closing cell	This event is a cell shutdown event, collecting time against cell shutdownoperations. The only parameter passedback is the cell hash (cellhash#).
Cell manager opening cell	This is a cell startup event. The only parameter passed back is, again, the cell hash (cellhash#).
Cell manager discovering disks	This is another cell startup event, passing back the cell hash (cellhash#). Like the other two events, no other parameters are provided.

Cell Smart Incremental Backup

Exadata has optimized RMAN (Recovery Manager) incremental backups by allowing offloading to the storage tier. As such, this event accrues wait time for Incremental Level 1 backups, where the processing has been offloaded to the storage tier. With Exadata, changes are tracked at the block level, allowing for faster backups of blocks changed since the last Incremental Level 0 backup. The storage tier is especially suited for this type of processing, thus the need for this new wait event.

Not every incremental backup triggers this wait event. Incremental Level 0 backups do not, as they are, essentially, full backups and don't rely on block change tracking. They are the starting point for any recovery operation utilizing incremental backups, which is why the most recent Incremental Level 0 backup supersedes any prior Incremental Level 0 backup when performing a restore and recovery absent a RECOVER ... UNTIL ... clause or a SET UNTIL TIME statement.

This event populates the cell hash (cellhash#) and nothing else. Normally, Oracle will reset or clear any parameters that are not passed by the current wait event, but, occasionally, values populated by prior wait events get through. The obj# parameter is one that could be populated in a 10046 trace file that records this event. In such cases, a non-negative obj# is meaningless. Oracle will populate the obj# with a -1, to show it was cleared from a prior event.

Cell Smart Restore from Backup

This event logs wait time spent doing a restore with RMAN. Just like the prior event, Exadata offloads this processing to the storage cells, which, again, are best suited for such operations, having direct access to the storage.

This event actually relates to the cell smart file creation event; both events record time for formatting of empty data blocks and initialization operations related to file creation.

The only parameter populated by this event is, again, the cell hash (cellhash#).

Idle Class/Other Class

The five wait events in these classes are rarely used in a properly operating Exadata system. We haven't found them on the systems we manage, and it's likely you won't either. There is one exception to this, the cell flash unkeep event, which will be covered in its own section. The remainder of these events are uninformative with respect to the P1, P2, and P3 values provided in the V$SESSION_WAIT view. Table 7-3 lists the events you're not likely to see and a basic description of the parameters supplied to Oracle.

Table 7-3. Rarely Reported Cell Wait Events

Event	Description
Cell manager cancel work request	The information provided by this event is Sparse, as none of the parameters that could be supplied are populated in V$SESSION_WAIT. We have yet to see this event in a 10046 Trace.
Cell worker online completion	This appears to be a cell startup event. The only parameter supplied is cell hash (cellhash# in a 10046 trace, P1 in the V$SESSION_WAIT view). This is another wait event that we haven't seen reported.
Cell worker retry	Another wait event that populates only the cell hash (cellhash#) and nothing else.
Cell worker idle	No parameters are supplied by this event, and we have not seen it reported on any of the systems we manage.

Cell Smart Flash Unkeep

This event logs time waiting while Oracle flushes blocks out of the Smart Flash Cache, but it doesn't get triggered for objects using the Smart Flash Cache in the default FIFO manner. This event tracks wait time for objects intended to be kept in the Smart Flash Cache (using the STORAGE(FLASH_CACHE KEEP) parameter). Operations that trigger this event would be table drops and truncates. An additional event associated with this wait is enq: RO fast object reuse, as the operation that triggers this event also triggers the buffer cache cleanout. Truncating or dropping a table also requires removal of any cached data from that object, and, on Exadata, there are two separate caches to be maintained.

The only parameter supplied by this event is the cell hash (cellhash#), to identify which cell was accessed for the truncated or dropped operation. No other parameters in the WAIT event in a 10046 trace, or in the V$SESSION_WAIT view, are populated.

Things to Know

The wait interface, which has already been expanded over the last few Oracle releases, experiences another expansion with Exadata: the addition of cell-specific events, which, in some cases, replace existing events found on non-Exadata systems. New events have also been added to monitor new mechanisms specific to Exadata.

The cell smart table scan event records time against Smart Scans, making this event an important one with respect to Exadata or systems using Exadata storage. This event usually replaces the direct path read event, although you can still find direct-path read waits on an Exadata system when queries do not qualify for a Smart Scan.

The cell smart index scan event reports time waited for index fast full scans; no other index access path triggers this wait.

The cell single block physical read event is the Exadata equivalent of the db file sequential read event on non-Exadata systems. It is most often associated with index access operations and table access by index rowid operations, but any single-block access operation can trigger this wait. It is, in our opinion, more accurately named than its non-Exadata equivalent, as the blocks read are single blocks and not necessarily sequential.

The cell multiblock physical read event collects time for sequential multiblock reads and is the replacement for the db file scattered read event. Again, we feel the Exadata event is better named, as it indicates that sequential collections of data blocks are read. The db file scattered read event records time against both sequential and nonsequential reads in non-Exadata systems, so its name is somewhat confusing.

Exadata provides a new event, cell list of blocks read, to record time against nonsequential, or scattered, block reads. This event can also replace the db file scattered read event, because the old event, as mentioned previously, records time against all multiblock reads, sequential or not.

Data block preparation is offloaded to the storage cells in Exadata and, because of this, a new event, named cell smart file creation, has been added. The name is somewhat of a misnomer, as it doesn't necessarily refer to file creation (although that is one operation that can trigger this wait), but usually collects time against data block formatting/reformatting, to prepare for new data. Operations that trigger this event include deletes, updates, database file creation, and file autoextension.

The cell statistics gather event is one that we feel is miscategorized, as it has nothing to do with disk I/O operations. Recording time against access of various V$ and X$ tables/views, it may be more accurately considered a System I/O or other wait-class event.

RMAN also has waits specific to Exadata, as some of the RMAN operations are offloaded to the storage cells. The cell smart incremental backup event records wait time experienced by Incremental Level 1 backups. Because an Incremental Level 0 backup is actually a full backup and starting point for the next series of Level 1 incremental backups, it is not a backup that triggers this event.

The cell smart restore from backup event collects wait times experienced by RMAN when performing a database restore, as operations specific to this wait are offloaded to the storage cells. Because the storage cells are the only servers in an Exadata system having direct access to the storage, it makes sense to offload these two RMAN operations.

Exadata has, as one of the performance enhancements, the Smart Flash Cache. When tables/indexes are created with the STORAGE(FLASH_CACHE KEEP) directive, the cell smart flash unkeep event can be triggered when these objects are truncated or dropped. These operations also trigger buffer cache cleanup, so trace files reporting this event usually report the enq: RO fast object reuse wait as well.

■ ■ ■

## CHAPTER 8

Measuring Performance

Exadata is a huge leap forward, with respect to its architecture. Unlike traditional commodity hardware configurations, Exadata provides a matched set of hardware and software. However, it is running the same Oracle 11.2.0.3 you can install on any non-Exadata platform. Thus, the same basic performance rules apply; the difference is the additional functionality of Smart Scans, the Smart Flash Cache, and offloading, to name a few. Because the purpose of this book is to make you familiar with, and work knowledgeably on, Exadata, it is the Exadata-specific performance metrics we will be covering. Additionally, we will cover Exadata-related performance topics and relevant internals.

Exadata provides plenty of performance metrics to use. That's the good news. Unfortunately, Exadata provides plenty of performance metrics to use. That's the bad news. It is good to have a vast array of metrics to examine in the quest for performance; the downside of that is you can get so lost in the wealth of performance data, you forget what you are looking for. Knowing what to look for, how to tell when things are good, and, more important, when things are bad can be difficult. The key to monitoring performance is not looking at every metric available but choosing metrics wisely. Why you are choosing specific metrics and what values you should be seeing are much more important.

The end user doesn't care how many I/Os per second Exadata can provide; she measures performance in terms of response time. Basically speaking, the faster things go, the happier the end user will be. Addressing performance issues should be a process of monitoring and optimizing the response time. This is where the Oracle Wait interface becomes a very useful tool. These wait events are discussed in Chapter 7. Exadata also supplies other metrics to provide additional information that can allow you to further enhance performance. Data such as the number of bytes saved by a Smart Scan, the I/O avoided by use of a storage index, and Smart Flash Cache statistics provide keys to improving performance. This chapter will discuss such metrics, how to get the data, and what the numbers mean. We will also discuss monitoring and troubleshooting Exadata performance problems using this information.

Measure Twice, Cut Once

Before we dive into the Exadata performance metrics, we have to review some key pieces of the Exadata system. Whether or not a query or statement uses a Smart Scan, the database servers ask the storage cells to actually retrieve the requested data. When a Smart Scan is in use, the storage cells also assist in processing that data through column projection and predicate filtering. These processes involve the cells reading the data or index blocks, filtering the desired rows, and extracting only the columns of interest. Storage indexes also contribute to this process, by allowing the storage cells to bypass 1MB units of data that do not contain the column values of interest. From the database server perspective, the storage cells are black boxes from which the desired data is dispensed. These "black boxes" also pass back to the database servers metrics that record how much work those storage cells have performed. The storage cells themselves provide a rich palette of performance metrics, many of which are not passed back to the database servers. However, you will find sufficient information from the storage cells available at the database server level to troubleshoot many performance issues.

Smart Scans are the lifeblood of Exadata; they are key to achieving performance levels beyond common commodity hardware configurations. It is important that you understand the performance metrics for Smart Scans, and with that thought in mind, we will discuss, again, some aspects of them.

Smart Scans, Again

In Chapter 2 we discussed Smart Scans and offloading at length; we won't go into that level of detail in this chapter. We will discuss important aspects you should know, in order to properly analyze the supplied metrics to make an informed diagnosis of performance issues.

Smart Scans require direct-path reads and full-table scans, index fast full scans or index full scans. The first step in troubleshooting performance issues regarding Smart Scans is to see if one of the qualifying full scans was used. The execution plan will give you that information, so it's the logical place to begin. Going back to a previous example, we can see the qualifying step in the following plan:

```
SQL> select *
  2  from emp
  3  where empid = 7934;

    EMPID EMPNAME                                        DEPTNO
--------- ---------------------------------------- ----------
     7934 Smorthorper7934                                    15

Elapsed: 00:00:00.21

Execution Plan
----------------------------------------------------------
Plan hash value: 3956160932

--------------------------------------------------------------------------------
| Id  | Operation                  | Name | Rows  | Bytes | Cost (%CPU)| Time     |
--------------------------------------------------------------------------------
|   0 | SELECT STATEMENT           |      |     1 |    28 |  6361   (1)| 00:00:01 |
|*  1 |  TABLE ACCESS STORAGE FULL | EMP  |     1 |    28 |  6361   (1)| 00:00:01 |
--------------------------------------------------------------------------------

Predicate Information (identified by operation id):
---------------------------------------------------

   1 - storage("EMPID"=7934)
       filter("EMPID"=7934)

Statistics
----------------------------------------------------------
      1  recursive calls
      1  db block gets
  40185  consistent gets
  22594  physical reads
    168  redo size
    680  bytes sent via SQL*Net to client
    524  bytes received via SQL*Net from client
      2  SQL*Net roundtrips to/from client
      0  sorts (memory)
      0  sorts (disk)
      1  rows processed

SQL>
```

As we stated in Chapter 2, simply because STORAGE is in the plan step, that is not a guarantee that a Smart Scan was executed. You have to dig deeper and see if direct-path reads were used. Other criteria also apply before it can be determined if a Smart Scan was used, such as the presence of column-projection data in the plan output. Predicate filtering also can take place with a Smart Scan. Storage indexes can also provide benefit, by allowing Oracle to bypass 1MB data segments that do not contain the column values of interest. Notice in the supplied plan that the full-scan step includes the keyword STORAGE and that the predicate information includes a storage() entry. Again, these do not guarantee that a Smart Scan was executed, only that the statement *qualifies* for Smart Scan execution. The absence of these items in a query plan does, however, indicate that a Smart Scan cannot occur. You may also see plans where the STORAGE keyword is present but the storage() predicate information is missing, indicating that no predicate offload was executed. In such cases, you may find that the query still benefited from column projection.

It is possible to have all of the previously mentioned criteria in an execution plan and still not execute a Smart Scan. Why? Remember that Smart Scans require direct-path reads; if no direct-path reads are executed, then no Smart Scan will be executed. Direct-path reads occur any time parallel execution is used but can also occur serially, especially if the _serial_direct_read parameter is set to TRUE. It is necessary when investigating Smart Scan performance to check the execution plan and any metrics indicating direct-path reads may have been used. Such metrics were discussed in Chapter 2, and the associated wait events were discussed in Chapter 6. Both sources of information will be used to troubleshoot Smart Scan performance.

Performance Counters and Metrics

The V$SQL and GV$SQL views provide two metrics we have used to prove Smart Scan execution, io_cell_offload_eligible_bytes, and io_cell_offload_returned_bytes. These are used to compute the percentage of data not read because a Smart Scan was executed. We provided this script in Chapter 2, but it is good to look at it again and understand what it reports:

```
SQL> select sql_id,
  2  io_cell_offload_eligible_bytes qualifying,
  3  io_cell_offload_eligible_bytes - io_cell_offload_returned_bytes actual,
  4  round((((io_cell_offload_eligible_bytes -
     io_cell_offload_returned_bytes)/io_cell_offload_eligible_bytes)*100, 2) io_saved_pct,
  5  sql_text
  6  from v$sql
  7  where io_cell_offload_returned_bytes> 0
  8  and instr(sql_text, 'emp') > 0
  9  and parsing_schema_name = 'BING';

SQL_ID        QUALIFYING   ACTUAL IO_SAVED_PCT SQL_TEXT
------------- ---------- ---------- ------------ --------------------------------
gfjb8dpxvpuv6 185081856   42510928        22.97 select * from emp where empid = 7934

SQL>
```

As a review, the io_cell_offload_eligible_bytes column reports the bytes of data that *can* be offloaded to the storage cells during query execution. The io_cell_offload_returned_bytes column reports the number of bytes returned by the regular I/O path. The difference between these two values provides the bytes actually offloaded during query execution. Using these two metrics can prove that a Smart Scan was executed. Two other columns can also provide information on Smart Scan and storage index usage. These are cell physical IO bytes saved by storage index and cell physical IO interconnect bytes returned by smart scan. Covered in Chapter 3, cell physical IO bytes saved by storage index reports exactly what it says, the total bytes that weren't read during a Smart Scan because the storage index allowed Oracle to bypass those 1MB blocks. An example from Chapter 3 follows as a refresher:

```
SQL> select *
  2  from v$mystat
  3  where statistic# = (select statistic# from v$statname where name = 'cell physical IO bytes
     saved by storage index');

     SID STATISTIC#      VALUE
---------- ---------- ----------
    1107        247 1201201152

SQL>
```

This value is reported at the session level from V$MYSTAT, and it's necessary to remember that this statistic is cumulative for the duration of the session. Querying V$MYSTAT before and after query execution will provide a delta showing the bytes saved for that particular query.

The cell physical IO interconnect bytes returned by smart scan reports the actual bytes returned from a Smart Scan operation. V$SQLSTATS reports this value, along with two other values, physical_read_bytes and physical_write_bytes, which can be used to provide a Smart Scan "efficiency," for want of a better term. This topic is covered in more depth in Chapter 10, but be aware that this "efficiency" can exceed 100 percent when sorts or index access paths that don't qualify for Smart Scan execution are used.

Knowing what the statement was waiting on also provides information on Smart Scan execution. Direct-path reads usually indicate Smart Scan activity, but not always. LOBs, index-organized tables, index scans that are not full or fast full scans, along with table fetch by rowid, may also use direct-path reads but do not qualify for Smart Scans. Thus, even though storage access has been noted in the execution plan and direct-path read waits have been recorded, a Smart Scan may not be the access method used by Oracle to process the query or statement.

Exadata wait events that signal that Smart Scans were not used are cell multiblock physical read and cell single-block physical read. The cell multiblock physical read wait applies not only to tables but to LOBs where the chunk size is greater than the database block size and Securefile reads. When the chunk size is less than or equal to the database block size, cell single block physical reads will be used. As discussed in Chapter 7, the cell single block physical read can apply to index access paths, but because such waits do not occur during index full scans and index fast full scans, a Smart Scan was not executed.

Users care about time, with respect to response time, so the first area where performance tuning should begin is the Exadata wait interface. Seeing where time is being spent by queries and statements can help pinpoint areas of poor performance. Knowing where the time sinks are gives you initial direction in addressing such performance problems and can possibly prove that the database is not at fault.

Dynamic Counters

The V$SYSSTAT and V$SESSTAT views provide a wealth of dynamic performance counters to aid you in diagnosing performance issues. Depending on where the session is spending its time, these views can help pinpoint areas that may require attention. As an example, if Oracle is using considerable CPU resources, one possible avenue of attack would be to see how the logical reads count increases for a given session. V$SYSSTAT provides the following list of read-related counters:

```
SQL> select name, value
  2  from v$sysstat
  3  where name like '%read%'
  4  /
```

NAME	VALUE
session logical reads	82777757613
session logical reads in local numa group	0
session logical reads in remote numa group	0
physical read total IO requests	21591992
physical read total multi block requests	12063669
physical read requests optimized	3355758
physical read total bytes optimized	41508200448
physical read total bytes	11935356259328
logical read bytes from cache	669321109651456
physical reads	1456537556
physical reads cache	43060982
physical read flash cache hits	0
physical reads direct	1413476574
physical read IO requests	21382598
physical read bytes	11931955658752
recovery blocks read	0
recovery blocks read for lost write detection	0
physical reads direct temporary tablespace	26335818
DBWR thread checkpoint buffers written	11428910
recovery array reads	0
recovery array read time	0
physical reads cache prefetch	36901401
physical reads prefetch warmup	233120
physical reads retry corrupt	0
physical reads direct (lob)	14262
cold recycle reads	0
physical reads for flashback new	0
flashback cache read optimizations for block new	0
flashback direct read optimizations for block new	0
redo blocks read for recovery	0
redo k-bytes read for recovery	0
redo k-bytes read for terminal recovery	0
redo KB read	0
redo KB read (memory)	0
redo KB read for transport	0
redo KB read (memory) for transport	0
gc read wait time	373
gc read waits	5791
gc read wait failures	0
gc read wait timeouts	180
gc reader bypass grants	0
Number of read IOs issued	5714868
read-only violation count	0
Batched IO vector read count	1455
transaction tables consistent reads - undo records applied	262
transaction tables consistent read rollbacks	15
data blocks consistent reads - undo records applied	16126989
no work - consistent read gets	77857741416
cleanouts only - consistent read gets	19160349

```
rollbacks only - consistent read gets                        187199
cleanouts and rollbacks - consistent read gets              1563685
table scans (direct read)                                    441631
lob reads                                                   9246167
index fast full scans (direct read)                          558680
securefile direct read bytes                                      0
securefile direct read ops                                        0
securefile inode read time                                        0
cell flash cache read hits                                  3355758

58 rows selected.

SQL>
```

V$SYSSTAT provides a view into the system-wide statistics, so pinpointing problems with a particular session will be difficult using this view. V$SESSTAT provides session-level statistics that will be much more useful when a particular session is a problem. Looking at the non-zero statistics for SID 1141 in one of our databases, we get the following output:

```
SQL> select sn.name, ss.value
  2  from v$sesstat ss join v$statname sn on sn.statistic# = ss.statistic#
  3  and ss.sid in (select sid from v$session where status ='ACTIVE')
  4  and ss.value > 0
  5  and ss.sid=1141
  6  order by 1, 2
  7  /

NAME                                  VALUE
----------------------------------- ---------------
cell flash cache read hits               246424
cell physical IO interconnect bytes  4037787648
cluster wait time                             2
enqueue releases                         246444
enqueue requests                         246444
ges messages sent                           758
in call idle wait time                 13559183
logons cumulative                             1
logons current                                1
messages received                             4
messages sent                                34
non-idle wait count                     2902944
non-idle wait time                        57613
physical read requests optimized         246424
physical read total IO requests          246441
physical read total bytes            4037689344
physical read total bytes optimized  4037410816
physical write total IO requests              2
physical write total bytes                32768
session pga memory                      7841624
session pga memory max                  7841624
```

```
session uga memory                          180736
session uga memory max                      180736
user calls2

24 rows selected.

SQL>
```

There are many more statistics available for a given session; the query filtered out those with a 0 value.

When to Use Them, and How

Now that you know where to find useful performance metrics and wait statistics, the next step is knowing how and when to use them to diagnose performance issues. Despite all of the available statistics and metrics you can use to dig deep into performance issues, the main concern, and driving force, behind performance evaluation and tuning is time. Users measure performance in how long a task takes to complete once started, and all of the I/O statistics in the world won't mean much to most of them. The first stop on the journey to performance is through an AWR report for the period in question. AWR provides information you'll need to find problems and begin the diagnosis process.

AWR reports are generated from regularly occurring snapshots of performance metrics and wait-event timings. This provides a way to generate reports based on the changes recorded between snapshots. With the information provided in an AWR report, it's possible to find long-running SQL statements, along with their associated SQL_id, so plans can be generated and analyzed. Additionally, the V$SESSTAT, V$SYSTEM_EVENT, and V$SYSTAT views can be used to drill down into the wait events and metrics to possibly uncover the underlying reason for the performance degradation. It's good to look at the "SQL Ordered by Elapsed Time" report to see problem statements and queries. It's not simply a matter of elapsed time but of elapsed time and number of executions, as long elapsed times, coupled with a high execution count, make the per-execution time small. For example, if the elapsed time is 7734.27 seconds and the number of executions is 1281, the average elapsed time per execution is around 6 seconds, a reasonable time by most standards. If, on the other hand, the elapsed time is 3329.17 and the number of executions is 3, then the average elapsed time per execution is approximately 1110 seconds. An elapsed time per execution of that magnitude is worthy of closer examination. This is where the V$SESSTAT, V$SYSTEM_EVENT, and V$SYSTAT views can provide additional detail.

Another good source of performance information is the 10046 trace; either in its raw form or in a report formatted by the tkprof utility. We often prefer tkprof-formatted output, as it provides an execution plan and the relevant wait events and times.

■ **Note** Wait information in a tkprof report is only provided when the 10046 trace event is set at level 8 or higher. Lower levels won't capture the wait statistics.

Looking at a portion of a tkprof-formatted trace file where waits were provided, the following data is available:

```
*****************************************************************************

SQL ID: 23bfbq45y94fk Plan Hash: 2983102491

DELETE FROM APP_RULE_TMP_STAGE
WHERE
 TMP_RULE_NAME = :B1
```

call	count	cpu	elapsed	disk	query	current	rows
Parse	1	0.00	0.00	0	0	0	0
Execute	22	9.38	125.83	25833	4732	493424	346425
Fetch	0	0.00	0.00	0	0	0	0
total	23	9.38	125.83	25833	4732	493424	346425

```
Misses in library cache during parse: 1
Misses in library cache during execute: 4
Optimizer mode: ALL_ROWS
Parsing user id: 113     (recursive depth: 1)
Number of plan statistics captured: 1
```

```
Rows (1st) Rows (avg) Rows (max)  Row Source Operation
---------- ---------- ----------  ---------------------------------------------------
         0          0          0  DELETE  APP_RULE_TMP_STAGE (cr=420 pr=3692 pw=0 time=26339915 us)
     44721      44721      44721    INDEX RANGE SCAN APP_RULE_TMP_STG_IDX2 (cr=377 pr=353 pw=0
time=1603541 us cost=36 size=7291405 card=3583)(object id 196496)
```

```
Elapsed times include waiting on following events:
  Event waited on                         Times  Max. Wait  Total Waited
  ---------------------------------------  Waited ----------  ------------
  library cache lock                           1      0.00          0.00
  row cache lock                              18      0.00          0.00
  library cache pin                            1      0.00          0.00
  Disk file operations I/O                     6      0.00          0.00
  cell single block physical read          25783      1.30        114.29
  gc cr grant 2-way                         1587      0.00          0.18
  gc current grant 2-way                   14205      0.00          1.53
  gc current grant congested                  69      0.00          0.00
  gc cr grant congested                       14      0.00          0.00
  cell list of blocks physical read           20      0.31          0.48
  gc current multi block request              12      0.00          0.00
  log buffer space                             2      0.83          0.86
********************************************************************************
```

The wait of interest in this statement is cell single block physical read, given its total elapsed time, which is reported in seconds. The execution plan gives us a clue that this could be a wait to consider with the INDEX RANGE SCAN step. Remember that using an INDEX RANGE SCAN disqualifies the statement for Smart Scan execution. Notice also that no parallel execution is used. Given the elapsed time for the statement, it would qualify for Auto Degree of Parallelism. Using parallel execution would likely have improved performance for this statement, by spreading out the I/O across multiple parallel query slaves, reducing the elapsed wait time.

Let Me Explain

We have covered query plans in relation to Smart Scans in Chapter 2. A review of that material can always be helpful.

There are three plan steps that can indicate possible Smart Scan activity:

> TABLE ACCESS STORAGE FULL
>
> INDEX STORAGE FULL SCAN
>
> INDEX STORAGE FAST FULL SCAN

Earlier in this chapter, we mentioned that the word *STORAGE* in a plan step only indicates the possibility of Smart Scan execution, because without direct-path reads, Smart Scans won't be triggered. Execution plans, however, can give you a good starting point for performance tuning. The absence of STORAGE in execution plan steps indicates that Smart Scans did *not* occur. If you examine the plan for a given statement and find the keyword STORAGE in one of the table or index access steps, you can use data found in V$SQL and GV$SQL to verify Smart Scan execution. As mentioned in Chapter 2, there are at least two columns in these views providing information on how beneficial the Smart Scan was to the query or statement. The two columns we covered are io_cell_offload_eligible_bytes and io_cell_offload_returned_bytes. We also supplied a query that can generate the I/O savings percentage realized, which was illustrated again earlier in this chapter, in the section "Performance Counters and Metrics."

Performance Counter Reference

There are many counters updated by Exadata, but the complete list will not be discussed here. We have chosen to describe those counters that we feel are the most "interesting" in terms of performance and troubleshooting. It is very likely that you won't have to dig this deep to solve most performance issues, as the wait interface and the SQL monitor, discussed in the next section, are usually sufficient diagnostic tools. It is good to be aware of these counters, which is why we provide them. We will list them by name and describe their purpose and the mechanisms behind them, to give you some insight into how Exadata does what it does.

cell blocks helped by commit cache

The commit cache is part of the consistent-read mechanism Oracle has used for years, except that this is implemented at the storage-cell level rather than the database-server level. As a review, consistent reads in a standard Oracle database on non-Exadata hardware involve reconstructing the row as of the time the query began, by using available undo, based on the lock byte being set. Two conditions are possible during consistent-read processing, the first being that the commit SCN is lower than the snapshot SCN (established at the start time of the query). In this case, Oracle can determine that the data in the block needs no reconstruction and can continue processing other blocks.

The second condition is that the commit SCN is greater than the snapshot SCN, and in this case, Oracle knows a rollback is necessary to return consistent data and, on non-Exadata systems, does this through the available undo records. To complicate matters further, commits don't always clean out every block that they touch; a threshold is set to limit block cleanout activity immediately after a commit. (This limit is 10 percent of the block buffer cache; any blocks in excess of that limit must wait for the next transaction that touches them to get cleaned out.)

This leaves data blocks in a state where the status of the transaction has to be established. Normally on non-Exadata systems, the database layer performs this processing. Imagine having to send these blocks back from the storage cells to the database layer to perform standard consistent-read processing via the undo records. For a few blocks, this might work on Exadata, but the possibility exists that an extremely large number of blocks would have to be processed in this manner. Performance would be slow, robbing Exadata of one of its key features. Because the undo data is not available to the storage cells (the storage cells have no access to the database buffer cache) and no storage cell communicates with any of the other storage cells, another mechanism has to be employed.

Exadata employs an optimization where the need for the database layer to process consistent-read requests is minimized. It is called the commit cache. The commit cache keeps track of which transaction ids have committed and which have not. By extracting the transaction id from the Interested Transaction List (ITL) in the data block, the storage cells can access this commit cache and see whether or not the referenced transaction has been committed. If information for that particular transaction id is not available in the commit cache, the storage cell requests that status from the database layer. Once received, it adds it to the commit cache, so the remaining storage cells need not make the request again.

Each time a storage cell finds transaction information it needs in the commit cache, the cell blocks helped by commit cache counter is increased by 1. Monitoring this counter during periods of high transactional activity can be very helpful when the wait interface and SQL monitor don't provide enough data to diagnose a performance problem. Seeing this counter increase during Smart Scans indicates that delayed block cleanout is being performed by the cells, required because the volume of data in an insert, update, or delete is greater than the cleanout threshold. The commit cache was designed for this very purpose and keeps the storage cells from continuously communicating with the database layer. It also significantly reduces the logical I/O at the database layer during Smart Scans.

cell blocks helped by minscn optimization

Another Exadata-specific consistent-read optimization is the Minimum Active SCN optimization, which keeps track of the lowest SCN for still-active transactions. This improves consistent-read performance by allowing Exadata to compare the transaction SCNs from the ITL with the lowest SCN of the oldest still-active transaction in the database. The database layer sends this information to the cell at the start of a Smart Scan operation. When the commit SCN is lower than the Minimum Active SCN passed to the cells, unnecessary communication between the database layer and the cells is avoided. Any transaction SCN found in the block's ITL that is lower than the Minimum Active SCN is known by the storage cell to be committed. Each block that gets helped by this mechanism increments the cell blocks helped by minscn optimization counter. With reference to performance, this optimization also reduces checks to the commit cache discussed previously. Because this is Exadata, and most likely the databases run on it are RAC databases, the Minimum Active SCN is RAC-aware. Actually known as the Global Minimum SCN, the MMON processes in each instance keep track of this SCN and update each node's SGA. The X$TUMASCN table contains the current Global Minimum SCN for the RAC cluster, as follows:

```
SQL> select min_act_scn
  2  from x$ktumascn;

MIN_ACT_SCN
-----------
   20695870

SQL>
```

The cell blocks helped by minscn optimization counter isn't one you will use on a regular basis, if at all. However, it is a good place to start looking when Smart Scans are interrupted by frequently reverting to block I/O to get transaction information from the database layer.

cell commit cache queries

This counter is incremented each time a Smart Scan queries the cell commit cache for a transaction status. This is done once for each uncommitted transaction found per block when the MinActiveSCN optimization didn't apply to the transaction SCN, meaning the transaction SCN was greater than or equal to the Minimum Active SCN. This counter and the cell blocks helped by minscn counter are closely related.

cell blocks processed by cache layer

This is one of four "layer" statistics collected by Exadata, reporting on the activity of the listed layer of processing. This particular statistic reports on the number of blocks actually processed by the storage cells for Smart Scan operations. When the cells pass back blocks to the database servers (block I/O mode), this statistic doesn't get incremented. It does get incremented when the cells actually process the blocks during Smart Scans. When a cell opens a block for a consistent read, the block cache header is checked, to ensure that the correct block is being read and that it is valid and not corrupted. The cache-layer process (Kernel Cache Buffer management, or KCB) performs these functions and reports the cell blocks processed by cache layer count back to the database.

When the database layer processes regular block I/O, one of two statistics, consistent gets from cache and consistent gets from cache (fastpath), can be updated. The storage cells, through CELLSRV, perform only consistent gets, not current mode gets. All current mode gets that are recorded in the db block gets from cache or the db block gets from cache (fastpath) come from the database layer. Any counts recorded in the cell blocks processed by cache layer counter provide data on how many logical reads the storage cells performed, either system-wide from V$SYSSTAT or at the session level through V$SESSTAT.

It is not unusual to find both database-layer and cell-layer processing in a query-execution plan. Smaller tables won't likely qualify for a Smart Scan and, thus, will be processed by the database server. Multi-table joins using both small lookup tables and large processing tables can produce such plans.

cell blocks processed by data layer

While the previous counter registered cell cache read activity, this statistic records physical blocks read from tables or materialized views. The data layer module, Kernel Data Scan (KDS), extracts rows and columns from data blocks, passing them on for predicate filtering and column projection. When the storage cell can perform all of the necessary work without database block I/O, this counter is incremented.

When the session-level count from this statistic is added to the session-level cell blocks processed by index layer count, you can determine if the storage cell did all of the consistent reads. The sum of those counters will equal the session-level count for the cell blocks processed by cache layer counter, if every block processed was read at the storage layer. If the sum is a lower number, then the database layer performed regular block I/O processing. The difference should be the number of blocks processed by the database servers.

cell blocks processed by index layer

The storage cells can process index blocks in a similar manner as table and materialized view blocks. This statistic records the number of index blocks processed by a Smart Scan of B*Tree and bitmap index segments.

cell blocks processed by txn layer

Because this counter records the number of blocks processed by the transaction layer, it will be beneficial to know what goes on in that layer. Looking at a basic explanation of how Smart Scans process consistent reads, let's go through and see what occurs during this process.

The cache layer, through KCB, opens the block and then checks the header, the SCN of the last modification, and the cleanout status. The transaction layer gets this block if the SCN of the last modification isn't greater than the snapshot SCN, because it hasn't been modified since the query started. If the SCN of the last modification is greater than the snapshot SCN, this indicates the block has been modified since the query started, requiring a rollback to the snapshot SCN. This causes the block to be passed back to the database layer for block I/O processing.

Should the block pass the first test, it is passed to the transaction layer to be processed by the Kernel Transaction Read Consistency process (KTR), which uses the Minimum Active SCN and the commit cache, reducing the amount of communication with the database layer. The transaction layer then performs processing of the data block to extract the requested information, in concert with the data and index layers, which are used to perform the consistent reads at the storage-cell level.

cell flash cache read hits

This counter was discussed in Chapter 4, so we'll only briefly mention it here. This is another cumulative metric, at both the session level and the instance level. The easiest way to monitor this is with a script we have provided in Chapter 4. We provide it here as well, as monitoring the Smart Flash Cache is a key part of performance troubleshooting.

```
SQL> select statistic#, value
  2  from v$mystat
  3  where statistic# in (select statistic# from v$statname where name = 'cell flash cache read hits');

STATISTIC#       VALUE
----------  ----------
       605           1

SQL>
SQL> select count(*)
  2  from emp;

  COUNT(*)
----------
   7340032

SQL>
SQL> column   val new_value endval
SQL>
SQL> select statistic#, value val
  2  from v$mystat
  3  where statistic# in (select statistic# from v$statname where name = 'cell flash cache read hits');

STATISTIC#       VAL
----------  ----------
       605         857

SQL>
SQL>
SQL> select &endval - &beginval flash_hits
  2  from dual;

FLASH_HITS
----------
       856

SQL>
```

This counter also provides the number of physical I/O requests, because accessing the Smart Flash Cache is physical, not logical, I/O.

cell index scans

Each time a Smart Scan starts on a B*Tree or bitmap index segment, this counter is incremented. As this requires the use of the index fast full-scan step in the execution plan and also must use direct-path reads, both of these conditions must be met for this counter to be incremented.

A Smart Scan is a segment-level operation, so a query running serially, on a non-partitioned index, will increment once for each of the index segments accessed. For partitioned index segments accessed in parallel, this counter can increase once for each partitioned segment accessed by each parallel query slave. Because partition segments can differ in size, it is possible that, for a given partitioned index, the segments can be accessed by different methods. Larger segments are likely to be accessed by direct-path reads, and, thus, this counter will be incremented. Smaller partitions may not trigger direct-path reads, and in those cases, Smart Scans won't be executed and the counter value won't increase.

cell IO uncompressed bytes

If you are not using compression, you won't see this statistic change, as it's only incremented when Smart Scan compression offloading occurs. This statistic reports the actual uncompressed size of the compressed data. If, for example, you have 10MB of compressed data that would be 20MB when uncompressed, the cell IO uncompressed bytes counter would increment by 20MB when that data is offloaded. The physical read total bytes counter would increment by 10MB, because that is the segment size. It isn't a problem to see the cell IO uncompressed bytes counter increase at a faster rate than the physical read total bytes counter, because, as noted, the physical read total bytes counter increments according to the segment size read, and the cell IO uncompressed bytes counter reports the total uncompressed bytes processed.

cell num fast response sessions

Oracle can elect to defer a full Smart Scan execution by choosing to perform a few block I/O operations at the outset, in an attempt to satisfy a query. FIRST_ROWS, FIRST_ROWS_n, and where rownum queries trigger this behavior, and when Oracle decides to not immediately execute a Smart Scan, this counter is incremented. To improve the efficiency and speed of queries, Oracle can avoid setting up a Smart Scan, in favor of a few block I/O operations, to satisfy a query. This counter reports how many times Oracle has done that since the instance was started. Just because this counter was incremented doesn't mean that a full Smart Scan wasn't executed, simply that Oracle tried to do as little work as possible to return the desired results.

cell num fast response sessions continuing to smart scan

After Oracle decides to defer running a Smart Scan to reduce the possible work done, it may be decided that to return the correct results to the calling session, a Smart Scan must be executed. When that switch is made, this counter is incremented. Because this occurs after Oracle initially decides to not run a full Smart Scan, the same triggering conditions apply—FIRST_ROWS, FIRST_ROWS_n, and where rownum queries are being run. Also, when this statistic is incremented, you may notice some db file sequential read waits. Even though most reads of this nature are reported as cell single block physical read wait events, the older named event can still be incremented on Exadata.

cell num smart IO sessions using passthru mode due to _____

There are three of these counters, where _____ can be either user, CELLSRV, or time zone. These counters indicate how many times a Smart Scan was initiated but converted to regular block I/O mode. When this happens, the blocks are passed through to the database servers and bypass cell processing. Smart Scan is actually reading the blocks but doing no local cell processing on them, sending them on to the database server for processing. Unless there are memory issues on the cells, you shouldn't see these counters increase, as pass-through processing shouldn't be occurring. If these counters start incrementing, it is a good sign that there are issues at the storage-cell level that need to be investigated.

cell physical IO bytes sent directly to DB node to balance CPU usage

This counter records how many times the cell CPU usage was so high that Oracle chose to fall back to pass-through mode, making the database servers perform regular block I/O to reduce the CPU load on the storage cells. Normally, you shouldn't see this counter increase. Again, if it does start incrementing, it's a sign of problems at the storage-cell level that have to be diagnosed. In older versions of Exadata, this counter was named cell physical IO bytes pushed back due to excessive CPU on cell.

chained rows processed by cell

Chained rows can be a problem in any database but especially so in Exadata, where disk groups are striped across all available disks and accessed by every available storage cell. In a non-Exadata database not using ASM, a chained or continued row will be in another block but will likely be on the same disk as the head of the chain. With ASM, and Exadata, the next piece of the row could be on another disk accessed by another storage cell. Remember that the storage cells do not communicate with each other, so when Oracle encounters a chained row, a Smart Scan will fall back to regular block I/O at the database layer, so the chained row can be processed. This is more efficient for chained-row processing, but it does slow down Smart Scans. The more chained rows there are, the slower the Smart Scan will be. If a Smart Scan can get the data it needs from the head row piece, then the Smart Scan won't lose any speed, and processing will appear to flow as it normally does. Should Oracle need to access any other piece of that chained row, then regular block I/O will be necessary, slowing down the Smart Scan.

This statistic, chained rows processed by cell, reports on the chained rows that were processed within a storage cell, that is, where the row pieces (or at least the ones Oracle needed to return results) are located within the storage accessed by a given storage cell. This is known as inter-block chaining, where the row piece is located in the same data block as the head row. This is a special case of row chaining for rows with more than 255 columns. The next piece is in the same block as the head and can be fetched with no additional effort.

chained rows rejected by cell

This counter records the chained rows where the next piece is not in the same block or cell, as described in the previous section. This statistic is incremented in, apparently, special cases, as we have not seen it incremented very often in the systems we manage. When this is incremented, the Smart Scan falls back to regular block I/O to process the row.

chained rows skipped by cell

This is the statistic most often incremented when a Smart Scan has to revert to regular block I/O. Again, it's incremented when a chained row is found and the remaining pieces reside across the entire storage stripe, spanning storage cells in the process. It isn't clear when the previous counter or this counter should be incremented in such situations. We have found that this counter is most often incremented when Smart Scans revert to regular block I/O to process chained rows.

SQL Statement Performance

It is important to know where an SQL statement spends its time during execution. VSQL, VSQL_MONITOR, V$SQL_PLAN_MONITOR, and V$ACTIVE_SESSION_HISTORY are good views to use to analyze SQL statement performance. An example using V$SQL follows, showing how the query benefited from Smart Scan optimizations:

```
SQL>select  sql_id,
  2  io_cell_offload_eligible_bytes qualifying,
  3  io_cell_offload_eligible_bytes - io_cell_offload_returned_bytes actual,
  4  round(((io_cell_offload_eligible_bytes -
     io_cell_offload_returned_bytes)/io_cell_offload_eligible_bytes)*100, 2) io_saved_pct,
  5  sql_text
  6  from v$sql
  7  where io_cell_offload_returned_bytes> 0
  8  and instr(sql_text, 'emp') > 0
  9  and parsing_schema_name = 'BING';
```

```
SQL_ID          QUALIFYING    ACTUAL  IO_SAVED_PCT SQL_TEXT
-------------   ----------  ----------  ------------ ------------------------------------
gfjb8dpxvpuv6   185081856   42510928        22.97 select * from emp where empid = 7934

SQL>
```

Note the following columns used from V$SQL:

```
io_cell_offload_eligible_bytes
io_cell_offload_returned_bytes
```

These two columns tell you how many bytes qualified for offload and how many bytes were actually returned as a result of Smart Scan offloading. The query provided computes the I/O bytes saved as a percentage of the total eligible bytes, so you can see how efficient the Smart Scan execution was for the query in question.

Things to Know

The intent of this chapter was not an exhaustive performance-tuning reference for Exadata, but, rather, an overview of what metrics and counters are available, what they mean, and when you should consider using them.

The cell metrics provide insight into statement performance and how Exadata executes statements. Dynamic counters such as cell blocks processed by data layer and cell blocks processed by index layer show how efficient the storage cells are in their processing. These counters are incremented every time a storage cell can complete data-layer and index-layer processing without passing data back to the database layer. Two reasons for the cells to pass data back to the database servers are consistent-read processing requiring undo blocks (regular block I/O) and chained-row processing where the chained pieces span storage cells. While the first condition can't be controlled entirely (transactions can be so large as to exceed the automatic block-cleaning threshold), the second, chained rows, can be addressed and possibly corrected.

The cell num fast response sessions and cell num fast response sessions continuing to smart scan counters reveal the number of times Oracle chose to defer a Smart Scan in favor of regular block I/O as an attempt to return the requested data with a minimum of work (the first listed counter) and how many times Oracle actually started a Smart Scan after the fast response session failed to return the requested data. These can give you insight into the nature of the statements submitted to your Exadata databases, by showing how often Smart Scans were averted because a small regular block I/O operation returned the requested data.

V$SQL also provides data that can be used to determine statement efficiency in the io_cell_offload_eligible_bytes and io_cell_offload_returned_bytes columns. These two columns can be used to calculate the percentage savings effected by a Smart Scan for a given query.

CHAPTER 9

Storage Cell Monitoring

By now, we've covered Exadata architecture enough for you to know that the storage cells are independent of the database servers and provide their own metrics and counters. Since the database servers don't directly communicate with the storage, it's up to the storage cells to provide the database servers with the requested data. To help with that task, the storage cells have their own CPUs and memory, which provide additional resources to assist in the processing of data. They also have their own O/S-level user accounts, two of which we will concern ourselves with in this chapter.

The accounts of interest are celladmin and cellmonitor, and the nature of the task determines which of the two accounts you will use. As you could probably guess, the cellmonitor account can access the counters and metrics but cannot perform any administrative tasks. The celladmin account, too, can access the metrics and counters but also has administrative privileges to start and stop all cell services. Accessing the storage cells is the only way to truly monitor cell performance and diagnose cell-related performance issues.

Talking to the Storage Cells

Communicating with the storage cells will require logging in to the storage cells, and Exadata provides two specialized accounts for that purpose. The first account we will discuss is the cellmonitor account, an account capable of accessing cells' performance metrics and counters. The cellmonitor account is a restricted account on the storage servers, having access only to its home directory and limited executable commands. The second account we will cover is celladmin, an administrative account with far more privilege and access to the storage cells at the operating-system level. Although the database servers do not directly communicate with the storage devices, it is possible to use ssh to log in to each available storage cell from any database server in the Exadata system, to check performance metrics.

■ **Note** As the storage servers are running a Linux kernel, the "root" account also exists on each available storage cell, and user equivalence (the ability to log in without a password) is configured for all servers in the Exadata system for that account. Unless you are a database machine administrator (DMA), you won't likely be granted "root" privileges. For enterprises where "root" access is associated with the system administrator (SA), the DBA will usually have access to both the celladmin and cellmonitor user accounts and their passwords. We will proceed with this chapter using the basic SA/DBA separation of duties.

Where Shall I Go?

The names and IP addresses of the available storage servers can be found in the /etc/hosts file on any of the database servers in the Exadata system. An example of how these entries would appear in the /etc/hosts file follows.

```
### CELL Node Private Interface details
123.456.789.3    myexa1cel01-priv.mydomain.com        myexa1cel01-priv
123.456.789.4    myexa1cel02-priv.mydomain.com        myexa1cel02-priv
123.456.789.5    myexa1cel03-priv.mydomain.com        myexa1cel03-priv
123.456.789.6    myexa1cel04-priv.mydomain.com        myexa1cel04-priv
123.456.789.7    myexa1cel05-priv.mydomain.com        myexa1cel05-priv
123.456.789.8    myexa1cel06-priv.mydomain.com        myexa1cel06-priv
123.456.789.9    myexa1cel07-priv.mydomain.com        myexa1cel07-priv
```

A simple ssh command connects you to one of the available storage cells as cellmonitor.

```
ssh cellmonitor@myexa1cel04-priv.mydomain.com
```

Unless you have passwordless ssh configured, a password will be required.

```
cellmonitor@myexa1cel04-priv.mydomain.com's password:
[cellmonitor@myexa1cel04 ~]$
```

You are now connected to storage cell 4, using the cellmonitor account. Connecting to the remaining storage cells uses the same procedure, just a different cell name. The available commands are the same on all storage cells, but we will provide examples from only one cell, to avoid possible confusion.

What Shall I Do?

The goal is to monitor and manage the storage cells, so that areas such as the Smart Flash Cache and Smart Scans are functioning normally. Examining the metrics available to both accounts is necessary, to ensure that Exadata is performing at its peak and no hardware/firmware/configuration errors are causing problems for the end users.

What's in a Name?

The cell metric names reported by cellsrvstat are fairly verbose, so they should not be difficult to understand. For example, the Smart I/O metrics have, in our estimation, clear and descriptive names.

```
Number of active smart IO sessions
High water mark of smart IO sessions
Number of completed smart IO sessions
Smart IO offload efficiency (percentage)
Size of IO avoided due to storage index (KB)
Current smart IO to be issued (KB)
Total smart IO to be issued (KB)
Current smart IO in IO (KB)
Total smart IO in IO (KB)
Current smart IO being cached in flash (KB)
Total smart IO being cached in flash (KB)
Current smart IO with IO completed (KB)
```

```
Total smart IO with IO completed (KB)
Current smart IO being filtered (KB)
Total smart IO being filtered (KB)
Current smart IO filtering completed (KB)
Total smart IO filtering completed (KB)
Current smart IO filtered size (KB)
Total smart IO filtered (KB)
Total cpu passthru output IO size (KB)
Total passthru output IO size (KB)
Current smart IO with results in send (KB)
Total smart IO with results in send (KB)
Current smart IO filtered in send (KB)
Total smart IO filtered in send (KB)
Total smart IO read from flash (KB)
Total smart IO initiated flash population (KB)
Total smart IO read from hard disk (KB)
Total smart IO writes (fcre) to hard disk (KB)
Number of smart IO requests < 512KB
Number of smart IO requests >= 512KB and < 1MB
Number of smart IO requests >= 1MB and < 2MB
Number of smart IO requests >= 2MB and < 4MB
Number of smart IO requests >= 4MB and < 8MB
Number of smart IO requests >= 8MB
Number of times smart IO buffer reserve failures
Number of times smart IO request misses
Number of times IO for smart IO not allowed to be issued
Number of times smart IO prefetch limit was reached
Number of times smart scan used unoptimized mode
Number of times smart fcre used unoptimized mode
Number of times smart backup used unoptimized mode
```

Such metrics make it an easy task to evaluate, for example, Smart I/O performance, as none of the metrics uses unclear abbreviations or names that may not accurately reflect the nature of the statistics reported.

Output from the cellcli interface can be difficult to read without the DETAIL keyword. This is why we prefer to use DETAIL, unless we are looking for specific metrics and want an abbreviated list of attributes. Both versions of the output produced from cellcli are provided in the next section.

Monitoring Basics
As cellmonitor

Available to you when connected as cellmonitor is CellCLI, the command-line interface to monitor the storage cell. A complete list of commands can be generated by typing help at the CellCLI> prompt.

```
[cellmonitor@myexa1cel04 ~]$ cellcli
CellCLI: Release 11.2.3.2.1 - Production on Wed Aug 07 13:19:59 CDT 2013

Copyright (c) 2007, 2012, Oracle.  All rights reserved.
Cell Efficiency Ratio: 234
```

```
CellCLI> help

HELP [topic]
   Available Topics:
        ALTER
        ALTER ALERTHISTORY
        ALTER CELL
        ALTER CELLDISK
        ALTER GRIDDISK
        ALTER IBPORT
        ALTER IORMPLAN
        ALTER LUN
        ALTER PHYSICALDISK
        ALTER QUARANTINE
        ALTER THRESHOLD
        ASSIGN KEY
        CALIBRATE
        CREATE
        CREATE CELL
        CREATE CELLDISK
        CREATE FLASHCACHE
        CREATE FLASHLOG
        CREATE GRIDDISK
        CREATE KEY
        CREATE QUARANTINE
        CREATE THRESHOLD
        DESCRIBE
        DROP
        DROP ALERTHISTORY
        DROP CELL
        DROP CELLDISK
        DROP FLASHCACHE
        DROP FLASHLOG
        DROP GRIDDISK
        DROP QUARANTINE
        DROP THRESHOLD
        EXPORT CELLDISK
        IMPORT CELLDISK
        LIST
        LIST ACTIVEREQUEST
        LIST ALERTDEFINITION
        LIST ALERTHISTORY
        LIST CELL
        LIST CELLDISK
        LIST FLASHCACHE
        LIST FLASHCACHECONTENT
        LIST FLASHLOG
        LIST GRIDDISK
        LIST IBPORT
        LIST IORMPLAN
        LIST KEY
```

```
        LIST LUN
        LIST METRICCURRENT
        LIST METRICDEFINITION
        LIST METRICHISTORY
        LIST PHYSICALDISK
        LIST QUARANTINE
        LIST THRESHOLD
        SET
        SPOOL
        START

CellCLI>
```

Because you are connected as cellmonitor, administrative commands such as ALTER, ASSIGN, CALIBRATE, DROP, EXPORT, and IMPORT are not available. These are reserved for the celladmin user account. DESCRIBE, LIST, and SET are available, as well as SPOOL, to send output to a file.

So what can you do as cellmonitor? You can perform monitoring tasks to ensure the cell is functioning properly. Note the long list of LIST commands. They are there to report on the important areas of storage cell operation, including the Smart Flash Cache. We'll start out by looking at the Smart Flash Cache.

```
CellCLI> list flashcache attributes all
        myexa1cel04_FLASHCACHE
FD_08_myexa1cel04,FD_10_myexa1cel04,FD_00_myexa1cel04,FD_12_myexa1cel04,FD_03_myexa1cel04,FD_02_
myexa1cel04,FD_05_myexa1cel04,FD_01_myexa1cel04,FD_13_myexa1cel04,FD_04_myexa1cel04,FD_11_myexa1
cel04,FD_15_myexa1cel04,FD_07_myexa1cel04,FD_14_myexa1cel04,FD_09_myexa1cel04,FD_06_myexa1cel04
2013-07-09T17:33:53-05:00                1488.75G        7af2354f-1e3b-4932-b2be-4c57a1c03f33
1488.75G        normal

CellCLI>
```

The LIST FLASHCACHE ATTRIBUTES ALL command returns values for all of the available attributes but puts the output in a form that can be difficult to read. You can narrow down the list and only report on selected attributes.

```
CellCLI> list flashcache attributes name, degradedCelldisks, effectiveCacheSize
        myexa1cel04_FLASHCACHE        1488.75G

CellCLI>
```

Notice that the attribute names are not included in the output for any of the LIST FLASHCACHE ATTRIBUTES statements. You can use the DESCRIBE command to provide the attribute names, as follows:

```
CellCLI> describe flashcache
        name
        cellDisk
        creationTime
        degradedCelldisks
        effectiveCacheSize
        id
        size
        status

CellCLI>
```

You can also get a more user-friendly output by using the LIST FLASHCACHE DETAIL command, as follows:

```
CellCLI> list flashcache detail
         name:                 myexa1cel04_FLASHCACHE
         cellDisk:
FD_08_myexa1cel04,FD_10_myexa1cel04,FD_00_myexa1cel04,FD_12_myexa1cel04,FD_03_myexa1cel04,FD_02_
myexa1cel04,FD_05_myexa1cel04,FD_01_myexa1cel04,FD_13_myexa1cel04,FD_04_myexa1cel04,FD_11_myexa1
cel04,FD_15_myexa1cel04,FD_07_myexa1cel04,FD_14_myexa1cel04,FD_09_myexa1cel04,FD_06_myexa1cel04
         creationTime:         2013-07-09T17:33:53-05:00
         degradedCelldisks:
         effectiveCacheSize:   1488.75G
         id:                   7af2354f-1e3b-4932-b2be-4c57a1c03f33
         size:                 1488.75G
         status:               normal
CellCLI>
```

The output is formatted at one line per attribute, with the names provided, so you know which attribute has what value. Looking at the attributes, the size is reported, and it's less than the 1600GB the Smart Flash Cache has in total. This is not a problem, since Flash Log is also configured from the Smart Flash Cache storage and consumes 512MB of the total cache size. Flash Log enables Oracle to write redo to both the redo logfiles and the flash storage, to speed up transaction processing. The writes that complete first signal Oracle that the transaction has been successfully recorded in the redo stream. This allows for faster transaction time and higher throughput, because Oracle isn't waiting on the redo log writes. You can report on the Flash Log just as you can the flash cache.

```
CellCLI> list flashlog detail
         name:                 myexa1cel04_FLASHLOG
         cellDisk:
FD_14_myexa1cel04,FD_05_myexa1cel04,FD_00_myexa1cel04,FD_01_myexa1cel04,FD_04_myexa1cel04,FD_07_
myexa1cel04,FD_09_odevx1cel04,FD_02_myexa1cel04,FD_08_myexa1cel04,FD_03_myexa1cel04,FD_15_
myexa1cel04,FD_12_myexa1cel04,FD_11_myexa1cel04,FD_06_myexa1cel04,FD_10_myexa1cel 04,FD_13_
myexa1cel04
         creationTime:         2013-07-09T17:33:31-05:00
         degradedCelldisks:
         effectiveSize:        512M
         efficiency:           100.0
         id:                   7eb480f9-b94a-4493-bfca-3ba00b6618bb
         size:                 512M
         status:               normal

CellCLI>
```

The total size reported between the Smart Flash Cache and the Flash Log for this cell is 1489.25GB, which is still less than the 1600GB allocated to the cache. Like physical disks, the "disks" used in the Smart Flash Cache also have to reserve space for operating-system management tasks, such as inode lists and the like. There is no need to worry, as the allocated space is more than enough to provide excellent performance from the Smart Flash Cache. Should the size be less than 1488.75GB, this is an indication that one or more of the flash disks have problems. We will cover that issue in a later section using the celladmin account.

You can also list details about the grid disks, the physical drives configured in the storage tier. LIST GRIDDISK ATTRIBUTES name, size reports the following output:

```
CellCLI> list griddisk attributes name, size;
         DATA_MYEXA1_CD_00_Myexa1cel04    2208G
```

```
        DATA_MYEXA1_CD_01_Myexa1cel04      2208G
        DATA_MYEXA1_CD_02_Myexa1cel04      2208G
...
        DBFS_DG_CD_02_Myexa1cel04          33.796875G
        DBFS_DG_CD_03_Myexa1cel04          33.796875G
        DBFS_DG_CD_04_Myexa1cel04          33.796875G
...
        RECO_MYEXA1_CD_00_Myexa1cel04      552.109375G
        RECO_MYEXA1_CD_01_Myexa1cel04      552.109375G
        RECO_MYEXA1_CD_02_Myexa1cel04      552.109375G
...
        RECO_MYEXA1_CD_11_Myexa1cel04      552.109375G

CellCLI>
```

The disk group name is part of the disk name, making it fairly easy to see the space, per disk, for each of the disk groups. More detailed information is available using LIST GRIDDISK DETAIL; a partial report follows:

```
CellCLI> list griddisk detail
        name:                   DATA_MYEXA1_CD_00_Myexa1cel04
        asmDiskgroupName:       DATA_MYEXA1
        asmDiskName:            DATA_MYEXA1_CD_00_MYEXA1CEL04
        asmFailGroupName:       MYEXA1CEL04
        availableTo:
        cachingPolicy:          default
        cellDisk:               CD_00_Myexa1cel04
        comment:
        creationTime:           2013-07-09T17:36:41-05:00
        diskType:               HardDisk
        errorCount:             0
        id:                     aa946f1e-f7c4-4fee-8660-4c69c830ef59
        offset:                 32M
        size:                   2208G
        status:                 active

Myexa1celMYEXA1CELMYEXA1CELMyexa1celMyexa1celMYEXA1CELMYEXA1CELMyexa1celMyexa1celMYEXA1CELMYEXA1
CELMyexa1celMyexa1celMYEXA1CELMYEXA1CELMyexa1celMyexa1celMYEXA1CELMYEXA1CELMyexa1celMyexa1celMYE
XA1CELMYEXA1CELMyexa1cel...

CellCLI>
```

This is a lot of information to process, and you don't really need all of it to monitor the grid disks. One benefit to using the DETAIL option to any of the LIST commands is that the entire attribute list is provided in an attribute: value output format. Some of the LIST commands produce a long list of output (like the LIST GRIDDISK DETAIL example), so you might want to wait until the output stops scrolling to take note of the available attributes. With an attribute list in hand, you can then report on attributes that interest you. For example, looking at the output from LIST GRIDDISK ATTRIBUTES name, celldisk, offset, size, status, a much more manageable and readable report is generated.

```
CellCLI> LIST GRIDDISK ATTRIBUTES name, celldisk, offset, size, status
        DATA_MYEXA1_CD_00_myexa1celMyexa1cel04    CD_00_myexa1celMyexa1cel04    32M
2208G           active
```

```
        DATA_MYEXA1_CD_01_myexa1celMyexa1cel04      CD_01_myexa1celMyexa1cel04      32M
2208G          active
myexa1celmyexa1celmyexa1celmyexa1celmyexa1celmyexa1celmyexa1celmyexa1celmyexa1celmyexa1
celmyexa1celmyexa1celmyexa1celmyexa1celmyexa1celmyexa1celmyexa1celmyexa1celmyexa1celmye
xa1cel...
        DBFS_DG_CD_03_myexa1celMyexa1cel04          CD_03_myexa1celMyexa1cel04      2760.15625G
33.796875G     active
        DBFS_DG_CD_04_myexa1celMyexa1cel04          CD_04_myexa1celMyexa1cel04      2760.15625G
33.796875G     active
        DBFS_DG_CD_05_myexa1celMyexa1cel04          CD_05_myexa1celMyexa1cel04      2760.15625G
33.796875G     active
myexa1celmyexa1celmyexa1celmyexa1celmyexa1celmyexa1celmyexa1celmyexa1celmyexa1celmyexa1
celmyexa1cel...
        RECO_MYEXA1_CD_00_myexa1celMyexa1cel04      CD_00_myexa1celMyexa1cel04      2208.046875G
552.109375G    active
        RECO_MYEXA1_CD_01_myexa1celMyexa1cel04      CD_01_myexa1celMyexa1cel04      2208.046875G
552.109375G    active
        RECO_MYEXA1_CD_02_myexa1celMyexa1cel04      CD_02_myexa1celMyexa1cel04      2208.046875G
552.109375G    active
myexa1celmyexa1celmyexa1celmyexa1celmyexa1celmyexa1celmyexa1celmyexa1celmyexa1celmyexa1
celmyexa1celmyexa1celmyexa1celmyexa1celmyexa1celmyexa1celmyexa1cel...

CellCLI>
```

During Exadata configuration, the disks are divided into slices, based on data found in the /opt/oracle.SupportTools/onecommand/onecommand.params file. By default, the SizeArr variable is set to 2208GB, which is the size for the slice allocated for the data disk group. Other slice sizes are derived from that initial setting. (It is possible to change the disk allocations; that process will be discussed in Chapter 11.) Each disk has 32MB configured for management processes and data, which explains the offset for the first available disk slice ASM can use. In the posted example, that first slice is allocated for the DATA_MYEXA1 disk group, and it's 2208GB in size. The next available slice is for the recovery disk group, and it's 565360MB in size. The final slice is for the DBFS disk group and provides 34608MB of storage. Each offset after the initial 32MB is the 32MB plus the size of the configured slice; it provides the "starting point" for each area of ASM configured storage on the disk.

The cellmonitor account is a good starting point for looking at the storage cells at the server level, but it's restricted, in that it's simply a monitoring account and provides no access to managing the cells. To dig deeper into the cells and provide additional statistics and metrics, you will have to use the celladmin account.

As celladmin

Connecting to the cells as celladmin is no different from connecting as cellmonitor; however, celladmin provides much more access to functionality and metrics. In addition to cellcli, the celladmin account can also access cellsrvstat, which can provide additional statistics and metrics not reported by cellcli.

When connected as celladmin, the cellcli interface provides the full list of functions provided earlier in this chapter. Since it is an administrative account, you can perform the following actions that cellmonitor cannot:

```
ALTER ALERTHISTORY
ALTER CELL
ALTER CELLDISK
ALTER GRIDDISK
ALTER IBPORT
ALTER IORMPLAN
```

```
ALTER LUN
ALTER PHYSICALDISK
ALTER QUARANTINE
ALTER THRESHOLD
ASSIGN KEY
CREATE CELL
CREATE CELLDISK
CREATE FLASHCACHE
CREATE FLASHLOG
CREATE GRIDDISK
CREATE KEY
CREATE QUARANTINE
CREATE THRESHOLD
DESCRIBE
DROP ALERTHISTORY
DROP CELL
DROP CELLDISK
DROP FLASHCACHE
DROP FLASHLOG
DROP GRIDDISK
DROP QUARANTINE
DROP THRESHOLD
EXPORT CELLDISK
IMPORT CELLDISK
```

Of the available metrics on the storage cells, the alert history is a good place to start looking for possible problems. Looking at the output from LIST ALERTHISTORY DETAIL, we see the following:

```
CellCLI> list alerthistory detail
        name:                  1_1
        alertMessage:          "Cell configuration check discovered the following problems:
Check Exadata configuration via ipconf utility Verifying of Exadata configuration file
/opt/oracle.cellos/cell.conf Error. Exadata configuration file not found
/opt/oracle.cellos/cell.conf [INFO] The ipconf check may generate a failure for temporary
inability to reach NTP or DNS server. You may ignore this alert, if the NTP or DNS servers are
valid and available. [INFO] You may ignore this alert, if the NTP or DNS servers are valid and
available. [INFO] As root user run /usr/local/bin/ipconf -verify -semantic to verify consistent
network configurations."
        alertSequenceID:       1
        alertShortName:        Software
        alertType:             Stateful
        beginTime:             2013-05-14T22:31:59-05:00
        endTime:               2013-06-20T11:36:18-05:00
        examinedBy:
        metricObjectName:      checkconfig
        notificationState:     0
        sequenceBeginTime:     2013-05-14T22:31:59-05:00
        severity:              critical
        alertAction:           "Correct the configuration problems. Then run cellcli command:
ALTER CELL VALIDATE CONFIGURATION   Verify that the new configuration is correct."
```

```
myexa1celmyexa1cel....

        name:                   4_1
        alertMessage:           "The disk controller battery is executing a learn cycle and may
temporarily enter WriteThrough Caching mode as part of the learn cycle. Disk write throughput
might be temporarily lower during this time. The flash drives are not affected. The battery
learn cycle is a normal maintenance activity that occurs quarterly and runs for approximately 1
to 12 hours.  Note that many learn cycles do not require entering WriteThrough caching mode.
When the disk controller cache returns to the normal WriteBack caching mode, an additional
informational alert will be sent.  Battery Serial Number : 6360  Battery Type       : iBBU08
Battery Temperature   : 35 C  Full Charge Capacity : 1342 mAh  Relative Charge      : 97 %
Ambient Temperature   : 22 C"
        alertSequenceID:        4
        alertShortName:         Hardware
        alertType:              Stateful
        beginTime:              2013-07-17T04:00:56-05:00
        endTime:                2013-07-17T10:09:16-05:00
        examinedBy:
        metricObjectName:       LUN_LEARN_CYCLE_ALERT
        notificationState:      0
        sequenceBeginTime:      2013-07-17T04:00:56-05:00
        severity:               info
        alertAction:            Informational.

        name:                   4_2
        alertMessage:           "All disk drives are in WriteBack caching mode.  Battery Serial
Number : 6360  Battery Type       : iBBU08  Battery Temperature   : 39 C  Full Charge
Capacity  : 1345 mAh  Relative Charge       : 52 %  Ambient Temperature   : 21 C"
        alertSequenceID:        4
        alertShortName:         Hardware
        alertType:              Stateful
        beginTime:              2013-07-17T10:09:16-05:00
        endTime:                2013-07-17T10:09:16-05:00
        examinedBy:
        metricObjectName:       LUN_LEARN_CYCLE_ALERT
        notificationState:      0
        sequenceBeginTime:      2013-07-17T04:00:56-05:00
        severity:               clear
        alertAction:            Informational.

CellCLI>
```

Here you can see the alert name, the message, the time frame for the alert, the severity, and the action, among
other attributes. Notice, also, the examinedBy attribute. This reports the user id or alias of the DBA or DMA who
examined the alert. Setting this attribute is a good idea, once the alert history has been read, as it allows other
DBAs or DMAs active on the system to know these alerts have been read. This is a fairly easy task to complete, as
it can be done for all alerts in the history or only on those that meet certain criteria, such as alertType='Stateful' or
alertShortName='Software.' You can set examinedBy for all alerts in the history, by using the following command:

```
CellCLI> alter alerthistory all examinedBy=dfitzj01
Alert 1_1 successfully altered
Alert 1_2 successfully altered
```

```
Alert 2 successfully altered
Alert 3_1 successfully altered
Alert 3_2 successfully altered
Alert 4_1 successfully altered
Alert 4_2 successfully altered

CellCLI>
```

If there are acknowledged and unacknowledged alerts, you will have to set examinedBy for the unacknowledged alerts by name; the WHERE clause is only available for the LIST command. You can find the unacknowledged alerts using the following command:

```
CellCLI> list alerthistory attributes name where examinedBy = ''
         1_1
         1_2
         2
         3_1
         3_2
         4_1
         4_2

CellCLI>
```

This gives you the names of all unacknowledged alerts. You can now update these by name, as follows:

```
CellCLI> alter alerthistory 1_1,1_2,2,3_1,3_2,4_1,4_2 examinedBy=dfitzj01
Alert 1_1 successfully altered
Alert 1_2 successfully altered
Alert 2 successfully altered
Alert 3_1 successfully altered
Alert 3_2 successfully altered
Alert 4_1 successfully altered
Alert 4_2 successfully altered

CellCLI>
```

In this case, all alerts were unacknowledged, but using ALL will cause you to lose any examinedBy values already set for acknowledged alerts. You should get into the habit of setting examinedBy for alerts as you read them, because exachk, the Exadata system validation utility, checks for unexamined alerts.

Some alerts notify you of actions you must take, such as firmware revisions for the storage servers. Others notify you of support issues Oracle has to address, such as faulty disks and PCIe cards. These alerts are informative and let you know what needs to be done, so you can decide who is to do the work. Actual hardware issues fall into the realm of Oracle Customer Support (OCS), and issues such as firmware upgrades can be done on-site by the DBA and/or SA.

Other metrics available to the celladmin user are generated by the **cellsrvstat** utility. Five categories of statistics are reported, with both cumulative and current delta values. Simply running the utility from the command prompt, without any additional parameters or qualifiers, produces the following output:

```
[celladmin@myexa1celMyexa1cel05 ~]$ cellsrvstat
===Current Time===                         Mon Aug 12 22:57:41 2013

== Input/Output related stats ==
Number of hard disk block IO read requests        0      670402182
Number of hard disk block IO write requests       0      682463432
```

Hard disk block IO reads (KB)	0	330820733723
Hard disk block IO writes (KB)	0	43747895151
Number of flash disk block IO read requests	0	1195284486
Number of flash disk block IO write requests	0	369512940
Flash disk block IO reads (KB)	0	10211102636
Flash disk block IO writes (KB)	0	6340334020
Number of disk IO errors	0	0
Number of reads from flash cache	0	1191640708
Number of writes to flash cache	0	67271278
Flash cache reads (KB)	0	10209174920
Flash cache writes (KB)	0	0
Number of flash cache IO errors	0	0
Size of eviction from flash cache (KB)	0	0
Number of outstanding large flash IOs	0	0
Number of latency threshold warnings during job	0	87255
Number of latency threshold warnings by checker	0	0
Number of latency threshold warnings for smart IO	0	0
Number of latency threshold warnings for redo log writes	0	1625
Current read block IO to be issued (KB)	0	0
Total read block IO to be issued (KB)	0	31352009247
Current write block IO to be issued (KB)	0	0
Total write block IO to be issued (KB)	0	42382773866
Current read blocks in IO (KB)	0	0
Total read block IO issued (KB)	0	31352009247
Current write blocks in IO (KB)	0	560
Total write block IO issued (KB)	0	42382773866
Current read block IO in network send (KB)	0	0
Total read block IO in network send (KB)	0	31352009247
Current write block IO in network send (KB)	0	0
Total write block IO in network send (KB)	0	42382773306
Current block IO being populated in flash (KB)	0	0
Total block IO KB populated in flash (KB)	0	1012902872

== Memory related stats ==		
SGA heap used - kgh statistics (KB)	0	1050259
SGA heap free - cellsrv statistics (KB)	0	209261
OS memory allocated to SGA (KB)	0	1259525
SGA heap used - cellsrv statistics - KB	0	1050264
OS memory allocated to PGA (KB)	0	21784
PGA heap used - cellsrv statistics (KB)	0	8723
OS memory allocated to cellsrv (KB)	0	22726298
Top 5 SGA consumers (KB)		
storidx:arrayRIDX	0	267676
storidx::arraySeqRIDX	0	267676
FlashCacheCtx	0	101609
Thread IO Lat Stats	0	98440
SUBHEAP Networ	0	81937
Top 5 SGA subheap consumers (KB)		
oracle_fp_init_scan:fplibCtx	0	206406797
oracle_fp_init_scan:fplibmd	0	170654364

```
            SageCacheInitScan : ctx                              0        13481725
            SageTxnInitScan : ctx                                0         8523711
            oracle_fp_reinit_md:fplibfmd                         0         2537710
Number of allocation failures in 512 bytes pool                 0               0
Number of allocation failures in 2KB pool                       0               0
Number of allocation failures in 4KB pool                       0               0
Number of allocation failures in 8KB pool                       0               0
Number of allocation failures in 16KB pool                      0               0
Number of allocation failures in 32KB pool                      0               0
Number of allocation failures in 64KB pool                      0               0
Number of allocation failures in 1MB pool                       0               0
Allocation hwm in 512 bytes pool                                0            1955
Allocation hwm in 2KB pool                                      0            1091
Allocation hwm in 4KB pool                                      0            2244
Allocation hwm in 8KB pool                                      0            2048
Allocation hwm in 16KB pool                                     0             963
Allocation hwm in 32KB pool                                     0            1068
Allocation hwm in 64KB pool                                     0            1621
Allocation hwm in 1MB pool                                      0            1725
Number of low memory threshold failures                         0               0
Number of no memory threshold failures                          0               0
Dynamic buffer allocation requests                              0               0
Dynamic buffer allocation failures                              0               0
Dynamic buffer allocation failures due to low mem               0               0
Dynamic buffer allocated size (KB)                              0               0
Dynamic buffer allocation hwm (KB)                              0               0

== Execution related stats ==
Incarnation number                                              0               6
Number of module version failures                               0               0
Number of threads working                                       0               1
Number of threads waiting for network                           0              19
Number of threads waiting for resource                          0               1
Number of threads waiting for a mutex                           0               0
Number of Jobs executed for each job type
            CacheGet                                             0      1485087768
            CachePut                                             0       680448625
            CloseDisk                                            0         9210374
            OpenDisk                                             0        11546018
            ProcessIoctl                                         0         4581873
            PredicateDiskRead                                    0        12992231
            PredicateDiskWrite                                   0           27125
            PredicateFilter                                      0        13896087
            PredicateCacheGet                                    0       139408284
            PredicateCachePut                                    0        79265728
            FlashCacheMetadataWrite                              0               0
            RemoteListenerJob                                    0               0
            FlashCacheResilveringTableUpdate                     0               0
            CellDiskMetadataPrepare                              0               0
```

```
SQL ids consuming the most CPU
        MYDB                                       0000000000000                82
        MYDB2                                      0000000000000                 1
        OKRA                                       1g3c5u9p6fpwr                15
        MYDB                                       bnrjgybpsu009                 2
        MYDB3                                      0000000000000                 1
END SQL ids consuming the most CPU

== Network related stats ==
Total bytes received from the network             0      969635109657
Total bytes transmitted to the network            0      122811940168
Total bytes retransmitted to the network          0                 0
Number of active sendports                        0               168
Hwm of active sendports                           0              1678
Number of active remote open infos                0              1975
HWM of remote open infos                          0              6472


== SmartIO related stats ==
Number of active smart IO sessions                0                 3
High water mark of smart IO sessions              0               186
Number of completed smart IO sessions             0           9006624
Smart IO offload efficiency (percentage)          0                 8
Size of IO avoided due to storage index (KB)      0       55764980592
Current smart IO to be issued (KB)                0              3072
Total smart IO to be issued (KB)                  0      366554357584
Current smart IO in IO (KB)                       0                 0
Total smart IO in IO (KB)                         0      365924276816
Current smart IO being cached in flash (KB)       0                 0
Total smart IO being cached in flash (KB)         0                 0
Current smart IO with IO completed (KB)           0              7776
Total smart IO with IO completed (KB)             0      375182446096
Current smart IO being filtered (KB)              0                 0
Total smart IO being filtered (KB)                0      375150215792
Current smart IO filtering completed (KB)         0             58848
Total smart IO filtering completed (KB)           0      365818995944
Current smart IO filtered size (KB)               0             10187
Total smart IO filtered (KB)                      0       29376577170
Total cpu passthru output IO size (KB)            0                 0
Total passthru output IO size (KB)                0                 0
Current smart IO with results in send (KB)        0                 0
Total smart IO with results in send (KB)          0      365498643760
Current smart IO filtered in send (KB)            0                 0
Total smart IO filtered in send (KB)              0       29283529373
Total smart IO read from flash (KB)               0                 0
Total smart IO initiated flash population (KB)    0                 0
Total smart IO read from hard disk (KB)           0      617450473088
Total smart IO writes (fcre) to hard disk (KB)    0        1365452520
Number of smart IO requests < 512KB               0          73658951
Number of smart IO requests >= 512KB and < 1MB    0          15965416
Number of smart IO requests >= 1MB and < 2MB      0           1146863
Number of smart IO requests >= 2MB and < 4MB      0          12189413
```

```
Number of smart IO requests >= 4MB and < 8MB          0        73111527
Number of smart IO requests >= 8MB                    0               0
Number of times smart IO buffer reserve failures      0               0
Number of times smart IO request misses               0          473544
Number of times IO for smart IO not allowed to be issued  0      30383972
Number of times smart IO prefetch limit was reached   0         5041176
Number of times smart scan used unoptimized mode      0               0
Number of times smart fcre used unoptimized mode      0               0
Number of times smart backup used unoptimized mode    0               0

[celladmin@myexa1celMyexa1cel05 ~]$
```

It's unnecessary to return all of that output if you're only monitoring the Smart I/O metrics. It's possible to monitor a single stat group, if you wish. As an example, we'll monitor the smartio stat group.

```
[celladmin@myexa1celMyexa1cel05 ~]$ cellsrvstat -stat_group=smartio

===Current Time===                          Sat Mar 16 15:29:33 2013

== SmartIO related stats ==
Number of active smart IO sessions                    0               2
High water mark of smart IO sessions                  0               3
Number of completed smart IO sessions                 0              18
Smart IO offload efficiency (percentage)              0               0
Size of IO avoided due to storage index (KB)          0       123950808
Current smart IO to be issued (KB)                10208           28576
Total smart IO to be issued (KB)               2652520      6416726632
Current smart IO in IO (KB)                       -4096           10176
Total smart IO in IO (KB)                      2642312      6416698056
Current smart IO being cached in flash (KB)           0               0
Total smart IO being cached in flash (KB)             0               0
Current smart IO with IO completed (KB)               0               0
Total smart IO with IO completed (KB)          2646408      6416688024
Current smart IO being filtered (KB)              -1024               0
Total smart IO being filtered (KB)             2646408      6416688024
Current smart IO filtering completed (KB)          1024            1024
Total smart IO filtering completed (KB)        2647432      6416687880
Current smart IO filtered size (KB)                   1               1
Total smart IO filtered (KB)                        394          966771
Total cpu passthru output IO size (KB)                0               0
Total passthru output IO size (KB)                    0               0
Current smart IO with results in send (KB)            0               0
Total smart IO with results in send (KB)       2646408      6416675592
Current smart IO filtered in send (KB)                0               0
Total smart IO filtered in send (KB)                393          966769
Total smart IO read from flash (KB)                   0               0
Total smart IO initiated flash population (KB)        0               0
Total smart IO read from hard disk (KB)        2642312      6292747248
Total smart IO writes (fcre) to hard disk (KB)        0               0
Number of smart IO requests < 512KB                  52          128995
Number of smart IO requests >= 512KB and < 1MB      260          604218
```

```
Number of smart IO requests >= 1MB and < 2MB             0            35
Number of smart IO requests >= 2MB and < 4MB           286        697848
Number of smart IO requests >= 4MB and < 8MB           299        723438
Number of smart IO requests >= 8MB                       0             0
Number of times smart IO buffer reserve failures        0             0
Number of times smart IO request misses                18         55773
Number of times IO for smart IO not allowed to be issued 0         10072
Number of times smart IO prefetch limit was reached      0             0
Number of times smart scan used unoptimized mode         0             0
Number of times smart fcre used unoptimized mode         0             0
Number of times smart backup used unoptimized mode       0             0

[celladmin@myexa1celMyexa1cel05 ~]$
```

The current statistics deltas are the first numbers displayed, and the cumulative statistics, from the cell start to the current time, are in the last numeric column. Because the first numbers listed are deltas, they can be negative between runs.

Seeing negative numbers shouldn't be a concern, but seeing several runs of 0's in the deltas should be a flag to check the queries, to see if they qualify for Smart Scans, and the storage cells, for alerts that could affect Smart Scan performance. We have seen systems where firmware mismatches caused Smart Scan issues when the affected disks were accessed. Upgrading the firmware solved the Smart Scan problems.

We use the following metrics when monitoring Smart I/O at the storage cell level:

```
Size of IO avoided due to storage index (KB)             0     123950808
Current smart IO to be issued (KB)                   10208         28576
Total smart IO read from hard disk (KB)            2642312    6292747248
Number of smart IO requests < 512KB                     52        128995
Number of smart IO requests >= 512KB and < 1MB         260        604218
Number of smart IO requests >= 1MB and < 2MB             0            35
Number of smart IO requests >= 2MB and < 4MB           286        697848
Number of smart IO requests >= 4MB and < 8MB           299        723438
Number of smart IO requests >= 8MB                       0             0
```

The size of IO avoided due to storage index (KB) provides you with another way to check for use of a storage index during a Smart Scan. You can see the current delta from the last two snapshots and the cumulative savings reported. current smart IO to be issued (KB) reports on the KB of data that qualify for Smart Scan processing as of the current snapshot, indicating that Smart Scans are active. The total smart IO read from hard disk metric reports the amount of data processed by Smart Scans that was read from the disks rather than from the cache. The number of smart IO requests metrics allow us to know the size ranges of the data requested by those scans and how many requests are generated for a given range, providing another measure of Smart Scan performance.

Sometimes execution plans get quarantined by Exadata. Usually, this is a result of an ORA-07445 error reported for O/S level failures. Additionally, the affected disk-storage region can be quarantined, which disables Smart Scans for that region, as well as for any queries using the quarantined plan or plans. The alert history will report such errors, and an example of such an alertMessage follows:

```
alertMessage: "ORA-7445: exception encountered: core dump
[kdzsBufferCUPiece()+35] [11] [0x000000000] [] [] []"
```

The following entry in the alert history shows an entry similar to the following:

```
alertMessage: "A SQL PLAN quarantine has been added. As a result,
Smart Scan is disabled for SQL statements with the quarantined SQL plan.
Quarantine id : 1 Quarantine type : SQL PLAN Quarantine reason :
 : 1dx1zzf5bwd07 SQL Plan details : {SQL_PLAN_HASH_VALUE=2181142203,
PLAN_LINE_ID=19} In addition, the following disk region has been
quarantined, and Smart Scan will be disabled for this region: Disk Region :
```

Such errors need to be addressed, but after they are corrected, the affected plans are still quarantined. To see which plans are quarantined, use the LIST QUARANTINE statement from cellcli. The command will display the following attributes for each quarantined plan:

```
name
cellsrvChecksum
clientPID
comment                   modifiable
crashReason
creationTime
dbUniqueID
dbUniqueName
incidentID
ioBytes
ioGridDisk
ioOffset
planLineID
quarantineReason
quarantineType
remoteHostName
rpmVersion
sqlID
sqlPlanHashValue
```

To clear the quarantine, use the drop quarantine command. If all issues that created quarantined plans have not been addressed, it is also possible to drop only the quarantined plans where the cause has been corrected. This uses the drop quarantine [name, name, name, name, ...] syntax and drops only the listed named quarantines. Once the quarantines are dropped, you should see Smart Scan performance restored for the once-affected plans.

It's best to use both accounts to monitor the storage cells on a regular basis, using cellmonitor for daily tasks and celladmin for those times when the output provided by the cellmonitor scripts indicate possible problems. It's a simple task to submit both cellcli and cellsrvstat commands to the storage servers from scripts on the database servers. For cellcli:

```
cellcli -e "command"
```

As an example:

```
[celladmin@myexa1celMyexa1cel05 ~]$ cellcli -e "list flashcache detail"
        name:                   myexa1celMyexa1cel05_FLASHCACHE
        cellDisk:
FD_11_myexa1celMyexa1cel05,FD_03_myexa1celMyexa1cel05,FD_15_myexa1celMyexa1cel05,FD_13_myexa1cel
Myexa1cel05,FD_08_myexa1celMyexa1cel05,FD_10_myexa1celMyexa1cel05,FD_00_myexa1celMyexa1cel05,FD_
```

```
14_myexa1celMyexa1cel05,FD_04_myexa1celMyexa1cel05,FD_06_myexa1celMyexa1cel05,FD_07_myexa1celMy
exa1cel05,FD_05_myexa1celMyexa1cel05,FD_12_myexa1celMyexa1cel05,FD_09_myexa1celMyexa1cel05,FD_02_
myexa1celMyexa1cel05,FD_01_myexa1celMyexa1cel05
         creationTime:           2013-07-09T17:33:53-05:00
         degradedCelldisks:
         effectiveCacheSize:     1488.75G
         id:                     8a380bf9-06c3-445e-8081-cff72d49bfe6
         size:                   1488.75G
         status:                 normal
[celladmin@myexa1celMyexa1cel05 ~]$
```

You need not enter the cellcli interactive interface to return data from cellcli. The cellsrvstat utility operates in a similar way, as the following example shows:

```
[celladmin@myexa1celMyexa1cel05 ~]$ cellsrvstat -stat_group=smartio -interval=1 -count=10

...
== SmartIO related stats ==
Number of active smart IO sessions                      0                 2
High water mark of smart IO sessions                    0                 3
Number of completed smart IO sessions                   0                44
Smart IO offload efficiency (percentage)                0                 0
Size of IO avoided due to storage index (KB)            0         139751400
Current smart IO to be issued (KB)                  10208             18368
Total smart IO to be issued (KB)                  2652520       13375858840
Current smart IO in IO (KB)                          -992             10240
Total smart IO in IO (KB)                         2642312       13375840472
Current smart IO being cached in flash (KB)             0                 0
Total smart IO being cached in flash (KB)               0                 0
Current smart IO with IO completed (KB)                 0                 0
Total smart IO with IO completed (KB)             2643304       13375830376
Current smart IO being filtered (KB)                    0                 0
Total smart IO being filtered (KB)                2643304       13375830376
Current smart IO filtering completed (KB)            1024              1024
Total smart IO filtering completed (KB)           2643304       13375830232
Current smart IO filtered size (KB)                     1                 1
Total smart IO filtered (KB)                          393           1999243
Total cpu passthru output IO size (KB)                  0                 0
Total passthru output IO size (KB)                      0                 0
Current smart IO with results in send (KB)              0                 0
Total smart IO with results in send (KB)          2642280       13375817944
Current smart IO filtered in send (KB)                  0                 0
Total smart IO filtered in send (KB)                  392           1999241
Total smart IO read from flash (KB)                     0                 0
Total smart IO initiated flash population (KB)          0                 0
Total smart IO read from hard disk (KB)           2642312       13236089072
Total smart IO writes (fcre) to hard disk (KB)          0                 0
Number of smart IO requests < 512KB                    52            265049
Number of smart IO requests >= 512KB and < 1MB        260           1284245
Number of smart IO requests >= 1MB and < 2MB            0                82
Number of smart IO requests >= 2MB and < 4MB          286           1446473
```

```
Number of smart IO requests >= 4MB and < 8MB          299        1510123
Number of smart IO requests >= 8MB                      0              0
...
```

This example also illustrates that `cellsrvstat` can in seconds automatically generate data for a specified number of runs at a specified interval. Automating these commands from the database servers uses `ssh` to log in to the storage cell and pass the desired command to the command prompt. An example for `cellsrvstat` follows:

```
echo "==========================================================================="
echo "================================ Cell 1 ===================================="
echo "==========================================================================="
/usr/bin/ssh celladmin@mytexa1cel01-priv.mydomain.com  "cellsrvstat -stat_group=smartio -
interval=$1 -count=$2"
echo "==========================================================================="
echo "================================ Cell 2" ====================================
echo "==========================================================================="
/usr/bin/ssh celladmin@myexa1cel02-priv.mydomain.com  "cellsrvstat -stat_group=smartio -
interval=$1 -count=$2"
echo "==========================================================================="
echo "================================ Cell 3" ====================================
echo "==========================================================================="
/usr/bin/ssh celladmin@myexa1cel03-priv.mydomain.com  "cellsrvstat -stat_group=smartio -
interval=$1 -count=$2"
```

■ **Note**   This script relies on passwordless login for `celladmin` to the various storage cells and, because of this, can run from cron. If passwordless login is not configured, the script can be run manually from the command prompt, and it will ask for the password before continuing. Since there are numerous resources describing how to set up passwordless access across servers, we won't discuss that here.

Once you have such a script written, it's another easy task to generate a logfile of the output on the database server. Simply create another script which calls this one, providing the desired parameters, and redirect the output to a local file, as follows:

```
/home/oracle/bin/cellsrvstat_smartio.sh 5 100 > /home/oracle/mydb/logs/cellsrvstat_smartio_`date
'+%m%d%Y%H%M%S'`.log
```

The output will be directed to the specified logfile on the database server, so you can examine the output without having to visit the storage cells directly.

You can also perform a similar operation using the dcli utility from the database server. Using the –c option allows you to specify a comma-delimited list of storage cell names dcli is to connect to. The entire command you want executed, including any supplied parameters, must be enclosed in single quotes. An example of generating a similar report on storage cells 4 and 5 follows.

```
$ dcli -c myexa1cel04,myexa1cel05 'cellsrvstat -stat_group=smartio interval=5 count=3'
myexa1cel04: ===Current Time===                                    Tue Sep 10 15:55:12 2013
myexa1cel04:
myexa1cel04: == SmartIO related stats ==
myexa1cel04: Number of active smart IO sessions                    0                    3
myexa1cel04: High water mark of smart IO sessions                  0                  191
myexa1cel04: Number of completed smart IO sessions                 0             44044288
myexa1cel04: Smart IO offload efficiency (percentage)              0                    6
myexa1cel04: Size of IO avoided due to storage index (KB)          0          113864506544
myexa1cel04: Current smart IO to be issued (KB)                    0                    0
myexa1cel04: Total smart IO to be issued (KB)                      0          531586293560
myexa1cel04: Current smart IO in IO (KB)                           0                    0
myexa1cel04: Total smart IO in IO (KB)                             0          530250520048
myexa1cel04: Current smart IO being cached in flash (KB)           0                    0
myexa1cel04: Total smart IO being cached in flash (KB)             0                    0
myexa1cel04: Current smart IO with IO completed (KB)               0                    0
myexa1cel04: Total smart IO with IO completed (KB)                 0          539827489136
myexa1cel04: Current smart IO being filtered (KB)                  0                    0
myexa1cel04: Total smart IO being filtered (KB)                    0          539642524176
myexa1cel04: Current smart IO filtering completed (KB)             0                    0
myexa1cel04: Total smart IO filtering completed (KB)               0          529809708672
myexa1cel04: Current smart IO filtered size (KB)                   0                    0
myexa1cel04: Total smart IO filtered (KB)                          0           33684733602
myexa1cel04: Total cpu passthru output IO size (KB)                0                    0
myexa1cel04: Total passthru output IO size (KB)                    0                    0
myexa1cel04: Current smart IO with results in send (KB)            0                    0
myexa1cel04: Total smart IO with results in send (KB)              0          526935373848
myexa1cel04: Current smart IO filtered in send (KB)                0                    0
myexa1cel04: Total smart IO filtered in send (KB)                  0           33558330216
myexa1cel04: Total smart IO read from flash (KB)                   0                    0
myexa1cel04: Total smart IO initiated flash population (KB)        0                    0
myexa1cel04: Total smart IO read from hard disk (KB)               0          822839718880
myexa1cel04: Total smart IO writes (fcre) to hard disk (KB)        0           4720157008
myexa1cel04: Number of smart IO requests < 512KB                   0            129319228
myexa1cel04: Number of smart IO requests >= 512KB and < 1MB        0             33944130
myexa1cel04: Number of smart IO requests >= 1MB and < 2MB          0              1917797
myexa1cel04: Number of smart IO requests >= 2MB and < 4MB          0             26218404
myexa1cel04: Number of smart IO requests >= 4MB and < 8MB          0             94846302
myexa1cel04: Number of smart IO requests >= 8MB                    0                    0
myexa1cel04: Number of times smart IO buffer reserve failures      0                    0
myexa1cel04: Number of times smart IO request misses               0               428373
myexa1cel04: Number of times IO for smart IO not allowed to be issued  0          51619053
myexa1cel04: Number of times smart IO prefetch limit was reached   0             13853892
myexa1cel04: Number of times smart scan used unoptimized mode      0                    0
myexa1cel04: Number of times smart fcre used unoptimized mode      0                    0
myexa1cel04: Number of times smart backup used unoptimized mode    0                    0
myexa1cel04:
...
```

```
myexa1cel05: ===Current Time===                                        Tue Sep 10 15:55:12 2013
myexa1cel05:
myexa1cel05: == SmartIO related stats ==
myexa1cel05: Number of active smart IO sessions                         0              3
myexa1cel05: High water mark of smart IO sessions                       0            190
myexa1cel05: Number of completed smart IO sessions                      0       13414701
myexa1cel05: Smart IO offload efficiency (percentage)                   0              6
myexa1cel05: Size of IO avoided due to storage index (KB)               0    122775633128
myexa1cel05: Current smart IO to be issued (KB)                         0              0
myexa1cel05: Total smart IO to be issued (KB)                           0    518860088328
myexa1cel05: Current smart IO in IO (KB)                                0              0
myexa1cel05: Total smart IO in IO (KB)                                  0    517153923160
myexa1cel05: Current smart IO being cached in flash (KB)                0              0
myexa1cel05: Total smart IO being cached in flash (KB)                  0              0
myexa1cel05: Current smart IO with IO completed (KB)                    0              0
myexa1cel05: Total smart IO with IO completed (KB)                      0    526712505064
myexa1cel05: Current smart IO being filtered (KB)                       0              0
myexa1cel05: Total smart IO being filtered (KB)                         0    526326301880
myexa1cel05: Current smart IO filtering completed (KB)                  0              0
myexa1cel05: Total smart IO filtering completed (KB)                    0    516527335136
myexa1cel05: Current smart IO filtered size (KB)                        0              0
myexa1cel05: Total smart IO filtered (KB)                               0     31742415677
myexa1cel05: Total cpu passthru output IO size (KB)                     0              0
myexa1cel05: Total passthru output IO size (KB)                         0              0
myexa1cel05: Current smart IO with results in send (KB)                 0              0
myexa1cel05: Total smart IO with results in send (KB)                   0    513421039080
myexa1cel05: Current smart IO filtered in send (KB)                     0              0
myexa1cel05: Total smart IO filtered in send (KB)                       0     31628785815
myexa1cel05: Total smart IO read from flash (KB)                        0              0
myexa1cel05: Total smart IO initiated flash population (KB)             0              0
myexa1cel05: Total smart IO read from hard disk (KB)                    0    778857687168
myexa1cel05: Total smart IO writes (fcre) to hard disk (KB)            0      4719981512
myexa1cel05: Number of smart IO requests < 512KB                       0        87530841
myexa1cel05: Number of smart IO requests >= 512KB and < 1MB            0        22106655
myexa1cel05: Number of smart IO requests >= 1MB and < 2MB             0          1379945
myexa1cel05: Number of smart IO requests >= 2MB and < 4MB             0         23696091
myexa1cel05: Number of smart IO requests >= 4MB and < 8MB             0         97340630
myexa1cel05: Number of smart IO requests >= 8MB                       0                0
myexa1cel05: Number of times smart IO buffer reserve failures        0                0
myexa1cel05: Number of times smart IO request misses                 0          1327742
myexa1cel05: Number of times IO for smart IO not allowed to be issued 0        56612486
myexa1cel05: Number of times smart IO prefetch limit was reached      0         6893531
myexa1cel05: Number of times smart scan used unoptimized mode         0                0
myexa1cel05: Number of times smart fcre used unoptimized mode         0                0
myexa1cel05: Number of times smart backup used unoptimized mode       0                0
myexa1cel05:
...
myexa1cel05:
$
```

The storage cell name is displayed, as well as the `cellsrvstat` report data for each interval reported. This also relies on passwordless `ssh` access to the storage cells; if that isn't established, it will be necessary to enter a password to connect to each cell in the list.

It is well worth the time and slight amount of effort to set up such monitoring of the storage cells using cron, as it will pay off in the long run. Troubleshooting Smart Scan and Smart Flash Cache issues can be made easier by having a baseline for current performance. Differences and deviations will be easier to spot and address, making troubleshooting time shorter and problem resolution faster.

Things to Know

There are two accounts you, as a DBA, should be aware of for the storage cells: `cellmonitor` and `celladmin`. The `cellmonitor` account is strictly a monitoring login and has restricted access to the storage cell directory structure.The `celladmin` account has far more access and privilege and is intended to be used for administrative duties.

The storage cells can be accessed by `ssh`; the addresses for the available storage cells are available in the `/etc/hosts` files on all available database servers in the Exadata system.

Two utilities exist for monitoring and managing the storage cells, `cellcli` and `cellsrvstat`. The `cellcli` utility is available to both `cellmonitor` and `celladmin`, with `cellmonitor` having a restricted set of available instructions. The `cellmonitor` account is intended for regular monitoring, using the `LIST` command set, which outputs statistics and metrics for various areas of the storage cell. The `celladmin` account is intended to allow the DBA to address issues reported by output generated by `cellmonitor`.

Both `cellcli` and `cellsrvstat` commands can be passed on the command line and `cellsrvstat` commands can be automated, in a way, by providing an interval, in seconds, and a count of executions to run of the given command. You can also restrict the output of `cellsrvstat` by using the -stat_group parameter to specify which group, or groups, you want to monitor. The available groups are smartio, io, mem, exec, and net.

Storage cell monitoring from the database server can be automated by using passwordless login to the storage cells and scripts, using `ssh` to connect to each storage cell and pass either `cellcli` or `cellsrvstat` commands to the cell you are connected to. The output can also be redirected to a logfile on the database server, by writing what is known as a "wrapper" script to redirect the output. This can establish a performance baseline for comparison, when the output indicates possible problem areas.

CHAPTER 10

■ ■ ■

Monitoring Exadata

Exadata is a complex system of interrelated components; monitoring them effectively is both an art and a science. Throughout this book, we have discussed monitoring options for various areas of Exadata. In this chapter, we will take this topic further and provide ways to monitor Exadata across both the database nodes and the storage cells. We will see how V$SQL and V$SQLSTATS can be used to monitor SQL statement performance and provide information on Smart Scan activity. We'll also look at the storage cells again, comparing the monitoring capabilities of the command-line interfaces and those of Oracle Enterprise Manager (OEM). We're not promising to make you a combination of Einstein and Rembrandt, but we will help you understand the available tools and techniques, so you can intelligently monitor your system.

The Database Layer

This is the layer the users will access, so we feel it's a logical starting point for a discussion on monitoring. We've discussed the wait interface in Chapter 7 and performance in Chapter 8. Now it's time to put them together and formulate a monitoring strategy.

Exadata's big selling point is the Smart Scan, and knowing what queries will and won't qualify for a Smart Scan is important. We covered these in Chapter 2, along with some monitoring steps, to see if Smart Scans were being executed. We will revisit that topic in the next section, using the V$SQL and V$SQLSTATS views.

Are We There Yet?

Exadata provides a wealth of metrics, counters, and statistics designed to report on what the system is doing for a given task. Simply because these metrics exist doesn't mean you should report everything Exadata records. You need a purpose and a direction when monitoring Exadata. Without purpose and direction, it's entirely possible you can be led down the wrong path, to solve the wrong "problem." Remember that monitoring should be designed to set an initial baseline, so that there is a solid foundation for comparison. Subsequent monitoring data should provide a window, relative to that baseline, showing how performance fares over time and data changes. You don't want to be chasing a moving target, if you can avoid it. Having no clear starting point only makes troubleshooting and problem resolution more difficult.

To design and implement an effective monitoring strategy, you need to step away from your normal role as DBA and look at the system from the user's perspective. Yes, you can drill down into the various metrics and statistics, wait events, and timers, but the end users don't care about that, really. Their main concern is how long their process or query takes to complete. If a process takes longer than the user thinks it should, the system is slow and needs tuning. Yes, it could very well be their query that needs attention, but to the user, it's the database causing the problem, and the database is your area of expertise. Users don't want to know that it's the 58th bit in the 32nd row of the ORDERS table that's at fault. They only want to see the problem corrected and response time reduced. Knowing that gives your monitoring process direction and purpose, the two items you need to effectively monitor the system.

Of course it's not just the user's claim of unsatisfactory performance that comes into play; it's also a matter of what acceptable and unacceptable performance may be. Simply because a monitoring script or tool reported "overly high CPU usage" doesn't mean the performance was unacceptable. You have to take into consideration how many sessions were active at the time and what those sessions were doing. Many tools set default thresholds for such alarms/reports, and those thresholds may not be appropriate for your system, so check these and set them to reasonable values, given your hardware, software, and user load. One size does not fit all, when it comes to monitoring.

Real-Time SQL Monitoring Reports

By far, the easiest way to monitor SQL performance is through Oracle Enterprise Manager 12c (OEM 12c), with the Diagnostic and Tuning Pack installed. Oracle will automatically monitor SQL statements run in parallel and serialized statements consuming five seconds or more of combined I/O and CPU time. It's also possible to monitor SQL statements with the /*+ MONITOR */ hint. Looking at a screenshot of the Performance window in OEM 12c in Figure 10-1, you can see the level of information presented.

Status	Duration	SQL ID	Session ID	Parallel	Database Time
✅	47.00 s	au7202yrjh9h	1429	2	45.39 s
✅	0.21 s	4ugrs1xkw14ab	2001	48	0.20 s
✅	0.29 s	4jxmx1k90z629	1534	48	0.29 s
✅	11.00 s	16wg2r96z0ucw	688	48	0.35 s
✅	24.00 s	0zc6aussjsfbn	2097		23.64 s
✅	9.00 s	6fqnmnqgrabyf	98		8.91 s
✅	21.00 s	0fgvzpwn70076	499		20.37 s
✅	4.00 s	9g86yth677d0h	2097		3.58 s
✅	125.00 s	agycayaa7msbg	1716	48	4878.09 s
✅	168.00 s	7kpxvuxsc8wv4	1716	48	4852.34 s

Figure 10-1. OEM 12c SQL monitoring pane

Among the details presented are the duration, the SQL ID, the session ID that ran the statement, the degree of parallelism for parallel execution, and a bar graph of the database time, broken down into the three categories for which time was recorded, CPU, User I/O, and Other. Green reports CPU time as a percentage of the total, blue the User I/O as a percentage, and orange the time (again as a percentage of the whole) recorded as Other. It's possible to "drill down" into the details for a specific SQL ID from the report by simply clicking on that SQL ID, shown in Figure 10-2.

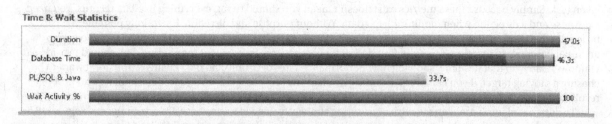

Figure 10-2. SQL ID Time & Wait window in OEM 12c

In addition to the enhanced execution plan (providing a time line, as well as the usual information), there are two sections above the plan providing time and wait statistics, along with I/O statistics. These are extremely helpful when diagnosing and troubleshooting performance issues on a per-statement basis. Not only is the "wall clock" time displayed (as the Duration bar), the time is broken down into its component pieces, so you can see where time was spent while executing the statement. Notice that Database Time, PL/SQL, and Java time, along with Wait Activity, are reported in the Time & Wait Statistics window. From the Database Time bar shown, the time is broken down into four wait categories: User I/O (blue), CPU (green), Cluster (white), and Application (red). Hovering the cursor over each of these areas reports what category is represented and the percentage of the total database time it represents. Such a breakdown is very helpful in determining where time is spent and, possibly, where improvements can be implemented. Likewise, hovering the cursor over the bars found in the I/O Statistics window reports the corresponding figures. Figure 10-3 illustrates this for the Time & Wait Statistics.

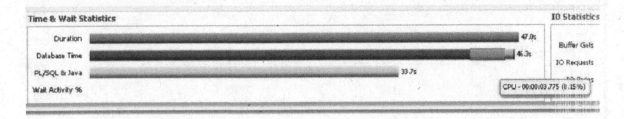

Figure 10-3. *Time & Wait Statistics breakdown*

Figure 10-4 shows this behavior for the I/O window.

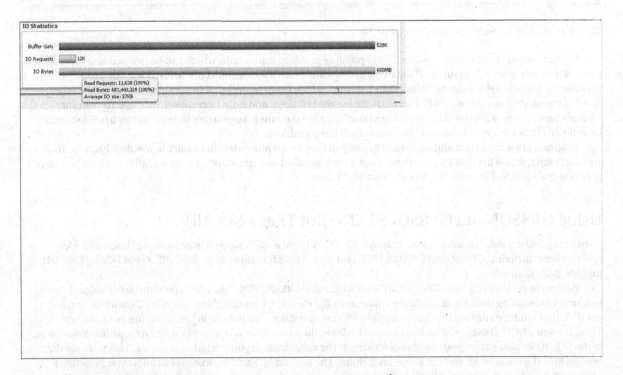

Figure 10-4. *I/O Statistics breakdown*

Through the tabs above the execution plan, you can see parallel wait statistics (for statements using parallel execution) as bar graphs and various other metrics as line graphs, the latter shown in Figure 10-5.

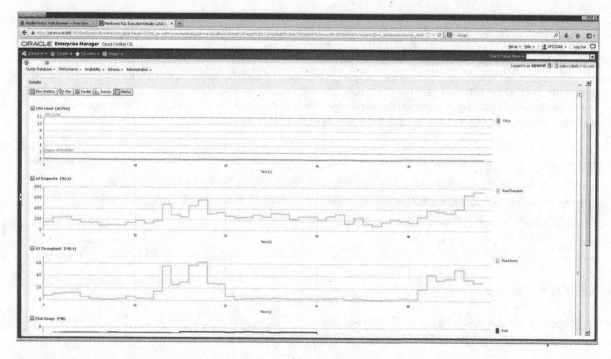

Figure 10-5. *SQL ID metric graphs from OEM 12c*

We use the Duration column to direct us to possible problem statements, which can be isolated and investigated to see if they are, indeed, a problem. If a statement has a duration of 993 seconds in the last hour, but had 1233 executions, the per-execution time is less than 1 second, which is not unacceptable performance. If, on the other hand, a statement has a duration of 79 seconds during the last hour, and only 1 execution, this SQL ID warrants further investigation. That the value reported in the Duration column is large bears little weight by itself. You must investigate further, in order to accurately determine if it is a problem.

Graphics are nice to have and fairly easy to use, but they aren't absolutely necessary to monitor Exadata. If you don't have access to OEM 12c, either because it isn't installed or it has stopped working, all is not lost. You can generate real-time SQL monitoring reports from SQL*Plus.

Using GV$SQL and GV$SQLSTATS (But That's Not All)

Generating real-time monitoring reports through SQL*Plus is not as difficult as it may seem, as Oracle provides several views, including GV$SQL and GV$SQLSTATS, and a packaged function (DBMS_SQLTUNE.REPORT_SQL_MONITOR), to provide this information.

Before we get to GV$SQL and GV$SQLSTATS, we will look at GV$SQL_MONITOR, which provides session-level execution monitoring data for all available instances in the cluster. Given that Exadata is a RAC environment, it's possible that multiple connections from an application may connect "round-robin" between the available nodes. Thus, the same SQL ID may exist on two or more nodes at the same time. It is important when monitoring execution at the SQL ID level to ensure you are always looking at the same session you started monitoring. This is where the session SID, the instance id, and the status are helpful. The session SID and the instance id allow you to isolate a session on a node for further monitoring. If the goal is to examine a currently running statement, ensure that the STATUS is reported as EXECUTING, so that monitoring over time will provide information you may need to troubleshoot a problem. Another view worth noting is GV$SQL_PLAN_MONITOR. This view is updated with plan-level monitoring data, updated in real time.

Looking at some examples using GV$SQL_MONITOR, GV$SQL_PLAN_MONITOR, GV$SQL, and GV$SQLSTATS should help you understand the power of these views and the information they can provide. We begin with GV$SQL_MONITOR and search for a specific SQL_ID, as follows:

```
SQL> select inst_id inst, sid, sql_plan_hash_value plan_hash, elapsed_time elapsed, cpu_time cpu_tm,
    fetches fetch, io_interconnect_bytes io_icon_byt, physical_read_bytes + physical_write_bytes
    tl_byt_proc, ((physical_read_bytes+physical_write_bytes)/io_interconnect_bytes)*100 offld_pct, status
  2  from gv$sql_monitor
  3  where status <> 'DONE'
  4  and sql_id = 'b1x37zg5a1ygr'
  5  and io_interconnect_bytes > 0
  6  /
```

INST	SID	PLAN_HASH	ELAPSED	CPU_TM	FETCH	IO_ICON_BYT	TL_BYT_PRC	OFFLD_PCT	STATUS
1	2	1747818060	329685	76988	0	8183808	8183808	100	DONE (ALL ROWS)
1	2222	1747818060	283095	100984	0	9199616	9199616	100	DONE (ALL ROWS)
1	1062	1747818060	240687	86987	0	9502720	9502720	100	DONE (ALL ROWS)
1	1810	1747818060	246776	85987	0	6201344	6201344	100	DONE (ALL ROWS)
1	201	1747818060	258911	46992	0	5505024	5505024	100	DONE (ALL ROWS)
1	1343	1747818060	232887	68989	0	7061504	7061504	100	DONE (ALL ROWS)
1	777	1747818060	280657	63990	0	6152192	6152192	100	DONE (ALL ROWS)
1	2094	1747818060	332745	54992	0	6520832	6520832	100	DONE (ALL ROWS)
1	966	1747818060	245549	79987	0	8028160	8028160	100	DONE (ALL ROWS)
1	1631	1747818060	273636	74988	0	9216000	9216000	100	DONE (ALL ROWS)
1	1530	1747818060	330327	89986	0	7454720	7454720	100	DONE (ALL ROWS)
1	1245	1747818060	239035	95985	0	8773632	8773632	100	DONE (ALL ROWS)
1	863	1747818060	288678	51992	0	6995968	6995968	100	DONE (ALL ROWS)
1	2004	1747818060	270000	41993	0	5562368	5562368	100	DONE (ALL ROWS)
1	1911	1747818060	258966	51992	0	6823936	6823936	100	DONE (ALL ROWS)
1	393	1747818060	323315	37993	0	4874240	4874240	100	DONE (ALL ROWS)
1	1724	1747818060	249028	72989	0	7421952	7421952	100	DONE (ALL ROWS)
1	1241	1747818060	36000	15998	1	40960	40960	100	DONE (ALL ROWS)
1	290	1747818060	234694	73989	0	6356992	6356992	100	DONE (ALL ROWS)
1	387	1747818060	264108	75988	0	8454144	8454144	100	DONE (ALL ROWS)
1	1431	1747818060	246059	75989	0	8011776	8011776	100	DONE (ALL ROWS)
1	482	1747818060	279164	51991	0	6692864	6692864	100	DONE (ALL ROWS)
1	493	1747818060	272336	69990	0	8347648	8347648	100	DONE (ALL ROWS)
1	1156	1747818060	274823	97985	0	11042816	11042816	100	DONE (ALL ROWS)
1	110	1747818060	261317	61991	0	7708672	7708672	100	DONE (ALL ROWS)

```
25 rows selected.
SQL>
```

There are 25 sessions running that same statement, all with different monitoring information. For Exadata, one of the key pieces of information is the IO_INTERCONNECT_BYTES, which indirectly reports the offload efficiency. If the sum of PHYSICAL_READ_BYTES and PHYSICAL_WRITE_BYTES equals the value in IO_INTERCONNECT_BYTES, the query or statement reaped the benefits of offloading with an efficiency of 100 percent. As we've pointed out before, ratios and efficiencies are relative numbers. But this ratio does give you a reasonable idea how much of the data was handled by offloading, which saves the database layer processing time. Notice that for every row in the results, the offload_pct is 100. You won't always see 100 percent offload efficiency, as multipart queries may have sections that will offload and sections that won't, as the following output illustrates.

INST	SID	PLAN_HASH	ELAPSED	CPU_TM	FETCH	IO_ICON_BYT	TL_BYT_PRC	OFFLD_PCT	STATUS
2	476	3140350437	7065006	2202665	142	85155840	83320832	97.845118	DONE (ALL ROWS)
1	869	484955222	6136552	5940097	127	147456	106496	72.222222	DONE (ALL ROWS)

Much of the output for statements from these two sessions was offloaded, but there was some output that wasn't, possibly because it needed traditional consistent-read processing at the database level. It's also possible to get percentages higher than 100.

INST	SID	SQL_ID	PLAN_HASH	ELAPSED	CPU_TM	FETCH	IO_ICON_BYT	TL_BYT_PRC	OFFLD_PCT	STATUS
2	1619	192t67rtdqrf8	4217233900	23380518	795879	2	61626560	127926272	207.58302	DONE (FIRST N ROWS)
2	1333	6m6y2y82sjpjx	627564094	4416403	1176820	1	57162056	77930496	136.33256	DONE (ALL ROWS)
2	1619	192t67rtdqrf8	4217233900	13716144	853870	2	63322304	129622016	204.70199	DONE (FIRST N ROWS)

An ORDER BY clause can cause this behavior, as it can up to double the read bytes processed by the query.

```
   INST_ID    SID  SQL_ID
---------- ------ --------------
SQL_TEXT
--------------------------------------------------------------------------------
SQL_PLAN_HASH_VALUE ELAPSED_TIME CPU_TIME FETCHES IO_INTERCONNECT_BYTES PHYSICAL_READ_BYTES PHYSICAL_WRITE_BYTES OFFLOAD_PCT STATUS
------------------- ------------ -------- ------- --------------------- ------------------- -------------------- ----------- ------
         2   1619  192t67rtdqrf8
select * from ad_parallel_update_units order by start_date desc
         4217233900    23380518   795879       2              61626560           127926272                    0 207.583016 DONE
                                                                                                                            (FIRST
                                                                                                                            N ROWS)

         2   1333  6m6y2y82sjpjx
Select TABLE_NAME, COLUMN_NAME, DEFAULT_LENGTH, DATA_DEFAULT
FROM SYS.USER_TAB_COLUMNS C WHERE 1=1
And default_length is not null
         1666543731     7998885  1801727       1              54386688            54386688                    0        100 DONE
                                                                                                                            (ALL
                                                                                                                            ROWS)

         2   1333  6m6y2y82sjpjx
Select TABLE_NAME, COLUMN_NAME, DEFAULT_LENGTH, DATA_DEFAULT
FROM SYS.USER_TAB_COLUMNS C WHERE 1=1
And default_length is not null
          627564094     4416403  1176820       1              57162056            77930496                    0 136.332563 DONE
                                                                                                                            (ALL
                                                                                                                            ROWS)

         2   1619  192t67rtdqrf8
select * from ad_parallel_update_units order by start_date desc
         4217233900    13716144   853870       2              63322304           129622016                    0 204.701989 DONE
                                                                                                                            (FIRST
                                                                                                                            N ROWS)
```

Index access can also increase the value for PHYSICAL_READ_BYTES above the value of IO_INTERCONNECT_BYTES. This is the case for SQL_ID 6m6y2y82sjpjx, as the plan shows.

Execution Plan

Plan hash value: 969465177

```
--------------------------------------------------------------------------------------------
| Id  | Operation                          | Name             | Rows | Bytes | Cost (%CPU)| Time     |
--------------------------------------------------------------------------------------------
|   0 | SELECT STATEMENT                   |                  |   28 |  3976 |  443   (1)| 00:00:01 |
|   1 |  CONCATENATION                     |                  |      |       |           |          |
|*  2 |   FILTER                           |                  |      |       |           |          |
|   3 |    NESTED LOOPS OUTER              |                  |    1 |   142 |   54   (0)| 00:00:01 |
|   4 |     NESTED LOOPS OUTER            |                  |    1 |   133 |   53   (0)| 00:00:01 |
|   5 |      NESTED LOOPS                 |                  |    1 |   129 |   52   (0)| 00:00:01 |
|   6 |       NESTED LOOPS OUTER          |                  |    1 |   107 |   51   (0)| 00:00:01 |
|   7 |        NESTED LOOPS OUTER         |                  |    1 |    98 |   49   (0)| 00:00:01 |
|   8 |         NESTED LOOPS             |                  |    1 |    72 |   48   (0)| 00:00:01 |
|*  9 |          TABLE ACCESS BY INDEX ROWID| OBJ$           |    5 |   215 |   47   (0)| 00:00:01 |
|* 10 |           INDEX RANGE SCAN        | I_OBJ5           |    5 |       |   43   (0)| 00:00:01 |
|* 11 |          TABLE ACCESS CLUSTER    | TAB$             |    1 |    12 |    2   (0)| 00:00:01 |
|* 12 |           INDEX UNIQUE SCAN       | I_OBJ#           |    1 |       |    1   (0)| 00:00:01 |
|* 13 |         TABLE ACCESS CLUSTER      | COL$             |    1 |    29 |    1   (0)| 00:00:01 |
|* 14 |          INDEX UNIQUE SCAN        | I_OBJ#           |    1 |       |    0   (0)| 00:00:01 |
|* 15 |        TABLE ACCESS CLUSTER       | COLTYPE$         |    1 |    26 |    1   (0)| 00:00:01 |
|* 16 |       TABLE ACCESS BY INDEX ROWID | OBJ$             |    1 |     9 |    2   (0)| 00:00:01 |
|* 17 |        INDEX RANGE SCAN           | I_OBJ3           |    1 |       |    1   (0)| 00:00:01 |
|* 18 |      INDEX RANGE SCAN             | I_USER2          |    1 |    22 |    1   (0)| 00:00:01 |
|* 19 |     INDEX RANGE SCAN              | I_USER2          |    1 |     4 |    1   (0)| 00:00:01 |
|* 20 |    INDEX RANGE SCAN               | I_HH_OBJ#_INTCOL#|    1 |     9 |    1   (0)| 00:00:01 |
|  21 |    NESTED LOOPS                    |                  |    1 |    29 |    2   (0)| 00:00:01 |
|* 22 |     INDEX SKIP SCAN               | I_USER2          |    1 |    20 |    1   (0)| 00:00:01 |
|* 23 |     INDEX RANGE SCAN              | I_OBJ4           |    1 |     9 |    1   (0)| 00:00:01 |
|* 24 |   FILTER                           |                  |      |       |           |          |
|* 25 |    HASH JOIN OUTER                |                  |   14 |  1988 |  387   (1)| 00:00:01 |
|  26 |     NESTED LOOPS OUTER            |                  |   14 |  1932 |  386   (1)| 00:00:01 |
|  27 |      NESTED LOOPS OUTER           |                  |   14 |  1806 |  358   (1)| 00:00:01 |
|  28 |       NESTED LOOPS OUTER          |                  |   14 |  1680 |  344   (1)| 00:00:01 |
|* 29 |        HASH JOIN                  |                  |   14 |  1316 |  330   (1)| 00:00:01 |
|  30 |         NESTED LOOPS             |                  |      |       |           |          |
|  31 |          NESTED LOOPS           |                  |   14 |  1008 |  328   (1)| 00:00:01 |
|* 32 |           TABLE ACCESS FULL       | COL$             |   14 |   406 |  300   (1)| 00:00:01 |
|* 33 |           INDEX RANGE SCAN        | I_OBJ1           |    1 |       |    1   (0)| 00:00:01 |
|* 34 |          TABLE ACCESS BY INDEX ROWID| OBJ$           |    1 |    43 |    2   (0)| 00:00:01 |
|  35 |         INDEX FULL SCAN          | I_USER2          |   63 |  1386 |    1   (0)| 00:00:01 |
|* 36 |        TABLE ACCESS CLUSTER       | COLTYPE$         |    1 |    26 |    1   (0)| 00:00:01 |
|* 37 |         INDEX RANGE SCAN          | I_HH_OBJ#_INTCOL#|    1 |     9 |    1   (0)| 00:00:01 |
|* 38 |       TABLE ACCESS BY INDEX ROWID | OBJ$             |    1 |     9 |    2   (0)| 00:00:01 |
|* 39 |        INDEX RANGE SCAN           | I_OBJ3           |    1 |       |    1   (0)| 00:00:01 |
|  40 |      INDEX FULL SCAN              | I_USER2          |   63 |   252 |    1   (0)| 00:00:01 |
|* 41 |     TABLE ACCESS CLUSTER          | TAB$             |    1 |    12 |    2   (0)| 00:00:01 |
|* 42 |      INDEX UNIQUE SCAN            | I_OBJ#           |    1 |       |    1   (0)| 00:00:01 |
|  43 |    NESTED LOOPS                    |                  |    1 |    29 |    2   (0)| 00:00:01 |
|* 44 |     INDEX SKIP SCAN               | I_USER2          |    1 |    20 |    1   (0)| 00:00:01 |
|* 45 |     INDEX RANGE SCAN              | I_OBJ4           |    1 |     9 |    1   (0)| 00:00:01 |
--------------------------------------------------------------------------------------------
```

Since the index access paths didn't qualify for a Smart Scan, they increased the PHYSICAL_READ_BYTES without adding the same amount to IO_INTERCONNECT_BYTES.

Another way to generate monitoring data with Oracle 11.2 is the DBMS_SQLTUNE.REPORT_SQL_MONITOR function.

```
select dbms_sqltune.report_sql_monitor(session_id=>&sessid, report_level=>'ALL',type=>'HTML') from dual;
```

The TYPE parameter can be either TEXT or HTML. We usually generate HTML reports, because they are easier to navigate and read in a web browser, as they preserve contextual (drill-down) information you can access with a right-click on the data item. Sample output for one of these HTML reports is shown in Figures 10-6a, 10-6b, and 10-6c.

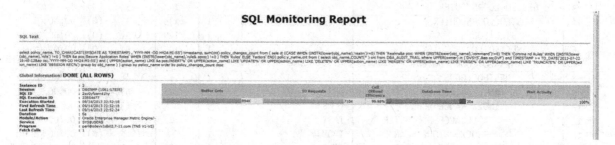

Figure 10-6a. *Global information output from DBMS_SQLTUNE.REPORT_SQL_MONITOR*

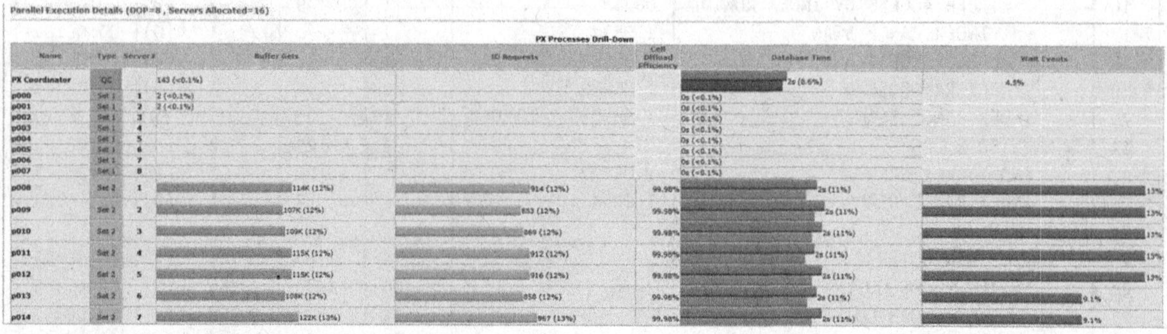

Figure 10-6b. *Parallel execution from HTML report*

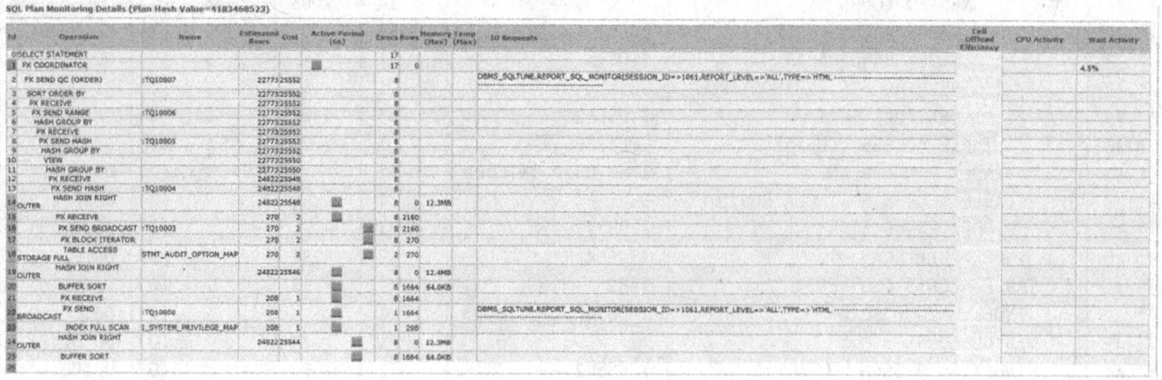

Figure 10-6c. *SQL Plan window from HTML report*

A text report for the same SID gives the same information.

```
--------------------------------------------------------------------------------
SQL Monitoring Report

SQL Text
--------------------------------
select policy_name, TO_CHAR(CAST(SYSDATE AS TIMESTAMP) , 'YYYY-MM-DD HH24:MI:SS'
) timestamp, sum(cnt) policy_changes_count from ( select (CASE WHEN (INSTR(lower
(obj_name),'realm')!=0) THEN 'Realms' WHEN (INSTR(lower(obj_name),'command')!=0)
 THEN 'Command Rules' WHEN (INSTR(lower(obj_name),'role') !=0 ) THEN 'Secure App
lication Roles' WHEN (INSTR(lower(obj_name),'rule') !=0 ) THEN 'Rules' ELSE 'Fac
tors' END) policy_name,cnt from ( select obj_name,COUNT(*) cnt from DBA_AUDIT_TR
AIL where
UPPER(owner) in ('DVSYS','DVF') and TIMESTAMP >= TO_DATE('2013-07-22 16:40:12','
YYYY-MM-DD HH24:MI:SS') and ( UPPER(action_name) LIKE 'INSERT%' OR UPPER(action_
name) LIKE 'UPDATE%' OR UPPER(action_name) LIKE 'DELETE%' OR UPPER(action_name)
LIKE 'MERGE%' OR UPPER(action_name) LIKE 'PURGE%' OR UPPER(action_name) LIKE 'TR
UNCATE%' OR UPPER(action_name) LIKE 'SESSION REC%') group by obj_name ) ) group
by policy_name order by policy_changes_count desc

Global Information
--------------------------------
 Status              : DONE (ALL ROWS)
 Instance ID         : 2
 Session             : DBSNMP (1061:17835)
 SQL ID              : 2sy0yfzam41hy
 SQL Execution ID    : 33554477
 Execution Started   : 09/14/2013 22:52:18
 First Refresh Time  : 09/14/2013 22:52:18
 Last Refresh Time   : 09/14/2013 22:52:24
 Duration            : 6s
 Module/Action       : Oracle Enterprise Manager.Metric Engine/-
 Service             : SYS$USERS
 Program             : perl@odevx1db02.7-11.com (TNS V1-V3)
 Fetch Calls         : 1
```

Global Stats

Elapsed Time(s)	Queuing Time(s)	Cpu Time(s)	IO Waits(s)	Application Waits(s)	Cluster Waits(s)	Concurrency Waits(s)	Other Waits(s)	Fetch Calls	Buffer Gets	Read Reqs	Read Bytes	Cell Offload
20	0.01	1.22	17	0.02	0.00	1.63	0.03	1	894K	7104	7GB	99.98%

Parallel Execution Details (DOP=8, Servers Allocated=16)

Name	Type	Server#	Elapsed Time(s)	Queuing Time(s)	Cpu Time(s)	IO Waits(s)	Application Waits(s)	Concurrency Waits(s)	Cluster Waits(s)	Other Waits(s)	Buffer Gets	Read Reqs	Read Bytes	Cell Offload	Wait Events (sample #)
PX Coordinator	QC		1.69	0.01	0.02	0.00	0.02	1.63	0.00	0.01	143			NaN%	os thread startup (1)
p000	Set 1	1	0.00		0.00	0.00					2			NaN%	
p001	Set 1	2	0.00		0.00	0.00					2			NaN%	
p002	Set 1	3	0.00							0.00				NaN%	
p003	Set 1	4	0.00		0.00									NaN%	
p004	Set 1	5	0.00							0.00				NaN%	
p005	Set 1	6	0.00							0.00				NaN%	
p006	Set 1	7	0.00											NaN%	
p007	Set 1	8	0.00		0.00									NaN%	
p008	Set 2	1	2.20		0.16	2.04			0.00		114K	914	869MB	99.98%	cell smart table scan (3)
p009	Set 2	2	2.34		0.16	2.18			0.00		107K	853	808MB	99.98%	cell smart table scan (3)
p010	Set 2	3	2.27		0.14	2.13			0.00		109K	869	828MB	99.98%	cell smart table scan (3)
p011	Set 2	4	2.19		0.15	2.04		0.00	0.00		115K	912	872MB	99.98%	cell smart table scan (3)
p012	Set 2	5	2.30		0.14	2.15			0.00		115K	916	874MB	99.98%	cell smart table scan (3)
p013	Set 2	6	2.21		0.15	2.06		0.00	0.00		108K	858	823MB	99.98%	cell smart table scan (2)
p014	Set 2	7	2.29		0.13	2.14				0.01	122K	967	930MB	99.98%	cell smart table scan (2)
p015	Set 2	8	2.21		0.15	2.06			0.00		103K	815	777MB	99.98%	cell smart table scan (2)

SQL Plan Monitoring Details (Plan Hash Value=4183468523)

Id	Operation	Name	Rows (Estim)	Cost	Time Active(s)	Start Active	Execs	Rows (Actual)	Read Reqs	Read Bytes	Cell OffLoad	Mem (Max)	Activity (%)	Activity Detail (# samples)
0	SELECT STATEMENT						17							
1	PX COORDINATOR					+1	17	0					4.00	os thread startup (1)
2	PX SEND QC (ORDER)	:TQ10007	22773	25552			8							
3	SORT ORDER BY		22773	25552			8							
4	PX RECEIVE		22773	25552			8							
5	PX SEND RANGE	:TQ10006	22773	25552			8							
6	HASH GROUP BY		22773	25552			8							
7	PX RECEIVE		22773	25552			8							
8	PX SEND HASH	:TQ10005	22773	25552			8							
9	HASH GROUP BY		22773	25550			8							
10	VIEW		22773	25550			8							
11	HASH GROUP BY		24822	25548			8							
12	PX RECEIVE		24822	25548			8							
13	PX SEND HASH	:TQ10004	24822	25548	1	+3	8	0				13M		
14	HASH JOIN RIGHT OUTER		270	2	1	+3	8	2160						
15	PX RECEIVE		270	2	1	+6	8	2160						
16	PX SEND BROADCAST	:TQ10003	270	2	1	+6	8	270						
17	PX BLOCK ITERATOR		270	2	1	+6	2	270						
18	TABLE ACCESS STORAGE FULL	STMT_AUDIT_OPTION_MAP	270	2			8							
19	HASH JOIN RIGHT OUTER		24822	25546	1	+3	8	0				13M		
20	BUFFER SORT			1			8	1664				65536		
21	PX RECEIVE			1			8	1664						
22	PX SEND BROADCAST	:TQ10000	208	1	1	+3	8	1664						
23	INDEX FULL SCAN	I_SYSTEM_PRIVILEGE_MAP	208	1	1	+3	1	208						
24	HASH JOIN RIGHT OUTER		24822	25544	1	+5	8	0				13M		
25	BUFFER SORT		208	1			8	1664				65536		
26	PX RECEIVE		208	1	1	+5	8	1664						
27	PX SEND BROADCAST	:TQ10001	208	1	1	+3	8	1664						
28	INDEX FULL SCAN	I_SYSTEM_PRIVILEGE_MAP	208	1	1	+3	1	208						
29	FILTER						8							
30	HASH JOIN RIGHT OUTER		24822	25543	1	+5	8	0				11M		
31	BUFFER SORT		181	1	1	+5	8	1448				81920		
32	PX RECEIVE		181	1	1	+5	8	1448						
33	PX SEND BROADCAST	:TQ10002	181	1	1	+5	8	1448						
34	INDEX FULL SCAN	I_AUDIT_ACTIONS	181	1	1	+5	1	181						
35	PX BLOCK ITERATOR		24822	25541	1	+5	8	0						
36	TABLE ACCESS STORAGE FULL	AUD$	24822	25541	3	+4	361	0	7104	7GB	99-98 %		96.00	Cpu (3)
														cell smart table scan (21)

Like the OEM reports we discussed earlier, the HTML version allows you to hover the cursor over a data bar and see the breakdown of I/O requests, database time, and wait activity, as shown in Figure 10-7.

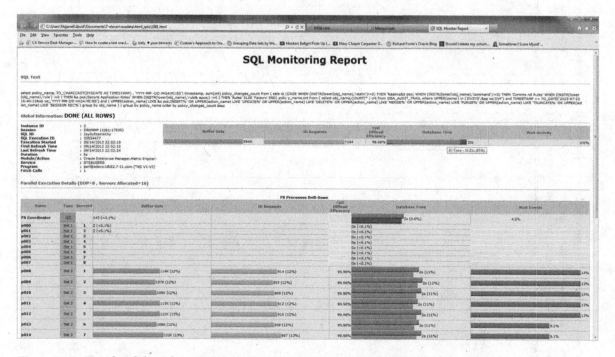

Figure 10-7. *Time breakdown from DBMS_SQLTUNE.REPORT_SQL_MONITOR HTML report*

If your Exadata system has Internet access and you are running Oracle 11.2.0.x, you can use a third option for the type parameter, 'ACTIVE', which generates an HTML-type report with active content that looks like the screens from OEM. Figure 10-8 illustrates how this type of report appears.

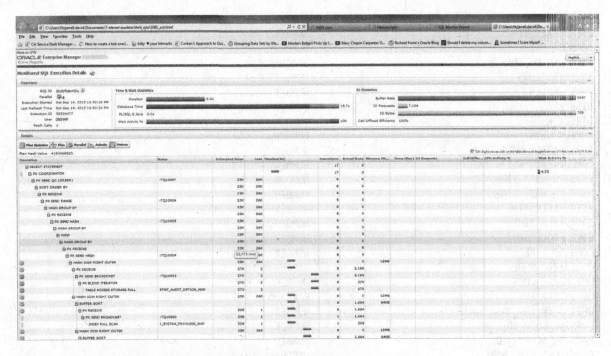

Figure 10-8. *Active DBMS_SQLTUNE.REPORT_SQL_MONITOR report*

As good as the reports generated with SQL Monitoring, AWR, ASH (Active Session History), and DBMS_SQLTUNE are, there is a limit to their effectiveness. By design, SQL Monitoring starts recording data after the I/O time, CPU time, or both combined exceed a five second limit; this usually means that only the longer-running queries and statements get monitored, even when you use the /*+ MONITOR */ hint. This leads back to the monitoring scripts and actions for databases, where AWR, Statspack, and ASH are not available. Those scripts and queries can still be useful with Exadata, especially when short-running queries are being examined, and those queries usually use V$SQL and, in more recent implementations, V$SQLSTATS.

For years, DBAs have relied on V$SQL to report data such as number of executions, buffer gets, disk reads, or parse calls. Looking at the definition of V$SQL, we find a wealth of data available.

```
SQL> desc v$sql
 Name                                      Null?    Type
 ----------------------------------------- -------- ----------------------------
 SQL_TEXT                                           VARCHAR2(1000)
 SQL_FULLTEXT                                       CLOB
 SQL_ID                                             VARCHAR2(13)
 SHARABLE_MEM                                       NUMBER
 PERSISTENT_MEM                                     NUMBER
 RUNTIME_MEM                                        NUMBER
 SORTS                                              NUMBER
 LOADED_VERSIONS                                    NUMBER
 OPEN_VERSIONS                                      NUMBER
 USERS_OPENING                                      NUMBER
 FETCHES                                            NUMBER
 EXECUTIONS                                         NUMBER
 PX_SERVERS_EXECUTIONS                              NUMBER
```

END_OF_FETCH_COUNT	NUMBER
USERS_EXECUTING	NUMBER
LOADS	NUMBER
FIRST_LOAD_TIME	VARCHAR2(76)
INVALIDATIONS	NUMBER
PARSE_CALLS	NUMBER
DISK_READS	NUMBER
DIRECT_WRITES	NUMBER
BUFFER_GETS	NUMBER
APPLICATION_WAIT_TIME	NUMBER
CONCURRENCY_WAIT_TIME	NUMBER
CLUSTER_WAIT_TIME	NUMBER
USER_IO_WAIT_TIME	NUMBER
PLSQL_EXEC_TIME	NUMBER
JAVA_EXEC_TIME	NUMBER
ROWS_PROCESSED	NUMBER
COMMAND_TYPE	NUMBER
OPTIMIZER_MODE	VARCHAR2(10)
OPTIMIZER_COST	NUMBER
OPTIMIZER_ENV	RAW(2000)
OPTIMIZER_ENV_HASH_VALUE	NUMBER
PARSING_USER_ID	NUMBER
PARSING_SCHEMA_ID	NUMBER
PARSING_SCHEMA_NAME	VARCHAR2(30)
KEPT_VERSIONS	NUMBER
ADDRESS	RAW(8)
TYPE_CHK_HEAP	RAW(8)
HASH_VALUE	NUMBER
OLD_HASH_VALUE	NUMBER
PLAN_HASH_VALUE	NUMBER
CHILD_NUMBER	NUMBER
SERVICE	VARCHAR2(64)
SERVICE_HASH	NUMBER
MODULE	VARCHAR2(64)
MODULE_HASH	NUMBER
ACTION	VARCHAR2(64)
ACTION_HASH	NUMBER
SERIALIZABLE_ABORTS	NUMBER
OUTLINE_CATEGORY	VARCHAR2(64)
CPU_TIME	NUMBER
ELAPSED_TIME	NUMBER
OUTLINE_SID	NUMBER
CHILD_ADDRESS	RAW(8)
SQLTYPE	NUMBER
REMOTE	VARCHAR2(1)
OBJECT_STATUS	VARCHAR2(19)
LITERAL_HASH_VALUE	NUMBER
LAST_LOAD_TIME	VARCHAR2(76)
IS_OBSOLETE	VARCHAR2(1)
IS_BIND_SENSITIVE	VARCHAR2(1)
IS_BIND_AWARE	VARCHAR2(1)

```
IS_SHAREABLE                         VARCHAR2(1)
CHILD_LATCH                          NUMBER
SQL_PROFILE                          VARCHAR2(64)
SQL_PATCH                            VARCHAR2(30)
SQL_PLAN_BASELINE                    VARCHAR2(30)
PROGRAM_ID                           NUMBER
PROGRAM_LINE#                        NUMBER
EXACT_MATCHING_SIGNATURE             NUMBER
FORCE_MATCHING_SIGNATURE             NUMBER
LAST_ACTIVE_TIME                     DATE
BIND_DATA                            RAW(2000)
TYPECHECK_MEM                        NUMBER
IO_CELL_OFFLOAD_ELIGIBLE_BYTES       NUMBER
IO_INTERCONNECT_BYTES                NUMBER
PHYSICAL_READ_REQUESTS               NUMBER
PHYSICAL_READ_BYTES                  NUMBER
PHYSICAL_WRITE_REQUESTS              NUMBER
PHYSICAL_WRITE_BYTES                 NUMBER
OPTIMIZED_PHY_READ_REQUESTS          NUMBER
LOCKED_TOTAL                         NUMBER
PINNED_TOTAL                         NUMBER
IO_CELL_UNCOMPRESSED_BYTES           NUMBER
IO_CELL_OFFLOAD_RETURNED_BYTES       NUMBER

SQL>
```

Unfortunately, V$SQL suffers from latch contention when queried without providing a SQL_ID, so if there are several queries active against this view, performance can be slow. In 10gR2, the V$SQLSTATS view was introduced, recording much of the same information as V$SQL but in a memory location and format that doesn't create latch contention with unqualified queries. Since V$SQLSTATS is, in our opinion, the view to use, we will discuss that here. Remember that the same basic type of queries used against V$SQLSTATS can also be used against V$SQL.

In Chapter 2, we discussed Smart Scans and how to prove they are working, and we used V$SQL to do that. We'll now use V$SQLSTATS to return similar information.

Looking at the definition for V$SQLSTATS, we see much of the same information that is available in V$SQL.

```
SQL> desc v$sqlstats
Name                                 Null?      Type
---------------------------------    --------   -------------------
SQL_TEXT                                        VARCHAR2(1000)
SQL_FULLTEXT                                    CLOB
SQL_ID                                          VARCHAR2(13)
LAST_ACTIVE_TIME                                DATE
LAST_ACTIVE_CHILD_ADDRESS                       RAW(8)
PLAN_HASH_VALUE                                 NUMBER
PARSE_CALLS                                     NUMBER
DISK_READS                                      NUMBER
DIRECT_WRITES                                   NUMBER
BUFFER_GETS                                     NUMBER
ROWS_PROCESSED                                  NUMBER
SERIALIZABLE_ABORTS                             NUMBER
FETCHES                                         NUMBER
```

EXECUTIONS	**NUMBER**
END_OF_FETCH_COUNT	NUMBER
LOADS	NUMBER
VERSION_COUNT	NUMBER
INVALIDATIONS	NUMBER
PX_SERVERS_EXECUTIONS	NUMBER
CPU_TIME	NUMBER
ELAPSED_TIME	**NUMBER**
AVG_HARD_PARSE_TIME	NUMBER
APPLICATION_WAIT_TIME	NUMBER
CONCURRENCY_WAIT_TIME	NUMBER
CLUSTER_WAIT_TIME	NUMBER
USER_IO_WAIT_TIME	NUMBER
PLSQL_EXEC_TIME	NUMBER
JAVA_EXEC_TIME	NUMBER
SORTS	NUMBER
SHARABLE_MEM	NUMBER
TOTAL_SHARABLE_MEM	NUMBER
TYPECHECK_MEM	NUMBER
IO_CELL_OFFLOAD_ELIGIBLE_BYTES	**NUMBER**
IO_INTERCONNECT_BYTES	**NUMBER**
PHYSICAL_READ_REQUESTS	NUMBER
PHYSICAL_READ_BYTES	NUMBER
PHYSICAL_WRITE_REQUESTS	NUMBER
PHYSICAL_WRITE_BYTES	NUMBER
EXACT_MATCHING_SIGNATURE	NUMBER
FORCE_MATCHING_SIGNATURE	NUMBER
IO_CELL_UNCOMPRESSED_BYTES	NUMBER
IO_CELL_OFFLOAD_RETURNED_BYTES	**NUMBER**

```
SQL>
```

V$SQLSTATS doesn't include the parsing user id, so you will need to use another method to isolate information you want to see. A possible rewrite of the V$SQL query used in Chapter 2 follows.

```
SQL> select      sql_id,
  2          io_cell_offload_eligible_bytes qualifying,
  3          io_cell_offload_eligible_bytes - io_cell_offload_returned_bytes actual,
  4          round(((io_cell_offload_eligible_bytes -
io_cell_offload_returned_bytes)/io_cell_offload_eligible_bytes)*100, 2) io_saved_pct,
  5          sql_text
  6          from v$sqlstats
  7          where io_cell_offload_returned_bytes > 0
  8          and io_cell_offload_eligible_bytes > 0
  9          and instr(sql_text, 'emp') > 0;

SQL_ID         QUALIFYING    ACTUAL IO_SAVED_PCT SQL_TEXT
------------- ---------- ---------- ------------ --------------------------------------------
gfjb8dpxvpuv6 185081856  185053096        99.98 select * from emp where empid = 7934
dayy30naa1z2p 184819712    948048          .51 select /*+ cache */ * from emp

SQL>
```

Since there could be a number of queries with "emp" as a substring, some of which don't qualify for a Smart Scan, it was necessary to include a condition that the io_cell_offload_eligible_bytes be greater than 0. Without that condition, the query generates a "divisor is equal to 0" error, which doesn't occur with the V$SQL version of the query.

There are some pieces of information not available in V$SQLSTATS.

COLUMN_NAME	DATA_TYPE	DATA_LENGTH
PERSISTENT_MEM	NUMBER	22
RUNTIME_MEM	NUMBER	22
LOADED_VERSIONS	NUMBER	22
OPEN_VERSIONS	NUMBER	22
USERS_OPENING	NUMBER	22
USERS_EXECUTING	NUMBER	22
FIRST_LOAD_TIME	VARCHAR2	76
COMMAND_TYPE	NUMBER	22
OPTIMIZER_MODE	VARCHAR2	10
OPTIMIZER_COST	NUMBER	22
OPTIMIZER_ENV	RAW	2000
OPTIMIZER_ENV_HASH_VALUE	NUMBER	22
PARSING_USER_ID	NUMBER	22
PARSING_SCHEMA_ID	NUMBER	22
PARSING_SCHEMA_NAME	VARCHAR2	30
KEPT_VERSIONS	NUMBER	22
ADDRESS	RAW	8
TYPE_CHK_HEAP	RAW	8
HASH_VALUE	NUMBER	22
OLD_HASH_VALUE	NUMBER	22
CHILD_NUMBER	NUMBER	22
SERVICE	VARCHAR2	64
SERVICE_HASH	NUMBER	22
MODULE	VARCHAR2	64
MODULE_HASH	NUMBER	22
ACTION	VARCHAR2	64
ACTION_HASH	NUMBER	22
OUTLINE_CATEGORY	VARCHAR2	64
OUTLINE_SID	NUMBER	22
CHILD_ADDRESS	RAW	8
SQLTYPE	NUMBER	22
REMOTE	VARCHAR2	1
OBJECT_STATUS	VARCHAR2	19
LITERAL_HASH_VALUE	NUMBER	22
LAST_LOAD_TIME	VARCHAR2	76
IS_OBSOLETE	VARCHAR2	1
IS_BIND_SENSITIVE	VARCHAR2	1
IS_BIND_AWARE	VARCHAR2	1
IS_SHAREABLE	VARCHAR2	1
CHILD_LATCH	NUMBER	22
SQL_PROFILE	VARCHAR2	64
SQL_PATCH	VARCHAR2	30
SQL_PLAN_BASELINE	VARCHAR2	30
PROGRAM_ID	NUMBER	22
PROGRAM_LINE#	NUMBER	22

```
BIND_DATA                       RAW                                     2000
OPTIMIZED_PHY_READ_REQUESTS     NUMBER                                    22
LOCKED_TOTAL                    NUMBER                                    22
PINNED_TOTAL                    NUMBER                                    22
```

For general monitoring tasks, those columns aren't necessary. If you do need to dig deeper into a problem, then you may need to use V$SQL to access memory, latch, or optimizer data for the query in question. We find that V$SQLSTATS does a good job for basic, routine monitoring of SQL statements and that it provides a lower overhead during busy periods of database activity.

The Storage Cells

Storage cell management was covered in Chapter 9, but we'll review some of that information here.

The Command Line

We feel that it's a good idea to review the command-line interfaces here. Remember that the storage cells offer both CellCLI and cellsrvstat to monitor the storage cells, and two accounts, cellmonitor and celladmin, to perform those tasks. For general monitoring, the cellmonitor account should provide the information you need through the CellCLI interface.

A common monitoring area for Exadata is the Smart Flash Cache. To fully monitor this area, it is necessary to connect to every available storage cell and generate a report. It's possible to send this to the storage cells via a script and have the output logged to the database server, which was illustrated in Chapter 9. An example of such a report, for storage cell 4, follows.

```
CellCLI> list flashlog detail
        name:                   myexa1cel04_FLASHLOG
        cellDisk:
FD_14_myexa1cel04,FD_05_myexa1cel04,FD_00_myexa1cel04,FD_01_myexa1cel04,FD_04_myexa1cel04,
FD_07_myexa1cel04,FD_09_ode vx1cel04,FD_02_myexa1cel04,FD_08_myexa1cel04,FD_03_myexa1cel04,
FD_15_myexa1cel04,FD_12_myexa1cel04,FD_11_myexa1cel04,FD_06_myexa1cel04,FD_10_myexa1cel 04,
FD_13_myexa1cel04
        creationTime:           2013-07-09T17:33:31-05:00
        degradedCelldisks:
        effectiveSize:          512M
        efficiency:             100.0
        id:                     7eb480f9-b94a-4493-bfca-3ba00b6618bb
        size:                   512M
        status:                 normal

CellCLI>
```

A command-line example, run on the storage cell, lists the same output but avoids using the command-line interface.

```
[celladmin@myexa1cel05 ~]$ cellcli -e "list flashcache detail"
        name:                   myexa1cel05_FLASHCACHE
        cellDisk:
FD_11_myexa1cel05,FD_03_myexa1cel05,FD_15_myexa1cel05,FD_13_myexa1cel05,FD_08_myexa1cel05,
FD_10_myexa1cel05,FD_00_myexa1cel05,FD_14_myexa1cel05,FD_04_myexa1cel05,FD_06_myexa1cel05,
FD_07_myexa1cel05,FD_05_myexa1cel05,FD_12_myexa1cel05,FD_09_myexa1cel05,FD_02_myexa1cel05,
FD_01_myexa1cel05
```

```
              creationTime:        2013-07-09T17:33:53-05:00
              degradedCelldisks:
              effectiveCacheSize:  1488.75G
              id:                  8a380bf9-06c3-445e-8081-cff72d49bfe6
              size:                1488.75G
              status:              normal
[celladmin@myexa1cel05 ~]$
```

As stated in Chapter 9, if you set up passwordless ssh connectivity between the database servers and the storage cells, you can run these commands from the database server command prompt and write a local logfile of the results.

One good CellCLI command worth noting is LIST METRICHISTORY. This command does just what you would think, listing the metric history for all known metrics in the storage cell, along with the time stamp indicating when the values were collected. The output will likely be a very long list, as you can see in the following abbreviated output:

```
CellCLI> list metrichistory attributes name, collectionTime, metricType, metricValue,
metricValueAvg where metricObjectName = 'DBFS_DG_CD_02_myexa1cel04'
...
     GD_BY_FC_DIRTY        2013-08-24T19:50:42-05:00    Instantaneous   0.000 MB
     GD_IO_BY_R_LG         2013-08-24T19:50:42-05:00    Cumulative      2,656 MB
     GD_IO_BY_R_LG_SEC     2013-08-24T19:50:42-05:00    Rate            0.000 MB/sec
     GD_IO_BY_R_SM         2013-08-24T19:50:42-05:00    Cumulative      207 MB
     GD_IO_BY_R_SM_SEC     2013-08-24T19:50:42-05:00    Rate            0.000 MB/sec
     GD_IO_BY_W_LG         2013-08-24T19:50:42-05:00    Cumulative      8,378 MB
     GD_IO_BY_W_LG_SEC     2013-08-24T19:50:42-05:00    Rate            0.000 MB/sec
     GD_IO_BY_W_SM         2013-08-24T19:50:42-05:00    Cumulative      60.191 MB
     GD_IO_BY_W_SM_SEC     2013-08-24T19:50:42-05:00    Rate            0.000 MB/sec
     GD_IO_ERRS            2013-08-24T19:50:42-05:00    Cumulative      0
     GD_IO_ERRS_MIN        2013-08-24T19:50:42-05:00    Rate            0.0 /min
     GD_IO_RQ_R_LG         2013-08-24T19:50:42-05:00    Cumulative      2,656 IO requests
     GD_IO_RQ_R_LG_SEC     2013-08-24T19:50:42-05:00    Rate            0.0 IO/sec
     GD_IO_RQ_R_SM         2013-08-24T19:50:42-05:00    Cumulative      4,086 IO requests
     GD_IO_RQ_R_SM_SEC     2013-08-24T19:50:42-05:00    Rate            0.0 IO/sec
     GD_IO_RQ_W_LG         2013-08-24T19:50:42-05:00    Cumulative      8,781 IO requests
     GD_IO_RQ_W_LG_SEC     2013-08-24T19:50:42-05:00    Rate            0.0 IO/sec
     GD_IO_RQ_W_SM         2013-08-24T19:50:42-05:00    Cumulative      1,326 IO requests
     GD_IO_RQ_W_SM_SEC     2013-08-24T19:50:42-05:00    Rate            0.0 IO/sec
...
```

The metrics listed may not be entirely clear from the abbreviations used in the names. A listing of each name and its meaning follows.

```
GD_BY_FC_DIRTY          Number of dirty MB cached for the griddisk
GD_IO_BY_R_LG           Griddisk I/O from large reads, in MB
GD_IO_BY_R_LG_SEC       Griddisk I/O from large reads per second, MB
GD_IO_BY_R_SM           Griddisk I/O from small reads, in MB
GD_IO_BY_R_SM_SEC       Griddisk I/O from small reads per second, MB
GD_IO_BY_W_LG           Griddisk I/O from large writes, in MB
GD_IO_BY_W_LG_SEC       Griddisk I/O from large writes per second, MB
GD_IO_BY_W_SM           Griddisk I/O from small writes, in MB
GD_IO_BY_W_SM_SEC       Griddisk I/O from small writes per second, MB
GD_IO_ERRS              Griddisk I/O errors
```

```
GD_IO_ERRS_MIN          Griddisk I/O errors per minute
GD_IO_RQ_R_LG              Griddisk large I/O read requests
GD_IO_RQ_R_LG_SEC         Griddisk large I/O read requests per second
GD_IO_RQ_R_SM           Griddisk small I/O read requests
GD_IO_RQ_R_SM_SEC         Griddisk small I/O read requests per second
GD_IO_RQ_W_LG             Griddisk large I/O write requests
GD_IO_RQ_W_LG_SEC         Griddisk large I/O write requests per second
GD_IO_RQ_W_SM             Griddisk small I/O write requests
GD_IO_RQ_W_SM_SEC         Griddisk small I/O write requests, per second
```

The only metric in that list reported as instantaneous is GD_BY_FC_DIRTY, which reports the current value for the MB of dirty cache blocks for the grid disk. The following metrics report cumulative values since cellsrv was started:

```
GD_IO_BY_R_LG
GD_IO_BY_R_SM
GD_IO_BY_W_LG
GD_IO_BY_W_SM
GD_IO_ERRS
GD_IO_RQ_R_LG
GD_IO_RQ_R_SM
GD_IO_RQ_W_LG
GD_IO_RQ_W_SM
```

The first four metrics are reported in MB; the remaining metrics are simply cumulative counts for the listed metrics. Additionally, there are rate metrics reported, as follows:

```
GD_IO_BY_R_LG  _SEC
GD_IO_BY_R_SM  _SEC
GD_IO_BY_W_LG_SEC
GD_IO_BY_W_SM_SEC
GD_IO_ERRS_MIN
GD_IO_RQ_R_LG  _SEC
GD_IO_RQ_R_SM_SEC
GD_IO_RQ_W_LG_SEC
GD_IO_RQ_W_SM_SEC
```

With the exception of GD_IO_ERRS_MIN, which reports the rate per minute for I/O error generation, these metrics report rates per second. These are current rates, updated at the time the metrics are reported. Read and write requests, as well as the actual I/O generated, will occur on a per-second basis. It should be unusual to generate I/O errors if the system is functioning properly. Notice the error metrics for this particular cell report 0 errors in total and 0.0 errors per minute. Impending disk failures or firmware mismatches can create I/O errors, but you should be informed of such impending failures by monitoring the alert history, which we covered in Chapter 9.

The collection interval is one minute, making the data volume very large after a prolonged period of uptime. Wildcard syntax does not work on the collectionTime attribute, so you won't be able to generate a report for a specific window of time. You can, however, restrict output to a specific minute if you wish, as follows:

```
CellCLI> list metrichistory attributes name, collectionTime, metricType, metricValue,
metricValueAvg where metricObjectName = 'DBFS_DG_CD_02_myexa1cel04' and collectionTime like
'2013-08-24T19:57:42-05:00'
         GD_BY_FC_DIRTY        2013-08-24T19:57:42-05:00    Instantaneous    0.000 MB
         GD_IO_BY_R_LG         2013-08-24T19:57:42-05:00    Cumulative       2,656 MB
```

GD_IO_BY_R_LG_SEC	2013-08-24T19:57:42-05:00	Rate	0.000 MB/sec
GD_IO_BY_R_SM	2013-08-24T19:57:42-05:00	Cumulative	207 MB
GD_IO_BY_R_SM_SEC	2013-08-24T19:57:42-05:00	Rate	0.000 MB/sec
GD_IO_BY_W_LG	2013-08-24T19:57:42-05:00	Cumulative	8,378 MB
GD_IO_BY_W_LG_SEC	2013-08-24T19:57:42-05:00	Rate	0.000 MB/sec
GD_IO_BY_W_SM	2013-08-24T19:57:42-05:00	Cumulative	60.191 MB
GD_IO_BY_W_SM_SEC	2013-08-24T19:57:42-05:00	Rate	0.000 MB/sec
GD_IO_ERRS	2013-08-24T19:57:42-05:00	Cumulative	0
GD_IO_ERRS_MIN	2013-08-24T19:57:42-05:00	Rate	0.0 /min
GD_IO_RQ_R_LG	2013-08-24T19:57:42-05:00	Cumulative	2,656 IO requests
GD_IO_RQ_R_LG_SEC	2013-08-24T19:57:42-05:00	Rate	0.0 IO/sec
GD_IO_RQ_R_SM	2013-08-24T19:57:42-05:00	Cumulative	4,086 IO requests
GD_IO_RQ_R_SM_SEC	2013-08-24T19:57:42-05:00	Rate	0.0 IO/sec
GD_IO_RQ_W_LG	2013-08-24T19:57:42-05:00	Cumulative	8,781 IO requests
GD_IO_RQ_W_LG_SEC	2013-08-24T19:57:42-05:00	Rate	0.0 IO/sec
GD_IO_RQ_W_SM	2013-08-24T19:57:42-05:00	Cumulative	1,326 IO requests
GD_IO_RQ_W_SM_SEC	2013-08-24T19:57:42-05:00	Rate	0.0 IO/sec

```
CellCLI>
```

You can write a script to generate a window of time, one minute at a time, as follows:

```
[oracle@myexa1db01 dbm1 bin]$ cellcli_metrichistory_window.sh
==================================================================================="
=================================== Cell 4 ========================================"
==================================================================================="
```

GD_BY_FC_DIRTY	2013-08-24T19:50:42-05:00	Instantaneous	0.000 MB
GD_IO_BY_R_LG	2013-08-24T19:50:42-05:00	Cumulative	2,656 MB
GD_IO_BY_R_LG_SEC	2013-08-24T19:50:42-05:00	Rate	0.000 MB/sec
GD_IO_BY_R_SM	2013-08-24T19:50:42-05:00	Cumulative	207 MB
GD_IO_BY_R_SM_SEC	2013-08-24T19:50:42-05:00	Rate	0.000 MB/sec
GD_IO_BY_W_LG	2013-08-24T19:50:42-05:00	Cumulative	8,378 MB
GD_IO_BY_W_LG_SEC	2013-08-24T19:50:42-05:00	Rate	0.000 MB/sec
GD_IO_BY_W_SM	2013-08-24T19:50:42-05:00	Cumulative	60.191 MB
GD_IO_BY_W_SM_SEC	2013-08-24T19:50:42-05:00	Rate	0.000 MB/sec
GD_IO_ERRS	2013-08-24T19:50:42-05:00	Cumulative	0
GD_IO_ERRS_MIN	2013-08-24T19:50:42-05:00	Rate	0.0 /min
GD_IO_RQ_R_LG	2013-08-24T19:50:42-05:00	Cumulative	2,656 IO requests
GD_IO_RQ_R_LG_SEC	2013-08-24T19:50:42-05:00	Rate	0.0 IO/sec
GD_IO_RQ_R_SM	2013-08-24T19:50:42-05:00	Cumulative	4,086 IO requests
GD_IO_RQ_R_SM_SEC	2013-08-24T19:50:42-05:00	Rate	0.0 IO/sec
GD_IO_RQ_W_LG	2013-08-24T19:50:42-05:00	Cumulative	8,781 IO requests
GD_IO_RQ_W_LG_SEC	2013-08-24T19:50:42-05:00	Rate	0.0 IO/sec
GD_IO_RQ_W_SM	2013-08-24T19:50:42-05:00	Cumulative	1,326 IO requests
GD_IO_RQ_W_SM_SEC	2013-08-24T19:50:42-05:00	Rate	0.0 IO/sec
GD_BY_FC_DIRTY	2013-08-24T19:51:42-05:00	Instantaneous	0.000 MB
GD_IO_BY_R_LG	2013-08-24T19:51:42-05:00	Cumulative	2,656 MB
GD_IO_BY_R_LG_SEC	2013-08-24T19:51:42-05:00	Rate	0.000 MB/sec
GD_IO_BY_R_SM	2013-08-24T19:51:42-05:00	Cumulative	207 MB
GD_IO_BY_R_SM_SEC	2013-08-24T19:51:42-05:00	Rate	0.000 MB/sec
GD_IO_BY_W_LG	2013-08-24T19:51:42-05:00	Cumulative	8,378 MB

GD_IO_BY_W_LG_SEC	2013-08-24T19:51:42-05:00	Rate	0.000 MB/sec
GD_IO_BY_W_SM	2013-08-24T19:51:42-05:00	Cumulative	60.191 MB
GD_IO_BY_W_SM_SEC	2013-08-24T19:51:42-05:00	Rate	0.000 MB/sec
GD_IO_ERRS	2013-08-24T19:51:42-05:00	Cumulative	0
GD_IO_ERRS_MIN	2013-08-24T19:51:42-05:00	Rate	0.0 /min
GD_IO_RQ_R_LG	2013-08-24T19:51:42-05:00	Cumulative	2,656 IO requests
GD_IO_RQ_R_LG_SEC	2013-08-24T19:51:42-05:00	Rate	0.0 IO/sec
GD_IO_RQ_R_SM	2013-08-24T19:51:42-05:00	Cumulative	4,086 IO requests
GD_IO_RQ_R_SM_SEC	2013-08-24T19:51:42-05:00	Rate	0.0 IO/sec
GD_IO_RQ_W_LG	2013-08-24T19:51:42-05:00	Cumulative	8,781 IO requests
GD_IO_RQ_W_LG_SEC	2013-08-24T19:51:42-05:00	Rate	0.0 IO/sec
GD_IO_RQ_W_SM	2013-08-24T19:51:42-05:00	Cumulative	1,326 IO requests
GD_IO_RQ_W_SM_SEC	2013-08-24T19:51:42-05:00	Rate	0.0 IO/sec
GD_BY_FC_DIRTY	2013-08-24T19:52:42-05:00	Instantaneous	0.000 MB
GD_IO_BY_R_LG	2013-08-24T19:52:42-05:00	Cumulative	2,656 MB
GD_IO_BY_R_LG_SEC	2013-08-24T19:52:42-05:00	Rate	0.000 MB/sec
GD_IO_BY_R_SM	2013-08-24T19:52:42-05:00	Cumulative	207 MB
GD_IO_BY_R_SM_SEC	2013-08-24T19:52:42-05:00	Rate	0.000 MB/sec
GD_IO_BY_W_LG	2013-08-24T19:52:42-05:00	Cumulative	8,378 MB
GD_IO_BY_W_LG_SEC	2013-08-24T19:52:42-05:00	Rate	0.000 MB/sec
GD_IO_BY_W_SM	2013-08-24T19:52:42-05:00	Cumulative	60.191 MB
GD_IO_BY_W_SM_SEC	2013-08-24T19:52:42-05:00	Rate	0.000 MB/sec
GD_IO_ERRS	2013-08-24T19:52:42-05:00	Cumulative	0
GD_IO_ERRS_MIN	2013-08-24T19:52:42-05:00	Rate	0.0 /min
GD_IO_RQ_R_LG	2013-08-24T19:52:42-05:00	Cumulative	2,656 IO requests
GD_IO_RQ_R_LG_SEC	2013-08-24T19:52:42-05:00	Rate	0.0 IO/sec
GD_IO_RQ_R_SM	2013-08-24T19:52:42-05:00	Cumulative	4,086 IO requests
GD_IO_RQ_R_SM_SEC	2013-08-24T19:52:42-05:00	Rate	0.0 IO/sec
GD_IO_RQ_W_LG	2013-08-24T19:52:42-05:00	Cumulative	8,781 IO requests
GD_IO_RQ_W_LG_SEC	2013-08-24T19:52:42-05:00	Rate	0.0 IO/sec
GD_IO_RQ_W_SM	2013-08-24T19:52:42-05:00	Cumulative	1,326 IO requests
GD_IO_RQ_W_SM_SEC	2013-08-24T19:52:42-05:00	Rate	0.0 IO/sec
GD_BY_FC_DIRTY	2013-08-24T19:53:42-05:00	Instantaneous	0.000 MB
GD_IO_BY_R_LG	2013-08-24T19:53:42-05:00	Cumulative	2,656 MB
GD_IO_BY_R_LG_SEC	2013-08-24T19:53:42-05:00	Rate	0.000 MB/sec
GD_IO_BY_R_SM	2013-08-24T19:53:42-05:00	Cumulative	207 MB
GD_IO_BY_R_SM_SEC	2013-08-24T19:53:42-05:00	Rate	0.000 MB/sec
GD_IO_BY_W_LG	2013-08-24T19:53:42-05:00	Cumulative	8,378 MB
GD_IO_BY_W_LG_SEC	2013-08-24T19:53:42-05:00	Rate	0.000 MB/sec
GD_IO_BY_W_SM	2013-08-24T19:53:42-05:00	Cumulative	60.191 MB
GD_IO_BY_W_SM_SEC	2013-08-24T19:53:42-05:00	Rate	0.000 MB/sec
GD_IO_ERRS	2013-08-24T19:53:42-05:00	Cumulative	0
GD_IO_ERRS_MIN	2013-08-24T19:53:42-05:00	Rate	0.0 /min
GD_IO_RQ_R_LG	2013-08-24T19:53:42-05:00	Cumulative	2,656 IO requests
GD_IO_RQ_R_LG_SEC	2013-08-24T19:53:42-05:00	Rate	0.0 IO/sec
GD_IO_RQ_R_SM	2013-08-24T19:53:42-05:00	Cumulative	4,086 IO requests
GD_IO_RQ_R_SM_SEC	2013-08-24T19:53:42-05:00	Rate	0.0 IO/sec
GD_IO_RQ_W_LG	2013-08-24T19:53:42-05:00	Cumulative	8,781 IO requests
GD_IO_RQ_W_LG_SEC	2013-08-24T19:53:42-05:00	Rate	0.0 IO/sec
GD_IO_RQ_W_SM	2013-08-24T19:53:42-05:00	Cumulative	1,326 IO requests
GD_IO_RQ_W_SM_SEC	2013-08-24T19:53:42-05:00	Rate	0.0 IO/sec

GD_BY_FC_DIRTY	2013-08-24T19:54:42-05:00	Instantaneous	0.000 MB
GD_IO_BY_R_LG	2013-08-24T19:54:42-05:00	Cumulative	2,656 MB
GD_IO_BY_R_LG_SEC	2013-08-24T19:54:42-05:00	Rate	0.000 MB/sec
GD_IO_BY_R_SM	2013-08-24T19:54:42-05:00	Cumulative	207 MB
GD_IO_BY_R_SM_SEC	2013-08-24T19:54:42-05:00	Rate	0.000 MB/sec
GD_IO_BY_W_LG	2013-08-24T19:54:42-05:00	Cumulative	8,378 MB
GD_IO_BY_W_LG_SEC	2013-08-24T19:54:42-05:00	Rate	0.000 MB/sec
GD_IO_BY_W_SM	2013-08-24T19:54:42-05:00	Cumulative	60.191 MB
GD_IO_BY_W_SM_SEC	2013-08-24T19:54:42-05:00	Rate	0.000 MB/sec
GD_IO_ERRS	2013-08-24T19:54:42-05:00	Cumulative	0
GD_IO_ERRS_MIN	2013-08-24T19:54:42-05:00	Rate	0.0 /min
GD_IO_RQ_R_LG	2013-08-24T19:54:42-05:00	Cumulative	2,656 IO requests
GD_IO_RQ_R_LG_SEC	2013-08-24T19:54:42-05:00	Rate	0.0 IO/sec
GD_IO_RQ_R_SM	2013-08-24T19:54:42-05:00	Cumulative	4,086 IO requests
GD_IO_RQ_R_SM_SEC	2013-08-24T19:54:42-05:00	Rate	0.0 IO/sec
GD_IO_RQ_W_LG	2013-08-24T19:54:42-05:00	Cumulative	8,781 IO requests
GD_IO_RQ_W_LG_SEC	2013-08-24T19:54:42-05:00	Rate	0.0 IO/sec
GD_IO_RQ_W_SM	2013-08-24T19:54:42-05:00	Cumulative	1,326 IO requests
GD_IO_RQ_W_SM_SEC	2013-08-24T19:54:42-05:00	Rate	0.0 IO/sec
GD_BY_FC_DIRTY	2013-08-24T19:55:42-05:00	Instantaneous	0.000 MB
GD_IO_BY_R_LG	2013-08-24T19:55:42-05:00	Cumulative	2,656 MB
GD_IO_BY_R_LG_SEC	2013-08-24T19:55:42-05:00	Rate	0.000 MB/sec
GD_IO_BY_R_SM	2013-08-24T19:55:42-05:00	Cumulative	207 MB
GD_IO_BY_R_SM_SEC	2013-08-24T19:55:42-05:00	Rate	0.000 MB/sec
GD_IO_BY_W_LG	2013-08-24T19:55:42-05:00	Cumulative	8,378 MB
GD_IO_BY_W_LG_SEC	2013-08-24T19:55:42-05:00	Rate	0.000 MB/sec
GD_IO_BY_W_SM	2013-08-24T19:55:42-05:00	Cumulative	60.191 MB
GD_IO_BY_W_SM_SEC	2013-08-24T19:55:42-05:00	Rate	0.000 MB/sec
GD_IO_ERRS	2013-08-24T19:55:42-05:00	Cumulative	0
GD_IO_ERRS_MIN	2013-08-24T19:55:42-05:00	Rate	0.0 /min
GD_IO_RQ_R_LG	2013-08-24T19:55:42-05:00	Cumulative	2,656 IO requests
GD_IO_RQ_R_LG_SEC	2013-08-24T19:55:42-05:00	Rate	0.0 IO/sec
GD_IO_RQ_R_SM	2013-08-24T19:55:42-05:00	Cumulative	4,086 IO requests
GD_IO_RQ_R_SM_SEC	2013-08-24T19:55:42-05:00	Rate	0.0 IO/sec
GD_IO_RQ_W_LG	2013-08-24T19:55:42-05:00	Cumulative	8,781 IO requests
GD_IO_RQ_W_LG_SEC	2013-08-24T19:55:42-05:00	Rate	0.0 IO/sec
GD_IO_RQ_W_SM	2013-08-24T19:55:42-05:00	Cumulative	1,326 IO requests
GD_IO_RQ_W_SM_SEC	2013-08-24T19:55:42-05:00	Rate	0.0 IO/sec
GD_BY_FC_DIRTY	2013-08-24T19:56:42-05:00	Instantaneous	0.000 MB
GD_IO_BY_R_LG	2013-08-24T19:56:42-05:00	Cumulative	2,656 MB
GD_IO_BY_R_LG_SEC	2013-08-24T19:56:42-05:00	Rate	0.000 MB/sec
GD_IO_BY_R_SM	2013-08-24T19:56:42-05:00	Cumulative	207 MB
GD_IO_BY_R_SM_SEC	2013-08-24T19:56:42-05:00	Rate	0.000 MB/sec
GD_IO_BY_W_LG	2013-08-24T19:56:42-05:00	Cumulative	8,378 MB
GD_IO_BY_W_LG_SEC	2013-08-24T19:56:42-05:00	Rate	0.000 MB/sec
GD_IO_BY_W_SM	2013-08-24T19:56:42-05:00	Cumulative	60.191 MB
GD_IO_BY_W_SM_SEC	2013-08-24T19:56:42-05:00	Rate	0.000 MB/sec
GD_IO_ERRS	2013-08-24T19:56:42-05:00	Cumulative	0
GD_IO_ERRS_MIN	2013-08-24T19:56:42-05:00	Rate	0.0 /min
GD_IO_RQ_R_LG	2013-08-24T19:56:42-05:00	Cumulative	2,656 IO requests
GD_IO_RQ_R_LG_SEC	2013-08-24T19:56:42-05:00	Rate	0.0 IO/sec

GD_IO_RQ_R_SM	2013-08-24T19:56:42-05:00	Cumulative	4,086 IO requests
GD_IO_RQ_R_SM_SEC	2013-08-24T19:56:42-05:00	Rate	0.0 IO/sec
GD_IO_RQ_W_LG	2013-08-24T19:56:42-05:00	Cumulative	8,781 IO requests
GD_IO_RQ_W_LG_SEC	2013-08-24T19:56:42-05:00	Rate	0.0 IO/sec
GD_IO_RQ_W_SM	2013-08-24T19:56:42-05:00	Cumulative	1,326 IO requests
GD_IO_RQ_W_SM_SEC	2013-08-24T19:56:42-05:00	Rate	0.0 IO/sec
GD_BY_FC_DIRTY	2013-08-24T19:57:42-05:00	Instantaneous	0.000 MB
GD_IO_BY_R_LG	2013-08-24T19:57:42-05:00	Cumulative	2,656 MB
GD_IO_BY_R_LG_SEC	2013-08-24T19:57:42-05:00	Rate	0.000 MB/sec
GD_IO_BY_R_SM	2013-08-24T19:57:42-05:00	Cumulative	207 MB
GD_IO_BY_R_SM_SEC	2013-08-24T19:57:42-05:00	Rate	0.000 MB/sec
GD_IO_BY_W_LG	2013-08-24T19:57:42-05:00	Cumulative	8,378 MB
GD_IO_BY_W_LG_SEC	2013-08-24T19:57:42-05:00	Rate	0.000 MB/sec
GD_IO_BY_W_SM	2013-08-24T19:57:42-05:00	Cumulative	60.191 MB
GD_IO_BY_W_SM_SEC	2013-08-24T19:57:42-05:00	Rate	0.000 MB/sec
GD_IO_ERRS	2013-08-24T19:57:42-05:00	Cumulative	0
GD_IO_ERRS_MIN	2013-08-24T19:57:42-05:00	Rate	0.0 /min
GD_IO_RQ_R_LG	2013-08-24T19:57:42-05:00	Cumulative	2,656 IO requests
GD_IO_RQ_R_LG_SEC	2013-08-24T19:57:42-05:00	Rate	0.0 IO/sec
GD_IO_RQ_R_SM	2013-08-24T19:57:42-05:00	Cumulative	4,086 IO requests
GD_IO_RQ_R_SM_SEC	2013-08-24T19:57:42-05:00	Rate	0.0 IO/sec
GD_IO_RQ_W_LG	2013-08-24T19:57:42-05:00	Cumulative	8,781 IO requests
GD_IO_RQ_W_LG_SEC	2013-08-24T19:57:42-05:00	Rate	0.0 IO/sec
GD_IO_RQ_W_SM	2013-08-24T19:57:42-05:00	Cumulative	1,326 IO requests
GD_IO_RQ_W_SM_SEC	2013-08-24T19:57:42-05:00	Rate	0.0 IO/sec
GD_BY_FC_DIRTY	2013-08-24T19:58:42-05:00	Instantaneous	0.000 MB
GD_IO_BY_R_LG	2013-08-24T19:58:42-05:00	Cumulative	2,656 MB
GD_IO_BY_R_LG_SEC	2013-08-24T19:58:42-05:00	Rate	0.000 MB/sec
GD_IO_BY_R_SM	2013-08-24T19:58:42-05:00	Cumulative	207 MB
GD_IO_BY_R_SM_SEC	2013-08-24T19:58:42-05:00	Rate	0.000 MB/sec
GD_IO_BY_W_LG	2013-08-24T19:58:42-05:00	Cumulative	8,378 MB
GD_IO_BY_W_LG_SEC	2013-08-24T19:58:42-05:00	Rate	0.000 MB/sec
GD_IO_BY_W_SM	2013-08-24T19:58:42-05:00	Cumulative	60.191 MB
GD_IO_BY_W_SM_SEC	2013-08-24T19:58:42-05:00	Rate	0.000 MB/sec
GD_IO_ERRS	2013-08-24T19:58:42-05:00	Cumulative	0
GD_IO_ERRS_MIN	2013-08-24T19:58:42-05:00	Rate	0.0 /min
GD_IO_RQ_R_LG	2013-08-24T19:58:42-05:00	Cumulative	2,656 IO requests
GD_IO_RQ_R_LG_SEC	2013-08-24T19:58:42-05:00	Rate	0.0 IO/sec
GD_IO_RQ_R_SM	2013-08-24T19:58:42-05:00	Cumulative	4,086 IO requests
GD_IO_RQ_R_SM_SEC	2013-08-24T19:58:42-05:00	Rate	0.0 IO/sec
GD_IO_RQ_W_LG	2013-08-24T19:58:42-05:00	Cumulative	8,781 IO requests
GD_IO_RQ_W_LG_SEC	2013-08-24T19:58:42-05:00	Rate	0.0 IO/sec
GD_IO_RQ_W_SM	2013-08-24T19:58:42-05:00	Cumulative	1,326 IO requests
GD_IO_RQ_W_SM_SEC	2013-08-24T19:58:42-05:00	Rate	0.0 IO/sec
GD_BY_FC_DIRTY	2013-08-24T19:59:42-05:00	Instantaneous	0.000 MB
GD_IO_BY_R_LG	2013-08-24T19:59:42-05:00	Cumulative	2,656 MB
GD_IO_BY_R_LG_SEC	2013-08-24T19:59:42-05:00	Rate	0.000 MB/sec
GD_IO_BY_R_SM	2013-08-24T19:59:42-05:00	Cumulative	207 MB
GD_IO_BY_R_SM_SEC	2013-08-24T19:59:42-05:00	Rate	0.000 MB/sec
GD_IO_BY_W_LG	2013-08-24T19:59:42-05:00	Cumulative	8,378 MB
GD_IO_BY_W_LG_SEC	2013-08-24T19:59:42-05:00	Rate	0.000 MB/sec

```
         GD_IO_BY_W_SM        2013-08-24T19:59:42-05:00    Cumulative   60.191 MB
         GD_IO_BY_W_SM_SEC    2013-08-24T19:59:42-05:00    Rate         0.000 MB/sec
         GD_IO_ERRS           2013-08-24T19:59:42-05:00    Cumulative   0
         GD_IO_ERRS_MIN       2013-08-24T19:59:42-05:00    Rate         0.0 /min
         GD_IO_RQ_R_LG        2013-08-24T19:59:42-05:00    Cumulative   2,656 IO requests
         GD_IO_RQ_R_LG_SEC    2013-08-24T19:59:42-05:00    Rate         0.0 IO/sec
         GD_IO_RQ_R_SM        2013-08-24T19:59:42-05:00    Cumulative   4,086 IO requests
         GD_IO_RQ_R_SM_SEC    2013-08-24T19:59:42-05:00    Rate         0.0 IO/sec
         GD_IO_RQ_W_LG        2013-08-24T19:59:42-05:00    Cumulative   8,781 IO requests
         GD_IO_RQ_W_LG_SEC    2013-08-24T19:59:42-05:00    Rate         0.0 IO/sec
         GD_IO_RQ_W_SM        2013-08-24T19:59:42-05:00    Cumulative   1,326 IO requests
         GD_IO_RQ_W_SM_SEC    2013-08-24T19:59:42-05:00    Rate         0.0 IO/sec
[oracle@myexa1db01 dbm1 bin]$
```

OEM

OEM 12c can also be used to monitor the storage cells, provided you have the System Monitoring plug-in for Exadata Storage Server installed. Although it may not provide all of the metrics reported by the command-line interface, it can give graphical representation of how the metric values change over time. Unfortunately, we do not have access to an OEM installation with this plug-in installed.

■ **Note** As we don't have access to the plug-in, our "choice" is the command-line interface. Others may choose OEM for the graphical representations it provides. The choice, ultimately, is yours to make. We, being old-school DBAs, prefer scripting to "flashy" graphic tools.

Adding the O/S Metrics

Oracle does a pretty good job of gathering performance statistics and metrics, but sometimes, especially when you encounter a bug situation, Oracle can miss the mark. It also has issues collecting and reporting low-level I/O data, such as that provided at the O/S level. In these situations, we turn to iostat, an O/S level utility that reports both the wait time and service time for I/O requests, something that Oracle cannot do.

The iostat utility can produce two types of reports, one for CPU utilization and the other for device utilization. When iostat is called without parameters, these two types are combined into a single output block, and an example of that follows.

```
[celladmin@myexa1cel04 ~]$ iostat
Linux 2.6.32-400.11.1.el5uek (myexa1cel04.mydomain.com)    08/29/2013

avg-cpu:  %user   %nice %system %iowait  %steal   %idle
           1.69    0.00    1.00    0.76    0.00   96.55

Device:            tps   Blk_read/s   Blk_wrtn/s   Blk_read   Blk_wrtn
sda              43.34     17678.69      2536.11   76052113157 10910095951
sda1              0.00         0.40         0.00    1724104       3566
sda2              0.00         0.00         0.00       6682          0
sda3             37.19     17595.97      2398.88   75696251195 10319754897
sda4              0.00         0.00         0.00       5598          0
sda5              5.17         1.14       128.00    4898908   550629320
```

sda6	0.26	34.13	0.00	146813324	3688
sda7	0.32	10.30	8.97	44302234	38601648
sda8	0.08	10.24	0.00	44052706	3568
sda9	0.05	6.83	0.00	29372810	3504
sda10	0.02	2.33	0.00	10020082	3504
sda11	0.17	17.28	0.25	74333114	1092256
sdb	40.52	14599.59	2521.14	62806099223	10845728471
sdb1	0.00	0.40	0.00	·1722690	3566
sdb2	0.00	0.00	0.00	6674	0
sdb3	34.50	14517.86	2383.92	62454489703	10255387417
sdb4	0.00	0.00	0.00	5598	0
sdb5	5.05	0.19	128.00	802666	550629320
sdb6	0.26	34.13	0.00	146811502	3688
sdb7	0.32	10.26	8.97	44156132	38601648
sdb8	0.08	10.24	0.00	44051066	3568
sdb9	0.05	6.83	0.00	29371066	3504
sdb10	0.02	2.33	0.00	10018098	3504
sdb11	0.17	17.28	0.25	74331628	1092256
sdc	35.50	15621.93	2358.42	67204113857	10145702504
sdd	43.31	18238.75	2411.67	78461434439	10374796825
sde	37.45	16292.94	2347.21	70090743919	10097464073
sdf	42.67	15401.76	2390.05	66256976848	10281761045
sdg	38.74	14337.09	2400.82	61676859523	10328104921
sdh	41.19	15494.96	2350.70	66657914894	10112485534
sdi	36.14	15339.71	2385.90	65990024896	10263942048
sdj	44.92	14766.18	2368.01	63522769026	10186958174
sdk	48.80	19425.04	2366.34	83564757833	10179786802
sdl	34.74	16006.00	2356.02	68856369043	10135375323
sdm	0.25	12.18	0.05	52388804	196296
sdm1	0.25	12.18	0.05	52385100	196296
md1	0.00	0.00	0.00	12560	0
md11	0.06	0.43	0.22	1854994	946160
md2	0.00	0.00	0.00	12848	0
md8	0.00	0.00	0.00	12616	48
md7	1.06	0.09	8.43	367218	36269392
md6	0.00	0.00	0.00	12774	120
md5	15.14	0.36	120.89	1551674	520072952
md4	0.00	0.01	0.00	57062	14
sdn	29.66	367.66	286.28	1581624255	1231530696
sdq	29.43	355.56	287.35	1529580431	1236147912
sdo	30.37	392.50	287.97	1688497023	1238832936
sdt	29.78	368.98	286.39	1587326255	1232021696
sdp	29.39	355.41	286.29	1528946047	1231606520
sdu	29.96	375.48	286.70	1615302159	1233365976
sds	29.72	368.07	286.62	1583404543	1233007976
sdr	33.92	493.72	286.80	2123954599	1233773728
sdy	29.20	352.04	291.22	1514424727	1252820440
sdx	29.23	359.17	286.09	1545115295	1230741224
sdw	30.19	373.09	291.31	1604988023	1253177480
sdv	29.80	368.34	288.12	1584564047	1239460224
sdac	29.00	347.57	287.43	1495213023	1236481216

```
sdab          28.98        349.61      288.36 1503994447 1240495096
sdz           34.75        540.44      286.27 2324924367 1231527200
sdaa          30.65        396.05      286.86 1703787199 1234049360

[celladmin@myexa1cel04 ~]$
```

The reports can be isolated using the -c option (to produce a CPU-only report) or the -d option (to produce a device-only report). For the device report the -x option can also be specified to produce a report with extended statistics. Looking at both forms of the iostat device report, you can see what additional statistics are reported. First up is the "regular" iostat device report.

```
[celladmin@myexa1cel04 ~]$ iostat -d
Linux 2.6.32-400.11.1.el5uek (myexa1cel04.mydomain.com)     08/29/2013

Device:          tps    Blk_read/s  Blk_wrtn/s    Blk_read    Blk_wrtn
sda            43.34     17677.25     2539.27  76057415661 10925374425
sda1            0.00         0.40        0.00     1724104        3566
sda2            0.00         0.00        0.00        6682           0
sda3           37.19     17594.54     2402.04  75701552203 10334934195
sda4            0.00         0.00        0.00        5598           0
sda5            5.17         1.14      128.00     4899732   550719152
sda6            0.26        34.12        0.00   146813324        3688
sda7            0.32        10.30        8.97    44302242    38610304
sda8            0.08        10.24        0.00    44052706        3568
sda9            0.05         6.83        0.00    29372810        3504
sda10           0.02         2.33        0.00    10020082        3504
sda11           0.17        17.28        0.25    74333778     1092944
sdb            40.52     14602.81     2524.33  62829441959 10861093803
sdb1            0.00         0.40        0.00     1722690        3566
sdb2            0.00         0.00        0.00        6674           0
sdb3           34.50     14521.09     2387.10  62477831559 10270653573
sdb4            0.00         0.00        0.00        5598           0
sdb5            5.05         0.19      128.00      802690   550719152
sdb6            0.26        34.12        0.00   146811502        3688
sdb7            0.32        10.26        8.97    44156132    38610304
sdb8            0.08        10.24        0.00    44051066        3568
sdb9            0.05         6.83        0.00    29371066        3504
sdb10           0.02         2.33        0.00    10018098        3504
sdb11           0.17        17.28        0.25    74332484     1092944
sdc            35.50     15623.32     2361.59  67220250345 10160892333
sdd            43.31     18239.34     2414.85  78475828335 10390026084
sde            37.46     16293.08     2350.37  70101955031 10112591593
sdf            42.68     15402.36     2393.21  66269586024 10296925275
sdg            38.74     14336.90     2403.96  61685381083 10343176536
sdh            41.20     15502.49     2353.87  66700399494 10127677980
sdi            36.14     15339.68     2389.08  65999899736 10279157674
sdj            44.92     14769.30     2371.17  63545804314 10202104613
sdk            48.81     19432.90     2369.51  83611198593 10194961456
sdl            34.75     16010.29     2359.19  68885217579 10150542364
sdm             0.25        12.18        0.05    52399172      196296
sdm1            0.25        12.18        0.05    52395468      196296
```

md1	0.00	0.00	0.00	12560	0
md11	0.06	0.43	0.22	1856514	946768
md2	0.00	0.00	0.00	12848	0
md8	0.00	0.00	0.00	12616	48
md7	1.06	0.09	8.43	367226	36277680
md6	0.00	0.00	0.00	12774	120
md5	15.14	0.36	120.89	1551714	520157664
md4	0.00	0.01	0.00	57062	14
sdn	29.66	367.70	286.26	1582041391	1231643376
sdq	29.44	355.59	287.33	1529927871	1236264000
sdo	30.38	392.53	287.96	1688884367	1238948184
sdt	29.78	369.01	286.37	1587689215	1232138712
sdp	29.39	355.44	286.28	1529296303	1231728176
sdu	29.97	375.53	286.68	1615731519	1233479056
sds	29.73	368.09	286.60	1583739183	1233122872
sdr	33.92	493.76	286.78	2124413863	1233898648
sdy	29.20	352.06	291.21	1514777647	1252946168
sdx	29.24	359.20	286.08	1545466895	1230858064
sdw	30.19	373.12	291.29	1605375927	1253298360
sdv	29.80	368.37	288.10	1584924095	1239580568
sdac	29.00	347.59	287.41	1495543487	1236597160
sdab	28.98	349.64	288.34	1504346895	1240616544
sdz	34.75	540.47	286.26	2325399199	1231644472
sdaa	30.65	396.09	286.84	1704198463	1234166016

```
[celladmin@myexa1cel04 ~]$
```

Next is the extended report.

```
[celladmin@myexa1cel04 ~]$ iostat -d -x
Linux 2.6.32-400.11.1.el5uek (myexa1cel04.mydomain.com)     08/29/2013
```

Device:	rrqm/s	wrqm/s	r/s	w/s	rsec/s	wsec/s	avgrq-sz	avgqu-sz	await	svctm	%util
sda	8.25	11.91	16.60	26.74	17677.00	2539.70	466.49	0.42	9.62	2.38	10.30
sda1	0.00	0.00	0.00	0.00	0.40	0.00	117.64	0.00	3.61	1.05	0.00
sda2	0.00	0.00	0.00	0.00	0.00	0.00	1.86	0.00	2.40	2.40	0.00
sda3	8.23	0.05	15.75	21.44	17594.29	2402.47	537.64	0.39	10.45	2.74	10.21
sda4	0.00	0.00	0.00	0.00	0.00	0.00	1.66	0.00	2.91	2.91	0.00
sda5	0.00	10.96	0.13	5.04	1.14	128.00	24.97	0.02	3.24	2.35	1.22
sda6	0.01	0.00	0.26	0.00	34.12	0.00	131.44	0.00	18.88	0.73	0.02
sda7	0.00	0.88	0.08	0.24	10.30	8.97	60.96	0.00	7.06	3.52	0.11
sda8	0.00	0.00	0.08	0.00	10.24	0.00	130.96	0.00	16.06	0.70	0.01
sda9	0.00	0.00	0.05	0.00	6.83	0.00	130.25	0.00	13.40	0.65	0.00
sda10	0.00	0.00	0.02	0.00	2.33	0.00	128.70	0.00	15.51	0.89	0.00
sda11	0.00	0.01	0.15	0.02	17.28	0.25	104.65	0.00	13.01	2.24	0.04
sdb	6.71	11.90	14.98	25.54	14603.11	2524.75	422.64	0.97	23.94	2.27	9.21
sdb1	0.00	0.00	0.00	0.00	0.40	0.00	111.99	0.00	9.61	0.96	0.00
sdb2	0.00	0.00	0.00	0.00	0.00	0.00	1.86	0.00	1.96	1.96	0.00
sdb3	6.69	0.04	14.25	20.25	14521.39	2387.52	490.09	0.95	27.46	2.64	9.12
sdb4	0.00	0.00	0.00	0.00	0.00	0.00	1.66	0.00	2.05	2.05	0.00
sdb5	0.00	10.96	0.01	5.04	0.19	128.00	25.38	0.01	2.43	1.57	0.79

sdb6	0.01	0.00	0.26	0.00	34.12	0.00	130.73	0.00	12.43	0.56	0.01
sdb7	0.00	0.88	0.08	0.24	10.26	8.97	60.95	0.00	7.05	2.46	0.08
sdb8	0.00	0.00	0.08	0.00	10.24	0.00	130.87	0.00	15.60	0.68	0.01
sdb9	0.00	0.00	0.05	0.00	6.83	0.00	130.24	0.00	17.31	0.72	0.00
sdb10	0.00	0.00	0.02	0.00	2.33	0.00	127.69	0.00	15.44	0.80	0.00
sdb11	0.00	0.01	0.15	0.02	17.28	0.25	104.70	0.00	14.88	1.63	0.03
sdc	7.24	0.00	14.71	20.79	15623.37	2362.02	506.56	0.14	4.05	2.69	9.53
sdd	7.61	0.00	21.10	22.21	18239.30	2415.28	476.91	0.94	21.79	2.19	9.46
sde	7.46	0.00	17.14	20.32	16293.03	2350.78	497.65	0.09	29.14	2.55	9.57
sdf	7.09	0.00	21.32	21.36	15402.34	2393.63	417.01	0.93	21.69	2.19	9.35
sdg	6.64	0.00	17.40	21.34	14336.81	2404.38	432.11	0.92	23.67	2.37	9.18
sdh	7.09	0.00	20.21	20.99	15503.33	2354.30	433.47	0.95	23.03	2.26	9.30
sdi	7.10	0.01	15.67	20.47	15339.57	2389.50	490.51	0.19	5.38	2.69	9.71
sdj	6.72	0.00	24.12	20.79	14769.54	2371.58	381.62	0.91	20.24	2.06	9.27
sdk	7.70	0.00	28.28	20.53	19433.71	2369.95	446.69	0.98	20.13	2.04	9.98
sdl	7.38	0.00	14.66	20.09	16010.68	2359.62	528.70	0.05	30.15	2.86	9.93
sdm	5.83	0.01	0.25	0.00	12.18	0.05	48.05	0.00	2.42	1.30	0.03
sdm1	5.83	0.01	0.25	0.00	12.18	0.05	48.05	0.00	2.42	1.30	0.03
md1	0.00	0.00	0.00	0.00	0.00	0.00	8.00	0.00	0.00	0.00	0.00
md11	0.00	0.00	0.03	0.03	0.43	0.22	10.95	0.00	0.00	0.00	0.00
md2	0.00	0.00	0.00	0.00	0.00	0.00	8.00	0.00	0.00	0.00	0.00
md8	0.00	0.00	0.00	0.00	0.00	0.00	8.00	0.00	0.00	0.00	0.00
md7	0.00	0.00	0.00	1.05	0.09	8.43	8.07	0.00	0.00	0.00	0.00
md6	0.00	0.00	0.00	0.00	0.00	0.00	7.99	0.00	0.00	0.00	0.00
md5	0.00	0.00	0.03	15.11	0.36	120.89	8.01	0.00	0.00	0.00	0.00
md4	0.00	0.00	0.00	0.00	0.01	0.00	17.27	0.00	0.00	0.00	0.00
sdn	0.00	0.00	21.82	7.84	367.71	286.26	22.05	0.00	0.13	0.12	0.37
sdq	0.00	0.00	21.57	7.87	355.59	287.33	21.84	0.00	0.13	0.12	0.36
sdo	0.00	0.00	22.49	7.89	392.54	287.95	22.40	0.00	0.13	0.12	0.38
sdt	0.00	0.00	21.95	7.83	369.02	286.37	22.00	0.00	0.14	0.13	0.38
sdp	0.00	0.00	21.57	7.82	355.45	286.28	21.83	0.00	0.13	0.12	0.36
sdu	0.00	0.00	22.12	7.85	375.54	286.68	22.10	0.00	0.14	0.13	0.38
sds	0.00	0.00	21.87	7.85	368.10	286.60	22.02	0.00	0.14	0.12	0.37
sdr	0.00	0.00	26.08	7.84	493.76	286.78	23.01	0.00	0.14	0.13	0.43
sdy	0.00	0.00	21.20	8.00	352.07	291.21	22.03	0.00	0.14	0.12	0.36
sdx	0.00	0.00	21.41	7.82	359.20	286.07	22.07	0.00	0.14	0.13	0.37
sdw	0.00	0.00	22.20	7.99	373.13	291.29	22.01	0.00	0.14	0.13	0.38
sdv	0.00	0.00	21.90	7.90	368.37	288.10	22.03	0.00	0.14	0.12	0.37
sdac	0.00	0.00	21.13	7.88	347.60	287.41	21.89	0.00	0.13	0.12	0.36
sdab	0.00	0.00	21.08	7.90	349.65	288.34	22.01	0.00	0.13	0.12	0.36
sdz	0.00	0.00	26.91	7.84	540.48	286.26	23.79	0.00	0.13	0.12	0.43
sdaa	0.00	0.00	22.80	7.85	396.10	286.84	22.28	0.00	0.13	0.12	0.37

```
[celladmin@myexa1cel04 ~]$
```

Both reports are beneficial, as they report different sets of monitoring data that can be very useful when digging into some performance issues or bugs.

The CPU report format, showing the columns and their meanings, is found in Table 10-1.

Table 10-1. *Iostat Values Reported in CPU Format*

%user	Shows the percentage of CPU utilization that occurred while executing at the user level (application).
%nice	Shows the percentage of CPU utilization that occurred while executing at the user level with nice priority.
%system	Shows the percentage of CPU utilization that occurred while executing at the system level (kernel).
%iowait	Shows the percentage of time that the CPU or CPUs were idle during which the system had an outstanding disk I/O request.
%steal	Shows the percentage of time spent in involuntary wait by the virtual CPU or CPUs while the hypervisor was servicing another virtual processor.
%idle	Shows the percentage of time that the CPU or CPUs were idle and the system did not have an outstanding disk I/O request.

The device report format is shown in Table 10-2.

Table 10-2. *Iostat Values Reported by Device Format*

Device:	This column gives the device (or partition) name, which is displayed as hdiskn, with 2.2 kernels, for the nth device. It is displayed as devm-n, with 2.4 kernels, where m is the major number of the device and n a distinctive number. With newer kernels, the device name as listed in the /dev directory is displayed.
tps	Indicates the number of transfers per second that were issued to the device. A transfer is an I/O request to the device. Multiple logical requests can be combined into a single I/O request to the device. A transfer is of indeterminate size.
Blk_read/s	Indicates the amount of data read from the device expressed in a number of blocks per second. Blocks are equivalent to sectors with 2.4 kernels and newer and, therefore, have a size of 512 bytes. With older kernels, a block is of indeterminate size.
Blk_wrtn/s	Indicates the amount of data written to the device, expressed in a number of blocks per second.
Blk_read	The total number of blocks read.
Blk_wrtn	The total number of blocks written.
kB_read/s	Indicates the amount of data read from the device, expressed in kilobytes per second.
kB_wrtn/s	Indicates the amount of data written to the device, expressed in kilobytes per second.
kB_read	The total number of kilobytes read.
kB_wrtn	The total number of kilobytes written.
MB_read/s	Indicates the amount of data read from the device, expressed in megabytes per second.
MB_wrtn/s	Indicate the amount of data written to the device expressed in megabytes per second.
MB_read	The total number of megabytes read.
MB_wrtn	The total number of megabytes written.
rrqm/s	The number of read requests merged per second that were queued to the device.
wrqm/s	The number of write requests merged per second that were queued to the device.

(continued)

Table 10-2. (*continued*)

r/s	The number of read requests that were issued to the device per second.
w/s	The number of write requests that were issued to the device per second.
rsec/s	The number of sectors read from the device per second.
wsec/s	The number of sectors written to the device per second.
rkB/s	The number of kilobytes read from the device per second.
wkB/s	The number of kilobytes written to the device per second.
rMB/s	The number of megabytes read from the device per second.
wMB/s	The number of megabytes written to the device per second.
avgrq-sz	The average size (in sectors) of the requests that were issued to the device.
avgqu-sz	The average queue length of the requests that were issued to the device.
await	The average time (in milliseconds) for I/O requests issued to the device to be served. This includes the time spent by the requests in queue and the time spent servicing them.
svctm	The average service time (in milliseconds) for I/O requests that were issued to the device.
%util	Percentage of CPU time during which I/O requests were issued to the device (bandwidth utilization for the device). Device saturation occurs when this value is close to 100 percent.
ops/s	Indicates the number of operations that were issued to the mount point per second.
rops/s	Indicates the number of read operations that were issued to the mount point per second.
wops/s	Indicates the number of write operations that were issued to the mount point per second.

The basic device report provides the tps, Blk_read/s, Blk_wrtn/s, Blk_read, and the Blk_wrt values. The remainder of the list in Table 10-2 is displayed in the extended device report. You should not be seeing large await times with a properly functioning Exadata system. On systems we manage, the largest await times we see are about 20 to 25 milliseconds for the physical disks and less than 1 millisecond for the flash disks. If you're seeing await times in the hundreds of milliseconds or longer on a regular basis for a given disk, further investigation is warranted, as the unit might be suffering from a firmware mismatch or impending device failure.

Because the database servers don't directly access the storage media, running an iostat device report to diagnose disk read/write issues won't provide any useful information regarding the ASM storage. However, don't forget that the database servers utilize CPU for all transactions, so an iostat CPU report should be generated when you generate a CPU report for the storage cells. By doing so, you minimize the chances of missing CPU-related issues that may occur only on the database server.

The device names reported by iostat are those found in the /dev hierarchy of directories on the server being monitored. Which cell disk is mapped to which device is reported by the CellCLI command list cell disk, specifying the name and deviceName attributes, as follows:

```
CellCLI> list celldisk attributes name, deviceName
         CD_00_myexa1cel04      /dev/sda
         CD_01_myexa1cel04      /dev/sdb
         CD_02_myexa1cel04      /dev/sdc
         CD_03_myexa1cel04      /dev/sdd
         CD_04_myexa1cel04      /dev/sde
         CD_05_myexa1cel04      /dev/sdf
         CD_06_myexa1cel04      /dev/sdg
```

```
CD_07_myexa1cel04        /dev/sdh
CD_08_myexa1cel04        /dev/sdi
CD_09_myexa1cel04        /dev/sdj
CD_10_myexa1cel04        /dev/sdk
CD_11_myexa1cel04        /dev/sdl
FD_00_myexa1cel04        /dev/sdv
FD_01_myexa1cel04        /dev/sdw
FD_02_myexa1cel04        /dev/sdx
FD_03_myexa1cel04        /dev/sdy
FD_04_myexa1cel04        /dev/sdz
FD_05_myexa1cel04        /dev/sdaa
FD_06_myexa1cel04        /dev/sdab
FD_07_myexa1cel04        /dev/sdac
FD_08_myexa1cel04        /dev/sdr
FD_09_myexa1cel04        /dev/sds
FD_10_myexa1cel04        /dev/sdt
FD_11_myexa1cel04        /dev/sdu
FD_12_myexa1cel04        /dev/sdn
FD_13_myexa1cel04        /dev/sdo
FD_14_myexa1cel04        /dev/sdp
FD_15_myexa1cel04        /dev/sdq

CellCLI>
```

The report shown should only have to be run once per storage cell on your Exadata system, provided you don't upgrade it to the next available configuration or if your Exadata system is a Full Rack. System upgrades, from Quarter Rack to Half Rack or Half Rack to Full Rack, will require you to run the report again, so that the new device mappings can be seen.

Knowing this information makes it easier to associate the device statistics reported by iostat -d to ASM disks and flash disks. Low-level I/O problems you might encounter can now be tracked and diagnosed by combining the output from the two utilities.

Things to Know

Exadata is well-instrumented across both the database and storage tiers, offering a large number of available metrics reporting on many aspects of the system. Choosing which metrics to report is an important task to prevent you from getting lost in an avalanche of data.

For monitoring to be effective, a baseline must be established, so that you have a known reference point to compare subsequent monitoring runs to. Comparing to a baseline provides a solid starting point from which to measure performance improvements and problems. Without such a baseline, every analysis is against a moving target, making the task much harder than it needs to be.

Oracle Enterprise Manager can be used to generate reports and graphs that represent performance metrics as they change over time. You still need a baseline to start from, and that baseline does not have to be for perfect performance. Remember: You're measuring performance changes relative to this baseline. You may find that when performance improves, you use that point of improvement as your new baseline.

OEM can also monitor the storage cells, if the System Monitoring plug-in for Exadata Storage Server is installed. This plug-in may not provide all of the metrics available from the command-line tools, but it can provide a view of how the storage statistics and metrics change over time.

Monitoring can also be performed outside of the Oracle Enterprise Manager by using scripts and command-line utilities to return the requested data. The storage cells offer both the `cellcli` and `cellsrvadmin` utilities, which report on various areas of the storage cells.

Oracle, no matter how well instrumented, doesn't report low-level I/O statistics, so it is necessary to go to the O/S for those. The `iostat` utility can provide a window into this low-level CPU and device activity. Two separate reports can be generated, one for CPU and one for devices, or both reports can be combined, by calling `iostat` without any command-line parameters.

The `cellcli` utility can report which cell disk is mapped to which hardware device, with the list `celldisk` command. The attributes of interest are name and deviceName. Knowing this mapping allows you to "translate" the output from the `iostat` device report, so you can monitor the ASM disks and see which, if any, may be experiencing problems.

## CHAPTER 11

Storage Reconfiguration

An Exadata system, by default, pre-allocates the bulk of the physical storage between the +DATA_MYEXA1 and +RECO_MYEXA1 disk groups and does so using an 80/20 split. During the preinstallation phase of purchase, Oracle supplies a worksheet to the DBAs, the network administrators, and the system administrators. Each group supplies information for the configuration process, with the DBAs and the network admins providing the bulk of that data. Once the worksheet is completed, discussions are held to clarify any ambiguous settings and to determine how the storage will be divided. It may not be apparent that the default settings need to be adjusted, so the system is configured with the standard 80/20 allocations. A third disk group, DBFS_DG, is also provided with approximately 32GB of space, and this disk group does not change in size.

It is possible, after configuration is complete, to change those allocations, but this is a destructive process that requires careful consideration. We have done this on an Exadata system destined for production, but it was done long before any production databases were created. It was also done with the assistance of Oracle Advanced Customer Support, and though we provide the steps to perform this reconfiguration, we *strongly* recommend you involve Oracle Advanced Customer Support in the process. The actual steps will be discussed, so that you will understand the entire process from start to finish. The goal of this chapter is to provide working knowledge of the storage-reconfiguration process. It may be best, if you are not comfortable performing such actions, to arrange with Oracle Advanced Customer Support to do this for you, should the need arise. Even if you don't do this yourself, it will be helpful to know what tasks will be run and what the end results will be. With that thought in mind, we'll proceed.

I Wish We Had More…

It may become apparent after the configuration has been completed, but before any databases (aside from DBM, the default database provided at installation) are created, that you may want or need more recovery storage than originally allocated, as an example. Or you may not be using the recovery area (an unlikely event) and would like to make the data disk group a bit larger, as another example. There is a way to do that before anything important gets created. We state again that reconfiguring the storage allocations is a *destructive* process that requires planning long before execution. We will demonstrate a process to distribute storage more evenly between the +DATA_MYEXA1 and +RECO_MYEXA1 disk groups, again with the caveat that proper planning is absolutely necessary and that Oracle Advanced Customer Support should be involved.

Redistributing the Wealth

Each disk in an Exadata system is logically divided into areas sometimes known as partitions, areas containing a fixed amount of storage determined at configuration time. Looking at how a single disk is configured on a standard Exadata installation, the following output shows how the various partitions are allocated:

```
CellCLI> list griddisk attributes name, size, offset where name like '.*CD_11.*'
        DATA_MYEXA1_CD_11_myexa1cel05    2208G           32M
        DBFS_DG_CD_11_myexa1cel05        33.796875G      2760.15625G
        RECO_MYEXA1_CD_11_myexa1cel05    552.109375G     2208.046875G

CellCLI>
```

■ **Note**   For UNIX/Linux systems, the terms *slice* and *partition* are used interchangeably in some sources. Both are used to indicate logical divisions of the physical disk. We will use the term *partition* in this text, as it is the most accurate terminology.

Notice that for a given disk, there are three partitions that ASM can see and use. Also note that for a given partition, the size plus the offset gives the starting "point" for the next partition. Unfortunately, the output from CellCLI cannot be ordered the way you might like to see it. The default ordering is by name in this example.

From the output provided, the first partition is assigned as the +DATA_MYEXA1 storage partition, starting after the first 32MB of storage. That 32MB is reserved for disk management by the operating system. The next partition available to ASM is assigned to the +RECO_MYEXA1 disk group, and the third partition is assigned to the +DBFS_DG disk group. The size of the disk groups is determined by the type of storage you select and the size of the Exadata rack that you've ordered. The system illustrated in this chapter uses high capacity disks, providing 3TB of storage per disk. High speed disks provide 600GB of storage per disk. The configuration process configures partitions for the data and recovery disk groups based on a parameter in the /opt/oracle.SupportTools/onecommand/onecommand.param file named SizeArr. Two systems were configured with the default storage division between +DATA_MYEXA1 and +RECO_MYEXA1. This resulted in an 80/20 allocation between these two disk groups. As mentioned previously, the output provided is for a standard Exadata configuration.

To change how ASM sees the storage, it will be necessary to delete the original configuration as the first step, so new partitions can be created across the physical disks. The next basic step is to create the new partitions and after that configure the ASM disk groups. Because the first step is to delete all configured partitions, this is not a recommended procedure when development, test, or production databases have been created on the Exadata system. We state again that this process is a destructive process and that no databases will remain after the initial steps of deleting the original logical disk configuration have completed. The GRID infrastructure is also deleted; it will be re-created as one of the 26 steps executed to define the new logical storage partitions.

■ **Note**   We ran this procedure on a newly configured Exadata system, with the assistance of Oracle Advanced Customer Support. *No important databases had been created on this system.* This is *not* a recommended operation when such databases exist on your system.

Looking at the V$ASM_DISKGROUP output you can see the original storage allocations. This is illustrated with the following output:

```
SQL> select name, free_mb, usable_file_mb
  2  from v$asm_diskgroup
  3  where name like '%MYEXA%';

NAME                              FREE_MB USABLE_FILE_MB
-----------------------------     --------- --------------
DATA_MYEXA1                       81050256       26959176
RECO_MYEXA1                       20324596        6770138

SQL>
```

You will see that when this process completes, the output from the illustrated query will report different values that are the result of the new storage settings. You should run this query both before the process starts and after the process finishes, to document the original storage and the newly configured storage.

With those notes in mind, we proceed with the steps necessary to reconfigure the storage.

Prepare

Not only are the logical storage areas redefined, but the "oracle" O/S user home is also re-created, so any changes made to that location must be preserved before executing this procedure. This needs to be done on all available database servers in your Exadata system, even if you have Oracle Advanced Customer Support perform the actual storage work. Thus, the first step to be executed is to preserve the "oracle" user home, either with tar (which originally was an acronym for *Tape ARchiver*, since in the olden days, the only media available was tape) or cpio (an acronym for *CoPy In/Out*, a "newer" utility relative to tar, designed to operate not only on tape but on block devices such as disk drives). These two utilities are provided at the operating-system level. If you choose tar, the following command will preserve the "oracle" O/S user's home directory:

```
$ tar cvf /tmp/oraclehome.tar ./*
```

In case you are not familiar with the tar command, the options provided perform the following actions:

```
c -- Create the archive
v -- Use verbose mode.  This will display all of the directories and files processed with their
associated paths
f -- The filename to use for the archive
```

Using the ./* syntax to specify the files to archive makes it easier to restore the files to any base directory you choose. It isn't likely that the "oracle" O/S user home will change names. Knowing this syntax can be helpful, if you want to copy a complete directory tree to another location, and it is our usual way to invoke tar to copy files and directories.

Using tar is not mandatory; you can also use cpio. If you are more comfortable with the cpio utility, the following command will archive the "oracle" O/S user home:

```
$ find . -depth -print | cpio -ov > /tmp/oraclehome.cpio
```

The options provided do the following:

```
o -- Copy out to the listed archive
v -- Verbose output, listing the files and paths processed
```

We recommend preserving the "oracle" user home directory before starting any storage reconfiguration, as it will be overwritten by the reconfiguration process. Preserve the existing "oracle" O/S user home on all available database servers, as all "oracle" O/S user homes will be rebuilt. Additionally, the "oracle" O/S user password will be reset to its original value, listed in the Exadata worksheet completed prior to delivery, installation, and initial configuration.

The file used for the Exadata configuration only allows you to specify the size of the data disk group partition. The recovery disk group partition size is derived from the value provided to size the data disk group. The DBFS_DG size is not affected by changing this value. This file cannot be modified until the original storage configuration has been deleted.

■ **Note** The commands listed for storage reconfiguration *must* be run as the "root" user. As this user has *unlimited power* at the O/S level, it *cannot* be stressed enough that caution *must* be exercised when executing these commands. If you are not comfortable using the "root" account, it would be best to make arrangements with Oracle Advanced Customer Support to reconfigure the storage to your desired levels.

You should have a good idea on what you want the storage reconfiguration to provide in terms of +DATA_MYEXA1 disk group and +RECO_MYEXA1 disk group sizes, and you should also have the "oracle" O/S user home preserved, either with tar or cpio. We now proceed with the actual process of reconfiguring the storage.

Additional tasks at this point include knowing what OEM agents are installed and noting whether or not the SCAN listener is using the default port. Reinstalling the OEM agents and reconfiguring the SCAN listener for a non-default port, if necessary, will have to be done as part of the restore steps, after the storage reconfiguration completes and the "oracle" O/S user home is restored. Steps to reinstall the OEM agents and reconfigure the SCAN listener will not be covered in this chapter, but it is good to know that they may need to be executed.

Act

You should be sufficiently prepared to begin the actual reconfiguration process. This first step drops the original storage configuration, including the configuration for the storage cells. Let's begin.

Act 1

Connect to database server 1 as the "root" user. You should see a # in the shell prompt indicating the login/su process was successful. You will now have to change directories to /opt/oracle.SupportTools/onecommand. This is where the scripts and configuration files that you will need to complete this operation reside. It's a good idea to know the available commands you can execute for this reconfiguration, and that information can be found by executing the following script with the listed parameters:

```
./deploy11203.sh -a -l
```

The following list will be displayed:

```
Step   0 = CleanworkTmp
Step   1 = DropUsersGroups
Step   2 = CreateUsers
Step   3 = ValidateGridDiskSizes
Step   4 = CreateOCRVoteGD
Step   5 = TestGetErrNode
Step   6 = DeinstallGI
Step   7 = DropCellDisk
Step   8 = DropUsersGroups
Step   9 = CheckCssd
Step  10 = testfn
Step  11 = FixAsmAudit
Step  12 = DropExpCellDisk
Step  13 = testHash
Step  14 = DeconfigGI
Step  15 = GetVIPInterface
Step  16 = DeleteDB
Step  17 = ApplyBP3
Step  18 = CopyCrspatchpm
Step  19 = SetupMultipath
Step  20 = RemovePartitions
Step  21 = SetupPartitions
Step  22 = ResetMultipath
Step  23 = DoT4Copy
Step  24 = DoAlltest
Step  25 = ApplyBPtoGridHome
Step  26 = Apply112CRSBPToRDBMS
Step  27 = RelinkRDSGI
Step  28 = RunConfigAssistV2
Step  29 = NewCreateCellCommands
Step  30 = GetPrivIpArray
Step  31 = SetASMDefaults
Step  32 = GetVIPInterface
Step  33 = Mychknode
Step  34 = UpdateOPatch
Step  35 = GetGroupHash
Step  36 = HugePages
Step  37 = ResetPermissions
Step  38 = CreateGroups
Step  39 = FixCcompiler
Step  40 = CollectLogFiles
Step  41 = OcrVoteRelocate
Step  42 = OcrVoteRelocate
Step  43 = FixOSWonCells
Step  44 = Dbcanew
Step  45 = testgetcl
Step  46 = setupASR
Step  47 = CrossCheckCellConf
```

```
Step 48 = SetupCoreControl
Step 49 = dropExtraCellDisks
Step 50 = CreateCellCommands
```

The following are three commands of interest for this step of the reconfiguration:

```
Step  6 = DeinstallGI
Step  7 = DropCellDisk
Step  8 = DropUsersGroups
```

These are the commands that will be executed to "wipe clean" the existing storage configuration and prepare it for the next step. Each command is run individually from the deploy11203.sh script. You must run these steps in the listed order, to ensure a complete removal of the existing configuration. The actual commands follow:

```
./deploy11203.sh -a -s 6
./deploy11203.sh -a -s 7
./deploy11203.sh -a -s 8
```

These steps will take approximately an hour to run on an Eighth Rack or Quarter Rack configuration and will provide output to the screen describing pending and completed tasks. We recommend that you run each command and watch the output provided. There should not be any errors generated from these processes; however, we feel it's best to be safe by watching the progress.

What do these steps do? Step 6 removes the GRID Infrastructure, basically the heart and soul of ASM (and RAC, but it's the link to ASM that we are concerned with in this operation). Once that infrastructure is gone, we are free to run Step 7 to drop the created grid disks and then the definitions for the partitions that ASM uses to recognize and access the storage. Last is the removal of the users and groups that access these partitions and grid disks. This is where the "oracle" user account gets dropped, along with its O/S home. Notice that only 3 steps are necessary to drop the existing storage configuration but 26 steps are necessary to re-create it.

Act 2

Once these operations have finished, it will be time to modify the storage array parameter to provide the storage division you want. The configuration file to edit is /opt/oracle.SupportTools/onecommand/onecommand.params. We use vi for editing such files, but you may wish to use emacs instead. Use whichever editor you are comfortable with. The parameter value to change is named SizeArr. For a standard default install, this line should look like the following entry:

```
SizeArr=2208G
```

It is good to know what value to use to obtain the desired storage division. Table 11-1 shows several SizeArr values and the approximate storage divisions created.

Table 11-1. *Some SizeArr Values and the Resulting Storage Allocations*

SizeArr Setting	Data Disk Group pct	Recovery Disk Group pct
2208	80	20
1932	70	30
1656	60	40
1487	55	45
1380	50	50

Remember that these percentages are approximations based on the default 80/20 storage allocation. We recommend that you use the standard shell script comment character, #, and comment that line, so you can preserve the original setting. You can now either copy the commented line or open a new line just below it and provide the following text:

```
SizeArr=<your chosen value>G
```

As an example, if you want to configure a 55/45 split on the available storage, the new line, based on the information in Table 11-1, would be as follows:

```
SizeArr=1487G
```

Once your edits are complete, there should be two lines listing SizeArr, as follows:

```
# SizeArr=2208G
SizeArr=1487G
```

This is the only change you will need to make to this parameter file, so save your work and exit the editor. You are now prepared to establish a new storage configuration.

Act 3

As in the previous operation, the deploy11203.sh script will be used, although with a greater number of steps. The following is the complete list of available steps for this part of the process:

```
Step   0 = ValidateEnv
Step   1 = CreateWorkDir
Step   2 = UnzipFiles
Step   3 = setupSSHroot
Step   4 = UpdateEtcHosts
Step   5 = CreateCellipinitora
Step   6 = ValidateIB
Step   7 = ValidateCell
Step   8 = PingRdsCheck
Step   9 = RunCalibrate
Step  10 = CreateUsers
Step  11 = SetupSSHusers
Step  12 = CreateGridDisks
Step  13 = GridSwInstall
Step  14 = PatchGridHome
Step  15 = RelinkRDSGI
Step  16 = GridRootScripts
Step  17 = DbSwInstall
Step  18 = PatchDBHomes
Step  19 = CreateASMDiskgroups
Step  20 = DbcaDB
Step  21 = DoUnlock
Step  22 = RelinkRDSDb
Step  23 = LockUpGI
Step  24 = ApplySecurityFixes
Step  25 = setupASR
Step  26 = SetupCellEmailAlerts
Step  27 = ResecureMachine
```

Unlike the first list, there are only 28 steps shown. As this is an existing Exadata installation, step 0, which validates the environment, and Step 27, which secures the machine, will not be run. This leaves the remaining 26 steps to reconfigure the storage and the storage cells. The following command will be used to complete the storage reconfiguration portion of this process:

```
./deploy11203.sh -r 1-26
```

The -r option executes the provided steps in order, as long as no step generates an error. If a step does generate an error, it stops at that step; any corrective action should be taken, and the deploy11203.sh script restarted with a modified list of steps. For example, if the execution stopped at step 21 due to errors, and the cause of the errors is corrected, the following command would restart the reconfiguration at the point it generated the error, as follows:

```
./deploy11203.sh -r 21-26
```

There should be no need to start the entire process from the beginning, should a problem arise midway through the execution.

For an Eighth Rack or Quarter Rack Exadata configuration, this last execution of the deploy11203.sh script will run for one and one-half to two hours. For larger Exadata configurations, this will run longer, as there will be a greater number of disks. Feedback will be provided by the script for each of the steps executed.

On a "clean" system—one that is still at the original configuration and without any new databases—we have experienced no errors or difficulties when reconfiguring the storage. It is a time-consuming process, but it should execute without issues.

■ **Note** We have executed this on a newly configured Exadata system, and it ran without difficulties. If you are planning on doing this on a system where other databases have been created, where other ORACLE_HOME locations exist, be advised that the steps provided here may experience problems related to these changes. The included database, commonly named DBM, will be re-created from scripts during the reconfiguration process. Be aware that restoring databases that were created after initial configuration was completed may cause errors due to the reallocated storage, especially if the +DATA_MYEXA1 disk group has been made smaller. In this situation, it is best to involve Oracle Advanced Customer Support.

Let's look at what each step accomplishes, at a basic level. Steps 1 and 2 are basic "housekeeping" actions, creating a temporary work directory and unzipping the software archives into that temporary work area. Step 3 starts the important aspects of this operation, which sets user equivalence (meaning passwordless ssh access) to all servers and switches for the "root" account. This is required, so that the remaining steps proceed without having to ask for a password. Step 4 updates the /etc/hosts file for the preconfigured storage cell IP addresses and server names for the Exadata system. This makes it easier to connect to other servers in the system, by using the server name rather than the IP address.

The next step, Step 5, creates the cellinit.ora file on the available storage cells. A sample of what the cellinit.ora contains (with actual IP addresses and port numbers obscured) follows.

```
#CELL Initialization Parameters
version=0.0
HTTP_PORT=####
bbuChargeThreshold=800
SSL_PORT=#####
RMI_PORT=#####
```

```
ipaddress1=###.###.###.###/##
bbuTempThreshold=60
DEPLOYED=TRUE
JMS_PORT=###
BMC_SNMP_PORT=###
```

This step also creates the `cellip.ora` file on the available database servers. Sample contents follow.

```
cell="XXX.XXX.XXX.3"
cell="XXX.XXX.XXX.4"
cell="XXX.XXX.XXX.5"
cell="XXX.XXX.XXX.6"
cell="XXX.XXX.XXX.7"
```

This file informs ASM of the available storage cells in the cluster.

Steps 6, 7, and 8 do necessary validation of the InfiniBand connectivity, storage cell configuration, and InfiniBand inter-process connectivity (IPC) between the database servers and the storage cells. Step 8 performs this validation by checking how the oracle executables are linked. IPC over InfiniBand is set by linking the oracle kernels with the `ipc_rds` option, and if this option is missing, IPC occurs over the non-InfiniBand network layer. Unfortunately, most database patches that relink the kernel do not include this parameter, because, I suspect, they are intended for non-Exadata systems. Thus, patching the oracle software can result in a loss of this connectivity, which can create performance issues by using a much slower network connection for IPC. The situation is easily rectified by relinking the oracle kernel with the `ipc_rds` option. One way to ensure that this occurs is to edit the script from the patchset where the oracle kernel is relinked. Another option is to simply perform another relink with the `ipc_rds` option before releasing the database to the users. The exact statement to use, copied from the command line on the database server, follows:

```
$ make -f $ORACLE_HOME/rdbms/lib/ins_rdbms.mk ipc_rds
```

This is also a check that the exachk script executes and output from that report lists the oracle kernels, which are not linked to provide RDS over InfiniBand connectivity.

Step 9 calibrates the storage, and it is a very important step. Each available storage cell has this run. First, CELLSRV is shut down, then the calibrate process is run. Output similar to the following will be generated.

```
CellCLI> calibrate;
Calibration will take a few minutes...
Aggregate random read throughput across all hard disk luns: 137 MBPS
Aggregate random read throughput across all flash disk luns: 2811.35 MBPS
Aggregate random read IOs per second (IOPS) across all hard disk luns: 1152
Aggregate random read IOs per second (IOPS) across all flash disk luns: 143248
Controller read throughput: 5477.08 MBPS
Calibrating hard disks (read only) ...
Calibrating flash disks (read only, note that writes will be significantly slower) ...
...
```

Once the calibrate step is complete for all storage cells, the cell disks and grid disks can be created, which is Step 12. Before that, though, the "oracle" O/S user is created, and the associated passwordless `ssh` access is established with Steps 10 and 11. After these steps complete, the grid disk partitions are created in Step 12, so they can be recognized by ASM. This is where your new setting takes effect and the desired ratio between +DATA_MYEXA1 and +RECO_MYEXA1 is established.

Next in line is setting up the GRID home by installing the GRID software (Step 13), patching the GRID home (step 14), relinking the GRID oracle executable to provide IPC over InfiniBand (Step 15), and running the GRID root.sh scripts (Step 16). These are the same actions you would take (with the exception of Step 15) on any other GRID installation. After the GRID software is installed and configured, the database software is installed and patched (Steps 17 and 18). Again, these are steps you would take on any system when you install and patch Oracle database software.

Since the grid disks are now created, it's a simple task to get ASM to recognize them and create the +DATA_MYEXA1, +RECO_MYEXA1, and +DBFS_DG disk groups in Step 19. This paves the way for creation of the DBM cluster database in Step 20, which is the default database provided with a "bare metal" Exadata installation. It is possible to change this database name in the configuration worksheet, but we haven't seen any installations where DBM isn't an available database. Once the DBM database is created, selected accounts are unlocked (Step 21), and a final relink of the DBM oracle executable, to ensure IPC over InfiniBand is functional, is executed (Step 22). The GRID Infrastructure is "locked" against any configuration changes in Step 23, then, in Step 24, any security fixes/patches are applied to the database home.

Step 25 may or may not be executed, and that depends on whether your enterprise has decided to allow Oracle direct access to Exadata via the Auto Service Request (ASR) server. This requires that a separate server be configured to communicate with Exadata to monitor the system and report back to Oracle any issues it finds, automatically generating a service request to address the issue. Such issues would be actual or impending hardware failures (disk drives, Sun PCIe cards, memory). The service request generates a parts order and dispatches a service technician to install the failed or failing parts. If you don't have a server configured for this, the step runs then terminates successfully, without performing any actions. If you do want this service and have the required additional server installed, this step configures the service with the supplied My Oracle Support credentials and tests to ensure the credentials are valid.

Step 26 sets up any desired cell alerts via e-mail. It requires a valid e-mail address that it uses and verifies. Having cell alerts e-mailed to you is convenient; you won't need to connect to the individual cells to list the alert history, so it saves time. This, too, is an optional step; you do not have to configure cell alerts to be e-mailed to you, but it is recommended.

At this point, your Exadata system is back to the state it was when it was installed, with the exception of the storage percentages that you modified. It's now time to restore the "oracle" O/S user home you had prior to starting this process.

Restore

Now that the storage has been reconfigured, it's time to address the re-created "oracle" O/S user homes and the reset "oracle" O/S password. Remember that the "oracle" O/S user was dropped as the last step of clearing the old storage configuration. Presumably you are still connected as "root," so at the shell prompt on each database server, you will type the following:

```
# passwd oracle
```

This will prompt you for the new "oracle" O/S user password, twice for confirmation. Because passwordless ssh access is configured for the "root" account, you can use ssh to connect to all other database servers from your "home base" on node 1. For those not familiar with ssh, the following command will connect you to database server 2:

```
# ssh myexa1db02
```

Change the destination server name to connect to the remaining database servers.

It is now time to restore the previous "oracle" O/S user home files and configuration. Use su to connect as "oracle." This will also put you at the user's home directory. If you used tar to archive the directory and its contents, the following command will restore the archived items:

```
$ tar xvf /tmp/oraclehome.tar . | tee oraclehome_restore.log
```

You may be prompted to overwrite existing files. With the exception of the .ssh directory, you should do so, as the files you are restoring are those which you configured prior to the storage reallocation. Remember that this process reestablished passwordless ssh connectivity for "oracle," and replacing the .ssh directory contents with those you saved prior to the reconfiguration could disable passwordless ssh, because the signatures in the saved authorized_keys file don't match the current values. Check the logfile for any errors you may have missed as the verbose output scrolled by and correct the listed errors. Use tar again to restore files or directories not created because of errors that have now been corrected. Should a second pass with tar be required, do *not* replace existing files when prompted.

If you used cpio to archive the directory and its contents, the following command will restore the archived items:

```
$ cpio -ivf ./.ssh < /tmp/oraclehome.cpio | tee oraclehome_restore.log
```

The cpio utility reads the archive specified; extracts the files and directories, except for the .ssh directory; and puts them in the current location. As explained in the tar example, you do not want to overwrite the .ssh directory contents, because the reconfiguration process reestablished passwordless ssh connectivity for "oracle," and overwriting those current files will disable that configuration. Once the archive restore is finished, you need to check the logfile for errors. Presuming there are none, you should be back to the "oracle" O/S user configuration you established before making changes to the storage allocations. If you do find errors in the restore, correct the conditions causing those errors and use cpio again to restore the files or directories that failed to create, due to errors.

Open another session and log in as "oracle," to see that all of the restored settings function as intended. If you have configured a way to set various ORACLE_HOME environments, that method should be tested, to ensure that nothing was missed in the archive of the "oracle" O/S user home or in the restore of those archived files and directories.

Act 4

Congratulations, you have completed the storage reconfiguration of your Exadata system. Looking at V$ASM_DISKGROUP, you should see output similar to the following, if you used the SizeArr setting from the example:

```
SYS> select name, free_mb, usable_file_mb
  2  from v$asm_diskgroup
  3  where name like '%MYEXA%';
```

NAME	FREE_MB	USABLE_FILE_MB
DATA_MYEXA1	52375300	17051522
RECO_MYEXA1	46920568	15638300

```
SYS>
```

The values of interest are those in the USABLE_FILE_MB column. From earlier in the chapter, the output of that query against the original storage allocations follows.

```
SQL> select name, free_mb, usable_file_mb
  2  from v$asm_diskgroup
  3  where name like '%MYEXA%';
```

NAME	FREE_MB	USABLE_FILE_MB
DATA_MYEXA1	81050256	26959176
RECO_MYEXA1	20324596	6770138

```
SQL>
```

There may be other tasks that you need to perform, depending on how you have the Exadata system configured, which include reinstalling any OEM agents you had running and, if it's not using the default port, reconfiguring the SCAN listener. Steps such as these are part of the preparation step prior to reconfiguration and should be noted prior to starting any storage reallocation.

Things to Know

Reconfiguring the storage allocations is possible on Exadata, but it is a destructive process that requires planning prior to execution.

It will be necessary to drop the existing storage configuration using the /opt/oracle.SupportTools/onecommand /deploy11203.sh script. This script will also be used, with different parameters, to create the new storage configuration.

Dropping the existing storage configuration is performed in three steps: dropping the GRID Infrastructure, dropping the cell disks, then dropping the associated user accounts and groups. Since the "oracle" O/S user will be dropped in this process, it is necessary to preserve the existing O/S user home on all available database servers in the Exadata system. This can be done with tar or cpio to create an archive of the directories and files in those locations.

There is a configuration file under /opt/oracle.SupportTools/onecommand named onecommand.params. It is this file that has to be edited to provide the new storage array size. The size provided in this file is for the +DATA disk group (the +DATA and +RECO disk group names usually include the Exadata machine name, for example, +DATA_MYEXA1 and +RECO_MYEXA1 for an Exadata machine named MYEXA1); the recovery disk group size is derived from this parameter's value.

The actual reconfiguration takes place using, once again, the /opt/oracle.SupportTools/onecommand /deploy11203.sh script and encompasses 26 separate steps. These steps reestablish user accounts, connectivity, software installations, disk partition creations, creation of the grid disks and ASM disk groups, creating the default DBM database, and applying database and security patches across the various homes. This part of the process also ensures that inter-process communication (IPC) uses InfiniBand, rather than the standard network, to avoid performance issues.

The next step you must execute is the restoration of all but the .ssh directory in the "oracle" O/S user's home directory. Since passwordless ssh connectivity was established by the reconfiguration procedure, overwriting those files would disable that functionality.

Finally, you must connect as the "oracle" user, preferably using an additional session, to verify that all functionality you established prior to the reconfiguration works, as expected.

Additional tasks you may need to perform include reinstalling OEM agents and reconfiguring the SCAN listener, if you changed it from using the default port.

CHAPTER 12

■ ■ ■

Migrating Databases to Exadata

An Exadata system, freshly installed and configured, has but one database, normally named DBM. As you might expect, it's a RAC database, so it exists on all available database servers. Exadata can run more than one database (either clustered or non-clustered), which is why you bought the system in the first place. Creating new databases isn't difficult, if you've built RAC databases before, and if you haven't, we'll provide instructions and guidance in this chapter, to help you along. However, you won't always be building truly "new" databases, because your goal is to migrate existing application databases to Exadata. There are a number of ways to accomplish this task. Some, such as the logical methods, require an empty database to work with, while others (the physical methods) will require only an init.ora file and the control files to get the process started. The aim of this chapter is to make migrating databases to Exadata as painless a task as possible.

Getting Physical

In these sections, we will discuss three options for physically migrating databases to Exadata: backups, transportable tablespaces, and standby databases. Each method has its advantages and disadvantages. Which method you choose is dependent on what migration strategy you have to use. Not all platforms are the same. Some are "big-endian," where the most significant byte of a data "word" is written to the lowest address in memory, and others are "little-endian," where the least significant byte of a data "word" is written to the lowest memory address.

If these concepts are unfamiliar, consider how data is stored in memory. The smallest unit of storage is the bit, which can have the value of either 0 or 1. Bytes, the next largest storage unit, are composed of 8 bits, and each byte of data can be represented either by the binary values of the bits of which it is composed or by hexadecimal digits that represent the same value. Thus the character "w" can be represented by the hexadecimal digits 6F or the binary value 01101111. In most of today's general-purpose computers, words are 4 bytes (32 bits) long, although some hardware architectures use words of different lengths (such as 64 bits).

Each memory address can store 1 byte, so each 32-bit word is divided into four single-byte values. The endian-ness of an operating system determines in which order the bytes will be written to memory. There are only two orders to choose from: big-endian or little-endian. To illustrate this behavior, the word *word* is composed of the following hexadecimal digits, listed in the order in which the letters appear:

6F
77
64
72

In a big-endian system, the bytes would be written as follows:

6F 77 64 72

In a little-endian system, the bytes would be reversed, as follows:

```
72 64 77 6F
```

If a source system is big-endian, then copying the data files directly to a little-endian system would result in unreadable data, because the destination operating system would be reading the bytes in the "wrong" order. Exadata runs Linux, a little-endian operating system. Migrating from big-endian operating systems, such as AIX or Solaris, for example, is possible but requires RMAN, either as the primary migration tool or as an additional utility, to convert the data files from big-endian to little-endian format.

Regardless of the endian-ness of the source system, RMAN is an excellent choice as a migration tool, especially because the database backup processes already in place can be used to generate the necessary backup set for migration. There are process changes you will have to make to migrate a database from a big-endian system to Exadata, so that RMAN can convert the data files to a little-endian format. These steps will be provided later in the chapter. Using RMAN to essentially clone the source database onto Exadata is relatively fast and brings over all of the internal database objects, regardless of data type. There will likely be objects that RMAN won't transfer, such as BFILES and directories, and there is a way to report those objects. Additional steps, which are discussed later in this chapter, can be performed to ensure those objects also get migrated.

Transportable tablespaces are also an option when only specific schemas have to be migrated. Tablespace dependencies are determined; the desired and dependent tablespaces are prepared; the metadata is exported; the tablespace files are transferred; and the tablespace metadata is imported into Exadata. Using this method requires that an empty database be created on Exadata, and the Database Configuration Assistant can perform that task. These general steps will be discussed in detail in another section.

A physical standby database can also be used to migrate a source database to Exadata. Basically using the same process as a standard RMAN database clone, a few additional steps, required for standby configuration and operation, will have to be performed. This method allows you to migrate the database to Exadata and keep it synchronized with the source database until the desired cutover date, when the standby is converted to a primary and all user traffic is redirected to Exadata. This method will also be covered in more detail later in this chapter.

Depending on the number of tablespaces to migrate, using transportable tablespaces might not be the method to use. RMAN, in our opinion, would be the physical method of choice, and data pump would be the method to use for a logical transfer of data. To aid in this migration, Oracle provides a view, V$TRANSPORTABLE_PLATFORM, that lists the operating systems RMAN can convert data files from and to and includes the endian-ness of that operating system. In the next section, we cover this view and how to use it to migrate a database from a system with different endian-ness to Exadata, running Linux, using RMAN.

Using Backups

Possibly the easiest method involves using the existing database backups to relocate a database to Exadata, because the backup strategy is already in place and has been tested to provide reliable results. This is the same procedure used to clone a database with RMAN, so it's reliable and repeatable.

■ **Note**   We have found it necessary to have external storage available for the backup pieces. This is especially true if you are migrating a database from a big-endian platform to Exadata, a little-endian platform, and using either transportable tablespaces or RMAN.

Looking at the steps involved to migrate a database to Exadata using RMAN backups, the procedure is straightforward. If a common storage device can be made available between the source server and the Exadata destination, it's even easier, as no transfer of backup pieces is necessary. Because we clone databases for testing and development purposes, we have access to an external storage array, which we use for backups of the desired databases. We will proceed with this discussion based on this configuration, and apart from having to copy backup pieces from the source machine to Exadata, the steps are identical.

■ **Note** The steps outlined in this section will migrate a database to a single-instance database on Exadata. There are additional steps to execute, should you want the migrated database to be a cluster database. Those steps will be covered at the end of this section and will apply to either of the RMAN methods described.

A recent backup of the source database is required before you begin. This process should also back up the control files and do so after the database backup is complete. This is necessary so that the backup just taken is found in the control files that will be restored. It's these control files you will use to start the database restore and recovery to Exadata. Additionally, a current copy of the init.ora or sp file from the source database is required, as are any necessary directory components, such as the diagnostic destination as defined for the source database. For a RAC database being migrated, the init.ora or spfile from each node will have to be copied to its respective location on the Exadata system. We recommend that you use tar or cpio to archive the diagnostic destination for the source database and transfer that archive to Exadata, where it can be restored. There may be situations where the full path for the diagnostic destination cannot be replicated on the Exadata system. In such cases, change directories to the directory listed in the init.ora file as the diagnostic_dest and archive from that point. An example for a database named TEST using tar follows:

```
$ cd /u01/oracle/11.2.0.3
$ tar cvf /obkups/diag_dest.tar ./diag/rdbms/test
```

The tar archive created would be transferred to the Exadata system. Change directories to the diagnostic_dest listed for the DBM database (because this is the ORACLE_HOME you will likely use for your transferred database) and restore the tar archive, as follows:

```
$ cd /u01/oracle/11.2.0
$ tar xvf /obkups/diag_dest.tar
```

This will restore the diag directory structure for the migrated database to the Exadata system. All that remains is to change the diagnostic_dest, background_dump_dest, core_dump_dest, and user_dump_dest values to the newly created location in the copied init.ora or spfile. During this process, the local archivelog destination also has to be created, and any necessary changes to that location string have to be made to the init.ora or spfile. If this is a RAC database being migrated, these steps will have to be performed on all nodes where this database will have running instances. To better explain this, presume this TEST database is a two-node RAC database. On database node 1 and on database node 2, the diag destination will have to be archived. Then the tar archive for node 1 will be copied to Exadata database node 1, and the tar archive for node 2 will be copied to Exadata database node 2. Each node will require the restore step to be run, and each copy of the init.ora or spfile will have to be modified to reflect any location changes.

Restoring the database to Exadata can be accomplished in two ways: by a simple restore-and-recovery session using only the backup pieces from the most recent backup, or by using the duplicate database command, which requires connecting to the source database as the auxiliary. We will presume that if you are able to copy the backup pieces from the source server to Exadata, you also have a valid SQL*Net connection to the source database. We will begin with a basic restore-and-recover scenario.

As mentioned previously, the first step is to ensure the availability of the backup pieces. It is presumed they are available on the Exadata system. With the init.ora or spfile in place, it is necessary to restore the control files from the current backup. Make note of the control file backup piece name, then issue the following command:

```
RMAN> restore controlfile from '<backup piece name>';
```

You should see the following output:

```
Starting restore at 27-JUL-13
 using channel ORA_DISK_1

channel ORA_DISK_1: restoring control file
 channel ORA_DISK_1: restore complete, elapsed time: 00:00:02
 Finished restore at 27-JUL-13
```

Now you can start and mount the database in preparation for the restore and recovery. If the source database is a RAC database, it will be necessary to set the cluster_database parameter to false before starting the restore and recovery. This is because the database must be mounted exclusive for the restore to be successful. From this point, it is a standard restore-and-recovery scenario, which should complete without error, presuming all of the configuration parameters in the init.ora or spfile are listing the correct locations on the Exadata system. If you set cluster_database to false before beginning the migration, you will have to set it back to true once the recovery is complete.

You may choose to clone the database from the source. The init.ora or spfile will have to be copied from the source database, so that the database can be started nomount on the Exadata system. Again, if this is a RAC database being migrated, the cluster_database parameter has to be set to false before starting the clone.

The clone process uses the duplicate database command to RMAN. Example commands for this process to duplicate the mytest database on a remote server to a database named test on Exadata follow (both databases use ASM):

```
connect target sys/<password>@mytest
connect auxiliary /
run {
  sql 'alter session set optimizer_mode=rule';
  allocate auxiliary channel c1 type disk ;
  allocate auxiliary channel c2 type disk ;
  allocate auxiliary channel c3 type disk ;
  allocate auxiliary channel c4 type disk ;
  allocate auxiliary channel c5 type disk ;
  allocate auxiliary channel c6 type disk ;
  duplicate target database to 'test'
       db_file_name_convert=('+DATA','+DATA_MYEXA1')
       logfile
          GROUP 11 ( '+DATA_MYEXA1','+RECO_MYEXA1' ) SIZE 512M,
          GROUP 12 ( '+DATA_MYEXA1','+RECO_MYEXA1' ) SIZE 512M,
          GROUP 13 ( '+DATA_MYEXA1','+RECO_MYEXA1' ) SIZE 512M,
          GROUP 14 ( '+DATA_MYEXA1','+RECO_MYEXA1' ) SIZE 512M ;
}
```

A shell script can also be written for this, making it easier to run and monitor the progress from a single session. The shell script would appear as in the following example:

```
export NLS_DATE_FORMAT='Mon DD YYYY HH24:MI:SS'
DATESTAMP=`date '+%y%m%d%H%M'`
MSGLOG=/home/oracle/clone/logs/dup_mytest_${DATESTAMP}.log

$ORACLE_HOME/bin/rman msglog $MSGLOG append << EOF
connect target sys/<password>@mytest
connect auxiliary /
run {
  sql 'alter session set optimizer_mode=rule';
  allocate auxiliary channel c1 type disk ;
  allocate auxiliary channel c2 type disk ;
  allocate auxiliary channel c3 type disk ;
  allocate auxiliary channel c4 type disk ;
  allocate auxiliary channel c5 type disk ;
  allocate auxiliary channel c6 type disk ;
  duplicate target database to 'test'
        db_file_name_convert=('+DATA','+DATA_MYEXA1')
        logfile
          GROUP 11 ( '+DATA_MYEXA1','+RECO_MYEXA1' ) SIZE 512M,
          GROUP 12 ( '+DATA_MYEXA1','+RECO_MYEXA1' ) SIZE 512M,
          GROUP 13 ( '+DATA_MYEXA1','+RECO_MYEXA1' ) SIZE 512M,
          GROUP 14 ( '+DATA_MYEXA1','+RECO_MYEXA1' ) SIZE 512M ;
}
EOF
```

This script would be run after the destination database has been started nomount and would be run in the background in no-hang-up mode. If this script were named clone_test_from_mytest.sh and located in the /home/oracle/clone directory, the command to do this would be as follows:

```
$ nohup $HOME/clone/clone_test_from_mytest.sh &
```

The duplicate process will now be running, and control will return to the shell prompt, so you can monitor the progress through the generated log file. This would be done with the following commands:

```
$ cd $HOME/clone/logs
$ ls -ltr *mytest*
...
dup_mytest_201307271343.log
$ tail -f dup_mytest_201307271343.log
```

The tail -f command is used to continually read the contents of a file that is actively being written, so you can see the entries as they occur. The script illustrated can also be used to refresh an existing destination database. If Oracle Managed Files are being used (they are on Exadata), it will be necessary to delete the existing files for the destination database before beginning the clone, because the data files won't be overwritten by the duplication process. All other steps will be executed as described previously in this section.

One good reason for using RMAN to migrate databases to Exadata is the fact that you can change the "endian-ness" of the data files if you need to. Exadata is using Linux, a little-endian operating system, but you may be migrating from AIX, a big-endian system. This will require that the data-file format be changed, and RMAN can do this task for you. You will need external storage available for the converted data files from the source database, because there isn't sufficient file-system storage available on Exadata. The first step in this process is to see which platforms are supported, and the V$TRANSPORTABLE_PLATFORM view provides this information, as follows:

```
SQL> select platform_name, endian_format
  2  from v$transportable_platform;

PLATFORM_NAME                                    ENDIAN_FORMAT
------------------------------------------------ --------------
Solaris[tm] OE (32-bit)                          Big
Solaris[tm] OE (64-bit)                          Big
Microsoft Windows IA (32-bit)                    Little
Linux IA (32-bit)                                Little
AIX-Based Systems (64-bit)                       Big
HP-UX (64-bit)                                   Big
HP Tru64 UNIX                                    Little
HP-UX IA (64-bit)                                Big
Linux IA (64-bit)                                Little
HP Open VMS                                      Little
Microsoft Windows IA (64-bit)                    Little

PLATFORM_NAME                                    ENDIAN_FORMAT
------------------------------------------------ --------------
IBM zSeries Based Linux                          Big
Linux x86 64-bit                                 Little
Apple Mac OS                                     Big
Microsoft Windows x86 64-bit                     Little
Solaris Operating System (x86)                   Little
IBM Power Based Linux                            Big
HP IA Open VMS                                   Little
Solaris Operating System (x86-64)                Little
Apple Mac OS (x86-64)                            Little

20 rows selected.

SQL>
```

RMAN can transport data files between any of the listed platforms, and the AIX to Linux migration is possible. The next step is to check for database objects that won't be transported by RMAN, such as directories, BFILES, and external tables. The following PL/SQL block will display these objects:

```
SQL> set serveroutput on
SQL> declare
  2    x boolean;
  3  begin
  4    x := sys.dbms_tdb.check_external;
  5  end;
  6  /
The following directories exist in the database:
SYS.ADMIN_BAD_DIR, SYS.ADMIN_LOG_DIR, SYS.ADMIN_DAT_DIR, SYS.XMLDIR, SYS.DATA_PUMP_DIR, SYS.ORACLE_
OCM_CONFIG_DIR
```

```
PL/SQL procedure successfully completed.

SQL>
```

Notice that the PL/SQL reports six directories that will have to be re-created once the database is migrated to Exadata. It is very likely that these directories will have new locations after the move to Exadata, so not only will the database locations have to change, but the directories themselves will have to be created on the Exadata system. A simple query can generate the necessary CREATE DIRECTORY statements, as follows:

```
SQL> column cr_dir format a132
SQL>
SQL> select 'create or replace directory '||directory_name||' as '''||directory_path||''';' cr_dir
  2  from dba_directories;


CR_DIR
--------------------------------------------------------------------------------------------------
create or replace directory ADMIN_LOG_DIR as '/u01/oracle/directories/log';
create or replace directory ADMIN_BAD_DIR as '/u01/oracle/directories/bad';
create or replace directory XMLDIR as '/u01/oracle/directories/rdbms/xml';
create or replace directory ADMIN_DAT_DIR as '/u01/oracle/directories/dat';
create or replace directory DATA_PUMP_DIR as '/u01/oracle/admin/mydb/dpdump/';
create or replace directory ORACLE_OCM_CONFIG_DIR as '/u01/oracle/directories/ccr/state';


6 rows selected.

SQL>
```

Spool this output to a file and edit the destination text to point to the newly created locations on Exadata. It is then a simple task of running the generated script in the migrated database to re-create these directories.

You will have to create a destination for the converted database files on the available external storage. In this example, we will use /obkups/db_convert as the destination for those files. Take a current backup of the source database, then shut down and start the source database in read-only mode. Connect RMAN to the target database and execute the CONVERT DATABASE command, as follows:

```
CONVERT DATABASE NEW DATABASE 'mydb'
        TRANSPORT SCRIPT '/obkups/db_convert/migratedb.sql'
        TO PLATFORM 'Linux IA (64-bit)'
        DB_FILE_NAME_CONVERT = ('/home/oracle/dbs','/obkups/db_convert');
```

RMAN will convert the database files and place them in the /obkups/db_convert directory, along with a copy of the pfile and the migration script. These files will have to be transferred to the Exadata system, if the external storage is not common to both servers. Once all of the generated files are transferred, you will have to edit the migration script, to enable restricted session. A sample migration script, including the edits, follows:

```
-- The following commands will create a control file and use it
-- to open the database.
-- Data used by Recovery Manager will be lost.
-- The contents of online logs will be lost and all backups will
-- be invalidated. Use this only if online logs are damaged.
```

```
-- After mounting the created controlfile, the following SQL
-- statement will place the database in the appropriate
-- protection mode:
--   ALTER DATABASE SET STANDBY DATABASE TO MAXIMIZE PERFORMANCE

STARTUP NOMOUNT PFILE='init_00bz4glk_1_0.ora'
CREATE CONTROLFILE REUSE SET DATABASE "MYDB" RESETLOGS  NOARCHIVELOG
    MAXLOGFILES 32
    MAXLOGMEMBERS 2
    MAXDATAFILES 32
    MAXINSTANCES 1
    MAXLOGHISTORY 226
LOGFILE
  GROUP 1 '/obkups/db_convert/archlog1'  SIZE 25M,
  GROUP 2 '/obkups/db_convert/archlog2'  SIZE 25M
DATAFILE
  '/obkups/db_convert/system01.dbf',
  '/obkups/db_convert/sysaux01.dbf',
  '/obkups/db_convert/mydatatbs01.dbf',
  '/obkups/db_convert/mydatatbs02.dbf',
  '/obkups/db_convert/mydatatbs03.dbf'
CHARACTER SET AL32UTF8
;

-- ALTER SYSTEM statement added to enable restricted session.

ALTER SYSTEM ENABLE RESTRICTED SESSION;

-- Database can now be opened zeroing the online logs.
ALTER DATABASE OPEN RESETLOGS;

-- No tempfile entries found to add.
--

set echo off
prompt ~~~~~~~~~~~~~~~~~~~~~~~~~~~~~~~~~~~~~~~~~~~~~~~~~~~~~~~~~~~~~~~~~~~~~~~~~~~~~~~~~~
prompt * Your database has been created successfully!
prompt * There are many things to think about for the new database. Here
prompt * is a checklist to help you stay on track:
prompt * 1. You may want to redefine the location of the directory objects.
prompt * 2. You may want to change the internal database identifier (DBID)
prompt *    or the global database name for this database. Use the
prompt *    NEWDBID Utility (nid).
prompt ~~~~~~~~~~~~~~~~~~~~~~~~~~~~~~~~~~~~~~~~~~~~~~~~~~~~~~~~~~~~~~~~~~~~~~~~~~~~~~~~~~

SHUTDOWN IMMEDIATE
-- UPGRADE option sets restricted session
STARTUP UPGRADE PFILE='init_00bz4glk_1_0.ora'
@@ ?/rdbms/admin/utlirp.sql
SHUTDOWN IMMEDIATE
```

```
-- NOTE: The startup below is generated without the RESTRICT clause.
-- Add the RESTRICT clause.
STARTUP RESTRICT PFILE='init_OObz4glk_1_0.ora'
-- The following step will recompile all PL/SQL modules.
-- It may take serveral hours to complete.
@@ ?/rdbms/admin/utlrp.sql
set feedback 6;
```

The database should now be created using the filesystem, instead of ASM, so now it's time to move the data files into the proper ASM disk groups. Make a copy of the pfile generated by the RMAN CONVERT process described earlier. Using RMAN, you will have to make another backup, this time using a script similar to the example that follows:

```
RUN
{
  ALLOCATE CHANNEL dev1 DEVICE TYPE DISK;
  ALLOCATE CHANNEL dev2 DEVICE TYPE DISK;
  ALLOCATE CHANNEL dev3 DEVICE TYPE DISK;
  ALLOCATE CHANNEL dev4 DEVICE TYPE DISK;
  BACKUP AS COPY
    INCREMENTAL LEVEL 0
    DATABASE
    FORMAT '+DATA_MYEXA1'
    TAG 'ASM_DB_MIG';
}
```

This puts the filesystem database files into the +DATA_MYEXA1 disk group. Archive the current log through RMAN, as follows:

```
SQL "ALTER SYSTEM ARCHIVE LOG CURRENT";
```

You are using a pfile, so it will be necessary to create an spfile in the ASM disk group. Use the following example to create the new spfile:

```
CREATE SPFILE='+DATA_MYEXA1/spfile<sid>.ora'
FROM PFILE='/obkups/db_convert/'init_OObz4glk_1_0.ora';
```

You are now ready to shut down the database cleanly. Create a new init<sid>.ora file in the $ORACLE_HOME/dbs directory with the following entry:

```
SPFILE='+DATA_MYEXA1/spfile<sid>.ora'
```

You will have to set the spfile parameters listed in the following example to ASM locations, as follows:

```
STARTUP FORCE NOMOUNT;
ALTER SYSTEM SET DB_CREATE_FILE_DEST='+DATA_MYEXA1' SID='*';
ALTER SYSTEM SET DB_RECOVERY_FILE_DEST_SIZE=100G SID='*';
ALTER SYSTEM SET DB_RECOVERY_FILE_DEST='+RECO_MYEXA1' SID='*';
ALTER SYSTEM SET CONTROL_FILES='+DATA_MYEXA1','+RECO_MYEXA1' SCOPE=SPFILE SID='*';
```

You can now switch to RMAN to migrate the control file into ASM, as follows, and mount the database.

```
RMAN> STARTUP FORCE NOMOUNT;
RMAN> RESTORE CONTROLFILE FROM '<original control file name and path>';
RMAN> ALTER DATABASE MOUNT;
```

Using RMAN, switch to the migrated data files, as shown, and recover the database.

```
SWITCH DATABASE TO COPY;
RUN
{
  ALLOCATE CHANNEL dev1 DEVICE TYPE DISK;
  ALLOCATE CHANNEL dev2 DEVICE TYPE DISK;
  ALLOCATE CHANNEL dev3 DEVICE TYPE DISK;
  ALLOCATE CHANNEL dev4 DEVICE TYPE DISK;
  RECOVER DATABASE;
}
```

Once the database is recovered, you can exit RMAN, connect with SQL*Plus, and open the database. You should now have your database migrated to Exadata and ASM. The next step is to drop the old tempfiles and re-create them in ASM, as follows:

```
SQL> ALTER DATABASE TEMPFILE '<existing tempfile name>' DROP;
SQL> ALTER TABLESPACE temp_tbs_name ADD TEMPFILE;
```

You will have to drop each tempfile individually. You may script this, if you like, to generate the ALTER DATABASE statements, to drop all of the tempfiles. The new tempfiles will be Oracle Managed Files, which makes the ADD TEMPFILE statement a single command that you will execute as many times as necessary to provide the desired temp space. Lastly, you will have to migrate the redo log groups to ASM and drop the old redo log groups. After that is complete, shut down the database cleanly and restart, to ensure there are no issues with the storage or ASM.

Exadata is designed with RAC in mind. At this point, the database you've migrated, either through a direct clone from a backup or from a different platform, is a single-instance database. It can be converted to RAC with the following steps. To start that process, some changes will have to be made to the spfile. The cluster_database, cluster_database_instances, and instance_number parameters will have to be set, as follows:

```
ALTER SYSTEM SET CLUSTER_DATABASE='TRUE' SID='*' SCOPE=SPFILE;
ALTER SYSTEM SET CLUSTER_DATABASE_INSTANCES=<number of instances> SID='*' SCOPE=SPFILE;
```

The following statement needs to be edited and run for each instance in the cluster:

```
ALTER SYSTEM SET INSTANCE_NUMBER=<instance number> SID='<instance_name>' SCOPE=SPFILE;
```

Shut down the local instance cleanly. On all of the nodes where instances for this database will run, you will have to put a copy of the init.ora file you just created, modifying the name to reflect the local instance SID. The next step is to register the database with cluster services, using the srvctl utility. The db_unique_name, the Oracle home, the instance name, and the spfile are required parameters. The following example illustrates adding the database mydb and instance mydb1 for database node myexa1db01:

```
srvctl add database -d mydb -i mydb1 -o /u01/oracle/product/11.2.0/dbhome_1 -p
/u01/oracle/product/11.2.0/dbhome_1/dbs/initmydb1.ora
```

For each node in the cluster that will be running an instance of this database, the step shown will have to be repeated, changing the instance name and pfile name accordingly. Next, it will be necessary to enable the database, as follows:

```
srvctl enable database -d mydb
```

You should now be able to start the cluster database using srvctl, as follows:

```
srvctl start database -d mydb
```

The database should start on all nodes successfully. You have now migrated a database to Exadata and converted it to RAC. Ensure that the listener and SCAN listener have registered this new database, by using the lsnrctl status command, which can report the status and services available from the conventional TNS listener and for the local SCAN address. The following example shows how to return database services registered with SCAN listener address LISTENER_SCAN2 on a two-node RAC cluster database.

```
$ lsnrctl status listener_scan2

LSNRCTL for Linux: Version 11.2.0.3.0 - Production on 04-OCT-2013 14:58:55

Copyright (c) 1991, 2011, Oracle.  All rights reserved.

Connecting to (DESCRIPTION=(ADDRESS=(PROTOCOL=IPC)(KEY=LISTENER_SCAN2)))
STATUS of the LISTENER
------------------------
Alias                     LISTENER_SCAN2
Version                   TNSLSNR for Linux: Version 11.2.0.3.0 - Production
Start Date                03-OCT-2013 15:25:02
Uptime                    0 days 23 hr. 33 min. 53 sec
Trace Level               off
Security                  ON: Local OS Authentication
SNMP                      OFF
Listener Parameter File   /u01/11.2.0/grid/network/admin/listener.ora
Listener Log File         /u01/11.2.0/grid/log/diag/tnslsnr/myexa1db01/listener_scan2/alert/log.xml
Listening Endpoints Summary...
  (DESCRIPTION=(ADDRESS=(PROTOCOL=ipc)(KEY=LISTENER_SCAN2)))
  (DESCRIPTION=(ADDRESS=(PROTOCOL=tcp)(HOST=XXX.XXX.XXX.XXX)(PORT=1523)))
Services Summary...
Service "dbm" has 2 instance(s).
  Instance "dbm1", status READY, has 2 handler(s) for this service...
  Instance "dbm2", status READY, has 1 handler(s) for this service...
Service "mydb" has 2 instance(s).
  Instance "mydb1", status READY, has 1 handler(s) for this service...
  Instance "mydb2", status READY, has 1 handler(s) for this service...
The command completed successfully
$
```

The mydb cluster database has successfully registered with the SCAN listener and can be accessed remotely.

Transporting Tablespaces

Transportable tablespaces are useful for migrating data for specific schemas or subsets of data, even from different operating platforms. However, to migrate across platforms, RMAN will also have to be used, to convert the data files to the correct endian format.

The process for transportable tablespaces is not complicated, but it does involve several checks prior to the move. The first check determines if the objects in the target tablespace or tablespaces are self-contained, meaning there are no dependencies in other tablespaces that aren't considered as the targets. Oracle offers a packaged procedure, DBMS_TTS.TRANSPORT_SET_CHECK, to report this information. As an example, the RETAIL_1 and RETAIL_2 tablespaces have to be migrated to Exadata. To determine if any other dependencies exist for this tablespace set, you would execute the following statement:

```
EXECUTE DBMS_TTS.TRANSPORT_SET_CHECK('retail_1,retail_2', TRUE);
```

Querying the TRANSPORT_SET_VIOLATIONS view will report any issues with this set of tablespaces.

```
SQL> SELECT * FROM TRANSPORT_SET_VIOLATIONS;

VIOLATIONS
--------------------------------------------------------------------------------
Constraint SALES_FK between table STORES.SALES in tablespace RETAIL_1 and table
STORES.UNIT in tablespace UNITLOC
Partitioned table STORES.MON_SALES is partialy contained in the transportable set
```

The output reports that the UNITLOC tablespace also has to be included in the tablespace set, and a bit of investigation is required to find all of the tablespaces containing partitions for the STORES.MON_SALES table. A second attempt, including the UNITLOC and the SALESPART_1, SALESPART_2, and SALESPART_3 tablespaces in the transport set, succeeds, as shown in the following example:

```
EXEC DBMS_TTS.TRANSPORT_SET_CHECK('retail_1,retail_2,unitloc,salespart_1,salespart_2,salespart_3', TRUE);

PL/SQL procedure successfully completed.

SQL> SELECT * FROM TRANSPORT_SET_VIOLATIONS;

no rows selected
```

You now have a complete transportable tablespace set, ensuring all of the data and constraints will be transferred to the destination database. The next step is to ensure that no transactions can be executed against the source data, by setting the desired tablespaces to read-only, using the following statements:

```
alter tablespace retail_1 read only;
alter tablespace retail_2 read only;
alter tablespace unitloc read only;
alter tablespace salespart_1 read only;
alter tablespace salespart_2 read only;
alter tablespace salespart_3 read only;
```

You are now ready to export the tablespace metadata for import into the destination database. Use expdp on the source system to generate this metadata export, using the TRANSPORT_TABLESPACES option, as follows:

```
expdp system/password DUMPFILE=retail_data.dmp DIRECTORY=tstrans_dir
transport_tablespaces = retail_1,retail_2,unitloc,salespart_1,salespart_2,salespart_3
transport_full_check=y
```

Using the TRANSPORT_FULL_CHECK=Y option verifies the tablespace check you made previously. If the transportable tablespace check fails for any reason, the export terminates unsuccessfully. Although this shouldn't occur if you have no output from the DBMS_TTS.TRANSPORT_SET_CHECK procedure, it is a good second check to execute when transporting tablespaces, to ensure there will be no issues once the tablespaces are migrated to Exadata. The TSTRANS_DIR location is, for this example, pointing to /obkups/tablespaces, which will be used as the source directory for the file transfers to Exadata.

If the source and destination systems have the same endian-ness, it's time to copy the tablespace files and the metadata export to Exadata. If the source tablespaces are using ASM, they will have to be copied out of ASM to the filesystem for transfer. This is the reverse of the step we provided to migrate data into ASM. The following example is provided:

```
RUN
{
  ALLOCATE CHANNEL dev1 DEVICE TYPE DISK;
  ALLOCATE CHANNEL dev2 DEVICE TYPE DISK;
  ALLOCATE CHANNEL dev3 DEVICE TYPE DISK;
  ALLOCATE CHANNEL dev4 DEVICE TYPE DISK;
  BACKUP AS COPY
    INCREMENTAL LEVEL 0
    DATAFILE file1,file2,...
    FORMAT '/obkups/tablespaces/'
    TAG 'FS_TBLSPC_MIG';
}
```

You will have to generate a list of the required data files, so you can modify the provided example to copy the desired data files. Execute the modified statement to copy the ASM data files into the desired directory. In this example, that is /obkups/tablespaces, for transport. You should now have all of the files necessary to transport the tablespaces to Exadata. Use scp to copy the contents of /obkups/tablespaces to an external location connected to the Exadata system. Copy the transferred data files into ASM using the same basic command you used to get the data files out of ASM, changing the destination to the desired Exadata ASM disk group. You will need a current list of the data files you just copied into ASM, so the metadata import will complete successfully. When you have that list, modify the following example and import the metadata using impdp:

```
impdp system/password DUMPFILE=retail_data.dmp DIRECTORY=tstrans_dir
TRANSPORT_DATAFILES=
  +DATA_MYEXA1/file1,
  +DATA_MYEXA1/file2,
...
```

The expectation is that you have created the necessary user accounts from the source database in the destination database, including all necessary privileges. The impdp utility will not create these accounts, so they must exist prior to executing the import. When the import has successfully completed, you will have to put the tablespaces back into read/write mode, as follows:

```
alter tablespace retail_1 read write;
alter tablespace retail_2 read write;
alter tablespace unitloc read write;
alter tablespace salespart_1 read write;
alter tablespace salespart_2 read write;
alter tablespace salespart_3 read write;
```

Please Stand By

A physical standby database is a good choice as a migration strategy, if the database has to be migrated to the new system at an earlier date than the application. Using a standby database keeps the data synchronized between the old production system and the new production system and allows for connectivity testing prior to the final move. The process to create a standby database is basically the same as the process provided earlier in this chapter that uses RMAN. Additional steps to configure a secondary archivelog destination, standby redo logs, and redo transport will be necessary. Those steps will not be discussed here, as they are available in the Oracle online documentation.

Using Oracle 11.2.0.3 it's possible to test the new database without affecting the standby configuration, by executing a switchover. This temporarily allows the standby to assume the primary role, providing an opportunity to test configurations and make necessary adjustments to the environment before the final move occurs. This also allows you to switch back to the primary without the necessity of a database rebuild.

On the date of cutover, it will be necessary to failover to the standby location, converting the standby to being the primary database. This will be a "one-way" move, as the source database will no longer be used and will not have to be rebuilt.

Post-migration Stuff

Packages, procedures, and views can be invalidated, owing to the migration, so it will be necessary to recompile those objects and correct any issues that may arise. It is a good idea to generate a list of invalid objects in the source database prior to the move. This will make it easier to know when you have succeeded in restoring all of the valid migrated objects from the source database. The following script will produce that list:

```
select owner, object_name, object_type, status
from dba_objects
where status <> 'VALID';
```

Spool the output to a file for later reference and transfer that file to Exadata. Run that same query again on the migrated database and execute $ORACLE_HOME/rdbms/admin/utlrp.sql to recompile the database objects, correcting any issues until the final list of INVALID objects matches the list generated from the source database.

If you were using a physical standby to migrate a database to Exadata, you would have to remove the spfile parameters that were necessary to establish the standby and possibly adjust the control file locations to reference multiple copies. (Usually, a standby uses a single standby control file.) Copy the existing control file to these additional locations.

Deprecated init.ora parameters could also be an issue, as the source database may be a release prior to 11.2.0.3 (the current release on Exadata). The alert log is a good place to find such parameters, so that they can be dealt with accordingly.

Although the BFILE columns will be replicated, the source files they point to will not. These files will have to be copied over to the Exadata system, and, once they are accessible to the database, the BFILE locators will have to be reassigned, based on the new locations.

You may find that other management tasks may be necessary, such as resizing extents, partitioning large tables, or compressing tables (such as archived tables or archived partitions). These tasks are also part of the post-migration list. Resizing extents and creating partitions can take a considerable amount of time, especially for large databases. Take such tasks into consideration when planning database migrations to Exadata, so that the end users will be aware that after the actual physical migration, tasks may still exist before the database can be made available for use.

That's Logical

Logical migration is also an option to Exadata. Such a migration would involve export and import, replication, or database links. Each of these options will be covered in the following sections.

Export and Import

The export and import utilities that are available depend on the release of Oracle you are migrating from. For releases earlier than 10.1, the original export and import utilities exist (exp and imp). These utilities are provided in all current releases of Oracle for backwards compatibility. For 10.1 and later releases, the newer Data Pump utilities (expdp and impdp) should be used.

Using an export-import strategy requires that an empty database be created on the Exadata system. This can be achieved by using the Database Configuration Assistant (DBCA), and this utility can create both single-instance and cluster databases. We recommend creating a new cluster database, because Exadata is built for RAC. We won't go into detail on how to create a database with DBCA, as the process is straightforward, and the GUI is intuitive.

When migrating older databases using the exp and imp utilities, it will be necessary to create the user account in the new Exadata database before importing any tables and data. If you're able to use the expdp and impdp utilities, this won't be necessary, as exporting a user exports the commands to create that user, commands that will be executed during the import process.

The compatibility matrix for the older export-import utilities is shown in Table 12-1.

Table 12-1. *Compatibility Matrix for the exp and imp Utilities*

Destination Release	Source Release
	| 7 | 8i | 9i | 10g | 11g
7	|yes | no | no | no | no
8i	|yes |yes | no | no | no
9i	|yes |yes |yes | no | no
10g	|yes |yes |yes | yes | no
11g	|yes |yes |yes | yes | yes

As expected, the older releases are not forward-compatible, so an export from an 8i database cannot be imported into a database using release 7. You can always use the exp and imp utilities from the oldest release, however, and later releases will be able to read and process the resulting dump file.

Table 12-2 lists the compatibility matrix for the expdp and impdp utilities.

Table 12-2. *Compatibility Matrix for the expdp and impdp Utilities*

Data Pump Dumpfile Version	Database Compatibility Setting	Can Be Imported into Target:			
		10gR1 10.1.0.x	10gR2 10.2.0.x	11gR1 11.1.0.x	11gR2 11.2.0.x
0.1	10.1.x	supported	supported	supported	supported
1.1	10.2.x	no	supported	supported	supported
2.1	11.1.x	no	no	supported	supported
3.1	11.2.x	no	no	no	supported

Use these matrices when planning your logical migration, using the export and import utilities, to avoid issues during the export and import process.

If you're using the export-import strategy, it's likely that you are transferring only a subset of the database data and tables. It is a good idea to export by schema or user, rather than by table name, because exporting a given user will capture all of the internal objects owned by that account. As we discussed previously in this chapter, it may be necessary to re-create directories and transfer BFILES to the Exadata system, as these objects won't be created on import. In the case of directories, the DDL to create the directory *is* captured. It's the location referenced in that DDL that won't exist on Exadata, and those locations will have to be created after the import is complete. If you cannot create the same location on Exadata as there was on the source server, you will have to create new locations and then re-create those directories to point to the new directories.

Cross-schema dependencies may exist for a given user account, and if that is the case, then some objects, such as views and integrity constraints, will fail to compile and will be invalid. The DBA_DEPENDENCIES view is useful for finding such dependencies, so you can export the necessary users to keep objects valid in the migrated schemas. A list of the user accounts having objects referenced by a given user can be generated with the following query:

```
select distinct referenced_owner
from dba_dependencies
where owner = '<user account>'
and referenced_owner <> '<user account>';
```

If you would rather have a list of the objects to reduce the size of the export, the following query can be used:

```
select referenced_owner, referenced_name, referenced_type
from dba_dependencies
where owner = '<user account>'
and referenced_owner <> '<user account>';
```

This will generate a list of the object name, object type, and owner, so only those objects will be in the export file. Remember that if you are only exporting a selected list of objects, you will have to perform an additional export after the original user export created, to transfer application tables and data to Exadata. The following example, for an 11.2.0.3 database, illustrates this concept:

```
#
# Export application user
#
expdp directory=dbmig_dir schemas=$1 dumpfile="$1"_mig.dmp logfile="$1"_mig.log
```

```
#
# Export dependent objects not owned by
# application user
#
expdp directory=dbmig.dir dumpfile="$1"_"$2".dmp logfile="$1"_"$2".log tables="$3"
```

This example takes three parameters, two user names, and a comma-delimited list of tables and presumes the list of tables is fairly short. If, for example, only a short list of tables is to be excluded, the command can be written as follows:

```
expdp directory=dbmig.dir schemas=$2 dumpfile="$1"_"$2".dmp logfile="$1"_"$2".log exclude="$3"
```

Now the table list is one of exclusion, and all tables for the user specified in parameter 2 will be exported, except those in the supplied list. The dumpfiles should be imported in reverse order, that is, for the user of the dependent tables, then for the application user. This will allow the import process to create and validate constraints and views for the application user without error.

Replication

Replication is another way to logically migrate a database to Exadata, and Streams or Golden Gate are the tools we would recommend for such a migration. Because Golden Gate has all of the Streams functionality built in, it is the more robust tool to use. We won't go into detail on a Golden Gate migration scenario, but we will mention a few areas you should be aware of with this type of migration.

Both Golden Gate and Streams impose limitations on the data types that will replicate to the destination server. The types that won't replicate follow:

BFILE

ROWID

User-defined types (including object types, REFs, varrays, and nested tables)

XMLType stored object relationally or as binary XML

The following Oracle-supplied types: **Any** types, **URI** types, spatial types, and media types

If your data contains such types, it might be better to use a physical method of migration, so that all data types, regardless, will be replicated. As mentioned previously, the files referenced by BFILE locators won't be copied, and it will be necessary to modify those locators once the source files have been copied.

Directories will also have to be re-created on the Exadata system, and, if the locations the directories reference change, the directory entries will have to be replaced. This was mentioned previously with the physical migration methods, but we feel it's important enough to repeat here.

Using Database Links

Database links can transfer data between two databases and, if the network bandwidth is sufficient, do so in a fairly efficient manner. You won't get the speed of a physical migration (a database restore can run relatively quickly), but you won't require external storage to house the files being transferred.

We suggest using one of the following two methods to transfer data over a database link:

```
INSERT
COPY
```

Because DDL is not allowed on remote databases through the `CREATE TABLE ... AS SELECT ...` statement, the destination tables will have to exist in the Exadata database prior to data migration. Also, LOB data is not accessible through a database link. Tables containing LOB columns are not eligible for migration through the `COPY` command and are probably best migrated through a physical method.

After migration, it will be necessary to go through the "Post-migration Stuff" section to resolve any issues caused by missing data, such as BFILES and directories.

Things to Know

Physical and logical methods can be employed to migrate databases to Exadata. Which method you use depends on availability of external storage and on the data types that have to be migrated.

Databases that include LOB data or BFILEs are best migrated using a physical methodology, as logical methods such as Golden Gate and Streams have restrictions on the data types they can replicate. Also, physical methods offer the possibility of migrating from a big-endian platform (such as AIX or Solaris) to Linux, a little-endian platform.

Big-endian platforms write the most significant byte first in the string, and little-endian platforms write the least significant byte first in the string. For example, the hexadecimal characters for the word *word* would be written with the *w* as the first byte. Little-endian platforms would store the word in reverse order, with the *d* in the first-byte position.

Three physical methods have been described: RMAN backups, transportable tablespaces, and physical standby databases. Each has its advantages, and the decision to select a particular method should be made based on the migration time line and the volume of data that has to be migrated.

RMAN backups will migrate the entire database to Exadata. RMAN can also be used to facilitate migration from different platforms, by converting the source data files to an endian format compatible with Linux.

Transportable tablespaces can be used to migrate subsets of data from the source database. An empty database will have to exist on the Exadata system. If the tablespaces are coming from a big-endian system, it will also be necessary to use RMAN to convert the data files to a little-endian format.

Physical standby databases make it possible for the database to be migrated well before the application is migrated. Using a standby keeps the destination database synchronized with the source while the application migration is in progress. A failover will have to be executed to convert the standby to a primary database for the final cutover.

Logical methods are also available, using export and import, replication via Streams or Golden Gate, and database links. All of the logical methods have restrictions on data types that will not migrate, and it is recommended that one of the physical methods be employed, if the database being migrated uses data types that won't replicate.

Export and import rely on the version of the source database. The export utility from the lowest Oracle release must be used to perform a successful logical migration.

Replication using Golden Gate or Streams won't copy BFILEs, user-defined types, or rowid columns, to name a few. You should be aware of the data types in use in the database being migrated, before choosing a method.

Database links can be used. The `COPY` command is the utility of choice for such migrations, but LOBs are not transferrable over a database link. Carefully consider the source data before choosing a final migration strategy.

Regardless of the method selected, objects such as BFILEs and directories will have to be addressed after the initial migration has completed. The files referenced by the source BFILE locators will have to be copied to Exadata, and the BFILE locators re-created using the new file locations. Directories will have to be created at the operating-system level, and the directory objects in Oracle will have to be replaced using the new directory locations.

Objects can be invalidated by a migration, so it is good practice to generate a list of invalid objects in the source database as a reference, when checking the destination database for objects invalidated by the migration. The `$ORACLE_HOME/rdbms/admin/utlrp.sql` script should be run post-migration to compile invalidated objects.

CHAPTER 13

■ ■ ■

ERP Setup—a Practical Guide

The purpose of this chapter is to provide readers with guidelines for setting up Oracle ERP (11i or R12) environments. Most of what you will find here is not necessarily specific to Exadata but to any Linux RAC environment. Exadata, however, has been described as "RAC-in-a-box," and as a result, the challenges will always be there with Exadata. Therefore, this seems like a good place to address these.

Oracle's standard for ERP is for each database to run from its own Oracle Home and for the listener for that database to have a dedicated, unique, SQLNet port. So, our first challenge comes with creating a new Oracle Home for each of the ERP databases. Exadata always comes with one Oracle Home and database ready to go. The simplest course of action is to simply clone that Oracle Home on each of the nodes. However, if you are installing a completely new version of the database compared to what was delivered with your Exadata machine, you can skip this section for the time being. But do not be surprised if you find that you have to clone that Home sometime in the future. In any event, cloning of Oracle Homes is a common practice for the ERP DBA.

Cloning the Oracle Home

In addition to the Grid Infrastructure Oracle Home (i.e., your ASM home), your Exadata cluster will be delivered with a standard database Oracle Home (on each node) and one database created using that Home. As a practical matter, you should leave this Home and database as is—for a reference point, if nothing else. Particularly on a dev/test cluster, you will likely need multiple Oracle Homes created for various purposes: dev, test, uat, etc. Use this "seeded" Oracle Home as the source for your first ERP Oracle Home and then patch it with the additional database patches that ERP is certainly going to need. You can then proceed to clone this Home for any additional ERP environments that you may require.

Unless you have specified otherwise to Oracle support, the "seed" database will likely be called DBM. In our example, its Oracle Home is /u01/app/oracle/product/11.2.0.3/dbhome_1. Our new database will be called ERPDEV. As root, do the following on all nodes in the cluster:

```
$ mkdir /u01/app/oracle/product/11.2.0.3/erpdevdb
$ cd /u01/app/oracle/product/11.2.0.3/dbhome_1
$ cp -r * /u01/app/oracle/product/11.2.0.3/erpdevdb/.
$ chown -R oracle:oinstall /u01/app/oracle/product/11.2.0.3/erpdevdb
```

Log in as the Oracle software owner and do the following—also on both nodes. When repeating the process on each node, be sure to set the LOCAL_NODE appropriately, as follows:

```
$ cd /u01/app/oracle/product/11.2.0.3/erpdevdb/clone/bin
```

237

```
$ perl clone.pl ORACLE_BASE=$ORACLE_BASE \
ORACLE_HOME=/u01/app/oracle/product/11.2.0.3/erpdevdb \
ORACLE_HOME_NAME=OraDb11g_ERPDEV \
'-O"CLUSTER_NODES={exadb01,exadb02}"' \
'-O"LOCAL_NODE=exadb01"'
```

The preceding command will ensure that the Oracle Home is registered in the central inventory. It is important to do the cloning properly, as it will have a huge impact on things down the road when it comes time to put in database patches, particularly the quarterly bundle patches. If the Oracle Home is not registered, you will not be able to patch it.

It is likely that additional database patches will have to be installed on top of this base version. Once additional patches are applied to this Oracle Home, then this can be the source for subsequent clones.

The SCAN Listener

While both ERP 11i and R12 can take advantage of the Single Client Access Name (SCAN) listener, its use is optional. At the time of this writing, all of the EBS clients are pre-11.2; therefore, EBS cannot make full use of the SCAN listener. If you are running 11i, then you may be discouraged from using the SCAN listener for your ERP database, because Autoconfig does not support it—although there are manual steps for setting it up. Also, if you are setting up a dev/test environment with several different databases, you will be setting up multiple listeners—one for each environment. Perhaps you are migrating an 11i database from another platform where the 1521 port (port pool zero, in Oracle ERP parlance) has been in use for many years and, therefore, may be difficult to change. In any event, you may find yourself in a situation where you do not want the SCAN listener running on the default 1521 port. In that case, you will have to reconfigure the SCAN listener to run on a different port. It does not really matter much which port you choose, but to keep things fairly simple, we will go with 1523.

There is a "My Oracle Support" note that outlines the steps as well (How to Modify SCAN Setting or SCAN Listener Port after Installation [ID 972500.1]). Using that note as a guide, we do the following:

First, modify the remote_listener and local_listener parameters for any existing non-ERP databases. On each of these databases, as SYS, execute the following:

```
SQL> alter system set remote_listener='exacluster-scan:1523' scope=spfile sid='*' ;
SQL> alter system set local_listener=
    '(DESCRIPTION=(ADDRESS_LIST=(ADDRESS=(PROTOCOL=TCP)(HOST=exa01-vip)(PORT=1523))))'
    scope=spfile sid='dbm1' ;
SQL> alter system set local_listener=
    '(DESCRIPTION=(ADDRESS_LIST=(ADDRESS=(PROTOCOL=TCP)(HOST=exa02-vip)(PORT=1523))))'
    scope=spfile sid='dbm2' ;
```

Set the environment for the Grid Oracle Home and do the same for ASM. Note that ASM does not have a remote_listener:

```
alter system set local_listener=  '(DESCRIPTION=(ADDRESS_LIST=(ADDRESS=(PROTOCOL=TCP)
(HOST=exa01-vip)(PORT=1523))))'
    scope=spfile sid='+ASM1' ;
alter system set local_listener=  '(DESCRIPTION=(ADDRESS_LIST=(ADDRESS=(PROTOCOL=TCP)
(HOST=exa01-vip)(PORT=1523))))'
    scope=spfile sid='+ASM2' ;
```

Shut down all databases.

```
$ srvctl stop database -d dbm
```

Now, we will set the environment for the Grid Oracle Home and change the listener port, as follows:

```
$ srvctl modify listener -l LISTENER -p "TCP:1523"
$ srvctl modify scan_listener -p 1523
$ srvctl stop scan_listener
$ srvctl start scan_listener
```

Restart the database(s), and that's all there should be to it.

```
$ srvctl start database -d dbm
```

Creating a Database

Whether performing a fresh installation or migrating from another server, you will have to create an empty database for your future full-blown ERP environment. In truth, this does not really differ from creating a database in any RAC environment where Oracle Managed Files are in use. The interesting part will come in the next section, when we discuss setting up the listener. For the sake of completeness, however, we must mention that, yes, a database gets created.

The simplest method is just to use dbca. Set the ORACLE_HOME and modify the PATH appropriately, as follows:

```
$ export ORACLE_HOME=/u01/app/oracle/product/11.2.0.3/erpdevdb
$ export PATH=$PATH:$ORACLE_HOME/bin
$ dbca
```

The steps for running dbca are well-documented, so we will not go into detail about that here. Make the usual choices regarding what disk group to use for your Oracle Managed Files, the character set to use, and various memory configuration choices. When complete, you may still want to adjust the redo log sizes and the storage parameters for the tablespaces (SYSTEM, UNDOTBS1 and 2, TEMP, USERS, etc.).

Once the database creation is complete, add the instance (the database will already have been added) to the oratab in each node in the cluster and use Oracle's oraenv utility to set your environment. Your oratab on node 1 should look something like the following:

```
+ASM1:/u01/app/11.2.0.3/grid:N
agent11g:/u01/app/oracle/GCAgents/oracle/MW/agent11g:N
dbm1:/u01/app/oracle/product/11.2.0.3/dbhome_1:N
erpdev1:/u01/app/oracle/product/11.2.0.3/erpdevdb:N
dbm:/u01/app/oracle/product/11.2.0.3/dbhome_1:N      # line added by Agent
erpdev:/u01/app/oracle/product/11.2.0.3/erpdevdb:N   # line added by Agent
```

The oratab for node 2 will be similar, the difference being that the instances local to that node (dbm2, erpdev2, etc.) will be listed.

Setting Up the Listener

Earlier, we moved the SCAN listener to 1523. Because port 1521 is now free, if we wish, we can create a new listener that uses that port. This listener will be specific to our ERPDEV database. Regardless of what port you do use, you will have to go through these steps to create a listener dedicated to your new database. The main point is that you cannot use the port that the SCAN listener is using.

Shut down the newly created ERPDEV database:

```
$ srvctl stop database -d erpdev
```

Under the $ORACLE_HOME/network/admin directory, create a new tnsnames.ora file with the following entries:

```
erpdev=
        (DESCRIPTION=
                (ADDRESS=(PROTOCOL=tcp)(HOST=exa01-vip)(PORT=1521))
                (ADDRESS=(PROTOCOL=tcp)(HOST=exa02-vip)(PORT=1521))
            (LOAD_BALANCE = yes)
            (CONNECT_DATA=
                (SERVER=DEDICATED)
                (SERVICE_NAME=erpdev)
            )
        )

erpdev1_LOCAL=
        (DESCRIPTION=
                (ADDRESS=(PROTOCOL=tcp)(HOST=exa01-vip)(PORT=1521))
        )

erpdev2_LOCAL=
        (DESCRIPTION=
                (ADDRESS=(PROTOCOL=tcp)(HOST=exa02-vip)(PORT=1521))
        )

erpdev_REMOTE=
        (DESCRIPTION=
            (ADDRESS_LIST=
                (ADDRESS=(PROTOCOL=tcp)(HOST=exa01-vip)(PORT=1521))
                (ADDRESS=(PROTOCOL=tcp)(HOST=exa02-vip)(PORT=1521))
                (ADDRESS=(PROTOCOL=tcp)(HOST=exa01-vip)(PORT=1523))
                (ADDRESS=(PROTOCOL=tcp)(HOST=exa02-vip)(PORT=1523))
            )
        )
```

Note the port 1523 references in the erpdev_REMOTE entry. These address entries will cause the database service to register with the default listener as well. Having the database registered with the default listener is required, if it becomes necessary to run dbca at any point in the future for this database. There are a variety of reasons why you may need to run dbca: to configure Database Vault or Oracle Internet Directory, for example.

Next, create the listener and tie it to this Oracle Home.

```
$ srvctl add listener -l erpdev -o $ORACLE_HOME -p 1521
$ srvctl setenv listener -l erpdev -T TNS_ADMIN=$ORACLE_HOME/network/admin
$ srvctl setenv database -d erpdev -T TNS_ADMIN=$ORACLE_HOME/network/admin
```

Start up the database and change its listener parameters.

```
$ srvctl start database -d erpdev

SQL> alter system set local_listener=
  '(DESCRIPTION=(ADDRESS=(PROTOCOL=tcp)(HOST=exa01-vip)(PORT=1521)))'
  sid='erpdev1' ;

SQL> alter system set local_listener=
  '(DESCRIPTION=(ADDRESS=(PROTOCOL=tcp)(HOST=exa02-vip)(PORT=1521)))'
  sid='erpdev2' ;

SQL> alter system set remote_listener='erpdev_REMOTE' ;
```

If you wish to also register the database with the SCAN listener, the remote_listener parameter may be set as follows:

```
SQL> alter system set remote_listener='erpdev_REMOTE','exacluster-scan:1523' ;
```

Data Migration

At this point, we have an empty database and a listener for that database. Unless this is a fresh install of Oracle ERP, the next (and most time-consuming) step is the migration of the existing database to our new, bright, shiny, Exadata database. The steps for migration are varied, based on the source platform, ERP version, and a host of other factors. Suffice to say, you will want to familiarize yourself with the copious "My Oracle Support" notes to get your database from point A to point Exadata. We cannot begin to attempt to cover that territory here. So, we will pick up at the point where the import is complete and Autoconfig has been run. Please see the list of MOS notes at the end of this chapter, which should provide a good basis for getting you through.

Environment Configuration

In a traditional, single-node ERP database environment, the SQLNet configuration files are stored under $ORACLE_HOME/network/admin/<context> where <context> is instance_server. It is Autoconfig that creates those files. Also, the env file that it creates sets TNS_ADMIN to that same $ORACLE_HOME/network/admin/<context> location. However, in a RAC environment, we want to use srvctl to manage the environment (i.e., start and stop the databases and the listeners). That being the case, we cannot have TNS_ADMIN set in such a way, as it would obviously have to be different on each node as the instance name changes.

Traditional single-node set-up:

```
TNS_ADMIN=$ORACLE_HOME/network/admin/erpdev_dbsrvr
$ORACLE_HOME/network/admin/erpdev_dbsrvr/tnsnames.ora
$ORACLE_HOME/network/admin/erpdev_dbsrvr/listener.ora
```

In addition, there will be an ifile parameter pointing to another file that can be used for custom settings. On Exadata (RAC), we are going to flip that around. Note in particular that we will not use the Autoconfig-generated listener.ora at all, as its entries are not applicable to RAC.

Be aware that the tnsnames.ora file that Autoconfig creates is generally full of errors in terms of what is needed for RAC. That file should be reviewed and adjustments made. The tnsnames.ora file that we created earlier can be used as a model for this. We then want to avoid these changes being overwritten as a result of subsequent runs of Autoconfig.

There are a few options for managing this.

1. Copy the file over the $ORACLE_HOME/network/admin/tnsnames.ora, i.e.,

    ```
    $ cd $ORACLE_HOME/network/admin/erpdev1_exadb01
    $ cp tnsnames.ora ../.
    ```

2. Rename the original file and add an ifile entry to $ORACLE_HOME/network/admin/tnsnames.ora that will point to it.

    ```
    $ cd $ORACLE_HOME/network/admin/erpdev1_exadb01
    $ cp tnsnames.ora tnsnames.ora.erpdev
    $ vi $ORACLE_HOME/network/admin/tnsnames.ora
    add → ifile=<ORACLE_HOME>/network/admin/erpdev1_exadb01/tnsnames.ora.erpdev
    ```

Because Autoconfig naturally restricts its activities to $ORACLE_HOME/network/admin/<context> directory, this option works nicely. Files under $ORACLE_HOME/network/admin will not be affected. Whatever you choose to do, this has to be communicated fully to anyone who may be either running Autoconfig on these servers in the future or adding entries to remote databases to the tnsnames.ora.

■ **Note**   The ifile entry has to have the full path. $ORACLE_HOME will not work there. Ensure use of the full path on both nodes.

Setting the Environment

Experienced ERP DBAs know that Autoconfig creates an env file under $ORACLE_HOME called <context>.env. Using the names we have been using throughout, we would have erpdev1_ exadb01.env on node 1, erpdev2_ exadb02.env on node 2, etc. However, the env file will have TNS_ADMIN set to $ORACLE_HOME/network/admin/<context>—which we are not using for the reasons previously discussed. You have to make accommodations for that by either commenting that out of the Autoconfig-generated env file or by creating another env file that calls that one and that has an unset TNS_ADMIN statement in it. I would recommend not modifying the generated env file, as it will get overwritten any time Autoconfig gets run, so you would have to remember to do the adjustment every time.

Create a file called <db>.env and put it in some directory in the path, such as /usr/local/bin. Our database name is erpdev, so we would have

```
$ cat erpdev.env
. /u01/app/oracle/product/11.2.0.3/erpdevdb/erpdev1_exadb01.env
unset TNS_ADMIN
echo;
echo "*************************************************"
echo "ORACLE_HOME...$ORACLE_HOME"
echo "ORACLE_SID....$ORACLE_SID"
echo "*************************************************"
echo;
```

Then, to simplify things further, add an alias definition in the .bash_profile:

```
alias erpdev='. /usr/local/bin/erpdev.env'
```

Then, setting the environment for one database or another is a snap.

```
$ erpdev
```

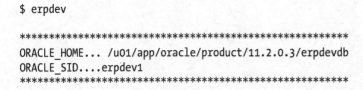

```
****************************************************
ORACLE_HOME... /u01/app/oracle/product/11.2.0.3/erpdevdb
ORACLE_SID....erpdev1
****************************************************
```

"My Oracle Support" Notes

Anyone who has worked with Oracle products should be familiar with "My Oracle Support," Oracle's site containing its knowledge base, patch downloads, and service-request system. You may also hear it referred to as *Metalink*, as that was its name for many years. Now, one often sees it referred to as "MOS." Whatever you call it, it is an invaluable resource.

The following is a list of pertinent notes that can be found there. Simply search on the reference ID, and the note should be first in the search results.

> Using Oracle 11g Release 2 Real Application Clusters with Oracle E-Business Suite Release 11i [ID 823586.1]

> Export/import notes on Applications 11i Database 11g [ID 557738.1]

> Interoperability Notes Oracle EBS 11i with Oracle Database 11gR2 (11.2.0) [ID 881505.1]

> How to Modify SCAN Setting or SCAN Listener Port after Installation [ID 972500.1]

Things to Know

Every ERP database must run from its own Oracle Home. Sharing of Oracle Homes between ERP databases is not allowed. This is a long-standing Oracle standard. In addition, each of the databases must have a dedicated listener.

The issue of the listener can be the most challenging. First, you must decide if the SCAN listener can simply stay on port 1521 or if it has to move. While you can use the SCAN listener, it is not practical to do so on a dev/test cluster, where you most likely will have multiple ERP databases running. Each of the databases will require its own listener port and, hence, its own listener. For the sake of consistency, we have found it best to have none of the databases use the SCAN listener as primary.

All that said, you still must have the database registered with the local listener, so that dbca will work. If it is not registered with the local listener, you will receive an error when you do try to run dbca. In fact, each database should be registered with both a named listener and port unique to that database and with the default listener. Remember that dbca is used for a variety of things, including adding instances to the database, registering the database with a Grid Control OMS, and configuring Database Vault—just to name a few.

Be sure to configure your $ORACLE_HOME/network/admin in such a way that subsequent runs of Autoconfig on the database tier do not compromise your TNS configuration. Fully communicate the configuration to anyone who may be running Autoconfig.

When setting your environment, be sure not to use the Autoconfig-generated TNS_ADMIN setting. The env file that Autoconfig generates is fine, but then the TNS_ADMIN variable must be unset.

Properly clone each ORACLE_HOME, so that it is registered with the central inventory. If the clone process is not followed, then the Home will not be registered, and you will not be able to apply quarterly patch bundles to it.

CHAPTER 14

■ ■ ■

Final Thoughts

You're here, at the final chapter of the book, and you've read and learned much by now. A lot of material has been covered, and you have a better idea of what Exadata is and what it can do. You also have a good working knowledge of the system and how to manage it. It was probably a daunting task at first, but, through reading this book and running the examples, you've gained an understanding of Exadata that will serve you well as you continue your career as an Exadata DBA or DMA.

You've Come Far, Pilgrim

When you started reading, you had probably just been told that Exadata was on its way and that you would be working with it. It's also likely that you had no real idea of how Exadata is configured or how it provided the exceptional performance everyone was talking about. Storage indexes and Smart Scans were foreign concepts, and the architecture of the system was like nothing you had seen before. You have come a long way since then.

Let us take a walk through the areas we have covered and highlight some of the material we have presented.

■ **Note**   This will not be a comprehensive list of all of the topics and material we have presented in previous chapters. Information on some areas may be more detailed than others, but know this chapter is not a comprehensive summary of the text.

We started, appropriately enough, at the beginning, and discussed the various configurations of an Exadata system. We did this to get you introduced to the hardware available on each of the currently available systems and to familiarize you with the resources available on each configuration. We also presented a short history of Exadata and how it has evolved to address different types of workloads, including OLTP.

The next stop on this journey took you to Smart Scans and offloading, two very important aspects of Exadata.

It has been said that Smart Scans are the lifeblood of Exadata, and we would agree. Smart Scans, as you learned, provide a "divide and conquer" approach to query and statement processing, by allowing the storage cells to perform tasks that, in conventional hardware configurations, the database server would have to perform. You also learned that offloading provides even more powerful tools to make data processing more efficient. Column Projection and Predicate Filtering allow the storage cells to return only the data requested by the query, by moving the data block processing to the storage layer. Column Projection, as you recall, allows Exadata to return only the columns requested in the select list and any columns specified in join conditions. This reduces the workload considerably, by eliminating the need for the database servers to perform conventional data block processing and filtering. This also reduces the volume of data transferred to the database servers, which is one way Exadata is more efficient than conventionally configured systems.

Predicate Filtering improves this performance even further, by returning data from only the rows of interest, based on the predicates provided. Other conditions necessary for Smart Scan execution were covered, including direct-path reads and full-table or index scans. Execution plans were explained, so that you would know what information to look for to indicate that Smart Scans were, indeed, being used, and other metrics were provided to further prove Smart Scan use. These additional metrics include the storage keyword in the Predicate information and two columns from the VSQL/GVSQL pair of views, io_cell_offload_eligible_bytes and io_cell_offload_returned_bytes. The following example, first offered in Chapter 2, shows how these column values provide Smart Scan execution information.

```
SQL>select  sql_id,
  2             io_cell_offload_eligible_bytes qualifying,
  3             io_cell_offload_eligible_bytes - io_cell_offload_returned_bytes actual,
  4             round(((io_cell_offload_eligible_bytes -
io_cell_offload_returned_bytes)/io_cell_offload_eligible_bytes)*100, 2) io_saved_pct,
  5             sql_text
  6  from v$sql
  7  where io_cell_offload_returned_bytes> 0
  8  and instr(sql_text, 'emp') > 0
  9  and parsing_schema_name = 'BING';


SQL_ID          QUALIFYING    ACTUAL IO_SAVED_PCT SQL_TEXT
-------------- ---------- ---------- ------------ --------------------------------------------
gfjb8dpxvpuv6  185081856   42510928        22.97 select * from emp where empid = 7934

SQL>
```

We also covered Bloom filters and how Exadata uses them to improve join processing. Bloom filters are part of the offloading process for qualifying joins, and their use makes joins more efficient. You can see that Bloom filters are in use through the execution plan for a qualifying query, as the following example, again first provided in Chapter 2, illustrates.

```
Execution Plan
----------------------------------------------------------
Plan hash value: 2313925751
```

Id	Operation	Name	Rows	Bytes	Cost (%CPU)	Time	TQ	IN-OUT	PQ Distrib
0	SELECT STATEMENT		218K	21M	1378 (1)	00:00:01			
1	PX COORDINATOR								
2	PX SEND QC (RANDOM)	:TQ10003	218K	21M	1378 (1)	00:00:01	Q1,03	P->S	QC (RAND)
3	HASH GROUP BY		218K	21M	1378 (1)	00:00:01	Q1,03	PCWP	
4	PX RECEIVE		218K	21M	1378 (1)	00:00:01	Q1,03	PCWP	
5	PX SEND HASH	:TQ10002	218K	21M	1378 (1)	00:00:01	Q1,02	P->P	HASH
6	HASH GROUP BY		218K	21M	1378 (1)	00:00:01	Q1,02	PCWP	
* 7	HASH JOIN		218K	21M	1376 (1)	00:00:01	Q1,02	PCWP	
8	PX RECEIVE		218K	11M	535 (1)	00:00:01	Q1,02	PCWP	
9	PX SEND BROADCAST	:TQ10001	218K	11M	535 (1)	00:00:01	Q1,01	P->P	BROADCAST
10	NESTED LOOPS		218K	11M	535 (1)	00:00:01	Q1,01	PCWP	
11	BUFFER SORT						Q1,01	PCWC	
12	PX RECEIVE						Q1,01	PCWP	
13	PX SEND BROADCAST	:TQ10000						S->P	BROADCAST
14	TABLE ACCESS BY INDEX ROWID	DEPT_INFO	1	27	1 (0)	00:00:01			
* 15	INDEX UNIQUE SCAN	DEPT_INFO_PK	1		1 (0)	00:00:01			
16	PX BLOCK ITERATOR		218K	5556K	534 (1)	00:00:01	Q1,01	PCWC	
* 17	TABLE ACCESS STORAGE FULL	EMP_DEPT	218K	5556K	534 (1)	00:00:01	Q1,01	PCWP	
18	PX BLOCK ITERATOR		1657K	75M	839 (1)	00:00:01	Q1,02	PCWC	
* 19	TABLE ACCESS STORAGE FULL	EMP	1657K	75M	839 (1)	00:00:01	Q1,02	PCWP	

```
Predicate Information (identified by operation id):
---------------------------------------------------
    7 - access("ED"."EMPID"="E"."EMPID")
   15 - access("D"."DEPTNUM"=20)
   17 - storage("ED"."EMPDEPT"=20)
        filter("ED"."EMPDEPT"=20)
   19 - storage(SYS_OP_BLOOM_FILTER(:BF0000,"E"."EMPID"))
        filter(SYS_OP_BLOOM_FILTER(:BF0000,"E"."EMPID"))

Note
-----
   - dynamic sampling used for this statement (level=2)

Statistics
----------------------------------------------------------
        60  recursive calls
       174  db block gets
     40753  consistent gets
     17710  physical reads
      2128  redo size
   9437983  bytes sent via SQL*Net to client
    183850  bytes received via SQL*Net from client
     16668  SQL*Net roundtrips to/from client
         6  sorts (memory)
         0  sorts (disk)
    250000  rows processed

SQL>
```

The presence of the SYS_OP_BLOOM_FILTER function in the plan output indicates the join was offloaded.

Functions can also be offloaded if they are found in the V$SQLFN_METADATA view; functions not found in this list will disqualify a query or statement from Smart Scan execution. Virtual columns can also be offloaded, which qualifies tables defined with virtual columns for Smart Scan execution.

Storage indexes were discussed in Chapter 3, and they are probably the most confusing aspect of Exadata, because this type of index is used to tell Oracle where *not* to look for data. Designed to assist in offload processing, storage indexes can significantly reduce the volume of data Oracle reads, by eliminating 1MB sections of table data. You learned that a storage index contains the barest minimum of data. You also learned that even though a storage index is small, it is undeniably mighty. Used to skip over 1MB sections where the desired data is *not* found, the resulting savings can be great. Of course, the good also comes with the bad, as a storage index can provide false positives, so that Oracle reads 1MB sections it doesn't need to, because the desired value falls within the minimum/maximum range recorded in the storage index, even though the actual value doesn't exist in that 1MB section of the table. To refresh your memory, the following example illustrates this.

```
SQL> insert /*+ append */
  2  into chicken_hr_tab (chicken_name, talent_cd, retired, retire_dt, suitable_for_frying, fry_dt)
  3  select
  4  chicken_name, talent_cd, retired, retire_dt, suitable_for_frying, fry_dt from chicken_hr_tab2
  5  where talent_cd in (3,5);

1048576 rows created.
```

```
Elapsed: 00:01:05.10
SQL> commit;

Commit complete.

Elapsed: 00:00:00.01
SQL> insert /*+ append */
  2  into chicken_hr_tab (chicken_name, talent_cd, retired, retire_dt, suitable_for_frying, fry_dt)
  3  select
  4  chicken_name, talent_cd, retired, retire_dt, suitable_for_frying, fry_dt from chicken_hr_tab2
  5  where talent_cd not in (3,5);

37748736 rows created.

Elapsed: 00:38:09.12
SQL> commit;

Commit complete.

Elapsed: 00:00:00.00
SQL>
SQL> exec dbms_stats.gather_table_stats(user, 'CHICKEN_TALENT_TAB', cascade=>true,
estimate_percent=>null);

PL/SQL procedure successfully completed.

Elapsed: 00:00:00.46
SQL> exec dbms_stats.gather_table_stats(user, 'CHICKEN_HR_TAB', cascade=>true,
estimate_percent=>null);

PL/SQL procedure successfully completed.

Elapsed: 00:00:31.66
SQL>
SQL> set timing on
SQL>
SQL> connect bing/#########
Connected.
SQL> alter session set parallel_force_local=true;

Session altered.

Elapsed: 00:00:00.00
SQL> alter session set parallel_min_time_threshold=2;

Session altered.

Elapsed: 00:00:00.00
SQL> alter session set parallel_degree_policy=manual;

Session altered.
```

```
Elapsed: 00:00:00.00
SQL>
SQL>
SQL> set timing on
SQL>
SQL> select /*+ parallel(4) */
  2  chicken_id
  3  from chicken_hr_tab
  4  where talent_cd = 4;

   CHICKEN_ID
---------------
     60277401
     60277404
...
     72320593
     72320597
     72320606
     72320626

4718592 rows selected.

Elapsed: 00:03:17.92
SQL>
SQL> select *
  2  from v$mystat
  3  where statistic# = (select statistic# from v$statname where name = 'cell physical IO bytes
saved by storage index');

           SID      STATISTIC#            VALUE
--------------- --------------- ----------------
           915             247                0

Elapsed: 00:00:00.01
SQL>
```

We feel this is a small price to pay for such efficiency.

Chapter 4 brought us to the Smart Flash Cache, a very versatile feature of Exadata, as it can be used as a read-through cache, a write-back cache, and even configured as flash disk usable by ASM. In addition to this functionality range, the Smart Flash Cache also has a portion configured as Smart Flash Log to make redo log processing more efficient. Log writes are processed both to disk, via the log groups, and to the Smart Flash Log, and the writes that finish first signal to Oracle that log processing has successfully completed. This allows Oracle to continue transaction processing at a potentially faster rate than using redo logs alone.

Chapter 5 brought us to parallel processing, an area that in conventionally configured systems can be both a help and a hindrance. Oracle 11.2.0.x provides improvements in the implementation and execution of parallel statements, which are available on any Exadata or non-Exadata configuration running this release of Oracle. It is the fact that Exadata was originally designed for data warehouse workloads, workloads that rely on parallel processing to speed the workflow, that makes it the ideal choice for parallel processing.

Certain configuration settings are necessary to enable the automatic parallel processing functionality, and a very important task, I/O calibration, is necessary for Exadata to actually act on these configuration settings. I/O calibration is a resource-intensive process and should not be run on systems during periods of heavy workloads. A packaged procedure, dbms_resource_manager.calibrate_io is provided to perform this task. Once the I/O calibration is complete, you will have to verify the parameters and settings found in Table 5-1 and Table 5-2.

Once you have everything set, you let Oracle take the reins; the users then reap the benefits of this improved parallel processing functionality. One of those benefits is parallel statement queuing, where Oracle will defer execution of a parallelized statement until sufficient resources are available. Querying the V$SQL_MONITOR view (or GV$SQL_MONITOR, to examine statements from all nodes in the cluster), where the status is QUEUED, will provide a list of statements waiting for sufficient resources to be released by parallel statements that finish execution. Provided you have set the resource limits correctly, this prevents the system from being overloaded, a vast improvement over the earlier parallel adaptive multiuser mechanism.

Another benefit is that Oracle will dynamically set the degree of parallelism (DOP) based on the available resources. One important item to note is that once the DOP is set by Oracle, it cannot be changed during execution, even if additional resources become available. The DOP is computed based on the estimated serial execution time for the given statement. A parameter, parallel_min_time_threshold, sets the threshold for serial execution time that will be the deciding factor for parallel execution. Remember that you can control whether queuing is enabled by setting the hidden parameter _parallel_statement_queuing to FALSE.

Another aspect of parallel execution is in-memory parallel execution. On the one hand, this can be desirable behavior, as disk I/O and traffic between the database servers and storage cells is eliminated, and the latency of memory is far lower than that for disk access. On the other hand, when this is active, Smart Scan optimizations are no longer available, because disk I/O is eliminated. Because the Smart Scan optimizations are eliminated, the database servers must perform all of the read processing that the storage cells would do, which increases the CPU usage. We also noted that we have not experienced in-memory parallel execution on any Exadata systems we've managed.

On to compression in Chapter 6. Exadata offers compression options not available on any non-Exadata platform, notably the Hybrid Columnar Compression (HCC) options. Those options are QUERY HIGH, QUERY LOW, ARCHIVE HIGH, and ARCHIVE LOW. These can significantly reduce the size of the selected tables; however, the compressed tables should be either inactive or subject to batch processing, including recompression, outside of the normal work hours. If HCC is used on actively updated tables, the compression level is silently changed to OLTP, and the original space savings are lost. Another aspect of using HCC is with respect to disaster recovery. If the recovery method is to simply restore the last good backup to a non-Exadata server or a server not using Exadata storage, the database could be unusable after the restore completes, because HCC isn't supported on non-Exadata storage. This is a situation correctable by uncompressing the tables, but by correcting it, you may run into space issues, if the destination server tablespaces were created based on the compressed size of the Exadata database.

Table 6-3 and Table 6-4 in Chapter 6 list the estimated and actual compression ratios for the various compression methods, including OLTP. Those tables will not be reproduced here, but it is a good idea to look at them again, if you are contemplating using a compression method to save space.

Wait events specific to Exadata were covered in Chapter 7. These wait events report on cell-related wait information. Seven of these wait events collect wait data under the I/O wait category, and the cell statistics gather event seems to be incorrectly included in this category. The cell single block physical read and cell multiblock physical read events essentially replace the older db file sequential read and db file scattered read events, respectively.

RMAN has Exadata-specific waits as well: cell smart incremental backup and cell smart restore from backup. The first wait collects time against incremental Level 1 backups and the second accrues wait time experienced by an RMAN restore. Because a Level 0 incremental is, essentially, a full backup, wait times experienced for those backups is not recorded.

Performance counters and metrics specific to Exadata were covered in Chapter 8. The intent of that chapter was to provide an overview of what metrics and counters are available, what they mean, and when you should consider using them.

The cell metrics provide insight into statement performance and how Exadata executes statements. Dynamic counters such as cell blocks processed by data layer and cell blocks processed by index layer show how efficient the storage cells are in their processing. These counters are incremented every time a storage cell can complete data-layer and index-layer processing without passing data back to the database layer. Two reasons for the cells to pass data back to the database servers are consistent-read processing requiring undo blocks (regular block I/O) and chained-row processing where the chained pieces span storage cells. While the first condition can't be controlled entirely (transactions can be so large as to exceed the automatic block-cleaning threshold), the second, chained rows, can be addressed and possibly corrected.

The `cell num fast response sessions` and `cell num fast response sessions continuing to smart scan` counters reveal the number of times Oracle chose to defer a Smart Scan in favor of regular block I/O, as an attempt to return the requested data with a minimum of work (the first listed counter), and how many times Oracle actually started a Smart Scan after the fast response session failed to return the requested data. These can give you insight into the nature of the statements submitted to your Exadata databases, by showing how often Smart Scans were averted because a small regular block I/O operation returned the requested data.

V$SQL also provides data that can be used to determine statement efficiency in the `IO_CELL_OPFLOAD_ELIGIBLE_BYTES` and `IO_CELL_OFFLOAD_RETURNED_BYTES` columns. These two columns can be used to calculate a percentage savings effected by a Smart Scan for a given query.

Chapter 9 went into storage cell monitoring, a very important aspect of Exadata, because some of the metrics are not passed back to the database servers. There are two accounts available outside of "root," and those are `cellmonitor` and `celladmin`. Which one you use really depends on what tasks have to be accomplished.

The `cellmonitor` account has access to the cell metrics and counters and can generate monitoring reports. It has limited access at the O/S level and cannot execute any of the administrative commands or functions from `cellcli`, the cell command-line interface. Basically speaking, the `LIST` commands are available to `cellmonitor`, and those are sufficient for monitoring the cells and verifying that they are functioning properly.

The `celladmin` account, as you would expect, has more power. In addition to generating reports like `cellmonitor`, it has the ability to execute the series of `ALTER`, `ASSIGN`, `DROP`, `EXPORT`, and `IMPORT` commands.

Besides `cellcli`, the storage cells can be monitored with `cellsrvstat` and, from any node in the cluster, `dcli`. The `cellcli` utility can also be run directly from the command line, by passing to it the command you wish to execute, as the following example illustrates.

```
[celladmin@myexa1cel03 ~]$ cellcli -e "list flashcache detail"
         name:                  myexa1cel03_FLASHCACHE
         cellDisk:              FD_00_myexa1cel03,FD_11_myexa1cel03,FD_02_myexa1cel03,FD_09_
myexa1cel03,FD_06_myexa1cel03,FD_14_myexa1cel03,FD_15_myexa1cel03,FD_03_myexa1cel03,FD_05_
myexa1cel03,FD_10_myexa1cel03,FD_07_myexa1cel03,FD_01_myexa1cel03,FD_13_myexa1cel03,FD_04_
myexa1cel03,FD_08_myexa1cel03,FD_12_myexa1cel03
         creationTime:          2012-08-28T14:15:50-05:00
         degradedCelldisks:
         effectiveCacheSize:    364.75G
         id:                    95f4e303-516f-441c-8d12-1795f5024c70
         size:                  364.75G
         status:                normal
[celladmin@myexa1cel03 ~]$
```

Using `dcli` from any of the database nodes, you can query all of the storage cells or a subset of them. Two options control how may cells will be polled: the `-g` option, where you pass a group file to `dcli` that contains all of the storage cell names, and the `-c` option, where you can specify, on the command line, a list of storage cells you want information from. When Exadata is configured, a group file named `cell_group`, among others, is created and can be used to poll all available storage cells, as follows:

```
[oracle@myexa1db01] $ dcli -g cell_group cellcli -e "list flashcache detail"
myexa1cel01: name:                  myexa1cel01_FLASHCACHE
myexa1cel01: cellDisk:              FD_07_myexa1cel01,FD_12_myexa1cel01,FD_15_
myexa1cel01,FD_13_myexa1cel01,FD_04_myexa1cel01,FD_14_myexa1cel01,FD_00_myexa1cel01,FD_10_
myexa1cel01,FD_03_myexa1cel01,FD_09_myexa1cel01,FD_02_myexa1cel01,FD_08_myexa1cel01,FD_01_
myexa1cel01,FD_05_myexa1cel01,FD_11_myexa1cel01,FD_06_myexa1cel01
```

```
myexa1cel01: creationTime:          2013-03-16T12:16:39-05:00
myexa1cel01: degradedCelldisks:
myexa1cel01: effectiveCacheSize:     364.75G
myexa1cel01: id:                     3dfc24a5-2591-43d3-aa34-72379abdf3b3
myexa1cel01: size:                   364.75G
myexa1cel01: status:                 normal
myexa1cel02: name:                   myexa1cel02_FLASHCACHE
myexa1cel02: cellDisk:               FD_04_myexa1cel02,FD_15_myexa1cel02,FD_02_
myexa1cel02,FD_11_myexa1cel02,FD_05_myexa1cel02,FD_01_myexa1cel02,FD_08_myexa1cel02,FD_14_
myexa1cel02,FD_13_myexa1cel02,FD_07_myexa1cel02,FD_03_myexa1cel02,FD_09_myexa1cel02,FD_12_
myexa1cel02,FD_00_myexa1cel02,FD_06_myexa1cel02,FD_10_myexa1cel02
myexa1cel02: creationTime:           2013-03-16T12:49:04-05:00
myexa1cel02: degradedCelldisks:
myexa1cel02: effectiveCacheSize:     364.75G
myexa1cel02: id:                     a450958c-5f6d-4b27-a70c-a3877430b82c
myexa1cel02: size:                   364.75G
myexa1cel02: status:                 normal
myexa1cel03: name:                   myexa1cel03_FLASHCACHE
myexa1cel03: cellDisk:               FD_00_myexa1cel03,FD_11_myexa1cel03,FD_02_
myexa1cel03,FD_09_myexa1cel03,FD_06_myexa1cel03,FD_14_myexa1cel03,FD_15_myexa1cel03,FD_03_
myexa1cel03,FD_05_myexa1cel03,FD_10_myexa1cel03,FD_07_myexa1cel03,FD_01_myexa1cel03,FD_13_
myexa1cel03,FD_04_myexa1cel03,FD_08_myexa1cel03,FD_12_myexa1cel03
myexa1cel03: creationTime:           2012-08-28T14:15:50-05:00
myexa1cel03: degradedCelldisks:
myexa1cel03: effectiveCacheSize:     364.75G
myexa1cel03: id:                     95f4e303-516f-441c-8d12-1795f5024c70
myexa1cel03: size:                   364.75G
myexa1cel03: status:                 normal
myexa1cel04: name:                   myexa1cel04_FLASHCACHE
myexa1cel04: cellDisk:               FD_08_myexa1cel04,FD_10_myexa1cel04,FD_00_
myexa1cel04,FD_12_myexa1cel04,FD_03_myexa1cel04,FD_02_myexa1cel04,FD_05_myexa1cel04,FD_01_
myexa1cel04,FD_13_myexa1cel04,FD_04_myexa1cel04,FD_11_myexa1cel04,FD_15_myexa1cel04,FD_07_
myexa1cel04,FD_14_myexa1cel04,FD_09_myexa1cel04,FD_06_myexa1cel04
myexa1cel04: creationTime:           2013-07-09T17:33:53-05:00
myexa1cel04: degradedCelldisks:
myexa1cel04: effectiveCacheSize:     1488.75G
myexa1cel04: id:                     7af2354f-1e3b-4932-b2be-4c57a1c03f33
myexa1cel04: size:                   1488.75G
myexa1cel04: status:                 normal
myexa1cel05: name:                   myexa1cel05_FLASHCACHE
myexa1cel05: cellDisk:               FD_11_myexa1cel05,FD_03_myexa1cel05,FD_15_
myexa1cel05,FD_13_myexa1cel05,FD_08_myexa1cel05,FD_10_myexa1cel05,FD_00_myexa1cel05,FD_14_
myexa1cel05,FD_04_myexa1cel05,FD_06_myexa1cel05,FD_07_myexa1cel05,FD_05_myexa1cel05,FD_12_
myexa1cel05,FD_09_myexa1cel05,FD_02_myexa1cel05,FD_01_myexa1cel05
myexa1cel05: creationTime:           2013-07-09T17:33:53-05:00
myexa1cel05: degradedCelldisks:
myexa1cel05: effectiveCacheSize:     1488.75G
myexa1cel05: id:                     8a380bf9-06c3-445e-8081-cff72d49bfe6
myexa1cel05: size:                   1488.75G
myexa1cel05: status:                 normal
[oracle@myexa1db01]$
```

You can specify certain cells to poll, if you suspect that only those cells are causing a problem, as shown in the following example.

```
[oracle@myexa1db01]$ dcli -c myexa1cel02,myexa1cel05 cellcli -e "list flashcache detail"
myexa1cel02: name:                      myexa1cel02_FLASHCACHE
myexa1cel02: cellDisk:                  FD_04_myexa1cel02,FD_15_myexa1cel02,FD_02_
myexa1cel02,FD_11_myexa1cel02,FD_05_myexa1cel02,FD_01_myexa1cel02,FD_08_myexa1cel02,FD_14_
myexa1cel02,FD_13_myexa1cel02,FD_07_myexa1cel02,FD_03_myexa1cel02,FD_09_myexa1cel02,FD_12_
myexa1cel02,FD_00_myexa1cel02,FD_06_myexa1cel02,FD_10_myexa1cel02
myexa1cel02: creationTime:              2013-03-16T12:49:04-05:00
myexa1cel02: degradedCelldisks:
myexa1cel02: effectiveCacheSize:        364.75G
myexa1cel02: id:                        a450958c-5f6d-4b27-a70c-a3877430b82c
myexa1cel02: size:                      364.75G
myexa1cel02: status:                    normal
myexa1cel05: name:                      myexa1cel05_FLASHCACHE
myexa1cel05: cellDisk:                  FD_11_myexa1cel05,FD_03_myexa1cel05,FD_15_
myexa1cel05,FD_13_myexa1cel05,FD_08_myexa1cel05,FD_10_myexa1cel05,FD_00_myexa1cel05,FD_14_
myexa1cel05,FD_04_myexa1cel05,FD_06_myexa1cel05,FD_07_myexa1cel05,FD_05_myexa1cel05,FD_12_
myexa1cel05,FD_09_myexa1cel05,FD_02_myexa1cel05,FD_01_myexa1cel05
myexa1cel05: creationTime:              2013-07-09T17:33:53-05:00
myexa1cel05: degradedCelldisks:
myexa1cel05: effectiveCacheSize:        1488.75G
myexa1cel05: id:                        8a380bf9-06c3-445e-8081-cff72d49bfe6
myexa1cel05: size:                      1488.75G
myexa1cel05: status:                    normal
[oracle@myexa1db01]$
```

Using dcli, you can redirect the output to a file. Setting up a script to perform this monitoring on a regular basis, writing the output to a dated log file, would be a good way to schedule this monitoring through cron.

Continuing with the monitoring theme, Chapter 10 discusses various ways to monitor Exadata at both the database level and the storage cell level and includes a discussion on real-time SQL monitoring. Both GUI and scripting methods are covered.

Establishing a baseline is a must, to ensure that any monitoring process you implement provides useful and usable information. Without a baseline, you are, at best, trying to hit a moving target. The baseline does not need to be established when performance is "good"; it simply has to be created to provide a point of reference for all subsequent monitoring data.

The GUI of choice for Exadata, in our view, is Oracle Enterprise Manager 12c (OEM12c), with the Diagnostic and Tuning Pack installed. With OEM12c configured in this manner, real-time SQL monitoring reports can be generated. Oracle will automatically monitor SQL statements run in parallel and also monitor serialized statements consuming five seconds or more of combined I/O and CPU time.

Oracle provides the GV$SQL, GV$SQLSTATS, and GV$SQL_MONITOR views (among others), which allow you to generate real-time SQL monitoring reports from within SQL*Plus. Also provided is the DBMS_SQLTUNE.REPORT_SQL_MONITOR procedure, which can generate HTML reports for a given sql_id. An example of how to call this procedure follows.

```
select dbms_sqltune.report_sql_monitor(session_id=>&sessid, report_level=>'ALL',type=>'HTML') from dual;
```

The TYPE parameter can have one of three values: TEXT, HTML, or, if you have an active Internet connection on the server, ACTIVE. The third value generates an HTML report that is very similar to the screens in OEM12c.

You can install the System Monitoring plug-in for Exadata Storage Server that configures OEM12c to access the storage cells, returning metric data, so they can be monitored from the same place as the database servers. If you do not have access to OEM12c, or if the Exadata storage plug-in is not installed, you can still monitor the storage cells from the command line. Both Chapter 9 and Chapter 10 provide ways to monitor the storage cells using command-line utilities. Reference those chapters for more detail and examples.

Chapter 11 introduced storage reconfiguration, a topic we felt needed to be discussed, regardless of whether you are or are not in need of reallocating your storage between the two major disk groups. As discussed, only three steps are necessary to drop the existing storage configuration. It's the rebuilding of that configuration that requires a 26-step process that includes disk partitioning, user account creation, grid disk creation, and re-creation of the storage cell initialization files on both the storage cells and the database servers.

Preparation is key to successfully changing the storage distribution between the +DATA_<system name> and +RECO_<system name> disk groups. As part of the process, the "oracle" O/S account is dropped and re-created on all available database servers in the cluster. As part of dropping the "oracle" O/S account, the O/S home directories for "oracle" on all available database servers are removed and re-created. Preserving those home directories is necessary before any of the actual storage reconfiguration steps are executed.

Once the storage reconfiguration steps have completed successfully, restoring the "oracle" O/S user homes is done, as well as reinstalling and reconfiguring any OEM agents that may have been lost during the reconfiguration process. The SCAN listener may also have to be reconfigured, if you have changed the port it is using from the default.

It is understood that you will need to migrate databases to the Exadata platform, and Chapter 12 addressed that task by providing both physical and logical methods of migration. Remember that not all systems are the same in terms of how memory values are written. Some are considered big-endian and others are little-endian. An operating system is one or the other; there is no other choice.

Physical methods include RMAN, physical standby databases, and transportable tablespaces. RMAN can allow you to migrate databases from a different platform, by converting the data files to the proper endian format. RMAN is also used with the transportable tablespace method when the operating systems are of different endian design.

Logical methods include export and import, database links, and replication, either with Streams or by using Golden Gate. Remember that replication imposes some restrictions on data types that will migrate. Physical methods of migration may be best.

Objects can be invalidated during migration. It is a good practice to generate, as a reference, a list of invalid objects in the source database, when checking the destination database for invalid objects. The $ORACLE_HOME/rdbms/admin/utlrp.sql script should be run post-migration, to compile invalidated objects.

Migrating Oracle ERP databases to Exadata can pose unique problems. Chapter 13 discusses these migrations. Every ERP database must run from its own Oracle Home. Sharing of Oracle Homes between ERP databases is not allowed. This is a long-standing Oracle standard. In addition, each of the databases must have a dedicated listener.

The issue of the listener can be the most challenging. First, you must decide if the SCAN listener can simply stay on port 1521 or if it has to move. While you can use the SCAN listener, it is not practical to do so on a dev/test cluster, where you most likely will have multiple ERP databases running. Each of the databases will require its own listener port and, hence, its own listener. For the sake of consistency, we have found it best to have none of the databases use the SCAN listener as primary.

You will need to have the database registered with the SCAN listener, so that dbca will work. Each ERP database will be registered with both a listener and port unique to that database and with the SCAN listener itself. Remember that dbca is used for a variety of things, including adding instances to the database, registering the database with a Grid Control OMS, and configuring Database Vault—just to name a few.

Be sure to configure your $ORACLE_HOME/network/admin in such a way as to ensure that subsequent runs of Autoconfig on the database tier do not compromise your TNS configuration. Fully communicate the configuration to anyone who may be running Autoconfig.

Properly clone each ORACLE_HOME so that it is registered with the central inventory. If the clone process is not followed, then the Home will not be registered, and you will not be able to apply quarterly patch bundles to it.

To DMA or Not to DMA

Exadata is a different system for a DBA to administer. Some tasks in this environment, such as running the exachk script, require root O/S privileges. This script can be run by the system administrator, and this will be the case if you are managing Exadata as a DBA. However, a new role has emerged relative to Exadata, that of the Database Machine Administrator, or DMA. Let's look at what being a DMA really means.

In addition to the usual DBA skillset, the DMA must also be familiar with, and be able to understand, the following management and monitoring commands on the specified systems.

On the compute nodes (database nodes):

> Linux: top, mpstat, vmstat, iostat, fdisk, ustat, sar, sysinfo

> Exadata: dcli

> ASM: asmcmd, asmca

> Clusterware: crsctl, srvctl

On the storage servers/cells:

> Linux: top, mpstat, vmstat, iostat, fdisk, ustat, sar, sysinfo

> Cell management: cellcli, cellsrvstat

Being a DMA also includes other areas of responsibility not associated with being a DBA. Table 14-1 summarizes the areas of responsibility for a DMA.

Table 14-1. *DMA Responsibilities*

Skill	Percent
System Administrator	15
Storage Administrator	0
Network Administrator	5
Database Administrator	60
Cell Administrator	20

The "Percent" column indicates the percentage of the overall Exadata system requiring this knowledge, and as you can see if you've been an 11g RAC administrator, you have 60 percent of the skillset required to be a DMA. The remaining skills necessary to be a DMA are not difficult to learn and master. We have covered the Cell Administrator commands you will need (cellcli, dcli), which furnish you with 80 percent of the skillset. Networking commands that you may need are ifconfig, iwconfig, netstat, ping, traceroute, and tracepath. You may, at some time, also need ifup and ifdown, to bring up or bring down network interfaces, although using these commands will not be a regular occurrence. The following example shows how to bring up the eth0 interface.

```
# ifup eth0
```

It seems like a daunting task, to become a DMA, but it really isn't that difficult. It *does* require a slightly different mindset, as you are now looking at, and managing, the entire system, rather than just the database. There will still be a need for a dedicated System Administrator and Network Administrator for your Exadata system, because, as a DMA, you won't be responsible for configuration of these resources, nor will you be responsible for patching and firmware upgrades. The DMA is, essentially, assisting these dedicated administrators by assuming the day-to-day tasks these resources would provide.

What You Don't Know, You Can Look Up

The IT world changes very rapidly, so you can't be expected to know it all. You can, however, know where to find information you need. The following resources are available to assist you in your journey through Exadata as a DBA or DMA.

> http://tahiti.oracle.com—The online Oracle documentation site
>
> www.oracle.com/us/products/database/exadata/overview/index.html—Oracle technology web site Exadata resources
>
> www.tldp.org/LDP/GNU-Linux-Tools-Summary/html/c8319.htm—Linux networking commands reference
>
> www.yolinux.com/TUTORIALS/LinuxTutorialSysAdmin.html—Linux system administration tutorial
>
> https://support.oracle.com—The My Oracle Support web site
>
> http://blog.tanelpoder.com/category/exadata/—Tanel Poder's Exadata blog, from an expert in performance tuning on Exadata
>
> http://kevinclosson.wordpress.com/kevin-closson-index/exadata-posts/—Kevin Closson's Exadata posts, an excellent resource for the storage tier
>
> http://arup.blogspot.com/—Arup Nanda's blog, where you can search for Exadata-related posts
>
> www.enkitec.com/—The Enkitec blog, from a company specializing in Exadata and sponsoring yearly Exadata-centric conferences
>
> http://jonathanlewis.wordpress.com/?s=exadata—Jonathan Lewis's excellent Exadata posts

These are the resources we regularly consult when questions arise. You may find others you prefer, but these are excellent sites to start from.

Things to Know

This chapter is not designed to be a crash course in Exadata; rather, it's intended to be a look back on areas we've covered, to bring a bit of perspective to your journey. When you began this odyssey, Exadata may have been just a name, shrouded in mystery and mentioned in reverent tones. As you progressed through this book, each step you took brought Exadata out of the fog and, hopefully, into focus, by replacing hype and rumor with fact and examples, so that you are now better prepared to assume the mantle of Exadata DBA or DMA.

Index

■ T, U

■ V

■ W, X, Y, Z

Get the eBook for only $10!

Now you can take the weightless companion with you anywhere, anytime. Your purchase of this book entitles you to 3 electronic versions for only $10.

is Apress title will prove so indispensible that you'll want to carry it with you erywhere, which is why we are offering the eBook in 3 formats for only $10 if u have already purchased the print book.

nvenient and fully searchable, the PDF version enables you to easily find and y code—or perform examples by quickly toggling between instructions and plications. The MOBI format is ideal for your Kindle, while the ePUB can be ized on a variety of mobile devices.

to www.apress.com/promo/tendollars to purchase your companion eBook.

Apress®
THE EXPERT'S VOICE™